INTRODUCTION TO

Sport Management

Theory and Practice

Mark Nagel
University of South Carolina, Columbia

Richard Southall
University of North Carolina at Chapel Hill

Kendall Hunt
publishing company

Book Team

Chairman and Chief Executive Officer   Mark C. Falb
President and Chief Operating Officer   Chad M. Chandlee
Vice President, Higher Education   David L. Tart
Director of Publishing Partnerships   Paul B. Carty
Editorial Manager   Georgia Botsford
Editor   Melissa M. Tittle
Vice President, Operations   Timothy J. Beitzel
Assistant Vice President, Production Services   Christine E. O'Brien
Senior Production Editor   Mary Melloy
Permissions Editor   Caroline Kieler
Cover Designer   Jenifer Chapman

Cover image © 2010, Shutterstock, Inc.

Kendall Hunt
publishing company
www.kendallhunt.com
Send all inquiries to:
4050 Westmark Drive
Dubuque, IA 52004-1840

Brief Contents

Contents

The initial inspiration to write this book occurred in 1999. While at the North American Society for Sport Management Conference (NASSM) in Vancouver, BC, this text's co-editors attended an academic presentation that detailed the need for and importance of theory in published sport-management research. The presenter, as well as many in the audience, made repeated comments denigrating "practical" research, devoid of any theoretical foundation. Later that day, the authors attended a different academic presentation, in which the presenter and members of the audience decried the lack of practical application in many of the articles currently being published in scholarly sport-management journals. A scan of each room revealed we were the only people who had attended both presentations. This simple observation confirmed the "chasm" we had sensed had developed between two academic sport-management "camps."

At the conclusion of that day's academic program, we continued discussing the relative importance of both theory and practice in the field of sport management and the distinct philosophical differences apparent in the sport-management academic community. It seemed then—and still appears now—that far too often neither "side" is able to acknowledge the other's contribution to sport management. One of our professional goals (established during those Vancouver conversations) was to constantly work to meld theory and practice in our future teaching and research activities. As doctoral students in 1999, neither of us contemplated eventually writing an Introduction to Sport Management textbook, but during our numerous conversations over the years, a discussion of integrating theory and practice was a constant theme. When we were approached about developing this text, one of the first things we discussed was the serendipity of this project based upon our "Vancouver" conversations.

Though the divide between theory and practice in sport-management research and curricula is less than it was in 1999, it is certainly greater than it could or should be in the future. There are still far too many research papers and presentations that leave people asking one of two questions: "How can this be applied to the real world?" or "Is there a theoretical foundation that underpins this research?" We hope this book is well received by both sport-management academics and practitioners, who recognize we have attempted to provide students with theoretical foundations from which to view current sport-industry issues.

The authors and interviewees are reflective of sport management's diversity. In addition, though each has a unique background and may be more or less theoretical in their perspective, they all hope sport-management students will enter the industry with the tools to succeed. Many of the chapters are designed to provide not only an introduction to a sport-management subtopic, but also a useful foundation from which a student will be well-prepared for specific sport-management courses as they progress in their academic program. In addition, there are specific chapters designed to help students better understand the many opportunities available in sport management and how to begin their career.

We also recognize this text may not satisfy every student's or faculty member's needs and that some readers may disagree with the order in which we present the material. However, we do hope each chapter provides sufficient detail, that upon completion students better understand the main activities a professional working in this "area" regularly undertakes and the major issues facing that functional area now and in the future. In addition, we are confident the end-of-chapter interviews reinforce the principles introduced and provide sound career advice.

To the students who we are privileged to have utilize this text, we want to welcome you to our field. Sport management is a wonderful discipline in which to work and conduct research. We hope your future career in sport management provides you with as much enjoyment as it has us.

Mark Nagel

Richard Southall

Student-Oriented Pedagogy

Because we recognize the importance of assessing student comprehension, we have included the following features in the chapters to facilitate student learning and to help instructors measure learning outcomes.

- **Chapter Objectives** help students focus on the overall concepts, theories, and skills discussed in the chapter.
- **Glossary of Key Terms** defines all the terms in the text; key terms are identified at the beginning and throughout each chapter.
- **Study Questions** located at the end of each chapter challenge and test the students' knowledge of the chapter content.
- **Learning Activities** are provided to help stimulate discussion and increase understanding of chapter concepts by turning knowledge into action.

The book contains 28 interviews with sport-management practitioners. The interviews come from a wide variety of practitioners and are provided to give the student a glimpse of real-world experience and detail specific strategies to begin and sustain a successful career in sport management.

The final chapter of the book is devoted to external resources from books to Web sites to provide the student a wealth of additional information on a wide range of sport-management topics.

Instructor Resources

The following resources are designed to aid instructors and were developed by the text's authors and contributors. The resources are available upon adoption of the text.

- **Test Bank.** The test bank offers several different types of questions to better assess student comprehension.
- **PowerPoint Slides.** Chapter content is provided in a PowerPoint format. Instructors may choose to use the presentations as they are provided or to add their own content and enrichment features.

Acknowledgments

I am indebted to numerous people who helped make this book a reality. Without the support of my family this project would not have been possible. My wife Leslie helped create a schedule that enabled me to work on this while my children, parents, siblings, and close friends showed patience when I was working to keep things moving toward completion. I am hopeful that I will have more time to devote to them now that the book is completed.

My coauthor Richard Southall provided ideas, insights, edits, and encouragement while we worked from initial idea to completed manuscript. It is always a pleasure to work with him on our numerous projects. Richard definitely makes me a better scholar and for this I am always grateful.

I must also thank the contributors who graciously provided their chapters and interviews for this book. The chapter authors remained patient and focused even when it seemed like we kept asking them to add content or make changes, while the interviewees were willing to provide their time and expertise so that readers would better understand the industry.

The faculty and staff in the Department of Sport and Entertainment Management at the University of South Carolina have consistently helped me to achieve my professional goals. Their ideas and encouragement were invaluable, especially during the development stage of the book.

Finally, I have had the pleasure of teaching hundreds of wonderful sport management students during my career. They have provided inspiration to search for new knowledge. While writing this book, I thought often of various conversations I have had with students inside and outside of the classroom. I hope that I have been able to teach them as much as they have taught me.

Mark Nagel

There are numerous people I need to thank for their help and support. My family (Deb, my wife, my children—Jason, Crystal and Elizabeth, my brothers and sisters, and my parents) has always believed in me and provided a lifetime of rich experiences upon which to draw. I want to thank them for making my life so worth living. I hope they know a simple "Thank you" does not convey the depth of my feelings.

To my close friends, including Drake, Cam, Dusty, Fritz, Billy, Sonny and Pam, Ellen, Allen, Linda, and Ron, thanks for allowing me to be part of your lives and have such wonderful conversations over the years.

My coeditor Mark Nagel was the driving force behind this project, keeping things moving forward from conception to completion, by providing leadership and inspiration. During the past decade-plus he has become not only a valued collaborator on numerous research activities, but a trusted friend and advisor. I appreciate him more than I can ever express.

I know I speak for Mark in thanking the book's chapter authors and interviewees, whose contributions make this a unique blend of sport-management theory and practice. Each chapter author willingly made suggested changes and edits, and gave us outstanding content for this book.

The interviewed sport practitioners openly shared their experiences and provided readers with an invaluable window on the sport industry. Without their willingness to share their expertise and knowledge this book would not have been possible.

The faculty and staff of the Department of Exercise and Sport Science, as well as the University of North Carolina Athletic Association, at The University of North Carolina at Chapel Hill have provided a vibrant and supportive environment in which to work. In addition, thank you to my sport-administration colleagues for their ideas and suggestions throughout this book's development.

Finally, I want to thank the many sport-management students I have had the honor of working with throughout my career. To the sport-management alumni of the University of West Georgia, who truly believed "close to home, close to each other, and close to perfection" was possible, thank you for setting the bar so incredibly high. Also, thanks to the students at The University of Memphis, who showed me what was possible when a dedicated group of students worked together for a common goal. Thank you for being the incubator. To the students at UNC, as well as CSRI interns, thank you for being wonderfully critical thinkers, challenging the status quo, and providing an opportunity to integrate theory and practice.

Richard Southall

We would both like to thank the people at Kendall Hunt, specifically Paul Carty, Melissa Tittle, and Mary Melloy for their support and patience throughout the writing and publishing process.

We gratefully acknowledge the constructive comments of the colleagues who provided content reviews. They include:

Suzannah Armentrout
Minnesota State University

Scott Armstrong
Olivet Nazarene University

Christina Belisle
Lesley University

Curtis Bickham
University of Wisconsin, Parkside

Robert Boland
New York University

Scott Bradshaw
Bucks County Community College

Martin Brett
DeSales University

Jennifer Breuer
Trinity University

Robert Brown
Daniel Webster College

Michael Burch
Virginia Commonwealth University

Steve Chen
Moorehead State University

Beth Cianfrone
Georgia State University

Dexter Davis
Niagara University

Paul Davis
Nebraska Wesleyan University

Larry Degaris
University of Indianapolis

Linda Draft
University of Wisconsin, Parkside

George Drops
National University

Chad Fagan
Northwood University

Annemarie Farrell
Ithaca College

Nicole Fennern
St. Mary's University

Michael Fetchko
La Roche College

Bob Foley
College of St. Joseph

Jaehyun Ha
College of St. Rose

Curt Hamakawa
Western New England College

Clark Haptonstall
Rice University

Brian Hofman
Ohio Northern University

Dee Jacobsen
Louisiana State University

Liz Jorn
Truman State University

DaeHyun Kim
University of Florida

Yongseek Kim
New Mexico Highlands University

Michael Klecan
Ocean County College

David Klenosky
Purdue University

Jordan Kobritz
Eastern New Mexico University

Myroslaw Kyj
Widener University

Robert Lade
Northwest Missouri State University

Seungeun Lee
York College

Mary Beth Leibold
Siena Heights University

Don Luy
Millikin University

Maria Macarle
Dowling College

Daniel Montgomery
Delta State University

Joy Moyer
Bucks County Community College

Steven Murray
Mesa State College of Colorado

Dr. Mark S. Nagel is presently an associate professor of Sport and Entertainment Management at the University of South Carolina. He is also the Associate Director of the College Sport Research Institute (CSRI) at The University of North Carolina at Chapel Hill. He also serves as an adjunct faculty member at the University of San Francisco (USF) and St. Mary's College of California. He is a former treasurer of the Sport and Recreation Law Association and the North American Society for Sport Management. Prior to working in academe, Dr. Nagel held numerous positions in sport management including campus recreation and athletic coaching. He was an assistant coach with the USF women's basketball team that advanced to the NCAA Tournament Sweet 16 in 1996.

Dr. Nagel has previously co-authored two widely utilized textbooks, *Financial Management in the Sport Industry* and *Sport Facility Management: Organizing Events and Mitigating Risks.* He has authored/co-authored over 25 peer-reviewed articles, 10 academic book chapters, and 14 articles in professional journals. In addition, he has contributed to multiple technical/research reports and wrote the Legal Guidelines and Professional Responsibilities chapter in the American Council on Exercise (ACE) Personal Trainer Manual.

Dr. Richard M. Southall is presently an assistant professor of Sport Administration and Director of the Graduate Sport-Administration Program at The University of North Carolina at Chapel Hill, where he is also Director of the College Sport Research Institute (CSRI). He is a former president of the Sport and Recreation Law Association (2004–2005).

He received his doctorate in Sport Administration from The University of Northern Colorado in 2001. His undergraduate degree (B.A.—summa cum laude) from Western State College of Colorado included concentrated coursework in English, history, and philosophy. Dr. Southall's areas of professional expertise include legal, political, marketing, sociocultural, and ethical issues in college sport; as well as sport facility and event management. In addition, he is a nationally-recognized expert on the business of big-time college sport, including the partners, products, structure, associations, and processes.

Dr. Southall has previously co-authored two widely-used sport-management textbooks, *Sport Facility Management: Organizing Events and Mitigating Risks* and *Bridging the Gap Ticket-Sales Training: Tips from the Pros.* He has authored/co-authored over 25 peer-reviewed articles dealing with such issues as: NCAA's institutional logics, university-policy responses to criminal behavior by college athletes, legal and marketing implications of National Football League ticket transfer policies, academic fraud scandals in college sport, and organizational culture dynamics in college-athletic departments. He has authored/co-authored 10 chapters in edited books and contributed to 35 technical/research reports. In addition, he has given more than 90 presentations (both refereed and invited) at national and international academic conferences.

About the Contributors

Matthew Bernthal Matthew Bernthal received his Ph.D. in marketing from The University of South Carolina, where he is an associate professor in the Sport and Entertainment Management Department. Bernthal teaches various courses in sport and entertainment marketing, and has consulted with numerous firms in the sport and entertainment industry. His research has appeared in the *Journal of Consumer Research, Sport Marketing Quarterly, Journal of Nonprofit and Public Sector Marketing, School Psychology International, Journal of Sport Behavior,* and other journals. His research primarily involves sport and entertainment consumer motivation and marketing ethics.

William Bowden Dr. William Bowden is president of Strategic Management Consultants. He holds degrees from Southern College, Southern Nazarene University, the University of Tulsa, and the University of Edinboro. A well-known athletic administration consultant, he specializes in working with business and educational institutions in developing leadership enhancement, continuous quality improvement programs and internal assessment programs. He is a former public school teacher, college professor and college administrator.

Jan Boxill Jan Boxill is Senior Lecturer and Director of the Parr Center for Ethics at UNC–Chapel Hill. Jan received her B.A., M.A., and Ph.D. in philosophy from UCLA. She specializes and teaches courses in ethics, social and political philosophy, and feminist theory. She is editor of *Sports Ethics* (Blackwell 2003) and *Issues in Race and Gender* (2000), and has written articles on ethics in sports, Title IX, and affirmative action. In 2006, she received the first Faculty Women's Advocacy Award. She is past president of the International Association for Philosophy in Sport and is a member of the Carolina Speakers Bureau.

Matthew Brown Dr. Matthew Brown has been at the University of South Carolina since 2005 where he teaches and researches in the areas of sport business and finance. His research has led to publications in journals like the *Journal of Sport Management, Sport Marketing Quarterly, Entertainment and Sport Law Journal,* the *International Journal of Sport Finance,* and *Sport Management Review.* In addition, Dr. Brown has made more than 40 national and international research presentations. Dr. Brown currently serves as the graduate director for the Department of Sport and Entertainment Management. Previously, he has served as the chief financial officer of the Southern Ohio Copperheads and treasurer of the Board of Directors of the Southern Ohio Collegiate Baseball Club.

Ronald Dick Dr. Ronald Dick is an Assistant Professor of Sport Marketing in the School of Business at Duquesne University. He previously was an Assistant Professor in Sport Management at James Madison University and an Associate Professor at the University of New Haven. He has 15 years experience in the NBA with the Philadelphia 76ers and New Jersey Nets. Dr. Dick has also served as the Assistant Dean for Sport Athletic Programs at Marian College (WI) and Assistant Athletic Director for Ticket Operations at the University of Houston. He has an Ed.D. from Temple University, an MBA from St. Joseph's University, and a B.S. from St. Joseph's University.

Ron Mower Ron Mower is a Ph.D. student in the Physical Cultural Studies program at the University of Maryland, College Park. In 2006, Ron graduated *Summa cum Laude* from the University of Maryland with a B.S. in Kinesiology and later completed a M.S. in Sport & Leisure Commerce from the University of Memphis in 2008. Drawing from a diverse range of theoretical frameworks, and across disciplinary boundaries of sociology, cultural studies, sport management, sport history, and organization studies, Ron's recent work revolves around issues of representing race and gender in transnational branding campaigns, the promotion and management of race in the NBA and NFL, and the visual uses of (sport) history in postmodern consumer culture. He is currently carrying out a socio-spatial mapping of, and conducting ethnographic fieldwork within, Baltimore City to examine the structures, forces, and processes impacting the differential access, provision, and quality of the Physical Activity Infrastructure (resources linked to health, physical activity, and sport) across the city's 55 Community Statistical Areas.

Brad Schultz Brad Schultz, Ph.D., an Associate Professor in the School of Journalism and New Media at the University of Mississippi, is the editor and creator of the *Journal of Sports Media,* a scholarly journal that publishes twice yearly. His research focuses on the effects of new media on sports journalism, and he has published nearly two dozen scholarly articles in various journals as well as three books. Before entering academia, Schultz spent 15 years in local sports television as an anchor, producer, news director, writer, videographer, and reporter. Schultz lives in Oxford, MS with his wife and two children.

Linda A. Sharp Linda A. Sharp is a Professor in the Sport Administration program at the University of Northern Colorado. She received her J.D. from Cleveland-Marshall College of Law and practiced corporate law before entering academe. Her research interests are the legal, ethical, and policy aspects of education, particularly higher education and sport. She is the lead author of the textbook *Sport Law: A Managerial Approach*. Professor Sharp is also a consultant on sport and higher education issues.

Jason Simmons Jason Simmons is a doctoral student in the sport administration program at the University of Louisville. He holds a master's degree in sport administration from Louisville and a bachelor's degree in history from the University of Nevada. He teaches undergraduate courses in sport facility management and sport communication. His research interests focus on fan-family conflict and the use of social media in sport communication.

Crystal Southall Crystal Southall is a Sport Administration doctoral candidate at the University of Northern Colorado in the School of Sport and Exercise Science, and a faculty member at Nebraska Wesleyan University, in Lincoln, NE. Her dissertation, entitled "Professional Basketball Consumer Behavior: An Analysis of the NBA Servicescape and Attendee Attitudes," examines the influence of involvement, loyalty, and sport servicescape in the creation of sport consumer attitudes and behaviors. Ms. Southall earned her M.S. in Sport and Leisure Commerce from the University of Memphis and her B.A. in History from the University of Colorado at Boulder.

Deborah Yow Dr. Deborah Yow is the director of athletics at North Carolina State University. Prior to arriving at NCSU, she served 16 outstanding years as the director of athletics at the University of Maryland. She serves as the current President of the national Division-IA Athletic Directors Association and is a member of the Board of Directors of the National Football Foundation, as well as the Board of Directors of USA Football and the NCAA Division-I Men's Basketball Academic Enhancement Committee. She has been honored by Street and Smith's Sports Business Journal as one of the 20 most influential people in intercollegiate athletics, was cited in The Chronicle of Higher Education in October 2007 as one of the "Ten Most Powerful People in College Athletics/The Builder" and she has received the Carl Maddox Sport Management Award presented by the United States Sports Academy for excellence in athletics administration.

CHAPTER 1

Do You Really Want to Work in the Sport Industry?

Mark Nagel • *University of South Carolina*
Richard Southall • *University of North Carolina at Chapel Hill*

After reading this chapter, you will be able to:

- Understand the difference between being a sport fan and a sport manager;
- Discuss the competitive nature of the sport-management field;
- Understand the importance of theory and practice as it applies to sport management education, research, and employment;
- Explain how various sport management functional areas are applicable to a sporting event.

KEY TERMS

Metadiscrete
  Experiential Learning

SWOT Analysis

I have been in both the college and professional sports ranks for 40 years. Having served as General Manager of the Philadelphia 76ers, Washington Wizards, New Jersey Nets, Portland Trail Blazers, and also as Executive Director of Philadelphia's Big 5: St. Joseph's University, Temple University, Villanova University, University of Pennsylvania, and LaSalle University; I have seen first-hand the explosion of sport and the importance of sales revenue.

There doesn't seem to be a day that goes by where I am not approached by an enthusiastic young person, or a concerned parent, and asked, "what is the best way to get a job working in sport?"

My reply to the question is always the same three-pronged answer: "Can you play? Can you coach? Can you sell?" Now, if your answers to the first two parts of my question are "no," then I would suggest you better be able to sell. Players and coaches are responsible for putting the "best product" on the floor or field. It's the front office staff's job to ensure that all of the duties leading up to and throughout each and every game are handled smoothly and efficiently. And with the economic demands facing franchises today, every person within the sound of your voice must be viewed as a potential customer.

The world of Sport Management has changed dramatically in my 40 years in the business, and the days of pledging to simply "work hard" and "learn on the job" are over. In today's market, the competition for front-office positions is as fierce as the battles being waged for a team roster spot or a coaching slot. If you are successful in selling yourself to a potential sports employer, you will be expected to arrive with the necessary tools to make an immediate contribution in the front office department to which you are assigned.

—John Nash

Introduction

Each year, throughout the United States and around the world, thousands of students enroll in sport-management classes. Since 1990 the number of sport-management academic programs has increased from a few dozen to over 250. This growth reflects students' escalating interest in sport and this academic major. However, though thousands of students annually enroll in sport management courses, for the vast majority, their initial attraction to sport management arises out of their previous experiences as an athlete or fan.

A typical initial exchange between a sport-management professor and a student enrolled in an introduction to sport management class may involve the professor asking, "Why do you want to major in sport management?" and the student responding, "I love SPORTS. I really enjoyed playing SPORTS in high school and want SPORTS to stay a part of my life" or "I have been a SPORTS fan my entire life and I want to be close to what I love." In some cases, a student might think that, since "SPORTS are fun to play and watch, a sport-management major will probably be enjoyable and easy."

These student responses reflect the perceptions of many non-sport management faculty and administrators. As many people involved in sport know, sport management is often viewed–by students, faculty, and the general public—as an "easy major," designed to keep college athletes eligible. As any sport marketer will attest, overcoming a negative product image is difficult, but can be accomplished through educating all relevant stakeholders (See Chapters 3 and 10). While there is certainly nothing wrong with having an interest in SPORTS, merely being a fan is not enough. Simply put, SPORT MANAGEMENT is the process of satisfying sports consumers' wants, needs and desires. While many of this book's authors were fans first, they are now sport managers; they work in the SPORT INDUSTRY. This change involves a fundamental shift in perspective. SPORTS CONSUMERS experience or "consume" the sport product. A SPORT MANAGER is usually "behind the curtain" or "backstage," and does not get to simply enjoy the game. A sport manager is involved in the sport-production process. FANS consume; MANAGERS direct the process.

When working in the sport industry, managers must always remember what it means to be a SPORTS FAN, as this memory assists them in selling the sport product. However, a sport manager CANNOT BE A FAN. If your goal is to someday regularly attend games, meet and interact with famous athletes and coaches, and spend your time being entertained in a luxury suite, a sport-management career should not be your goal.

Going Pro in Something Other Than Sport

For years, one of the National Collegiate Athletic Association's (NCAA) marketing campaigns has included the tagline, "There are more than 400,000 'student athletes' and most of them will go pro in something other than sports" (Brown, 2009, para. 4). This marketing slogan is consistent with Oriard's (2010) discussion of the difficult and unlikely path for college football players who aspire to a professional football career, since of the approximately 54,000 college football players each year, roughly 1,000 will sign a National Football League (NFL) contract, only about 330 will actually make an NFL roster, and only approximately 165 will have a four-year (or longer) NFL career.

Just as few college athletes will become professionals, not all sport-management students will become sport managers. However, even though it may be difficult to land a sport-industry job, and even more challenging to carve out a career in sport, majoring in sport management can result in profound positive effects for the vast majority of students, many of whom go ". . . pro in something other than the sport industry." The knowledge, skills, and attitudes students can develop by majoring in sport management can stay with them their entire working career, whether in the sport industry or not.

While there may not be hundreds of thousands of sport-management majors who graduate each year, with hundreds of sport management programs in North America alone, there is a great deal of competition for any sport-industry job. In addition, just like you, students from other majors, including business, journalism, liberal arts, and so on are also attracted to SPORTS. The competition for internships, as well as part-time or full-time entry-level positions, is fierce. It is not uncommon for people wanting to break into the sport industry to "settle for" performing multiple internships before landing a full-time sport-industry job.

In addition to fierce competition, entry-level sport-industry jobs are usually low-paying positions, with the expectation of long days and numerous responsibilities. The excitement fans associate with attending a sport event is the result of many sport managers doing their job. The sport-entertainment product does not magically appear; it is planned, developed, and managed by and through a host of trained professionals. Simply stated, working in the sport industry is hard work, with long hours, and (at least initially) low pay. If your primary motivation is potential initial salary, the sport industry is probably not the place for you. While working for low pay is not an ideal situation, it allows new sport managers to discover if they truly have a passion for a sport-industry career. Those who are able to "work through" the initial few years of low pay and long working hours usually find a sport management career is more enjoyable and fulfilling than many other career options. Many established sport managers remark they have friends who wish they would have pursued a career based upon a love for the industry rather than the size of the initial paycheck.

Speaking openly and honestly about the state of the sport industry today is not meant to discourage you from pursuing a sport-business career. Part of becoming a sport-business professional is identifying and understanding the sport-industry's pros and cons. The importance of performing a **SWOT** (Strengths, Weaknesses, Opportunities, and Threats) analysis will be discussed in several chapters in this text. Being honest about the sport-industry's job prospects is part of performing a career SWOT analysis. In this context you should perform a SWOT analysis on yourself as well as the sport industry.

SWOT
An investigation that determines an organization's strengths, weaknesses, opportunities, and threats.

Where Theory and Practice Lead to Action

Just as there is a difference between being a sports consumer and being a sport manager, there is sometimes a "disconnect" among sport-management faculty. This disconnect is often the result of faculty who see themselves as either "theoreticians" or "practitioners." This chasm can be graphically represented as a bimodal distribution (see Fig. 1.1) in which faculty members seemingly feel they must choose between either a "theory" or "practice" perspective. This text's

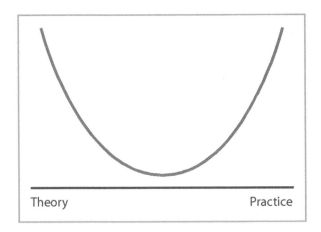

FIGURE 1.1

Current Sport Management Faculty Focus

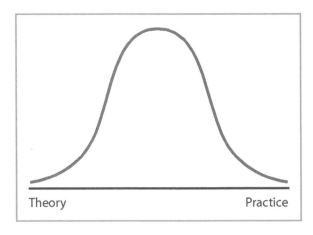

FIGURE 1.2

Ideal Sport Management Faculty Focus

design, format, and content proposes abandoning this polarizing, either-or worldview and adopting a more "normal" distribution (see Fig. 1.2.) in which sport-management faculty and students, as well as sport-industry practitioners, recognize that theory informs practice, and theory must be validated in the "real" world.

If sport management, as an academic discipline, wants to serve the needs of students and the sport industry, it seems logical that it can no longer be fragmented into two camps whose members seldom talk to each other. Sport-industry practitioners need to be aware of and utilize solid research, based upon sound theoretical frameworks, and sport-management researchers need to reach out to offer practical solutions to sport-industry needs. In addition, this new "normal" should become sport-management's organizational culture, or "how we do things in sport-management education." Fundamentally, sport-management education should be theoretically grounded, but practically oriented. Figure 1.3 illustrates the interlocking relationship between theory and practice that should occur.

Just as researchers must reach out to the sport industry, basing and testing practical decisions against existing theories would fundamentally improve the sport industry. Such an approach would free sport-managers from having to reinvent the proverbial wheel or make the same mistakes over and over again in order to learn how

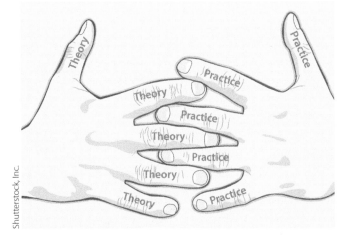

Shutterstock, Inc.

FIGURE 1.3

Molding Theory and Practice Creates Stronger Research and More Effective Practitioners

Metadiscrete experiential learning

A learning model, in which staff from partnering sport businesses serve as instructional leaders and facilitators alongside sport-management faculty, that "...enhances student understanding of entrepreneurship, sales, sponsorship, event management, and marketing research within the context of the university's sport management program" (Southall, Nagel, LeGrande, & Han, 2003, p. 23). Greater knowledge gain is possible because in a metadiscrete experience, the roles of teacher and practitioner are not separate and distinct, but are dual aspects of the same function.

to effectively manage. Such an integrated, new-normal approach to sport-management education ultimately results in stronger internship experiences and a greater likelihood of career success, and has become an accepted theoretical sport-management educational model: **metadiscrete experiential learning** (Southall, Nagel, LeGrande, & Han, 2003; Irwin, Southall, & Sutton, 2007; Southall & Dick, 2010).

Integration of Sport-Management Functional Areas

Just as a sport organization's "organizational chart" identifies specific functional areas, this text is divided into identifiable chapters that represent facets of the sport industry. However, just as functional areas—and the duties and responsibilities of employees within these functional areas—do not exist in a vacuum, this text's chapters are not discrete silos of information. Sport management involves integrating theory and practice in order to manage (i.e., plan, organize, supervise, develop, control, implement, and evaluate) across functional areas. As you continue your sport-management education, do not myopically focus on a functional area in which you think you want to work.

As many of the interviews throughout this text highlight, it is crucial to "SEE THE BIG PICTURE." In the sport industry every functional area is part of the sport product. Too many students say, "I want to work in _____. I don't need to know anything about _____." Top-level sport managers synthesize information related to many functional areas in order to make informed decisions.

As you continue your sport-management education, you will undoubtedly develop an area of interest and a desire to work or become an expert in a specific functional area. That is to be expected; however, it is important to always remember how you and your area of expertise fit into the sport product. Dissecting a hypothetical college-sport event can help identify the interconnections.

Fundamentally, the decision to sponsor a college athletic program and at what level to compete is based on beliefs within society about whether or not sport is or is not consistent with a university's mission. For many, college sport is the tie that binds the institution's various communities (faculty, staff, students, alumni, local residents, etc.) together. On many campuses, particularly those that compete at the NCAA Division-I level, athletics is a dominant

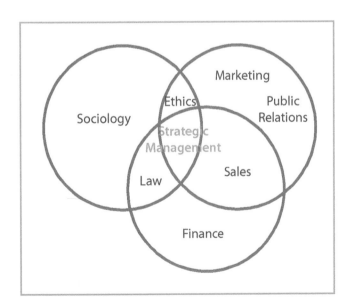

FIGURE 1.4

The Interlocking Components of Sport Management Decision Making subculture, with large financial outlays for scholarships, facilities, coaches and administrators, and travel. For other schools, such as those that compete in the NCAA Division-III level, intercollegiate athletic opportunities are offered, but there are no athletic scholarships, coaches typically also work as faculty members, and minimal travel budgets are provided. Some other campuses do not offer intercollegiate athletics at all, preferring to offer only intramural opportunities for students. The institution's view of athletics' importance can change. In the last ten years, numerous NCAA Division-II institutions have enhanced their commitment to athletics and have sought membership in the more "prestigious" —and more expensive—NCAA Division-I level. Some Division-III members have also developed their programs to compete at the Division-II level.

Though many of these moves have been to "higher" levels, there have been some institutions that have deemphasized "big-time" athletics on their campuses. The University of Chicago once competed at the highest level of athletics (Jay Berwanger won the first Heisman Trophy in 1935.). The University of Chicago later left the Big Ten Conference and decreased its financial commitment to its intercollegiate athletic program. More recently, Birmingham-Southern College moved from NCAA Division I to Division III. Ironically, though Birmingham Southern College eliminated their athletic scholarships as a condition of Division III membership, they were able to increase overall academic and need-based scholarships to students on campus while also increasing the total number of intercollegiate athletic opportunities.

If a school commits to sponsoring an athletic department (at whatever level), then it must prepare to manage the various sporting events that will occur on its campus. An event cannot occur without a facility. Even outdoor sports such as cross-country require some sort of a venue, as well as facilities for spectators, race officials, and members of the media. In addition to the "playing field" and areas for spectators and the working press during the competition, facility managers are responsible for event elements, such as parking, concessions, and restrooms. Fundamentally, a facility must provide a safe environment. In addition, it should be designed and operated in a manner that either maximizes potential revenue streams, or minimizes operational expenses.

Once an event has been scheduled in an identified facility, various athletic-department functional areas must execute their roles to ensure the event's success. If one of the goals is to have spectators at the event, the sales staff must work to sell tickets, sponsorships, and, in some cases, media rights. These can be done locally, regionally, nationally, or, in some cases, globally. In their initial representation, sport events have a short shelf life; once the event is completed there is not an additional opportunity to sell any unused tickets. The sales staff has to work to identify potential customers and to attempt to tie the potential customers' wants, needs, and desires to the benefits the event offers.

Typically, sales staffs work closely with marketing departments. It is much easier to sell tickets and sponsorships to events that are well known among various consumer groups and across various business sectors. An efficient marketing department can generate revenue well in excess of the salaries and overhead necessary for its operation. Though the sales department and marketing departments will typically work to identify potential customers and media rights holders, the public-relations department will also interact with various potential customers and the media.

Public-relations departments typically focus upon two main areas: community relations and media relations. While the marketing and sales departments typically focus on sales for specific events, the community-relations component of a public-relations department will focus upon generating goodwill among various constituent groups. In some cases, such groups may not want to or be able to attend an event, but are still potentially important. Reading to kids in schools, visiting hospitals, and interacting with senior citizen groups are typical community-relation activities. Though these constituent groups may not immediately buy tickets to events, generating goodwill by interacting with them can help build overall athletic-department support in the community.

Separate from such community relations, the public-relations department's media-relation component typically involves attracting members of the press to events and then working to enhance their experience so members of the media will produce positive accounts of the event. In addition, media-relations departments also work with non-attending media outlets to help promote event or department activities and accomplishments, through press releases and media guides.

As various departments prepare for the event, all personnel must adhere to various legal requirements. Facility operations, marketing and sales activities, and public-relations initiatives must adhere to local, state, and national laws. Sport events often involve activities that may be inherently dangerous for participants and spectators. Ensuring the safety of participants and attendees is an important legal requirement. In addition, laws governing employee behavior must be followed. With an eye toward minimizing litigation, aspects of scheduling and event operations are detailed in contracts and other important legal documents. An athletic department will typically employ at least one person specifically responsible for legal affairs, but the more knowledge all departmental staff members have about the law and its application to operating an event, the more likely the sport event will be successfully managed.

Though laws establish required behaviors, ethical standards are also an important consideration when conducting an event. Everyone must establish their own ethical standards, but it is important that such individual standards are consistent with organizational policies and procedures, and the organization's culture. A difference in opinion regarding what is ethical can lead to conflicts within an organization. In 1990, the National Basketball Association (NBA) banned the use of courtside advertising for "liquor" company sponsorships. In 2009, the NBA rescinded the rule, resulting in extensive discussion among a variety of individuals and organizations (Hollencamp, 2009). Though it was certainly "legal" for the NBA to allow its teams to sell liquor advertisements, some believed it had declined to do so until the economic downturn resulted in a heightened need for revenues. Numerous critics noted the league regularly conducts public-relations campaigns aimed at helping children and other constituents and that increased advertising for liquor companies contradicted those other messages (Hollencamp). In addition, the fact that not every NBA franchise elected to sell liquor advertising once the ban was lifted, reflected the different ethical standards of NBA owners and franchises related to this potential revenue stream.

Organizing an event involves a variety of financial decisions. To remain financially viable, any organization must generate revenues that exceed expenses. A college sport event will have a variety of revenue sources and potential expense areas. It is ultimately an athletic director's responsibility to ensure the athletic department is not operating in a financial deficit and therefore is a drain on the university. Over the past 10 years, there have been numerous examples where athletic departments have lost money. In some cases money from the institution's general fund has been utilized to cover these losses. On other campuses, student fees have been raised to ostensibly balance the books. In some cases, since generating additional revenue (whether by utilizing institutional resources, selling more tickets or increasing media rights, or raising student fees) is not an option, some athletic departments have had to cut costs, either by reducing team budgets, or, in some cases, by eliminating teams from their athletic programs.

Event management requires the analysis of a variety of factors across the various functional areas. The need to undertake strategic management actions to predict, identify, and solve problems is critical to an organization's success. Though most organizations typically do not have a position titled "strategic manager," the ability to analyze available resources, identify potential opportunities, and take actions necessary to benefit the entire organization is needed in every functional area.

Conclusion

Sport management is a popular area of academic study. Though having an interest in sports is certainly helpful, a career in sport management is not just becoming an adult fan. For many graduating students, working in the sport industry is an attractive career choice. It is important for sport-management students to recognize that each year there are many more applicants for sport-management positions than there are job openings, so throughout their undergraduate education, students should prepare themselves to be a competitive candidate for a variety of sport-industry positions. Since there is so much interest in sport management, employers typically can offer low paying jobs that require long hours to entry-level employees. Though this reality may be initially discouraging, if new sport managers can maintain their focus during the early phase of their career, higher pay in an enjoyable job will likely result.

A final word of unsolicited advice: during this course, and throughout your sport-management career, remember the importance of integrating theory and practice. A strong theoretical foundation can be immensely valuable for making informed practical decisions. Remember, each sport-management sub-area covered in this text does not exist in a silo. Decisions made in one area typically impact many other, if not all, areas of a sport organization. Highly successful sport managers learn to recognize the importance of every facet of the organization, and remember to always SEE THE BIG PICTURE!

Good luck on your sport-management journey!

Interview

INTERVIEW 1.1

Todd Koesters
Vice President, Marketing & Sales
Churchill Downs Entertainment Group

Q: Can you briefly describe your career path?

A: I completed my undergraduate studies at The Ohio State University (OSU) with a BA in English and then graduated from Capital University Law School and Ohio University (OU) in a joint degree program in law and sports administration and facility management. My paid and unpaid internships while in school included working at OSU in the Athletic Compliance Office, serving as a legal intern for the Ohio Civil Rights Commission, and working as the External Operations Director for the Mid-American Conference's Men's and Women's Swimming and Diving Championships hosted by OU.

After graduate school, I completed an internship with a small NASCAR-specific marketing agency called Agency Won and then accepted my first full time job in sport management with the same company. During my time there I worked on several NASCAR marketing programs and was then exposed to the world of agency acquisitions and holding companies when Agency Won merged with a holding company called Disson, Furst and Partners (DF&P). DF&P was a collection of niche sports and event agencies that offered expertise in multiple disciplines.

The business experiences learned during that merger proved invaluable to my career in sport management.

Following my time with DF&P, I accepted an Account Executive position with GMR Marketing, a leader in event, lifestyle and sport marketing. My job with GMR was in their newly formed Sports Division and included opening their Charlotte Office in my house. As we grew the business—and following an 18-wheeled truck unloading its cargo onto my driveway—my wife was able to convince my bosses that GMR needed a real office that did not include our garage as the fulfillment center. My 10-year stay at GMR shaped the foundation of my development as a marketer in the sport management industry and taught many invaluable lessons for business and life.

After leaving GMR in the fall of 2009, I joined Churchill Downs Entertainment Group, a wholly owned subsidiary of Churchill Downs Incorporated, that was formed in 2009. I currently serve as Vice President, Marketing and Sales. Though the Kentucky Derby is certainly our signature event, the company owns multiple racetracks and our newly formed subsidiary is tasked with expanding our entertainment offerings. Our first event in July 2010 was a 3-day music festival at the iconic track. The festival was named HullabaLOU and included more than 65 performances from acts such as Bob Jovi, Kenny Chesney and the Dave Matthews Band.

Q: What have been some of the biggest challenges you have faced during your career?

A: Determining a career path is always a challenge, particularly when the industry is continually changing. I am constantly setting new goals for myself. From the time I decided to work in sports, I had to figure out what specific subarea I would devote my concentration. Once I decided to work for an agency, there were multiple opportunities, some of which were presented to me, and others that I created. I have constantly had to determine how short-term career decisions can build toward a longer-term set of goals. Oddly enough, one primary long-term goal I set for myself after making the agency decision was achieved by the time I was 31 years old. I realized what I thought would be a "final" destination point was really just the starting point of a new phase in my career. When I was in school, my vision and understanding of job titles and responsibilities was naive. Early in my career I thought the end destination involved having a fancy job title, good salary, and extensive professional responsibilities. I realize now those things are certainly nice to have, but they are not really part of the big picture in my overall setting of career goals. I think a lot of people in sport management realize after a few years in their career that finding a place where you are challenged and fulfilled is much more important than the short-term needs that most of us concentrate on when we are in school. There is always much more that can be done in this industry as new challenges regularly present themselves.

Q: You have had a chance to teach some sport management classes and to mentor a variety of interns and employees. How do you help people conceptualize the sport management industry?

A: I have found a model that helps students better understand how the sport industry functions and what potential opportunities may exist. The first portion of the

model involves determining how an organization should be categorized. Sport organizations will typically operate as one of the following:

1. **Property**—Teams, athletic departments, venues, and leagues and their employees (athletes, coaches, front office staff, etc.) typically operate as a property. When many students initially think of sport management, they often narrowly define the industry as only involving the property. One of the reason entry-level pay is often low in this sector is because most sport management students narrow their focus to working for a team, college athletic department, league, etc. and many of these entities may only have a few dozen full-time employees and turnover occurs less often than in other industries or sport management sectors.

2. **Sponsor**—Companies who pay to be associated with the property. For many students, the countless number of companies that sponsor various sporting events are too often not seen as part of the sport industry or as potential employers. Companies such as Coca-Cola or MillerCoors have dozens or even hundreds of employees who work to identify and evaluate sport properties for potential sponsorship investments. In many cases career opportunities with sponsors may not appear as "glamorous" as working for a team. However, since most sponsors operate more like a "normal" business, salaries for employees tend to be higher and there is more room for potential advancement because the company does a variety of things inside and outside of sport.

3. **Broadcast Rights Holders**—Television, radio, Internet, and other telecommunications companies are an integral component of the sport industry. Though some may view these entities as sponsors, they fulfill a different role. Technological advances are certainly changing the entire sport industry and broadcast rights holders are no exception.

4. **Agencies**—Any company who represents the interest of others in the buying and selling of

sports. Most students know that players and coaches typically retain agents. Few students know that companies such as IMG, CBS Collegiate Sports Properties, and Learfield Communications, Inc. often represent colleges in their negotiations with sponsors and broadcast rights holders. Fewer students are aware of companies such as GMR Marketing that help sponsors enhance the value of their relationships with properties. Ticketing companies such as Ticketmaster or Stubhub are agencies that provide a service specific to a particular facet of the sport industry.

Once the organization can be categorized, the "space" in which it operates must be determined. Organizations can operate and wield influence

1. Locally

2. Regionally

3. Nationally

4. Globally

Understanding the extent to which a sport organization operates is important. In some cases, certain aspects of an organization may operate in different areas. For instance, the Pittsburgh Steelers of the National Football League sell tickets and sponsorships primarily in their local and regional market. In this case, their local market is the Pittsburgh metropolitan area and their region is most of Pennsylvania, excluding the Philadelphia metropolitan market. However, due to the NFL's national media agreements, the Steelers have been able to build their brand identity throughout the United States. Though this brand-building may occur nationwide, the Steelers are unlikely to sell many tickets or sponsorships outside of their region. However, they do sell licensed merchandise throughout various areas of the United States.

Though the NFL is the most popular and powerful sport league brand in the United States, the limited American football participation in most of the world is somewhat limiting the NFL's international initiatives (compared to other leagues such as the National Basketball Association and Major League Baseball). The NFL has been playing and broadcasting games in various international markets, but much of their marketing efforts in many countries have been focused on explaining what American football is and why it is exciting. NFL franchises like the Steelers would certainly like to expand their international presence, but doing so takes time, effort, and a financial commitment. Currently, most NFL teams have focused a large percentage of their attention on their local and regional initiatives.

Analyzing an organization's characteristics and geographic areas of influence is important, as it will help an organization better understand where to allocate resources and when to potentially alter their current practices. Students can utilize this model to better understand the industry and better prepare for interviews with potential employers.

Q: As you teach students to better understand and apply this model, what specific skills do you emphasize?

A: One of the things that irritates me is the term "sports marketing." It is amazing the number of students I speak with who say they want a career in sports marketing but they do not know the first thing about *marketing*. In my current position I am a marketer who leverages sports to achieve sales and marketing goals. The way I explain it to students is there are two ways to look at it depending upon word placement. There is the "SPORTS business" with the first word being more important than the second. People who work in the SPORTS business are typically involved with "talent." Players, coaches, general managers, scouts, etc. would fall into this category. Most of the students in sport management programs will work in the BUSINESS of sport. This world involves sales, marketing, sponsorship evaluation, accounting, administration, and various other functional areas. General business principles are critical, though they must be applied differently in sport than in some other industries. If students want to work in the BUSINESS of sports, classes taken and skills developed should reflect an understanding of business and how various principles apply to the subareas discussed earlier.

Q: What publications do you regularly read?

A: I have referred to my copy of *Kellogg on Marketing* by the Kellogg Marketing Faculty at Northwestern University so often that the binding is becoming worn! I also regularly read *Harvard Business Review, USA Today* and *The Wall Street Journal* and of course the *SportsBusiness Journal* and *SportsBusiness Daily.* I also try to regularly read *Advertising Age, Brand Week,* and *Event Marketer Magazine* as time permits.

I think it is important to stay on the cutting edge in the industry so I typically buy 15+ new books a year from the business section of the local bookstore. I also regularly buy books that cover the BUSINESS of sports but rarely buy books covering the SPORTS business.

Q: As you work and study the industry, what trends do you see emerging?

A: Three areas of importance in the BUSINESS of sport industry include: (a) globalization (Thomas Friedman's book *The World is Flat* has accurately discussed many of the major issues in the world), (b) Technology trends which enable active engagement with customers, and (c) financial escalation of rights fees and ticket prices during a strained economy.

Q: Do you advise students to potentially pursue a graduate degree?

A: Absolutely. Graduate school is an investment in your future that will pay dividends in the short and long run. I chose a joint masters degree and JD because there were not as many options in sport management as there are now. Law school was beneficial for me in a variety of ways. One only needs to look at a history of league commissioners and other prominent BUSINESS of sport leaders to see how attorneys have impacted the industry. Pursuing a law degree is certainly not a requirement for success. There are now many good MBA and MSA programs around the country. There are also some that focus too much on the "fan" side of sports and not enough on the BUSINESS of sport.

Q: Is there any additional advice you would like to provide?

A: In this industry, as well as life in general, nothing replaces hard work and dedication. Everyone, even people with industry "connections," are going to have to undertake tasks that are not glamorous or exciting early in their career (and often even later in their career). The more you can do now while you are students, the better you will be prepared to seize opportunities as they are presented. Do not ever feel you are entitled to anything. This has been one of the biggest downfalls for many graduate students. Earning an MBA or MSA is certainly important, but it does not make one immune to needing to prove yourself in an organization.

References

Brown, G. (2009, January 8). Women's Lacrosse. *The NCAA News.* Retrieved March 13, 2010 from http://www.ncaa.com/sports/w-lacros/spec-rel/010809aaa.html

Hollencamp, K. (2009, February 10). Anti-alcohol organizations blast NBA's ad policies. Retrieved March 14, 2010 from http://news.medill.northwestern.edu/chicago/ news.aspx?id=115141

Irwin, R.L., Southall, R.M., & Sutton, W.A. (2007). Pentagon of sport sales training: A 21st century sport sales training model. *Sport Management Education Journal,* 1(1), 18–39.

Oriard, M. (2009). *Bowled over.* Chapel Hill, NC: University of North Carolina Press.

Southall, R.M., & Dick, R.J. (2010, March). Assessing sport-sales training effectiveness: Development of a baseline sample. Paper presented at the Association of Marketing Theory and Practice, Hilton Head, SC.

Southall, R.M., Nagel, M.S., LeGrande, D., & Han, M.Y. (2003). Sport management practica: A metadiscrete experiential learning model. *Sport Marketing Quarterly,* 12(1), 27–36.

CHAPTER 2

Socio-Cultural Aspects of Sport

Richard M. Southall • *University of North Carolina at Chapel Hill*
Crystal Southall • *School of Sport and Exercise Science, University of Northern Colorado*

After reading this chapter, you will be able to:

- Critically investigate the nature of sport in social and cultural contexts;
- Identify sociological theories often used to examine sport;
- Detail elements of organizational culture theory;
- Define institutional logics theory and discuss various sports as institutions;
- Utilize presented sociological, cultural, or institutional theories to analyze a given sport-industry issue.

KEY TERMS

Commodification

Conflict Theory

Cultural Hegemony

Functionalist Theory, or Functionalism

Institutional Logics

Organizational Culture

Introduction

Sports is human life in microcosm.

—Howard Cosell

When students are asked what they like about sports, one of the most-often listed and enduring appeals is the "love of competition" and the fact that athletes win or lose on the basis of their athletic talent. Inherent in this meritocracy is the notion of a "level playing field," on which athletes compete based on one consistently enforced set of rules. As most every American sport fan of your professor's age is aware, this democratic notion of competition was personified in Jesse Owens' display of athletic prowess at the 1936 Berlin Olympics. The functionalist perspective on his multiple gold-medal performances is that they were the result of his strength, power, and skill, not his race, class, or politics.

Suppose you were asked a simple question: "Should a sport's rules be enforced?" How would you answer? Most every student would answer, "Yes." But, the answer may not be so simple. This is the essence of a socio-cultural examination of sport and the subject of this chapter. As we continue through this chapter, we hope to provide you with an opportunity to see how a simple question may have more than one possible answer.

Specific to our question, sports' rules are intended to insure that one team or competitor does not gain an unfair advantage over another. Claims of a "home-court" advantage do not extend to a game's fundamental rules, and it is presupposed such an advantage does not include "cheating" or "fixing" a game's outcome. Fundamental rule violations in baseball (committing a balk), football (pass interference), basketball (traveling or fouling), and skiing (missing a gate) must be penalized, since to not do so would violate the fairness of athletic competition, which is one of sports' allures.

But what about other types of on-the-court or field behaviors that do not directly affect this level-playing field, but are still often penalized (sometimes harshly), with such penalties often affecting the game's outcome. These penalized actions, such as in football taking off a helmet after scoring a touchdown or engaging in excessive end-zone celebrations, "trash-talking" or taunting after a spectacular dunk in basketball, or arguing a call with an umpire in baseball, do not actually take place during play.

A simple answer to our initial question would be, "All sports require rules. Just as in society, a sport's rules should be enforced."

But as you will find as you continue studying the sport industry, thoughtful examination of sport-related issues requires sport managers to have at least a rudimentary understanding of some fundamental sociological and cultural theories. In addition to acquiring such theoretical knowledge, in order for sport-management students to be better informed, they should be willing and able to critically examine the sport industry and discuss political, social, and cultural sport-related issues.

Many students are interested in a sport-industry career because they "love" sport. Many of you may be current or former athletes. In addition, many students in an introduction to sport management course are also currently sport fans. For many students, to hear or see the "business of sport" described as a capitalist economy predicated on controlling labor costs and maximizing consumption in order to increase revenue production is a foreign concept. Brohm's (1975) contention that the commodified sport industry's global development paralleled the rise of colonial imperialism also threatens many students' long-held belief that sport involvement is based on athletes, fans, and coaches' "Love of the Game." Initially, it might seem disheartening to discuss sport in the context of modes of production, an accumulation ethic, and a social structure designed to support the recurring production of athletes, sport events, and stadia.

Many sport-management students have not been exposed to some of the sociological or cultural concepts in this chapter. Perhaps some of you will find some of these theoretical discussions obtuse and overly abstract. In addition, since some of the theories and perspectives presented in this chapter call into question accepted view of sports, students may either ignore or denigrate them. We recognize this is not a sport-sociology course, but an introduction to sport management course. However, this chapter's purpose is to stimulate discussion and allow faculty and students to openly and critically examine the sport industry. Since sport-management students must undergo a transformation from being simply sport consumers (i.e., fans) to sport managers, this chapter is designed to provide students some theoretical tools, which they may utilize during this transition. As students may discover, becoming a sport manager is a journey that will affect the way in which they view sport.

Cultural Hegemony_____
A concept that a culturally diverse society can be ruled or dominated by one of its social classes. Cultural hegemony may also be seen as the dominance of one social, political, or economic group over another group.

A Sociological and Cultural Examination of Sport

Sociology is the study of the organization of people within a society and their social relationships. Sociology also extends to the investigation of constructed organizations and institutions, and the processes through which people are linked. These social processes reflect repetitive and recurring organizational and institutional patterns characterizing individual and group choices. Culture consists of the ways in which life is created and organized by people within a particular society. As we will discuss later in this chapter, we construct social, organizational, and institutional "meaning," through, our social relationships, organizations, and institutions. A socio-cultural investigation of sport involves viewing sport within social, organizational, and institutional settings.

Some sport sociologists contend that spectator and participatory sport industries reflect the dominance of what Southall and Nagel (2009) described as "jock capitalism." Jock capitalism encapsulates the development of corporatized, commercial sport as cultural hegemony (Donnelly, 1996: Sack, 1987). In this context of sport as **cultural hegemony,** people who have societal power reproduce this privilege in the sport industry through promoting "entertaining and fun" sport forms that reinforce the values and orientations that encourage capitalist business expansion and profit maximization, and support their positions of power.

Shutterstock Images © 2010

We construct meaning through our social relationships, organizations, and institutions.

This cultural hegemony is succinctly expressed in the sport-industry maxim, "Nothing happens until we sell something," and in the Sales and Revenue Generation in Sport chapter's focus on the importance of sales and revenue generation in the sport industry. However, it should be noted the commercialized sport-industry is neither monolithic nor completely unified. Rather, it is a complex of layered *socio-cultural structures* (classes), each of which may have its own "mission," culture, and dominant logic. In addition, class members may often coexist with those from other classes. For students considering a sport-industry career, it is appropriate to investigate some theoretical perspectives from which to examine the industry in which they want to work. Later in this chapter students will be introduced to sociological theories from which the sport industry may be viewed (functionalist theory and conflict theory). In addition, stakeholder theory will be utilized to examine sport organizations' internal and external relationships. And, finally, a more recently developed theoretical perspective—the theory of institutional logics—will be presented as a means to investigate various sport-industry institutions.

Throughout this chapter, we will return to our initial scenario involving the need for rules in sport, and a discussion of sportsmanship, in order to dissect our initial answer and investigate how and why different people within the sport landscape may adopt different points-of-view on a given issue. In addition, the presented theories will be used to provide context for our discussions. The next section introduces two commonly utilized sport-sociology theories: functionalism, and conflict theory.

Sociological Theories and Practice

Functionalism

Prior to enrolling in an introduction to sport-management course, most students' sport consumption involves attending sport events, watching or listening to broadcasts, reading a daily newspaper's sport-section or sport magazine—such as *Sports Illustrated* or *ESPN: The Magazine;* and perusing websites, including Yahoo Sports, ESPN.com, SI.com, and Rivals.com. Much of this consumption is mediated reproduction (Southall & Nagel, 2008), which is primarily uncritical and statistically oriented, consisting of game summaries and celebration of celebrity athletes, home-town franchises, or mega sport events. Much mainstream sport journalism mythologizes athletes' heroic, almost superhuman athletic accomplishments, or sport's redeeming social qualities, including teamwork, discipline, hard work, and courage. Within this context, sport is often described as apolitical and a shining example of a meritocracy, where the participants are judged only on their athletic ability.

The sociological theory encapsulated in such sport consumption is **functionalist theory** or **functionalism**. Functionalism consistently supports the status quo in which sport teaches participants and spectators societal values by which they should live. In this theory sport unites people, overcoming economic, gen-

Functionalist Theory, or Functionalism_____

A sociological theory in which society is viewed as an organized system of interrelated parts held together by shared values and social processes that minimize differences and promote consensus among people (Coakley, 2008).

der, ethnic, or national barriers. Sport provides a mechanism through which appropriate goals can be set and met. Such goal-setting in sport translates to societal cooperation in which members of society fulfill their duties and obligations, allowing for society to provide for the common good.

Consistent with a functionalist view, sport has been trumpeted as a fortress that represents a consensus of societal values and holds the wall against radical elements (Oriard, 2010). In addition, at various times, functionalists have imbued specific sports, such as American football, with the ability to impart valuable lessons of loyalty, teamwork, and fundamental societal beliefs in family, friends, and faith (Wallace, 1951). In the United States, since at least the 1950s, in addition to an emphasis on pageantry, many large-scale sport events have also included religious and political undercurrents, represented by the inclusion of the national anthem (since World War II), fireworks, giant American flags, patriotic music, and military flyovers.

However, it should be noted a functionalist perspective may often exaggerate sport's positive effects. In addition, in many societies there has been a long history of intertwining politics and sport; with the effect that both become entangled in the public's mind with a society's values. Sport, whether in the form of the Olympics or high-school sports, has often been seen as the bastion of the common person. Such a traditional view of sport tends to minimize the possibility that sport is socially constructed and may disproportionately benefit some groups or individuals and exploit others.

Many sport events have political undertones.

Applying Theory to Practice— Unsporting Behaviors

Going back to our discussion of unsporting behaviors (i.e., verbally taunting or insulting an opponent), it is evident such on-field or court behaviors by football and basketball players are routinely penalized, and almost universally criticized by a segment of fans because they detract from the "essence of the game." (Note: This "fan segment" will be the basis for our conflict-theory discussion later in this chapter.) Through the years, in college or professional sports, "antics" such as taunting and "trash talking," choreographed and excessive celebrating, dancing, dunking, uniform dress-code violations, or removing a helmet while on the field have all been deemed to be unsporting and criticized by most coaches, media and fans.

Consistent with a functionalist perspective, sport fosters societal values of teamwork, fair play, honesty, and humility. Since inherently in team sports the "team" is paramount, it makes sense that team members should refrain from any actions that call attention to ones' self. Trash talking and taunting are fundamentally rude and "thuggish" and often provoke physical violence. In addition to these "civil" guidelines, some actions were (or are) banned for safety reasons (hanging on the rim after a dunk in a basketball game) or because they delay or detract from the game action. Just as "There's no crying in baseball," there should not be excessive celebration in sports. Decorum in sport, as in society in general, allows for societal cooperation and for everyone to get along nicely. For a functionalist the answer to our question remains, "All sports require rules. Just as in society, a sport's rules should be enforced." (Note: Such a viewpoint is consistent with the Deontological ethical framework presented in Chapter 7—Ethics and Ethical Decision Making.)

Conflict Theory

Conflict Theory_____
Sociological theory emphasizing social and political inequalities and the resulting economic and power differentials; a conflict theory analysis focuses on the inherent and endemic conflicts that arise from economic disparities.

In contrast to functionalism, which emphasizes sport's positive social characteristics, **conflict theory** emphasizes social and political inequalities and the resulting economic and power differentials that occur in the sport context. A conflict-theory analysis of sport focuses on the inherent and endemic conflicts that arise from economic disparities. Rather than occurring as a result of members of society performing their "natural" duties, social order is maintained through a political economy, in which certain groups (e.g., rich and powerful) maintain their economic advantage through coercion and exploitation. The media, business entities, political systems, educational institutions, and sport are examples of institutions that shape society's political economy. In this theory, sport, similar to other societal institutions, is shaped by society's economic structures. Contrary to functionalism, conflict theorists contend societal order results not from consensus, but from economic power and the use of such power to exploit labor.

Studying jock capitalism from a conflict perspective often results in the following issues being raised:

- Sport as an "opiate of the masses" or "beer and circus" (See Sperber, 2001.)
- Increased professionalism in college sport
- Exploitation of minority athletes in college sport
- Sport as a tool of militarism/nationalism
- Sport and sexism
- Sex and racism
- Public subsidization of professional sport

Applying Theory to Practice— Unsporting Behaviors

One criticism of the sportsmanship justification for penalizing such behaviors is the inconsistency of such penalties and criticisms. Similar behaviors by athletes of different ethnicities often receive different interpretations and different sanctions by sport leagues, organizations, and fans. Often, it is pointed out, rule-making and enforcing individuals, as well as many of the offended fans, are ethnically different from the "offensive" athletes. In addition, what is acceptable behavior in one sport setting is roundly criticized in another (e.g., in professional football the "Lambeau Leap," in which Packers players jump into the end zone stands after a touchdown is a time-honored tradition, but in college football an "excessive celebration" penalty may result from nothing more than a too exuberant a high-five.). In addition, fighting is tolerated in hockey, but not in football, basketball, and many other sports.

Fighting may be acceptable in hockey but not in other sports.

An example of this double standard is the consistent fines that Terrell Owens and Chad Ochocinco (National Football League wide receivers) have accrued over the years. Both players have been consistently criticized for their unsporting behaviors, and their excessive and choreographed behaviors. Such criticism has focuses on their behaviors as disrespectful to their opponents and to the game of football (as it is "meant to be played"). Meanwhile, college basketball coaches often argue with referees, use foul language in public, and yell at their players. Some sport sociologists suggest that while such actions by coaches may be criticized, they are more often excused as necessary elements of coaching and often helpful in maintaining player discipline.

In the context of sports, penalties are designed to compensate for participant actions that result in an unfair competitive advantage. The penalties are necessary to restore and maintain a "level playing field." However, in the case of "unsporting" behaviors, it is hard to see how engaging in them provides much, if any, competitive advantage, since most of them have to do with behavior that takes place outside the real-time competition itself. They have little, if any, influence on the outcome of the contest.

From a conflict-theory perspective, a relevant and often overlooked point specific to these "institutionalized" behavioral penalties in football and basketball (in the United States) are most often assessed to black male athletes. The disproportionate number of such penalties is because they more often engage in such behaviors, which reflect a distinctive black male urban culture (Andrews and Majors, 1999; Simons, 2003). These penalties quite often occur during a "stoppage in play" or after a score. In football, for example, celebrating by taking off one's helmet, taunting, and inciting the crowd occur after play has stopped. In basketball, some of the behaviors such as inciting the crowd, trash talking, and taunting, or hanging on the rim, most often do not take place during play. Interestingly, while one function of trash talking is to intimidate or "get into the head" of an opponent (which may provide some small competitive advantage), most often the overall competitive effect of these unsporting behaviors is minor compared to "competitive advantage" behaviors.

Since the behaviors under discussion do not produce a competitive advantage in the first place, penalizing them places one team at a competitive *disadvantage* and may contribute to an "uneven playing field."

Chad Ochocinco has garnered both adulation and criticism for his flamboyant, premeditated touchdown celebrations.

The penalties, in fact, contradict the level-playing-field justification for penalizing rule violations. Most penalties attempt to compensate for the competitive advantage gained by the offending team and restore the "level playing field." Interestingly, in United States professional football and basketball, the competitive disadvantage of such behaviors is compounded by frequent player suspensions, which preclude the punished athletes from playing in subsequent game(s).

As a result of a history of social and economic exclusion from white society, as well as a historical clustering in certain sports (e.g., football and basketball), American black male athletes have developed a set of distinctive behavioral cultural patterns (Boyd, 2003; Lane, 2007). These patterns are distinct from the white middle-class society's behavioral expectations (Andrews & Majors, 1999; Kochman, 1981). Many of the behavioral patterns exhibited in these penalized behaviors are associated with a subculture that has the following social markers: male, African-American, inner-city, "hip-hop" sports. "Talking smack" in sports is synonymous with African-American verbal aggressiveness. However, Gates' (1998) theory of African-American literary criticism argues such verbal aggressiveness is part of a long African oral tradition of "signifying" (i.e., saying one thing and meaning something else). Therefore, trash talking, celebration dances, and other expressive behaviors serve multiple functions for the black athlete; they both heighten competitive motivation and add enjoyment to the game (Boyd; de Jonge, 1993; Eveslage & Delaney, 1998; Lane).

Based upon their adoption of a functionalist perspective, many whites (especially those in positions of authority and power in sport) interpret these behaviors as the epitome of poor sportsmanship and offensive to white male upper and middle-class sensibilities. Specific to football and basketball, these sports' appropriate or "sporting" behaviors perpetuate the beliefs and attitudes of a predominantly white economic and political system maintained through control of institutions such as schools, media, and sports. To functionalists, these behaviors show a lack of humility, demean and embarrass an opponent, call attention to an individual, and serve to incite a crowd. In addition, these black males' aggressive behaviors play on white fear of them, leading to physical aggression, which may cause the game to get out of control. As a result these behaviors, which are inconsistent with "accepted" cultural norms, are frequently penalized and labeled "deviant, thuggish, immature, etc." Within the context of sport, this sporting ideology (represented in the institutionalizing of behavioral penalties) supports and maintains the dominant group's cultural hegemony.

Approaches to Sport Socialization

As can be seen, two different theoretical perspectives result in two distinctive analyses of the same situation. The disagreements are based on each theory's inherent fundamental assumptions. These theoretical differences fuel many "heated" sport-issue discussions among fans, students, faculty members and sport industry professionals. They form the story-lines for many elements of sports-talk radio and TV, sport blogs, websites, and Twitter posts. As you spend time, both in and out of class, talking about sport and sport-management issues, remember a theory's assumptions are at the heart of the various expressed points-of-view.

Sociological theories help sport management students investigate how members of society undergo socialization, an active process through which each societal member develops ideas of who they are and what is important to them. This socialization is interactive and ongoing. Each of us influence and is influenced by others, and interpret and accept or reject the social cues and signals. Various sociological theories provide different socialization perspectives. A functionalist looks at socialization as a process of learning society's rules and roles. A functionalist approach to sport socialization is most interested in studying who and what causes people to participate in sports and the effects (most often assumed to be positive) that sport participation produces. This approach assumes sport participation prepares athletes to assume roles as productive members of society. Most often a functionalist socialization perspective operates from the underlying assumption that sports participation is a "good" thing.

A conflict-theory approach to sport socialization assumes that, while such socialization is an internal and interactive process, its primary purpose in our society is to support capitalism's need to influence societal members in order for them to become sport consumers and sport managers within the existing economic system. This perspective looks at how our existing sport structures replicate and support racist, sexist, militaristic, and apolitical orientations among consumers, participants, and managers. This perspective focuses on how the existing economic system often disproportionately denies sports opportunities to poor and minority athletes, consumers, and sport managers.

A Multiple-Perspective Approach?

After this brief introduction to these two sociological perspectives, a sport-management student may have several questions:

- Is there a correct perspective?
- I want to work in the sport industry. How can I adopt a conflict perspective and still work in this field?
- I think sport is a good thing. What purpose does it serve to focus on the negative?
- Instead of adopting a single perspective, is it possible to utilize some elements from more than one theory, while conceding sport may have positive and negative effects?

Adopting a multiple-perspective approach may allow students interested in exploring a sport-management career to concede our modern sport industry may legitimize existing economic and political power structures.

Such a multiple-perspective approach does not depoliticize a sociological examination of the sport industry. It allows that facets of the privatized corporate sport industry, as it is presently constructed, may have negative social implications. In addition, this approach also contends sport does not necessarily have to exclusively exhibit these characteristics, but can also be more egalitarian and inclusive. However, it should be recognized that elements of a more democratic sport culture may not be totally accepted within the modern sport industry in which many sport-management students seek employment. This envisioned "hybrid" sport culture may not be the "idealized" sport culture envisioned by sport-management students or those who presently work in the sport industry. As a result, sport-management students who are sympathetic to such a perspective, but also aspire to be sport managers, may need to reevaluate their career aspirations and make a series of ethical decisions (See Chapter 7: Ethics and Ethical Decision Making) throughout their careers.

Examining Sport Organizations and Sport as an Institution

In addition to investigating sport's place in society, in order to examine where they might fit within the sport industry, sport-management students should be able to examine sport organizations and institutions. Two theoretical frameworks useful in examining individual sport organizations as institutions within society are **organizational culture**, and **institutional logics**. In order to use these frameworks, it is necessary to spend some time discussing each theory's elements. We will first define and delineate the fundamentals of organizational culture theory and then do the same for the theory of institutional logics. Finally, using both theories, we will examine specific sport organizations and sport as institutions.

Organizational Culture Theory

Definitions of Organizational Culture

There have been numerous definitions proposed for organizational culture. The concept of 'culture' has its roots in anthropology and sociology, and organizational studies focusing on organizational behavior and psychology. While not the first researcher to define organizational culture, Schein (1984) developed an often-cited definition:

> Organizational culture is the *pattern of basic assumptions* that a *given group* has *invented, discovered, or developed in learning to cope* with its *problems of external adaptation and internal integration,* and that have *worked well enough to be considered valid,* and therefore, to be *taught to new members* as the correct way to *perceive, think, and feel* in relation to those problems (p. 46). (Emphasis in original.)

Schein (1983) also summarized these patterns of basic assumptions as:

1. The organization's relationship to its environment—Is this relationship one of dominance, submission, harmonizing, finding an appropriate niche, or some combination of the above.

Organizational Culture_____

Pattern of basic assumptions that a given group has invented, discovered, or developed in learning to cope with its problems of external adaptation and internal integration, and that have worked well enough to be considered valid, and therefore, to be taught to new members as the correct way to perceive, think, and feel in relation to those problems (Schein, 1984).

Institutional Logics_____

A set of material practices and symbolic construction, which constitutes an institution's organizing principles. Such institutional logics (a) determine what are considered acceptable or un-acceptable operational means, (b) establish routines, (c) guide the evaluation and implementation of developed strategies, and (d) create precedent for further innovation.

2. The nature of reality and truth—This involves linguistic and relational rules that define what is a "fact" and whether truth is "discovered" or "revealed."
3. The nature of human nature—Centered on questions of what it means to be human, is human nature intrinsically "good or evil."
4. The nature of human activity—What is the right thing to do, based on the above assumptions? What is work and what is play?
5. The nature of human relationships—What is the right way for people to relate to each other, and distribute power and love? (p. 16)

In short, an organization's culture is its organizational "reality."

Consistent with this definition, Peterson, Cameron, Jones, Mets, and Ettington (1986) noted that organizational culture serves to emphasize an organization's unique or distinctive character, which provides a subordinating meaning to members, is deeply embedded and enduring, and is not malleable, changing primarily by cataclysmic events or through slower, intensive, and long-term efforts.

Dominant Culture and Subcultures

Schein's (1984) definition of culture presupposes that an organization must *own* a culture in order for that culture to exist. As a result, an organization's cultural beliefs are its taken-for-granted beliefs. Similar to societal norms, an organization's culture forms the basis of an organization and its members' view of reality. According to this view, such accepted organizational beliefs are not open to interpretation.

However, Martin and Siehl (1983) offered a variation on Schein's single-level "given-group" approach and proposed that an organization's culture often consisted of a dominant culture and at least three subcultures that may exist at any time in an organization. A dominant culture "expresses, through artifacts, core values shared by a majority of the organization's members" (p. 53). According to Koene, Boone, and Soeters (1997) a coherent organizational culture emerges ". . . through the social interaction between organization members" (Koene et al., p. 276). In addition, an organization's dominant culture is strengthened ". . . by weeding out individuals with different opinions and hiring employees with personal views congruent with those of other organization members" (p. 277).

Sport organizations often have strong dominant cultures, and all members of the organization are expected to adhere to the dominant culture. Those members who do not subscribe to this dominant culture will often be asked or forced to leave the organization. Research on college sport reveals that it is quite common for newly hired coaches to "run-off" a former coach's players who do not share his/her organizational culture values (Hill, Mitchell, & Southall, 2010). For example, in 2009 the University of Kentucky's men's basketball program had a 60 percent roster turnover (Hill, et al., 2010). The pronouncement that a sport organization is "going in a different direction" may often reflect an attempt to shift a franchise or program's organizational culture.

Since sport organizations, like many other entities, expect members to adhere to the organization's culture, prior to seeking employment with a sport organization, sport-management students should attempt to learn as much about "how things are done" within the organization, so they can ascertain the extent to which their personal values are consistent with the organization's cultural values.

Types of Subcultures

Even though sport organizations may have a dominant organizational culture, not every organizational member will completely internalize the organization's dominant cultural values. Such members may be part of what have been called organizational subcultures. Martin and Siehl (1983) contend such subcultures exist in all organizations. They identified one type of organizational subculture as an *enhancing* subculture. This subculture reflects O'Reilly and Chatman's (1986) idea of extreme organizational value internalization. An enhancing subculture exists in an ". . . organizational enclave in which adherence to the core values of the dominant culture would be more fervent than in the rest of the organization" (pp. 53–54). The members of an enhancing subculture think of themselves and are viewed by others as "true believers."

In sport, members of an enhancing subculture may engage in what Coakley (2009) referred to as *overconformity,* the unquestioned acceptance of cultural norms. Overtraining, utilizing performance-enhancing-drugs (PEDs), working long hours, ignoring family and friends in order to accomplish organizational goals are all examples of overconformity. Such extreme adherence to organizational norms may create conditions that result in blind faith in an ideal, a leader, or belief system.

Another type of organizational subculture is an *orthogonal* subculture. An orthogonal subculture is comprised of members who accept the core values of the dominant culture, but have separate, though not conflicting, assumptions, values, beliefs, and possibly goals that are unique to their particular group. This group's dominant content themes are still congruent with the dominant culture's content themes, but the members also have unique points of emphasis. For example, a sport franchise's coaching staff and its marketing and sales staff may share the core values of the franchise's dominant culture, while still having separate values specific to their roles within the organization. Coaches are focused on winning games, while the marketing and sales staffs are focused on getting fans in the stands! There is no fundamental conflict between these two goals, but most often coaches are not concerned with the marketing mix, and may actually view in-game promotions as intruding upon the game.

A third type of subculture is a *counterculture.* Counterculture members possess core values in direct opposition to the dominant culture and represent a challenge to the dominant culture. Martin and Siehl (1983) proposed that a counterculture's artifacts and practices often "ridicule" elements of the dominant culture's values, and actually support a competing alternate set of values. Members of a counterculture may engage in *underconformity* or deviance based upon ignoring or rejecting organizational norms (Coakley, 2009). Martin and

Siehl contend strongly-centralized organizations that permit decentralized diffusions of power are more likely to give rise to nonconforming subcultural enclaves. Such enclaves may include a charismatic challenger who may later be absorbed by the organization in an attempt to deal with the *counterculture.* This absorption is accomplished by giving the challenger ". . . limited power, some formal structural autonomy, and a tacit mandate to gather followers and create a nonconforming enclave" (p. 54) that the organization will seek to control. This absorption of the charismatic leader by the dominant culture actually serves, in many ways, to isolate the countercultural threat. By granting the counterculture some measure of autonomy, innovative ideas and practices may arise. If the results are beneficial to the organization, they can be co-opted by the dominant culture and embraced. On the other hand, if the deviance is not advantageous to the organization, it has been isolated.

In sport the identification of countercultures has often been seen as a direct challenge to an organization's legitimacy. Since many sport organizations are highly structured, with strong "chains of command," countercultures are often not tolerated. College football in the 1960s, including the integration of the Southeastern Conference (SEC) and the changing relationship between coaches and players, has been viewed as an example of societal changes that resulted in the development of subcultures within college football programs that challenged their dominant organizational cultures (Oriard, 2010).

Applying Theory to Practice—Big-Time College Athletic Departments

Intercollegiate athletic departments are increasingly diverse organizations. Not surprisingly, organizational culture research has found members of NCAA Division-I college athletic departments are highly competitive and value having a good reputation. However, it has also been found that since coaches and administrators often have divergent organizational backgrounds, distinct subcultures exist both between and within athletic departments (Putler & Wolfe, 1998; Southall, 2001; Southall, Wells, & Nagel, 2005).

Division-I university athletic departments' subcultures can be broken down into three basic "enclaves." These subcultures are (a) female non-revenue sport coaches, (b) male non-revenue sport coaches, and (c) revenue sport coaches. Not surprisingly, there are significant differences in these coaches' perceptions of departmental expectations regarding winning. As might be expected, the male-revenue-sport coaches' subculture places a higher value on winning and revenue-production. They also feel more constrained by departmental and NCAA rules than any other group (Southall, 2001; Southall et al., 2005). Interestingly, research has also revealed NCAA Division-I women's basketball coaches' views are more similar to those held by male revenue-sport coaches than other women's sport coaches. This suggests revenue-production status, not gender of the sport, may be a critical factor. In addition, the fact that the number of women coaching women's college teams is at an all-time low (42.8%) (Metcalfe, 2008) may also be a factor.

Such research is of interest to managers, since they need to be aware of a subculture's values and determine if the subculture is an enhancing, orthogonal, or counter-culture. If it is determined that the subculture is, in fact, a counter-culture (with values at odds with the stated values of the organization), the organization should take steps to address this situation. In any sport organization, not everyone is on the same page when it comes to core organizational or cultural values. Like any organization, a college athletic department may often reflect a complex and chaotic clash of organizational values. This is important, since research has found organization members who do not agree with an organization's predominant espoused value system are more likely to engage in organizational deviance (e.g., flout NCAA compliance regulations, not support a marketing campaign, or not pay attention during emergency management planning meetings) (Santomier, Howard, Piltz, & Romance, 1980; Padilla & Baumer, 1994). Athletic directors must work to develop a cohesive workforce, while still equitably managing their department. It should come as no surprise that subcultures exist within professional franchises, parks and recreation departments, or high-school sport teams. Any sport organization is an intricate product of complex, interdependent factors and people, all of whom operate to fulfill their own wants, needs, and desires. In addition, it is important that students who wish to work in the sport industry recognize that since cultural values are creations of people interacting with one another, they cannot be mandated by an outside organization (e.g., the NCAA, National High School Federation, or NFL Commissioner's Office).

Theory of Institutional Logics

A theory useful in examining sport as an institution is the theory of institutional logics. While organizational culture theory focuses on individual organizations, institutional-logics theory applies to sport as an institution that encompasses many sport organizations. It has been argued that Western society's major institutions, including Christianity, capitalism, the family, democracy, and the bureaucratic state, have logics that guide action (Friedland & Alford, 1991). In addition to investigations focused on the societal level, there have been field or industry-level examinations in various industries, including financial services (Lounsbury, 2002), educational publishing (Thornton, 2002), professional sport in the United States (Cousens & Slack, 2005), English rugby union (O'Brien & Slack, 2004), and American college sport (Southall & Nagel, 2008; Southall et al., 2008).

From this theoretical perspective, sport, as an institution, as Friedland and Alford (1991) noted has ". . . a central logic—a set of material practices and symbolic construction—which constitutes its organizing principles and which is available to organizations and individuals to elaborate" (p. 248). Such institutional logics determine what are considered acceptable or unacceptable operational means, establish routines, guide the evaluation and implementation of developed strategies, and create precedent for further innovation (Duncan & Brummett, 1991; Friedland & Alford; Nelson & Winter, 1982; Washington &

Ventresca, 2004). These logics manifest themselves as generalized expectations that allow individuals within sport to engage in coherent, well understood, and acceptable activities. In this sense, then, institutional logics influence how people working within sport communicate, enact power, and determine what behaviors to sanction and reward (Barley & Tolbert, 1997). Eventually, these logics become taken-for-granted "facts" reflected in particular unquestioned courses of action.

Similar to individual organizations, as institutions develop competing institutional logics may emerge. Such conflict most often results in the emergence of a dominant logic that works to establish local-meaning frameworks that guide strategy and structure by focusing the attention of decision makers towards those issues that are most consistent with the perceived dominant logic and away from those issues that are deemed to be inconsistent (Thornton, 2002).

Applying Theory to Practice— Bowl Championship Series Football Broadcasts

Just as it is important to identify the organizational culture of a sport franchise or athletic department to which they have submitted an application, students should be familiar with a sport's overarching material practices and organizing principles. Within a specific sport (e.g., NCAA Football Bowl Subdivision [FBS]) and a specific sport product [Bowl Championship Series (BCS) television broadcasts] there are great opportunities to apply institutional logics theory. As you read the section, pay attention to how the specific research results are discussed in relation to the theory, and how the theory provides a context for better understanding the sport product.

BCS Bowl-Game Telecasts

There is no question NCAA Division-I college sport in general—and big-time college football in particular—occupies a central place in American culture. In his 2009 State of the Association address, Dr. Myles Brand (late President of the NCAA) noted: "[College sport] has become integral to many of our universities and colleges, institutions which are the guardians of our traditions and histories and the harbingers of our futures. College sports generates (sic) a significant economic impact in communities all across the country" (National Collegiate Athletic Association, 2009, para. 14).

University administrators, as well as NCAA Football and BCS executives, and network broadcast partners, rarely—if ever—directly address possible conflicts between educational and commercial logics within the field of college-sport. However, they all acknowledge the need for increased commercialism in college sport. Since 2003, the NCAA and member D-I universities have consistently embraced increased college-sport commercialization. In fact, the NCAA and university presidents have been applauded by corporate partners for their recognition that ". . . there should be more, not less, [commercialism] as long as it stays within the framework of amateurism and promotes the accomplishments of the athletes and their teams" (Smith, 2009, p. 28). This sense of cooperation is evident in the statement of Tim McGhee, executive director of corporate sponsorship at AT&T, an NCAA corporate champion, ". . . I see an NCAA that is more responsive to corporate partners and how we market our products and services" (Smith, p. 28).

However, Bob Lawless, NCAA Executive Committee Chair, seemed to recognize the possibility of such conflict, noting "There's a realization that when you receive a certain amount of revenue from a network that they're going to generate revenue in order to meet the agreement of the contract" (National Collegiate Athletic Association, 2002, para. 6). However, according to The NCAA News, college presidents are unperturbed with ". . . a corporate partner essentially 'sponsor[ing]' the NCAA's educational mission," as long as it is ". . . done well and tastefully" (National Collegiate Athletic Association, para. 2, 6).

Previous research of college-sport broadcasts revealed the apparent existence of two competing institutional logics, (e.g., educational and commercial) within the college-sport field (Southall & Nagel, 2008; Southall et al., 2008). There is evidence to suggest a commercial logic has been dominant for almost as long as the NCAA has been in existence, and college football has been broadcast. A primary reason why U.S. universities and colleges developed sport programs was to enhance their resources and increase visibility (Oriard, 2009; Washington and Ventresca, 2004). This is exemplified by the aggressive pursuit of television rights fees by NCAA members since the early 1950s (Dunnavant, 2004), as well as universities' willingness to engage in seemingly fratricidal litigation (e.g., *Board of Regents v. NCAA*) in order to clear the way for commercial-revenue maximization (Oriard; Washington, 2004).

A primary justification for big-time college football at the highly visible FBS or BCS level relates to such athletic contests' potential to communicate (both to fans in stadiums and those watching on TV or the Internet) universities' educational stories (Gerdy, 2006). In particular, if BCS broadcasts are vehicles through which this "educational" purpose is pursued, these broadcasts' content—the images portrayed and messages conveyed—of such telecasts, should reflect intercollegiate athletics' stated values and communicate higher-education's expressed purposes. However, if such messages that reflect commercialized logics are dominant and the BCS's organizational legitimacy is based upon its market position, then the arrangement's paramount mission—exhibited through BCS telecasts—should be to build and enhance the BCS's competitive market position. The results, in Tables 2-1 and 2-2, summarize the non-football-specific content (e.g., commercials, inserted commercial graphics, public service announcements) from an analysis of the five 2009 BCS telecasts (Southall, Southall, & Dwyer, 2009). This content (i.e., The "stuff" you fast-forward past if you have "Tivoed" the game, and the graphic that always tells you the game action is about ready to resume!) offers evidence a commercial institutional logic now dominates big-time college football.

TABLE 2.1

BCS Broadcast Nonprogram Category Summary

Category	Mean (M) per Broadcast
Advertising Commercials	47 min, 43 sec
NCAA Public Service Announcements	2 min, 13 sec
Corporate Public Service Announcements	60 sec
Graphic Advertisements	25 min, 32 sec
Graphic Advertisements with verbal commentary	12 min, 48 sec
Academic Graphics (e.g., player majors)	11 sec
Educational Commentary	16 sec

Table 2.1 clearly illustrates how pervasive the selling of non-sport products is during a sport event. In an average BCS Bowl-game broadcast there are almost 90 minutes of commercial messages. Conversely, in a "college" football game, in which the teams are ostensibly sponsored by institutions of higher "education," there is less than 30 seconds of educational messages. Citing the increased commercialization and professionalization of college sport apparent in studies such as this one, some critics of college sport have called on the U.S. Congress to rescind college sports' tax exempt status.

As Table 2.2 highlights, Bowl Championship Series broadcasts provide little evidence of an educational institutional logic. While the primary messages

TABLE 2.2

BCS Broadcast Educational Messaging Summary

Game	Graphic with Academic Information (positive or negative)		Educational Messages by Commentators (positive or negative)	
	Units	Time	Units	Time
Allstate Sugar Bowl	—	—	1 (pos)	15 sec
FedEx National Championship	—	—	—	—
FedEx Orange Bowl	9 (pos)	53 sec	5 (1 pos; 4 neg)	60 sec
Rose Bowl presented by CITI	—	—	—	—
Tostitos Fiesta Bowl	—	—	1 (pos)	7 sec
TOTAL	9 (pos)	53 sec	7 (3 pos; 4 neg)	82 sec

conveyed during any college-sport contest will, of course, be related to the game itself, within BCS telecasts, discussions of higher education, academics, or broader university missions of teaching, research, or service did not occur. In fact, the 2009 BCS National Championship and Rose Bowl broadcasts contained no educational messaging, while the Tostitos Fiesta Bowl contained only seven seconds of such messaging.

BCS bowl-game broadcasts do indeed offer evidence of a "partnership" among FBS stakeholders, but contrary to rhetoric espoused by NCAA and university officials, as well as corporate and broadcast partners, it seems as if this "amateur" sport partnership is built on commercial, not educational, values. While for most American sport fans there is ". . . nothing wrong with money and making it, especially if you can use it to further your mission" (Brown, 2002, p. 4), concerns regarding college sport's lack of academic credibility—at least in reference to the educational value of BCS bowl-game broadcasts—appear to be accurate. At least one NCAA faculty athletic representative (FAR) has expressed such a concern, "The problem comes when the money diverts you from what you're supposed to be doing" (Brown, p. 4). During BCS bowl-game broadcasts, the public is overwhelmingly bombarded with commercial messages. While the BCS member schools may promote their football "brands," at least during their sport products' telecasts, these universities' educational mission is rarely, if ever, mentioned. Citing this seeming disconnect between higher-education's espoused educational institutional logics (i.e., a commitment to undergraduate and graduate education, research, etc.) and a quasi-professional sport broadcast, in which viewers are inundated with advertisements for non-sport products, some critics have argued the NCAA's "collegiate" model has effectively become no more than a point of differentiation to separate NCAA-licensed games and participating teams from other professional televised sport leagues and events.

For our purposes here, it is important for sport-management students to recognize how a theory, in this case institutional-logics theory, can be used to make sense of a sport product through data analysis. While a college-sport fan may simply watch a BCS telecast and sarcastically gripe, "It's too bad this game is interrupting these great commercials!" a researcher views the same game and attempts to understand why there are almost 90 minutes of commercials in a BCS broadcast. Then, perhaps using an ethical framework from Chapter 7—Ethical Decision Making, a social critic might make a judgment about whether or not the broadcast is consistent with the sponsoring organization's public mission statement.

Conclusion

This chapter's purpose is to illustrate that there is more to studying sport than simply watching SportsCenter, reading a box score, or following a fantasy-football player's progress each week. This chapter has focused on a "different" method of viewing sport as a social and organizational world. Sport is an integral part of many of our lives. Many of you reading this book aspire to a sport management career. Many sport-management students have been—or still are—athletes. Many have been a "fan" as long as they can remember, with a favorite player, team, or sport.

Sport is part of many cultures. It is comprised of human beings and constructed and shaped by those same people. Not all sports are the same; they vary just as the people who compete, view, and manage them vary. To truly understand and appreciate sport and the sport industry, sport-management students need to be willing and able to use socio-cultural theories and apply them to real-world sport situations.

Study Questions

1. Define functionalism, and conflict theories. To which theory are you most sympathetic? Why do you think this is so?
2. Do you think professional or college football and basketball players should be penalized for celebratory or "trash-talking" behaviors? If so, why? If not, why not? What elements of the sociological theories presented do you think make the most sense in supporting your position?
3. What is the definition of organizational culture? What types of organizational subcultures do Martin and Siehl identify? Given what you know about college sport on your campus, do you agree with the analysis of the organizational culture of college sport presented? Why or why not? What experiences can you draw on to support your position?
4. What do you think is the purpose of big-time college sport? Do you agree with the analysis of college-sport's institutional logics presented in this chapter? If so, why? If not, why not?

Learning Activity

Watch a sport-event broadcast and pay attention to the non-program messages that are represented during the course of the broadcast. What messages are found within the broadcast? What commercials and graphics are displayed? What do the commentators discuss? From this exercise, what conclusions can you draw, if any, regarding the sport's institutional logics?

References

Andrews, V. (1996). Black bodies white control: The contested terrain of sportsmanlike conduct. *Journal of African American Men, 2*(1), 33–60.

Andrews, V. (1997). African American player codes on celebration, taunting and sportsmanlike conduct. *Journal of African American Men, 2*(2-3), 57–92.

Barley, S.R., & Tolbert, P.S. (1997). Institutionalization and structuration: Studying the links between action and institution. *Organization Studies, 18*, 93–117.

Boyd, T. (2003). *Young, black, rich & famous: The rise of the NBA, the hip hop invasion, and the transformation of American culture.* Lincoln, NE: University of Nebraska Press.

Brand, M. (2009, January 15). The 2009 NCAA State of the Association speech. *The NCAA News Online.* Retrieved September 23, 2009 from http://www.ncaa.org/ wps/ncaa?ContentID=43942

Brohm, J. (1978). *Sport: A prison of measured time.* London: Ink Links.

Brown, G.T. (2002, March 18). The $6 billion plan: NCAA wants TV contract to increase revenue, decrease tension between scholarly mission and commercial image. *The NCAA News.* Retrieved May 5, 2006 from http://www. ncaa.org/wps

Coakley, J.J. (2008). *Sport in society* (10th ed.). Boston, MA: McGraw Hill.

Duncan, M.C., & Brummett, B. (1991). The mediation of spectator sport. In L.H. Vande Berg & L.A. Wenner (Eds.), *Television criticism: Approaches and applications* (pp. 367–387). New York: Longman.

Dunnavant, K. (2004). *The fifty-year seduction: How television manipulated college football, from the birth of the modern NCAA to the creation of the BCS.* New York: St. Martin's Press.

Eveslage, S., & Delaney, K. (1998). Talkin' trash at Hardwick High: A case study of insult talk on a boys' basketball team. *International Review for the Sociology of Sport, 33*(3), 239–54.

Friedland, R., & Alford, R.R. (1991). Bringing society back in: Symbols, practices, and institutional contradictions. In W.W. Powell & P.J. DiMaggio (Eds.), *The new institutionalism in organizational analysis* (pp. 232–262). Chicago: University of Chicago.

Gates, H. (1998). *The signifying monkey: A theory of African American literary criticism.* New York: Oxford University Press.

Gerdy, J.R. (2006). *Air ball: American education's failed experiment with elite athletics.* Oxford, MS: University Press of Mississippi.

Mitchell, C., Hill, D., & Southall, R.M. (2010, April). *Understanding the commonality of roster turnover on NCAA men's basketball teams.* Paper presented at the annual Scholarly Conference on College Sport, Chapel Hill, NC.

Lane, J. (2007). *Under the boards: The cultural revolution of basketball.* Lincoln, NE: University of Nebraska Press.

Martin, J., & Siehl, C. (1983). Organizational culture and counterculture: An uneasy symbiosis. *Organizational Dynamics, 12,* 52–64.

Metcalfe, J. (2008, May 18). Women coaches are few in women's sports: In push to win, some wonder if role models lost. *AZcentral.com.* Retrieved April 1, 2010, from http://www.azcentral.com/news/articles/2008/05/18/20080518women coaches0518.html

National Collegiate Athletic Association. (2002, March 18). CEOs don't blink on corporate tag. *NCAA News.* Retrieved October 4, 2009, from https://www.ncaa.org/wps/wcm/connect/ncaa/ncaa/ncaa+news/ncaa+news+online/2002/association- wide/ceos+don_t+blink+on+corporate+tag+-+3-18-02

Nelson, R.R., & Winter, S.G. (1982). *An evolutionary theory of economic change.* Cambridge, MA: The Belknap Press of Harvard University Press.

O'Reilly III, C.A., & Chatman, J.A. (1996). Cultures as social control: Corporations, cults, and commitment. *Research in Organizational Behavior, 18,* 157–200.

Oriard, M. (2009). *Bowled over: Big-time college football from the sixties to the BCS era.* Chapel Hill, NC: The University of North Carolina Press.

Padilla, A., & Baumer, D. (1994). Big-time college sports: Management and economic issues. *Journal of Sport and Social Issues, 18,* 123–143.

Peterson, M.W., Cameron, K.S., Jones, P., Mets, L.A., & Ettington, D. (1986). *The organizational context for teaching and learning: A review of the research literature.* Ann Arbor, MI: National Center for Research to Improve Postsecondary Teaching and Learning, University of Michigan.

Putler, D.S., & Wolfe, R.A. (1999). Perceptions of intercollegiate athletic programs: Priorities and tradeoffs. *Sociology of Sport Journal, 16,* 301–325.

Santomier, J.P., Howard, W.G., Piltz, W.L., & Romance, T.J. (1980). White sock crime: Organizational deviance in intercollegiate athletics. *Journal of Sport and Social Issues, 4 (2),* 26–32.

Sack, A.L. (1987). College sport and the student-athlete. *Journal of Sport and Social Issues, 11(1/2),* 31–48.

Sack, A. (2009). Clashing models of commercial sport in higher education: Implications for reform and scholarly research. *Journal of Issues in Intercollegiate Athletics,* 76–92. Retrieved December 13, 2009, from http://csri-jiia.org/documents/puclications/research_articles/2009/JIIA_2009

Schein, E.H. (1983, Summer). The role of the founder in creating organizational culture. *Organizational Dynamics,* 13–28.

Schein, E.H. (1984). Coming to a new awareness of organizational culture. *Sloan Management Review, 25(2),* 3–16.

Simons, H. D. (2003). Race and penalized sports behaviors. *International Review for the Sociology of Sport, 38(1),* 5–22.

Smith. M. (2009, September 21-27). 'The right man at the right time': NCAA's Brand brought academic reform, a respect for need to generate revenue. *Street & Smith's SportsBusiness Journal, 12(21),* 1, 28–29.

Southall, R.M. (2000). *A study of organizational culture of Mountain West Conference - intercollegiate athletic departments.* Published doctoral dissertation. University of Northern Colorado.

Southall, R.M., Wells, D.E., & Nagel, M.S. (2005). Organizational culture perceptions of intercollegiate athletic department members. *Applied Research in Coaching and Athletics Annual, 20,* 65–93.

Southall, R.M, Nagel, M.S., Amis, J., & Southall, C. (2008). A method to March Madness: Institutional logics and the 2006 National Collegiate Athletic Association Division I men's basketball tournament. *Journal of Sport Management, 22(6),* 677–700.

Southall, R.M., & Nagel, M.S. (2008). A case-study analysis of NCAA Division I women's basketball tournament broadcasts: Educational or commercial activity? *International Journal of Sport Communication, 1(4),* 516–533.

Southall, R.M., Southall, C., & Dwyer, B. (2009). 2009 Bowl Championship Series telecasts: Expressions of big-time college-sport's commercial institutional logics. *Journal of Issues in Intercollegiate Athletics, 2,* 150–176.

Sperber, M. (2001). *Beer and circus: How big-time college sports is crippling undergraduate education.* New York: Henry Holt and Company.

Thornton, P.H. (2002). The rise of the corporation in a craft industry: Conflict and conformity in institutional logics. *Academy of Management Journal, 45,* 81–101.

Washington, M. (2004). Field approaches to institutional change: The evolution of the National Collegiate Athletic Association 1906-1995. *Organization Studies, 25,* 393–414.

Washington, M., & Ventresca, M. J. (2004). How organizations change: The role of institutional support mechanisms in the incorporation of higher education visibility strategies, 1874–1995. *Organization Science, 15,* 82–97.

The United States Sport Industry

Mark S. Nagel • *University of South Carolina*

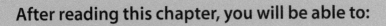

After reading this chapter, you will be able to:

- Explain the breadth of the United States sport industry;
- Identify and describe selected organizations working within the sub-industries of the United States sport marketplace;
- Describe potential internship and entry level employment opportunities in sport management.

KEY TERMS

Football Bowl
  Subdivision

Football
  Championship
  Subdivision

Independent Teams

Licensed Merchandise

Introduction

The vast majority of entry-level sport-management students will answer the question "What do you want to do in your sport management career" with one of the following responses:

1. "Become a general manager of a franchise in the National Basketball Association (NBA), National Football League (NFL), National Hockey League (NHL), or Major League Baseball (MLB)."
2. "Become an athletic director at a National Collegiate Athletic Association (NCAA) Division-I athletic department, preferably one that is a member of one of the largest conferences (Big 10, Big 12, ACC, SEC, PAC-10, or Big East)."
3. "Become a player agent."

While each of these choices is a potential career option, they are certainly not indicative of the breadth of the sport-management industry. The above-listed positions typically generate extensive media attention, so most students, parents, and non-sport management faculty tend to think sport-management graduates primarily work in these subsectors of the industry. Though positions in these areas do exist, there are usually few such entry-level positions available and higher-ranking positions are especially scarce. For instance, there are only 32 NFL teams, meaning there are only 32 NFL general managers. Mathematically, students have a higher likelihood of becoming a member of the United States Congress than of becoming an NFL, NBA, NHL, or MLB general manager.

In addition to there being few opportunities, general managers, athletic directors or prominent player agents are often people who were high-level athletes. Though certainly not a requirement, being a well-known former athlete can often provide a spring-board to eventual success as a general manager, athletic director, or player agent. It is wonderful if a student desires to someday obtain one of these positions, and, while students should not be discouraged from pursuing a career path with these eventual outcomes as the primary goal, they should understand the reality of the situation. Becoming a NCAA Division-I athletic director, general manager, or prominent sport agent requires intellect, determination, countless hours of learning, and years of preparation. Though it is highly unlikely that obtaining one of those positions will occur, by setting an "ultimate" goal, along with smaller goals that serve as steps along the way, either that final goal will be achieved or other career opportunities will present themselves. While this advice may seem "cliché-like," it is actually true.

This chapter discusses various subsectors of the sport industry that may provide internship opportunities and eventual employment. It is designed to provide students with a broader perspective of the industry than a "traditional" view of sport management that consists of only involving college and professional sport employment or becoming an agent. The categories are certainly not exhaustive as the sport industry is constantly evolving, with new subsectors emerging almost daily. Regardless of your career path (Just a note: By enrolling in a sport-management class your career has already begun!), be prepared to work long hours in order to achieve your career goals. Remember, your career will not develop overnight. The adage, "You learn in your 20s and begin to earn in your 30s" is certainly applicable to the sport-management industry. Maintain your focus while working diligently and good things will eventually happen.

Professional Sport

Professional sport franchises have two distinct sets of employees. The "talent" side of the organization deals with preparing the team to achieve on-field success. The general manager, player-personnel director, coaches, full-time scouts (and certainly the players) usually receive salaries considerably higher than those earned by employees on the organization's "business" side. Players, coaches, and general managers also typically receive extensive media attention and are readily identified by fans and many members of the team's local community. The desire to work on the "talent" side of professional sports is what initially attracts many students to sport-management programs. However, in the vast majority of cases, sport-management students will be hired to work in the business side of the organization. It is certainly possible, but extremely rare, for a sport-management student who is not a former college or professional sport player to be hired by a professional sport franchise to work on the "talent" side of the organization. Most sport-management students who work for a professional sport franchise will be employed in one or more of a variety of sport business areas (e.g., marketing, finance, game operations, sales, etc.).

When most students think of working in professional sports, they focus upon the NBA, NHL, NFL and MLB as likely employers. These leagues tend to attract large fan bases and have games that are often televised. Potential internship or employment openings at these organizations usually attract hundreds of applicants and therefore have extremely low salaries. Much of the "compensation" for working for a franchise in one of these leagues is the ability to say that you work for the team. Sport franchises realize there are often hundreds of potential employees who would "love" to work for their organization, so they often keep salaries low and demand long working hours, particularly for those employees who have been with the team for less than five years.

Professional sport franchises from the "Big 4" leagues tend to have distinct compartmentalized divisions in marketing, sales, game operations, finance, media relations, human resources, and law. Interns or entry-level employees hired to work for these teams may find they work almost exclusively in one area and do not get exposed to very many facets of the organization. Working exclusively in the marketing department certainly enables an intern or entry-level employee to learn detailed aspects of marketing, but it may not be conducive to understanding how the other departments interact in order for the franchise to operate effectively.

Though not nearly as popular as teams in the "Big 4" sports leagues, there are many other professional-sport franchises. Sports such as soccer, lacrosse, and

Independent Teams_____

Baseball teams that operate without a direct affiliation with any Major League Baseball franchise.

volleyball have financially viable professional leagues, and the NBA, NHL, and MLB also have extensive minor-league systems. In baseball, there are also **independent teams** that operate without the direct support of a major-league affiliate. Most students do not initially consider a career working with franchises other than those in the "Big-Four" leagues, but often there are much greater career advancement opportunities in these situations. For instance, though not the norm, it is not uncommon for general managers of minor league baseball teams to be hired prior to reaching their 35th birthday. It is also not uncommon for talented interns to be promoted quickly after an internship with a "minor league" franchise. There are many prominent sport managers who have achieved great success in (so called) minor-league sport, who refuse "major-league" job offers because their "minor-league" careers are fulfilling.

Since the team's overall staff is much smaller, minor-league sports franchise employees (including interns) typically have multiple areas of responsibility within the organization. For instance, an NBA team will likely have at least five marketing department staff members. Each employee will likely have a narrowly defined job description. However, a NBA D-League franchise will have a much smaller marketing staff that will, most likely, have daily interaction with members of many different departments. By being thoroughly exposed to the smaller organization's various facets, skills are developed that can be applied to future work activities. Even more prominent minor league sports, such as Triple-A teams in minor-league baseball, will present opportunities for employees to see and understand how the various aspects of the organization function. For instance, it is not uncommon for every member of a minor-league franchise, including the general manager, to help pull the tarp during rain delays.

In addition, the world of professional sports is not limited to "team" sports. There are numerous organizations that operate tournaments for professional athletes in sports such as tennis, golf, fishing, boxing, mixed martial arts, and track and field. Though events such as the United States Open Tennis Championship or Professional Golf Association (PGA) Championship garner extensive media attention, there are other internship and employment opportunities in these sports, since tournaments are held most weekends during the year. Sports such as mixed martial arts and lacrosse have only recently launched viable leagues, but they are growing—in both popularity and employment opportunities.

The growth of NASCAR over the past 15 years is an excellent example of an emerging professional sport and the potential for growth. For many years, automobile racing was seen as a niche sport in the United States, with little national interest beyond the Indianapolis 500 each spring. Until the 1990s, NASCAR was perceived primarily as a "southern" sport that did not generate much national media attention. However, as NASCAR racing became more popular, various NASCAR employees were recognized for their expertise in a variety of sport business areas, particularly sponsorship sales and fulfillment. While NASCAR has recently faced numerous challenges, with a concurrent slowdown in television ratings and revenue, its rise as a "major-league" sport is an indication that "niche" professional sport organizations can provide excellent employment opportunities.

Though working for a team is certainly one of the most popular potential sport management careers, professional-sport opportunities are not limited to team-sport franchises. Each professional sport league has a league office. League office employees are charged with creating a fair environment for all league participants, enhancing the league's brand, and developing league revenue sources. Most leagues have a commissioner or league president who oversees the league office. For instance, Major League Baseball has a commissioner who hires a staff that schedules games, hires and supervises umpires, negotiates media contracts, and markets the league. Minor League Baseball (MiLB) has a President responsible for all of the affiliated minor-league baseball teams. In addition, each minor league (e.g., Midwest League, Southern League, etc.) has a President who hires and manages a full-time staff, as well as league interns.

Working for a professional sport league does not offer the emotional highs and lows associated with an individual franchise, because team employees have a vested interest in each game's results. The day-to-day excitement of working for an individual franchise can be intense, especially at the end of the season when a team is in the playoffs. Though "business-office" staff do not directly influence the outcome on the field, they certainly contribute to franchise success by marketing to fans and providing a positive game-day experience. In recognition of their contributions, most professional sport organizations reward all full-time employees, not just the coaches and players, with rings and other awards if the team wins a championship.

To truly understand the professional sport environment and to determine if it is a good fit, students should seek out volunteer and internship opportunities with individual franchises—as well as league offices. It certainly is appropriate to pursue positions with a "major-league" franchise or league, if that is your primary goal, but do not fail to at least consider a "minor league" position, since many wonderful career opportunities are available.

College Sport

When most people think of intercollegiate athletics, they tend to focus upon **Football Bowl Subdivision** (FBS) football bowls and the NCAA Division-I Men's and Women's Basketball Tournaments. Though these are certainly the most watched college athletic events, they are a small fraction of the total opportunities in college athletics. The NCAA is divided into three divisions (I, II, III). Currently, there are *1089 member schools* with *347* in Division I, *295* in Division II, and *447* in Division III. The NCAA organizes championships in 23 different sports with schools offering opportunities for men and women to compete.

To be eligible to be a member of Division I, an institution must offer at least seven sports for men and seven for women (or six for men and eight for women) with at least two team sports for each gender. Division-I members may offer athletic scholarships and most schools recruit potential athletes from various regions

Football Bowl Subdivision__
A segment of the National Collegiate Athletic Association that is comprised of schools playing the highest level of football (formerly known as Division IA).

Division-I football teams usually compete in large stadiums while Division-II or Division-III programs typically have much smaller facilities.

of the country. Though nearly every Division-I athletic department is part of a regional conference, most teams schedule some competition with schools outside of their immediate geographic area. Division-II institutions must sponsor at least five sports for men and five for women (or four for men and six for women) with two team sports for each gender. Though Division-II institutions may offer athletic scholarships, their recruitment efforts are usually regionally based. In addition, athletic-competition travel tends to be local or regional. Division-III institutions must offer at least five sports for men and five for women. They are not permitted to offer athletic scholarships ("What's the difference . . . ," n.d.).

Division I is further separated into three divisions (formerly known as IA, IAA, IAAA). Division-IA institutions that offer "big time" football compete in the Football Bowl Subdivision (FBS), while D-IAA schools—now **Football Championship Subdivision** (FCS)—do not provide as high a financial commitment to their football programs. Division IAAA members do not field D-I football teams. It is important to remember that all Division-I schools compete for the same championships in all sports besides football. Except for a few rare instances, schools must compete at the same level for all of their sports. Such instances are often in Olympic sports (e.g., skiing, hockey, wrestling, etc.).

The various NCAA divisions roughly approximate varying philosophical perspectives and financial commitments to intercollegiate athletics. Division-I programs tend to provide coaches with greater financial resources for scholarships, personnel, and equipment, upgraded facilities, large travel budgets, and extensive opportunities to compete against other schools across the nation. Most Division-II institutions offer athletic-related scholarships across a variety of sports, but travel and expenses are typically much lower than in Division I. Division-III members, while still committed to intercollegiate athletic competition, in most instances have deemphasized a highly commercialized approach to

Football Championship Subdivision_____

A segment of the National Collegiate Athletic Association that is comprised of Division-I schools that are not playing at the highest level of football competition (formerly known as Division IAA).

college sport. According to the division's mission statement, member institutions prohibit athletic-related scholarships and ". . . place highest priority on the overall quality of the educational experience and on the successful completion of all students' academic programs." (NCAA, n.d., para. 1).

Most NCAA members have maintained their current affiliation for many years. However, each year a handful of members attempt to move divisions. In most cases, the movement is prompted by a desire to enhance athletic commitment and "upgrade" to a higher division. Most schools rationalize such a move (from Division III to Division II or from Division II to Division I) as a means to enhance the institution's "marketability." Competing at a high level of intercollegiate athletics is perceived by many to be critical to attracting and retaining students, since competing at the Division I-level offers a greater opportunity to be mentioned on ESPN's *SportsCenter* and in other media outlets. Though examining the specifics regarding the costs and benefits of moving up a division is beyond the scope of this chapter and book, a focus on athletic-department expansion and increased use of college sport as a marketing platform has resulted in concern among many faculty, students, alumni and administrators regarding institutional priorities. These concerns have resulted in a small number of schools "downgrading" their NCAA status. Recently, Birmingham Southern College realized an increase in overall athletic participation and an increase in campus minority enrollment, university giving, and applicant quality after it moved from Division I to Division III.

Though the importance placed upon winning and academic achievement may differ by sport and NCAA Division, regardless of division, athletic directors' and athletic department staff roles are similar. Athletic directors are expected to hire coaches and other staff members, manage an athletic department's budget, generate revenues to insure the department's financial viability, and interact with various on- and off-campus constituencies. Reflecting the enhanced commitment to the business of intercollegiate athletics, the vast majority of coaches and athletic department personnel who work at Division I-institutions tend to not maintain formal roles in other areas of the university. However, at many Division-II and (especially) D-III institutions, coaches and athletic department staff members often teach classes and assume other campus roles.

Students wishing to eventually work in college athletics should develop and fully understand their personal philosophy of the relationship between athletics and academics before pursuing potential college sport internships. At Division-I institutions, a primary focus (and some would argue the only focus) is winning. Athletes' education and character development, while still ostensibly important, are often secondary, particularly in revenue-generating sports. At the Division-II and Division-III levels facilities typically are not as lavish, and media attention is often non-existent. As a result, there is often less commercial intrusion, which may allow athletes to maintain more focus on their academic and social development. At most Division-III institutions, coaches and administrators are evaluated primarily on how well their program contributes to students' education.

The Division-I focus on winning, particularly in revenue sports, is not necessarily a "bad" thing, but sport-management students must attempt to insure that philosophy and expectations match a university's mission and goals. If a student's personal values are incongruent with those of the athletic department in which they work, frustration often occurs. Having a general idea of expectations and the work environment prior to taking a job in college athletics can alleviate potential philosophical disagreements.

Though most students seeking employment in college athletics will gravitate toward a job at an individual school, there are additional administrative positions available at the NCAA as well as other college sport-governing bodies. Each Division-I conference maintains a league office and employs a full-time staff. Certainly, conferences such as the Southeastern Conference (SEC) and the Big Ten Conference have many more staff members than the West Coast Conference (WCC) or the Western Athletic Conference (WAC), but all conference employees attempt to market the conferences' brand and enhance athletic-related revenue streams. Much like working for a professional sport league, NCAA and conference administrators will not have the emotional highs and lows of individual school employees.

There are also opportunities outside of the NCAA umbrella. The National Association of Intercollegiate Athletics (NAIA) governs sport activities for member NAIA schools. Though not as large as the NCAA, the NAIA currently has over 300 member institutions, and organizes championships in 13 sports. The NAIA maintains a full-time staff that works to organize championships and market NAIA members. In addition, though their athletic departments will likely be small compared to NCAA Division-I institutions, every NAIA school will have athletic employment opportunities.

Intercollegiate athletics opportunities are also offered at many junior colleges. Junior college athletic department administrators are also often members of the physical education faculty. Since junior colleges typically attract students from the local area, rather than from throughout the country, such athletic department budgets are often much more limited. However, many states organize championships for a variety of sports at the junior college level. These championships can attract local media attention and fans. The National Junior College Athletic Association (NJCAA) works to promote the efforts of junior college athletics.

College Sport License Holders

The development and expansion of the business of intercollegiate athletics has resulted in the proliferation of numerous college sport marketing companies. Since many athletic departments do not have adequate personnel with the expertise to evaluate and sell sponsorship inventory, negotiate media rights to athletic department content, and seek advertisers, they often partner with third-party license holders. As these license holders have proliferated, they have provided excellent internship and employment opportunities for sport management students.

There are a variety of college-sport licensees. One of the most important people in the development of this sub-industry is Jim Host. In the 1970s, Host established Jim Host & Associates, which provided assistance to college athletic departments looking to outsource some or all of their marketing activities. After initially working with the University of Kentucky, Host's company became more and more successful. As Host expanded his influence throughout the industry, other competitors entered the marketplace. Currently, prominent college sport marketing companies include ISP Sports, Learfield Sports Properties, and Nelligan Sports Marketing, Inc.

In 2007, International Management Group (IMG) purchased Host Communications and combined it with recently acquired Collegiate Licensing Company (CLC), an entity that had initially been established to assist colleges and universities to create and expand their **licensed merchandise** sales, to form IMG College. The merger established IMG College as the nation's largest provider of marketing services to the college sport industry.

Licensed Merchandise _____
Granting another entity the right to produce products that bear a trademarked logo.

Though the aforementioned companies provide a variety of marketing services to college athletic departments, there continues to be new opportunities for college sport consulting. In 2009, Georgia Tech hired the Aspire Group to organize its ticket sales for football and men's basketball games. It was believed to be the first time an athletic department outsourced its ticketing operations to a third party (Lombardo & Smith, 2009). It is likely many future employment opportunities in college athletics will involve working for an outside entity, rather than directly for the athletic department.

Youth Sports

Professional and intercollegiate athletics typically generate significantly higher attendance and greater media attention than organized youth sports; however, over the past 10 years high school athletics has become dramatically more commercialized. At many high schools, since the athletic director is no longer expected to teach classes, his/her energy can be fully devoted to selling tickets, executing fund raising initiatives, seeking sponsorship agreements, and raising awareness of the high school's athletic exploits in the media. High school football and basketball games are increasingly being broadcast on local or regional television and radio stations, or sport networks. In addition, ESPN has recently dramatically increased its coverage of selected games. It is not uncommon for prominent high school athletic teams to travel via airplane to participate in prestigious tournaments. As many high school athletic departments have begun to model their structure and activities after prominent colleges, athletic directors with advanced sport business skills are needed.

Other youth sport activities have also recently seen dramatic changes. Little League Baseball and the Amateur Athletic Union (AAU) have long attracted thousands of participants, but the scheduling and marketing of their athletic contests now mimics commercialized sport properties. Not only are Little League

World Series games televised live on ESPN, but most regional championships are also covered extensively by the media. AAU tournaments in a variety of sports no longer merely attract parents and close friends of the participants. With much of the college recruiting for some sports (such as basketball and volleyball) occurring during summer AAU tournaments, fans have begun to attend, and media outlets have begun to cover, some of these events in the hopes of seeing the "next" great college players before they have graduated from high school.

With the growing emphasis on commercialized youth sports, parents now often insist that their children's sporting activities be organized and operated like "professional" sport entities. Some affluent parents have also retained "performance" coaches to work with their child—in some cases before their son or daughter has enrolled in junior high school. The increased emphasis that parents have placed upon organized, elite youth sport activities is of grave concern to many people. During much of the 20th century young kids participated in athletics without direct parental organization or supervision (Coakley, 2009). Sport was as much about "play" as it was about winning. Participants (children) often amended rules to allow for a more competitive and "fun" environment. While some sociologists lament the current state of youth sports, with today's emphasis on adult-organized and directed youth sports, there are opportunities for sport-management graduates to establish, organize, and promote youth sport events.

Olympic Sports

In 1896 the first "modern" Olympic Games took place in Athens, Greece. Though the "first" Olympics attracted "only" 14 nations and 241 athletes, the games slowly expanded during the first half of the 20th century. Since it was impractical to hold competitions for many popular sports, such as skiing and ice-skating, during the summer, in 1924 the first Winter Olympic Games were held in Chamonix, France. As the Olympics continued to attract larger contingents of athletes and greater media attention, they became an outlet for countries' nationalism. During the 1936 Summer Olympics in Berlin, the Nazi Party utilized the Games as the focal point to demonstrate the "rebirth" of Germany after World War I. Despite Adolf Hitler's propaganda campaign about the Aryan "master race," United States' track star Jesse Owens won four gold medals to become the hero of the 1936 Olympics.

Though the popularity of the Olympics grew following World War II, many Olympic Games have been marred by tragedy, financial problems, and political turmoil. During the 1972 Munich Games, members of the *Israeli Olympic team* were taken *hostage* and eventually murdered by *Black September,* a militant group with ties to the Palestinian *Fatah* organization. By the end of the ordeal, the death toll stood at 17. The terrorists eventually killed eleven *Israeli athletes* and *coaches* and one West German *police officer.* Five of the eight Black September members were killed during a failed rescue attempt. Though certainly not as tragic as the loss of life in Munich, the 1976 Montreal Games were a financial disaster as millions of dollars of facility investments required decades for the citizens of Montreal and the rest of Canada to repay. At the height of the "Cold War," the United States and many of its allies boycotted the 1980 Moscow Games in protest of the Soviet Union's invasion of Afghanistan. By 1984, there was considerable concern about the financial viability of the Los Angeles Games, especially after the Soviet Union and other "Eastern Bloc" countries boycotted the Games in retaliation for the 1980 boycott. Despite concerns, the financial and marketing success of the 1984 Summer Olympics changed the Olympic movement.

The 1984 Summer Olympics generated a profit and changed the way future Olympic Games would be organized.

Peter Ueberroth served as the Executive Director of the 1984 Summer Olympics. Where all of the proceeding Olympic Games were primarily financed and operated by government entities, Ueberroth organized the Los Angeles Games as a private entity. Ueberroth managed the Olympics as a separate, stand-alone business and he solicited extensive sponsorship and licensed merchandise sales to generate revenue. The Los Angeles Olympics were such a financial success that Ueberroth was named *Time Magazine's* Man of the Year. Cities and countries that had viewed hosting the Olympics as a financial risk, changed their opinion of hosting future games. The Los Angeles Olympics caused many worldwide sporting events to become "mega-events" requiring extensive and highly-trained staffs in order to solicit bids, develop financial plans, schedule facilities, organize event employees, and maximize revenue opportunities. Today, sport-management students have the opportunity to pursue an Olympics-based career, whether working for the International Olympic Committee (IOC), United States Olympic Committee (USOC), one of the USOC's national sport governing bodies (NGO), or for a potential host city.

The Olympic Games are not the only mega-event to attract competitors and spectators from throughout the world. In 1948 Sir Ludwig Guttman organized the first sport competition for injured soldiers from World War II. Guttman's event would grow and eventually be called the Paralympics. Starting in 1988 with the Seoul Olympics, the Paralympics have been held in the Olympic host city shortly after the Olympic Games have concluded. The Paralympics, as well as other sporting events for the disabled, have grown in popularity. Much like the Olympics, the Paralympics must be organized and managed. With thousands of athletes and spectators attending, there are numerous career opportunities in this area.

Sport Facilities

Regardless of the size or scope of a sporting event, facilities will be needed to insure the event is successful. Even outdoor events, such as cross-country races, require facilities for spectators, members of the media, and race officials.

Certainly, major professional sports facilities and Division I athletic department facilities receive considerable media attention, but there are also many potential career opportunities associated with smaller venues. As discussed in chapter 11, sport facilities may include stadiums (both indoor, outdoor, and retractable roofed) for events such as football and soccer games, arenas for events such as basketball and volleyball games and facilities designed specifically for sports such as tennis, swimming, auto racing, horse racing, and dog racing.

Though high profile "competitive" sport facilities tend to initially attract sport management students, there are also numerous opportunities to work in recreation and fitness facilities. Most communities have private and publicly-owned recreation centers that offer general recreation opportunities as well as scheduled events such as tournaments. Over the past 10 years, colleges and universities have come to realize on-campus recreation centers can be utilized to recruit and retain students (as well as faculty and staff). Most campuses have at least one recreation center, and offer extensive intramural programs. Military bases, both in the United States and throughout the world, also offer recreation opportunities. These facilities require professional, part-time, and volunteer staff members to insure operational efficiency. Though NFL stadiums and NBA arenas receive extensive television exposure, community recreation centers or on-campus recreation facilities all need trained staff to operate and maintain. Such employees establish budgets, organize programs, insure the safety of equipment, and attract and retain customers.

Over the last 15 years, as the importance and complexity of managing sport facilities has increased, numerous private management companies have offered sport facility-management services. Though there are numerous private management companies that offer such full-scale management, three organizations currently dominate the marketplace. SMG World is the leading provider of management for arenas, convention centers, stadiums, and theatres throughout the world. It currently manages nine stadiums, 40+ theatres, 50+ convention centers, and 50+ arenas, with more than 1.5 million seats. IMG continues to expand its operations and influence in the sport facility marketplace ("SMG at a glance," n.d.).

Global Spectrum, a division of the Philadelphia-based sports and entertainment company Comcast-Spectacor, calls itself the "fastest growing firm in the public-assembly facility management field ("Company background," n.d.). Founded in 1974, Global Spectrum presently manages five ice facilities, seven performing-arts centers, 32 arenas, 25 convention centers, and eight stadiums ("Venue list," n.d.). Global Spectrum is expanding its global presence, with offices in the United States, Canada, the United Kingdom, and Singapore.

AEG Live has only recently begun soliciting facility-management contracts, but its recent successes have been impressive. AEG Live has signed contracts with some of the top-grossing facilities in the world. It currently oversees the development of L.A. Live, a 4-million square foot, $2.5 billion sport, residential, and entertainment district ("About us," n.d.). AEG has committed to expanding its presence in the sport facility-management field.

Each of these companies offers extensive internship and entry-level employment opportunities. Since SMG, Global Spectrum, and AEG manage multiple facilities around the world, there are tremendous opportunities to advance your career, if you are able and willing to relocate. It is not uncommon for these companies to "fast-track" exceptional students from internships to full-time employment and from entry-level employment to middle-management.

In addition to full-service facility-management companies, there are also potential sport management employment opportunities in firms that offer specific services in subsectors of facility management. Since selling food and beverages is a critical revenue stream for most sporting events, many facilities have outsourced concession-sales responsibilities to private companies. Though there are many food-service companies, a few dominate the marketplace. Aramark is the largest sport concessionaire and it continues to expand its presence in the United States and in international markets. Other prominent concessionaires include Centerplate, Delaware North Sportservice, Levy, and Ovations Food Services (owned and operated by Comcast Spectacor). Much like the large full-scale facility management companies, these concessionaires have multiple accounts across the country, providing employees many opportunities for career advancement.

Though crowd safety has always been an important issue, after the terrorist attacks on 9/11 most facilities and events realized they needed to reassess their crowd-management practices. There are many companies that work directly or indirectly with sporting events to create a safe environment. Contemporary Services Corporation (CSC) is the best known. With multiple offices throughout the United States and accounts with many of the top college and professional sport teams, CSC is a leader in providing staffing for sport-event crowd management.

Most live sport events require patrons to purchase tickets to gain entry to the facility. For many years, tickets were sold primarily at a facility's box office. By the 1970s, tickets could be purchased over the phone with a credit card, but the sales process was still inefficient. In 1976, two Arizona State students founded Ticketmaster—a company that designed software that allowed for "remote" ticket sales. In the 1980s, as Ticketmaster developed and enhanced its technology, it quickly became the industry leader. With the proliferation of the Internet in the 1990s, Ticketmaster captured nearly the entire sport and entertainment ticketing industry. In 2010, it merged with Live Nation. Though many students may not have an interest in working for Ticketmaster, it is important to understand how its operations impact nearly every aspect of live sport and entertainment events.

There are a variety of other employment opportunities in sport facility and event management. Sport events cannot function without sports and office equipment, landscaping, trash removal, and a myriad of other services. There are many lesser-known companies that work intimately within the sport industry. In addition, there are companies that have not even been established that will provide future employment opportunities. For instance, in 1981 Sports

Team Analysis and Tracking Systems (STATS, Inc.) was established by John Dewan. In the early 1980s, statistical analysis (particularly in sports) was often seen as a "fringe" activity reserved solely for "nerds." Since 1981 the importance of sport statistical analysis (as well as statistical analysis in all aspects of business) has grown tremendously and companies such as STATS, Inc. (now STATS LLC) play an important role in the industry. Many students reading this book will likely have ideas for aspects of the sport industry that have not yet been contemplated. Do not discount emerging ideas or companies as they may become a critical component of the sport industry in the future!

Licensed Merchandise

In the 1950s, New York Yankee's General Manager George Weiss was asked about having a Yankee Cap Day. He supposedly replied, "Do you think I want kids in New York wearing Yankee hats?" Certainly, the use of team or league logos on hats, shirts, jackets, sweaters, and various other articles of clothing and other products has greatly expanded since the 1950s. Today, any sport executive would welcome the opportunity for logoed merchandise to be worn by fans, especially when the fans pay for the "privilege" of being associated with the sport organization.

Most teams, leagues, and athletic department sell licenses that permit third parties to produce various products that display a sport organization's name and logo. The profit margin on sales of licensed merchandise can be quite high. One only has to look at the price of a plain sweatshirt sold at a department store, and compare it to the price of a sweatshirt bearing a college or university logo, to see the profits generated through licensed merchandise sales. The cost of ink is likely pennies, but the addition of a school logo on a plain piece of clothing can double, triple, or even quadruple the product's price!

Licensed merchandise sales are a critical component of most sport organizations' revenue plans. The tremendous profit margins available through the sale of licensed merchandise have led most sport organizations to devote at least one employee to this area. For extremely popular sport teams, an entire franchise division or functional area may work to investigate potential licensing opportunities, negotiate licensing contracts, and insure that counterfeit merchandise is not sold. In order to maximize profits, sport leagues typically create league-wide licensing agreements. These league agreements typically disburse revenues to each team, which enables every team (though their individual sales may fluctuate each year due to team performance and other factors) to receive a more consistent revenue stream.

Companies that design and sell apparel have been interested in utilizing sport logos for many years. Recently, various non-traditional products and services have sought associations with sport organizations. Some college athletic departments offer their fans the opportunity to purchase licensed products as varied as seat cushions, plates, silverware, glasses, futons, toilet seat covers, DVDs, photographs, and other new-media products. Some schools and professional sport franchises have even begun offering officially licensed urns and coffins for fans who wish to be buried in "their" school or team colors (Jones, 2008).

Sport Media

Sport events typically attract the attention of fans, and therefore are often covered by various media outlets. Certainly, sport organizations seek to maximize media exposure. Most hire employees to work with the media to generate positive publicity. In addition, media-relations departments must also prepare and handle potential crises that develop. An organization that is not prepared for a crisis will likely experience significant negative feedback from fans and other constituents who view the sport entity as unprepared, uncaring, or unprofessional in their dealings with the media.

The media industry has changed dramatically over the past 100 years. The primary mode of information gathering for most sport consumers has progressed from newspapers to radio to television to the Internet. Changes in media platforms have resulted in employment opportunities and in alterations to some established sport norms. In addition to a proliferation of satellite and cable TV networks and delivery options, many professional and college leagues and conferences now have their own cable sports networks. The NFL, NBA, and MLB all have their own networks. The Mountain West Conference (Mtn) and Big Ten Conference (Big Ten Network) have led the way in college sport. Individual franchises (such as the New York Yankees with the YES Network) as well as individual schools (such as the University of Texas) have developed their own cable networks.

The Internet's "viral" nature (through the sharing of files, video sharing-websites, blogs, digital networks, and "old-fashioned" email) has enabled bloggers to wield significant influence in the sport industry. For many years, many sport franchises did not view Internet writers as "real" journalists. Today, most teams have begun to recognize prominent bloggers are an important part of their media constituencies. As technology continues to evolve, the need for sport organizations to tell their "story" through the media will not change, but the platforms by which that story is conveyed will undoubtedly be much different. Students seeking employment in sport media should understand the unique nature of sport media relations, and prepare for continued rapid changes in the future.

Sports Agents

Though being a "player agent" is probably the number one career non sport-management people think of when sport management is mentioned, an infinitesimal fraction of sport-management students will ever work as a player agent.

Though multimillion-dollar athlete contracts and movies like Jerry Maguire make the layperson think there are numerous player agents and many of them are financially successful, in reality only a few player agents make substantial salaries. For every Scott Boras, Leigh Steinberg or David Falk, there are thousands of other agents who have considerably more dreams than clients. In many years, the reported number of agents exceeds the number of players in several sports.

Though the player-agent industry now involves millions of dollars, the first athlete-agent agreement began with little more than a handshake. In 1960, Attorney Mark McCormack noticed that golfer Arnold Palmer had established his career as a successful performer. With television rapidly increasing its coverage of golf tournaments, McCormack approached Palmer about managing his endorsement opportunities. McCormack's success with Palmer's career attracted other golfers such as Jack Nicklaus and Gary Player. McCormack's agency, IMG, would eventually sign numerous other golfers and tennis players. Later, IMG expanded its agency to represent athletes from other sports, as well as entertainers, politicians, and models. IMG also began to manage sport and entertainment events.

The success of McCormack and IMG led other individuals to work in the player agent business. During the 1970s, numerous attorneys expanded their business to include athlete representation. As the value of player contracts escalated in the 1980s, many individuals became full-time agents rather than attorneys who "also" represented athletes. In the 1990s many prominent agents began to expand their client services. Instead of merely negotiating player contracts, most large agencies began to design marketing and sponsorship campaigns, offer financial advice, retain nutritionists, personal trainers, and sport psychologists, and perform statistical analysis of their clients' athletic performance. Currently, most "successful" agents represent many clients and allow their past successes to supplement their recruiting efforts.

Becoming a prominent player agent is one of the most difficult sport-career paths. Competition within the industry is fierce, with some agents notoriously circumventing established rules, laws, and ethical guidelines (See Chapter 5—Ethics and Ethical Decision Making) to attract clients. The actions of players, coaches, parents, and "advisors" can make the life of an agent difficult—particularly since most agents rely on their commission as a primary source of income and are therefore usually not in a position to say "No" to most requests. Few sport-management students realize an agent's long hours, tough working conditions, and stressful lifestyle. Students wishing to become an agent should seek opportunities to work for an established agency. Though most agents are reluctant to share their secrets regarding recruitment and retention of clients—for fear of training someone to eventually become their competition—there are typically opportunities to work for agents doing a variety of tasks such as coordinating athlete appearances and researching marketing opportunities. Students who desire to become an agent should not abandon that dream, but should realize the incredibly tough environment in which player agents operate.

Athlete Foundations

With the large salaries that some professional athletes earn, there is often a pressure to "give back" to the community. Most prominent athletes have either established charitable foundations or work closely with organizations that attempt to enhance the livelihood of various constituents. Athletes can generate positive publicity through their charitable work with schools, hospitals, and other entities that serve the community. There are potential internship and employment opportunities working for athlete foundations. This has become especially important over the past five years as many athletes have been publicly chastised and, in some cases prosecuted, for allowing family members and close friends to improperly operate their charitable foundation. With an increased emphasis on operating athlete foundations as a legitimate non-profit organization, many of these organizations have sought sport management students for internships and entry-level employment.

Sport Tourism

Though tourism is one of the world's oldest industries, many components of organized sport tourism in the United States have only been developed in the past 30 years. In the United States, the 1904 St. Louis (Missouri) World's Fair was organized in concert with the 1904 Olympic Games. Hosting both events was designed to maximize the number of tourists who would visit St. Louis. Despite the success of the 1904 Olympics, most sport events in the first third of the 20th century were primarily viewed as "local" events. However, during the height of the Great Depression, the 1932 Los Angeles Olympics attracted many spectators who spent money in the Los Angeles area. In 1939, the National Baseball Hall of Fame and Museum was opened in Cooperstown, New York. Despite the ongoing economic depression, the induction of the first class of baseball hall of famers generated substantial onsite attendance and national media attention. Other sports and leagues would later establish their own Hall of Fames to attract tourists.

In the United States, the link between sports and tourism has continued to grow. Various companies, particularly those in the restaurant, hotel, and car-rental industries, reap economic benefits when sport events attract tourists from outside the community. Tourists who spend money generate "economic impact," which can spur employment opportunities and enhance tax receipts. Certainly, most cities' convention and visitors bureaus attempt to attract as many sport events, and sport tourists, as possible.

Attracting sport events to a local community is perceived to be important enough for many municipalities that agencies specifically tasked with attracting such events have been established. The San Jose Sports Authority (SJSA) is an excellent example of an agency established to attract sport events to a community, in order to attract tourists and generate economic activity. Long overshadowed by

Courtesy David Eadie

The San Jose Sports Authority works to bring events such as the Rock 'n' Roll San Jose Half Marathon, with an estimated economic impact of over $16 million annually, to San Jose.

San Francisco and Oakland to the north, the City of San Jose established the SJSA in 1991. Since its creation, the SJSA has worked to bring sport events such as the NCAA Division-I Women's Final Four, NCAA Division-I Men's Basketball Western Regional Finals, Major League Soccer All-Star Game, Siebel Classic (Senior PGA event), and numerous U.S. Olympic trials to San Jose.

There are numerous opportunities to work in sport tourism and new opportunities are continually being developed. Recently, travel companies have developed sport tourism packages that offer organized tours of stadiums and other sport facilities in a variety of cities. It is likely that sport tourism opportunities will continue to expand in the future, making this an important potential outlet for internships and employment opportunities.

Employment Placement

The growth of the sport industry and the proliferation of sport organizations have resulted in the creation of companies that specialize in helping sport management students find internships and entry-level employment. In addition, many such organizations link established sport management professionals to sport organizations that need specific skills. For instance, TeamWork Online (through its web-based services) assists sport organizations in finding employees and employees finding open sport-management positions. Six Figure Sports is another company that specializes in helping sport organizations seeking employees, but their focus is typically upon executive-level searches. It is likely that as the sport industry continues to develop, additional organizations that provide employment consulting will be established, creating additional sport-management employment opportunities.

Sport Sponsors

The importance of sport sponsorship has grown over the past 20 years—both for sport entities and for local, regional, national and international companies. With sports becoming a larger component of many individuals' everyday lives, many organizations have realized that they must actively attempt to understand sport sponsorship and its potential costs and benefits. Many Fortune 500 companies have staff members specifically tasked with evaluating sport-sponsorship opportunities. Sport-management graduates often have a unique understanding of what makes a sport athlete, team, league, or event worthwhile for potential sponsorship. Though working in the corporate world may not seem as "exciting" as working for a team or league, there are some potential benefits. Most Fortune 500 companies offer much higher salaries than those in other sport-industry sectors. In addition, though employees are expected to work diligently, especially during sponsored events, there tends to be a more "reasonable" expectation of working hours and better fringe benefits (excluding the opportunity to be a part of a potential championship team). Even if a company does not have a division devoted specifically to sport-sponsorship, most organizations task their marketing staffs with exploring all possible outlets to enhance their brand. There are many sport-management graduates working in "marketing" for non-sport organizations who maintain a close contact to the industry through marketing and sponsorship opportunities.

Conclusion

Opportunities for internships and entry-level employment in the United States' sport management industry are extremely diverse. There are myriad avenues for students to pursue. Certainly, developing a knowledge base by studying the industry is important for future success, but understanding the nuances of various subsectors can only be accomplished by working in that industry area. Students should begin to explore potential opportunities immediately, as no employer will ever tell an applicant that they have "too much experience" for a sport-management position.

CHAPTER

Interview

INTERVIEW 3.1

Tom Regan
Associate Professor of Sport and Entertainment Management
University of South Carolina

In the nine years that Dr. Regan served as chair of the University of South Carolina Department of Sport and Entertainment Management, the undergraduate program expanded to over 500 students, new faculty were hired, a master's program was created, and plans to start a doctoral program were implemented. Throughout Dr. Regan's tenure as chair, the academic requirements consistently increased and USC's graduates positively impacted numerous areas of sport and entertainment management. Through Dr. Regan leadership, USC's sport and entertainment management undergraduate program has become one of the best in the country and its graduate program is in position to begin to attract quality students from throughout the world.

Q: Can you briefly describe your background and career path?

A: I was born and raised in Miles City, Montana, one of six children of blue-collar working parents. I attended the University of Wyoming on a baseball scholarship and graduated with undergraduate (1979) and master's (1981) degrees in Accounting. My first job after gradua-

tion was as a staff accountant for Fox and Co. CPA's (later Fox/Grant Thorton after a merger). After two years I took a job as the senior accountant at Natural Gas Processing Company. Within six months I became the controller and worked for the next eight years with NGP, Wyoming Gas Co. and other entities we purchased.

I then wanted to do something that involved my passions of sport and business. The University of Northern Colorado had a new sport management doctoral program. Though I was initially concerned about some aspects of the new program, I enrolled and enjoyed taking courses that conformed to my business background. I finished my degree by writing my dissertation on the Economic Impact of the Denver Broncos. After graduation in May 1991, I took an academic position at the University of South Carolina in the Department of Sport Administration (since renamed) under the tutelage of Dr. Guy Lewis, who started the University of Massachusetts sport management program many years before. USC's program was attractive because it was business oriented rather than physical education or recreation focused.

I have stayed at the University of South Carolina in the Department of Sport and Entertainment Management since my initial appointment. After being tenured and promoted in 1997, I was named the Department Chair, a position I held for over nine years. During that time the department grew from 151 students and three full-time tenure tract faculty members to over 500 students and 10 full time faculty members.

Q: What have been the biggest challenges your have encountered during your career?

A: Balancing work and family is always a challenge. I have tried to never let work get in the way of being at my children's games or significant events. I can work later in the day, at home or on weekends to make sure I keep my priorities in order. Everyone needs to maintain balance in their mental, social, spiritual and physical lives. Properly juggling home and work lives often takes planning and commitment.

The academic world often reacts slowly to change and accomplishing goals quickly can sometimes be a challenge. Working within a bureaucracy is often difficult and a university has multiple layers of approval for most activities.

Q: What are the most important skills for sport management students to develop?

A: • Interpersonal communication (writing, especially activities outside of Twitter/Texting)
• Entrepreneurship (ability to problem solve and incorporate ideas from various aspects of business
• Public speaking
• Sales—the ability to sell is critical
• Accounting
• Strategic Management—this is often the difference between the manager and the subordinate.

Q: What classes do you recommend students take while an undergraduate (especially electives)?

A: • Public speaking
• Accounting
• Finance

• Marketing
• Sales
• Graphic design (helps with sporting events—creating brochures, etc.)
• Foreign language—It is a global economy and foreign language skills are invaluable.
• Computer skills—this is essential. At a minimum a comprehensive understanding of MS Office is needed but additional skills are helpful.

Q: How do you teach students to understand that sport management extends beyond becoming an agent or a general manager of a professional sport franchise?

A: • There are more neo-natal surgeons than General Managers of a professional sport franchise. Considering how difficult it is to become a surgeon, students should consider the likelihood of becoming a GM.
• I tell the students who are interested in being an agent to go to law school and build the agency **after** they have established a solid practice as an attorney. You have to make a living, and agency work is a dog-eat-dog world where lots of financial resources and contacts are needed. If you do not have a client, you are not an agent!
• I tell them to read biographies of successful sport managers from a variety of fields.

Q: Where are the best places to find jobs in sport management presently? Where do you see the largest areas of growth for sport management jobs in the future?

A: • Jobs that are related to facilities (professional, college, and interscholastic sport and entertainment venues of all sizes) are available. The challenge for many facilities is how they will pay for the debt that was accumulated to build the venue. Increasing the number of events is the likely answer and there will be jobs in that area of the business.
• Largest area of growth will be international events in Asia. Many Asian countries have a growing middle class with disposable income and free time, which means they will be looking for opportunities to spend some of that money.

Q: Do you typically advise undergraduate students to pursue graduate school?

A: For students who want to pursue a career in college athletics a master's degree is required. For other fields it is not required, but the skills that can be learned in graduate schools can certainly help. Specific careers (agent—law) do require a specified graduate degree, but there are many successful sport managers who do not have a graduate degree.

Study Questions

1. Describe the main areas of potential sport management employment?
2. Why are entry-level salaries in major professional sport and Division I athletics low compared to other industries?
3. What specific companies contract with college athletic departments to handle various marketing opportunities?
4. What specific companies provide facility management services for sport and entertainment events?
5. How can a sport management graduate work actively in sport without actually working for a company that primarily offers sport-related products or services?
6. Conduct research regarding the various sub-industries described in this chapter. What other companies exist that could provide internship and employment opportunities?

References

About us. (n.d.). Retrieved March 10, 2010 from http://www.aegworldwide.com/08_corporate/about_us.html

Coakley, J. (2009). *Sports in society* (9th ed.). New York: McGraw-Hill.

Company background. (n.d.). Retrieved March 10, 2010 from http://www.global-spectrum.com/default.asp?lnopt=1&sn1opt=1&sn2opt=1&month=4&year=2010&newsID=0

Jones, A. (2008, February 13). Regents board approves logos on coffins. The Atlanta Journal-Constitution. Retrieved March 14, 2010 from http://www.ajc.com/metro/content/metro/stories/2008/02/13/coffin_0214.html

Lombardo, J. & Smith, M. (2009, May 25). Ga. Tech hands ticket sales to Aspire Group *SportsBusiness Journal.* Retrieved March 27, 2010 from http://www.sportsbusinessjournal.com/article/62558

NCAA. (n.d.). Division III philosophy statement. Retrieved April 12, 2010 from http://www.ncaa.org/wps/portal/ncaahome?WCM_GLOBAL_CONTEXT=/ncaa/NCAA/Legislation%20and%20Governance/Committees/Division%20III/General%20Information/d3_philosophy_stmt

SMG at a glance. (n.d.). Retrieved March 14, 2010, from http://wwwsmgworld.com/worldwide_venues.aspx

Venue list. (n.d.). Retrieved March 13, 2010, from http://media.eventbooking.com/57957_st.pdf

What's the difference between Division I, II and III? (n.d.). Retrieved March 14, 2010 from http://www.ncaa.org/wps/portal/ncaahome?WCM_GLOBAL_CONTEXT=/ncaa/ncaa/about+the+ncaa/membership/div_criteria.html

Sport in the Global Marketplace

Ronald L. Mower • *Physical Cultural Studies, University of Maryland*

After reading this chapter, you will be able to:

- Understand and analyze some of the key transformations in the global (cultural) economy and the role that sport plays within it;
- Compare and contrast specific examples of how sport constitutes, and is constituted by, intricate processes of global interconnectivity;
- Synthesize an array of basic global theories to interpret and explain the character and influence of sport in diverse global contexts;
- Think critically about issues facing the production and management of sport in nations possessing different politics, cultures, technologies, and economic infrastructures;
- Enter the global sport marketplace with an appreciation for new technologies, cultural differences, and the need for new solutions in a complex global age.

KEY TERMS

Commodification

Complex Connectivity

Cultural (Symbolic) Production

Global Heterogenization

Global Homogenization

Global Hybridity

Sport is probably the most universal aspect of popular culture. It crosses languages and countries to captivate spectators and participants, as both a professional business and a pastime

—Miller, Lawrence, McKay, & Rowe, 2001, p. 1)

Globalization is like putting together a jigsaw puzzle: it is a matter of inserting a multiplicity of localities into the overall picture of a new global system

—Morley & Robins, 1995, p. 116

Contemporary sport has a cultural and economic impact throughout the globe. It surpasses national boundaries as it presents itself through media (satellite TV, Internet, radio), products (merchandised apparel, sporting goods equipment), and services (live games, ticket sales, concessions). Certainly consumption of sport changed dramatically in the 20th century with the advent of television, and in the 21st century with the prevalence of the Internet. Technologies of instantaneous mass communication not only link disparate peoples across the globe, but also alter the way information is accessed, thereby affecting the influence, presentation, and role of sport in daily lives. Further, despite economic crises and security threats, modes of global transportation facilitate rapid business/tourist travel or permanent migration to any location on the planet. Conceivably, one could ride the ferry from Amsterdam to London, fly from London to New York, take a bus from New York to Baltimore, and still get home in time to catch a few late innings of the Orioles on the Mid-Atlantic Sports Network (MASN); all the while surfing the net to catch the latest SportsCenter highlights, chatting with family in California, sending text messages to friends in New Zealand, and listening to reggae music on the all encompassing I-phone. These diverse technologies of travel and communication interact with sport in some important ways. If viewed from a socio-cultural perspective, the multifarious expressions of global sport can be said to constitute, and be constituted by, their interrelatedness to the structures, institutions, and processes that comprise contemporary society. As such, sport, the way it is played, by whom, and for what purpose, is reflective of the broader economic, technological, and cultural forces at work in any given country. This idea is extremely important for sport managers seeking to understand how global processes are inherently tied to, and reflective of, sport in its various iterations.

With the continuous growth of international sporting competition, and professional leagues in numerous sports from all over world vying to expand into foreign markets, tomorrow's sport managers face not only numerous challenges but also unique opportunities to shape the workings of the global sport marketplace (see Table 4.1 for a glimpse of current global sporting leagues). Within this chapter, some basic theories and key issues affecting the global sport marketplace will be discussed to inform your conceptualization of managing effectively, ethically, and with a prescient sense of sport's local, national, and global character. As the opening quotes to this chapter might suggest, globalization (and the globalization of sport in particular) is an extremely complex process, with the term itself being quite protean in nature; used differently and having various meanings within academic and professional circles. Given the degree of dispute concerning its meaning and influence, globalization is even more confusing and misunderstood amongst the general population who are affected by it every day, often without realizing its broader significance. Thus, in order to succeed in an increasingly complex global market, even the most modest position in sport management and/or marketing would benefit from acquiring a more global perspective informed through an understanding of global processes affecting the interplay between culture and commerce.

TABLE 4.1

Major Sporting Leagues and Organizations around the Globe

- **Australian Rules Football**
  Australian Football League
  Victorian Football League
  West Australian Football League

- **Auto Racing**
  National Association of Stock Car Auto Racing (NASCAR)
  Formula 1
  National Hot Rod Association (NHRA)

- **Baseball**
  Major League Baseball (MLB)
  Nippon Professional Baseball (Japan)
  Puerto Rican Professional Baseball League
  Korean Baseball Organization

- **Basketball**
  National Basketball Association (NBA)
  Women's National Basketball Association (WNBA)
  Ligue Nationale de Basketball (France)
  Baltic Basketball League (BBL; Latvia, Lithuania,
    Estonia and Sweden)
  Super Basketball League (SBL; Taiwan)
  Fédération Internationale de Basketball (FIBA)

- **Bowling**
  Professional Bowlers Association (PBA)

- **Boxing**
  International Boxing Federation (IBF)
  World Boxing Association (WBA)

- **Cricket**
  International Cricket Council (ICC)
  National Elite League Twenty20 (Kenya)
  Women's National Cricket League (Australia)
  Indian Premier League (IPL)
  Major League Cricket (U.S.)
  National Cricket League of Bangladesh

- **Curling**
  Canadian Curling Association

- **Football**
  National Football League (NFL)
  United Football League (U.S. league in beginning
    stages of development)
  Arena Football League (Canceled 2009 season)
  Canadian Football League (CFL)

- **Golf**
  Professional Golf Association (PGA)
  Ladies Professional Golf Association (LPGA)
  European Tour

- **Hockey**
  National Hockey League (NHL)
  American Hockey League
  Kontinental Hockey League (Russia, with teams also
    in Belarus, Kazakhstan, and Latvia) Deutsche
    Eishockey Liga (Germany)

- **Hurling**
  Gaelic Athletic Association (GAA)
  National Hurling League (Ireland)

- **Lacrosse**
  Major League Lacrosse (MLL)
  National Lacrosse League (NLL)
  Major Series Lacrosse (Canada)

- **Rugby**
  Rugby Football League (RFL)
  Rugby Union (RU)
  Super League (England, Wales, France)
  National Rugby League (Australia, New Zealand)
  Professional Rugby League (Russia)

- **Soccer**
  FA Premier League (England)
  Primera División de México (Mexico's Premier
    Division)
  Campeonato Brasileiro (Brazil)
  Major League Soccer (MLS; U.S.)
  Professional Football League (Trinidad & Tobago)

- **Tennis**
  Association of Tennis Professionals (ATP)
  Women's Tennis Association (WTA)

*Note: This list is by no means exhaustive; there are hundreds of sporting leagues and organizations not listed here, including entire sports not mentioned as well. The International Olympic Committee (IOC) alone recognizes over 200 international sport federations and non-governmental organizations that promote, develop, and organize global sport competitions.

Before discussing the global interconnectivity of sport commerce and culture, it must be noted that both critical and complementary theories from a range of disciplines will be presented throughout this chapter. While there are vast literatures sometimes contradicting the basic values and ideals of one another about the topic—some lauding the pursuit of efficient operations and enhanced profit margins, others criticizing human rights abuses and increasing wealth/health disparities—this chapter will present just a glimpse of the complexities involved in globalization, and particularly that of the globalization of sport. Ultimately, it is hoped that a greater understanding of such issues, and the ability to think critically about them, will translate into more effective problem-solving and management in the future. Discussion of various global sport properties, transnational corporations (TNCs), and sport-related businesses will arise throughout the chapter, culminating in some more detailed explanations of careers in global sport-related commerce and in particular, that of a sport practitioner for Visa Europe.

Basic Theories in the Globalization Debate

In order to grasp the place of sport within processes of globalization, we must first understand what globalization is, and take at least a cursory look at some theories of globalization emanating from disciplines as diverse as political science, economics, and sociology. First, as technological capacities and modes of transportation have continued to increase, the rate at which ". . . goods, capital, people, knowledge, images, crime, pollutants, drugs, fashions, and beliefs . . . flow across territorial boundaries" has intensified (McGrew, 1992, p. 66). In this sense, our existence in a "global age" (Albrow, 1996) has been described as a compression of time (instantaneous global mass communication) and space (rapid global mass transportation) where, hypothetically speaking, our globe is shrinking (Harvey, 1989). No matter what our country of origin, our ancestors as recently as the early 20th century envisioned the world much differently than we do today. While we send messages instantly to remote locations across the globe using our Blackberry, imagine the time it took to compose a handwritten letter, and have it shipped via railroad, horse, or ship across the states or across the oceans. Further, with the time it took to communicate or travel globally, many cultures maintained a degree of autonomy and isolation from people of different cultures in distant regions. The world seemed a much larger place, with many different ideologies, politics, economies, cultural practices (like sport), and social relations that were completely unknown or misunderstood by the majority of the worlds' population outside of any given locality and its immediate reach.

Today, however, the barriers that once separated disparate peoples and cultures have largely dissipated, leading to new connections and dependencies in a global world order in which the spatial organization of social relations is altered through transcontinental or inter-regional **flows** and **networks** of activity (Held, McGrew, Goldblatt, & Perraton, 1999; Maguire, Jarvie, Mansfield, & Bradley, 2002). As an important conception of the global condition, John Tomlinson stated that globalization is, "an empirical condition of the modern world: what I shall call—**complex connectivity**. By this I mean the rapidly developing and ever-densening network of interconnections and interdependencies that characterize modern social life" (1999, p. 2, *emphasis added*). In other words, complex connectivity refers to the development of various **networks** of organizations, governing bodies, and corporations (an idea we will come to shortly) and the connected and dependant nature with which they operate and/or conduct business, resulting in a rapid **flow** of exchange (see also Castells, 1997). With this in mind, the increased connectivity of the global age indicates that no country, region, city, or individual is completely isolated from (or rather, unaffected by) the broader processes, practices, and products of the global marketplace (McLuhan & Powers, 1989). It is important to understand that not only can this intensified **interconnectivity** produce positive outcomes like the ability to communicate widely or to break down cultural barriers, but it also presents the possibility of negative outcomes when irresponsible decisions are made without concern for others. In a more disturbing and sobering aspect, events occurring in country X can have implications and effects for people in country Y, whether by intervention or the lack thereof during environmental or natural disasters, economic crises, political strife, or war and terrorism. In many cases, the problems arising from the international relations of countries are due to established hierarchies of power, cultural differences, and disparate ideological values. While not as dramatic, sporting institutions face similar barriers, as sport is intricately tied to the cultural values and political ideals of particular nations and regions. Sports marked as being distinctly American (basketball, football, baseball) or European (soccer, cricket, rugby), for example, have developed over time and represent many years of political ideals, technological innovations, cultural changes, and national identities that resonate with people sharing those common points of reference. As a global sport manager, expanding into foreign markets or working in a foreign market requires a sensitivity and understanding of such differences to make informed decisions that are both profitable for your organization and ethical toward the consumers and country in which you operate.

Understanding the managerial context is a vital part of operating efficiently and effectively in any market. This means that in order to be successful, one must have a working knowledge of the conditions and factors that may influence or effect business. For example, since sport is linked to broader political, technological, and cultural forces, it has tremendous power to influence, impose, or alter the lived experiences and identities of people, communities, and nations. Likewise, individuals, communities, and nations have power to influence the production of sport in various ways. Thus, within foreign markets in particular, having knowledge of the cultural differences, political ideologies, and common business practices of the locality will be a valuable asset in making difficult decisions and in ensuring success. As one potential barrier to foreign expansion,

Complex Connectivity_____
Tomlinson's (1999) notion of an ever-densening network of global interconnections and interdependencies that characterize modern life. Rapid increases in technology, modes of communication, travel, and trade have enabled an intensification of global flows. For example, the speed at which intangibles (ideas and information services) and tangibles (products and people) can circle the globe is either instantaneous (Internet, Cable TV, Satellite) or quite swift (plane, train, ship). As a result, cultures and peoples that were once so detached are now incredibly connected and dependant upon each other, especially in realms of politics and economics.

negative perceptions of Western developed nations (the United States and United Kingdom for example) sometimes hinder the reception of brand names, sport leagues, and products emanating from such countries. Some scholars have described such sentiments as being critical of the unequal power structures (the "west and the rest") and corporate ambitions of western developed nations (especially the U.S.) for imposing distinct cultural, economic, and political forms upon poorer developing nations, sport being an important part of this process (see, for example, Hall, 1992). Or, as noted by Kuisel (2003), "the import by non-Americans of products, images, technologies, practices, and behavior that are closely associated with America/Americans" has been defined as **Americanization** (p. 96). Nevertheless, while globalization has often been attributed to various processes of Americanization, the complexities of global relations cannot be reduced to a unidirectional flow. We can see some obvious examples of globalization's multi-directional flow just by looking at the cultural and ethnic diversity of America: the international foods we eat, languages spoken, prevalence of foreign-made products, growing popularity of soccer, and so on. While the outcomes of these processes traverse both the negative aspects of capitalist globalization and the positive aspects of multiculturalism and flow of ideas, they also denote the complex and irreducible nature of globalization as a dispersed phenomenon. It is within this conception that we can see political, economic, cultural, and technological **networks** playing a role in the development of interdependencies and interconnections between and within nations (see Table 4.2). In addition to global events like the Olympics and the World Cup, for example, the World Baseball Classic (WBC) demonstrates the development of global networks through the coming together of nations and the shared technological platforms that each country (in varying degrees) uses to stream media coverage of the event to their home nations. Furthermore, although baseball is widely known as a distinctly American sport, events like the WBC indicate the extent to which the game has been spread through various modes of global travel and communication technologies. As interconnected and interdependent networks continue to intensify the means and ease with which global flows occur, three main theoretical frameworks or paradigms (ways of viewing and thinking about something) have emerged from the scholarly community to describe our condition in the global age: global **homogenization**, global **heterogenization**, and global **hybridity**.

Global Homogenization

As the term suggests, global homogenization refers to a condition in which everything is the same or in the process of becoming uniform and undifferentiated; a convergence of cultures, ideas, politics, etc. Global corporations like Nike, McDonalds, Coca-Cola, and Wal-Mart are often discussed as being primary proponents of global *homogenization* due to their involvement in scouring the globe for cheaper production costs, new markets, and raw materials. Since their presence is felt and known nearly everywhere in the world, the conditions relative to their overwhelming success often call into question the extent to

Global Homogenization___
Theory that countries, nations, corporations, politics, economies, and cultures are becoming increasingly the same. More specifically, it generally cites three main forces responsible for the global diffusion of ideas, information, products, and so on, and an accelerated level of cultural convergence/sameness/uniformity: (1) Free market liberal economics, (2) Global corporate structures and technologies and (3) A consumer capitalist culture. In relation to sport, the processes and structures of global sporting organizations and events can be said to operate much the same, mainly due to the adoption of principles of American business and corporate structure.

TABLE 4.2

Various Networks of Global Connectivity

Political Networks

- Global government organizations
  United Nations (UN)
  World Bank (WB)
  World Health Organization (WHO)
- Regional political structures
  European Union (EU)
- Regional military alliances
  NATO
- Global non-governmental organizations
  Red Cross/Red Crescent
  Greenpeace
  Amnesty International

Economic Networks

- As economies globalize, corporations look beyond national boundaries for raw materials, production, and markets.
  This was possibly due to changes since 1980:
  I. Increased deregulation of economic protectionist policies; tariff and quota barriers loosened.
  II. Opening of financial markets, and establishment of a truly global financial structure.
  III. Increased foreign investment in national markets.
  IV. Emergence of truly global corporations.

Technological Networks

- Advances have radically changed the speed and scope of global transport and communications technologies.
- Transport Technologies
  With the development of the jet-liner we are now in an age of RAPID GLOBAL MASS TRANSPORTATION
- Communications Technologies!
  With the development of satellite television and internet technologies, we are now in an age of INSTANTANEOUS GLOBAL MASS COMMUNICATION.
- TV—people in US can watch European soccer and Europeans can watch NFL (satellite)

Cultural Networks

- Political, economic, and technological shifts have increased the rate of flow of objects, images, and people across national, regional, and global space. This has led to the emergence of:
  I. Diasporic populations: New waves of immigration and establishment of ethnically diverse communities.
  II. A new global multiculturalism: Greater flow of previously indigenous cultural practices and styles.
  III. A new global monoculturalism: Increased spread and influence of culturally homogenizing global products, practices, and images.

Reprinted by permission of D.L. Andrews.

which they are exploiting or altering the economies, cultures, and politics of foreign nations to make them more like America; thereby simplifying and increasing profitability in the mode of production and consumption in transnational business. With regard to sport, then, we can see definitive relationships between the overzealous expansionism of western thought, politics, economics,

© Tatiana Markow/Sygma/Corbis

McDonalds is an example of a company that has experienced some resistance as it expanded operations throughout the world.

and cultural values and the global diffusion of popular sporting forms as constitutive elements in the flattening of cultural difference. In other words, according to this theory, the fact that you can go practically anywhere in the world and still have access to ESPN, McDonalds, Coke products, Nike, and a range of other distinctly American products and brand images denotes the scale and scope of global *homogenization*. Over ten years ago, managers in predominantly American sports (basketball and baseball primarily) realized the need to, or were already actively engaged in, seeking out new markets globally, recognizing that there were:

> fans willing to buy into the excitement of American-style entertainment. . . . Sports leagues are discovering what Coca-Cola., McDonald's Corp., Disney Co. and the makers of Marlboro cigarettes figured out long ago: The trappings of America's consumer culture will sell overseas (Alms, 1994, p. 1D).

With the aforementioned success of other American corporations overseas, it is perhaps not surprising that NBA commissioner David Stern famously quoted so long ago: "There are 250 million potential NBA fans in the U.S., and there are 5 billion outside the U.S. . . . We like those numbers" (Comte, 1993, p. 42). Since that time, the NBA has become a leader in establishing overseas networks and tapping new markets to become a "multifaceted marketing and entertainment conglomerate incorporating over 20 divisions, including NBA Properties, NBA Entertainment, NBA International, and NBA Ventures" (Andrews, 2006, p. 95). It also does not hurt when international players like Yao Ming, just one of many foreign born players for example, bring an almost cult-like following to the league that helps establish a significant consumer market, inspire a new talent pool of NBA hopefuls, and generate more lucrative broadcasting contracts overseas. If the 2008 Beijing Olympics is any indication, the degree of Chinese support for Team USA (Kobe Bryant had the highest jersey sales in China during 2008, for example; see "Kobe Bryant," 2008), combined with the increasing industrial boom and prosperity of China's economy, will likely bode well for the NBA's future in the country. Already broadcasted in over 215 countries in 41 different languages, the NBA's expansion into China has produced considerable results. In 2007, the NBA's own global website proclaimed that the NBA had recently:

> . . . added 24 TV partners in China and currently has relationships with 51 TV stations that provided NBA programming to 34 million viewers per week and more than 1.2 billion viewers for the 2006–07 season. With 20% of traffic to NBA.com coming from China, basketball is rapidly growing in popularity . . . ('NBA China,' 2007, para. 8).

With regard to its global homogenizing effects, it is not only that basketball is generally played the same way (at least in terms of basic rules and tenets of the game) in China or Australia that it is in America, but it also is broadcast or communicated in the same fashion all across the globe denoting the technological and economic uniformity in the global sport structure. Even if some of the players might look different, the tangential aspects of its production (media broadcasting, merchandising, sponsorship, management and labor, marketing, display of physical movement, mass spectatorship, and the emotional and visceral attachment of spectators) would appear to affirm the homogenization thesis as a credible and applicable way of viewing this phenomenon.

Courtesy Richard Southall

China built new facilities such as the Bird's Nest to host global sport competitions such as the Olympic Games and ParaOlympic Games.

Global Heterogenization

While homogenization suggests a creeping uniformity, what do we make of the deeply held national and local cultural traditions, values, and allegiances so central to sports' ubiquitous global success? Another way of viewing global sport processes is that sport, unlike other institutions, depends upon the appeal of locality, difference, and uniqueness. In this sense, the notion of **global heterogenization** suggests that, in fact, nations, cultures, and peoples are becoming more differentiated, not less; opposed to the idea of global uniformity and holding dearly to the particularities of their own local cultures. As suggested by David Rowe (2003), "the social institution of sport is so deeply dependent on the production of difference that it repudiates the possibility of comprehensive globalization while seeming to foreshadow its inevitable establishment" (p. 282). In other words, the success of sporting teams and leagues is dependent on consumers' affiliations with a particular place, albeit a town, city, or country. More specifically, sport has the capacity to (re)define the unique cultural and national meanings, histories, and ideals of a country and its citizens due to the visceral and emotional attachment fans maintain with their sporting teams, places, and heros. Just think about your favorite sport and team for a moment. How did you fall in love with that particular sport and team? Was it influenced by the country, region, or locality in which you were raised? Or could it be the cultural meanings associated with a particular team, player, or coach that resonated with your own identity? Many fans of the Pittsburgh Steelers will, to varying degrees, cite the hard work mentality, blue-collar tradition, and masculine toughness associated with the historical memory of past Steelers teams, and their geographic and historical location in a once thriving industrial economy of steel production, as reason for their allegiance. The particular values, beliefs, and cultural norms associated with that team and its city reflects the importance of locality in defining a particular social grouping and imagined community (an

Global Heterogenization___

Largely in response to the real and/or perceived threat of globally homogenizing forces, this theory asserts that countries, nations, corporations, politics, economies, and cultures are actually becoming more differentiated, not less. In this sense, local difference has intensified by both the reaction to global uniformity by local cultures and through corporations' realization of the value of cultural niches and marketing of local difference. Sport has been argued to play a considerable role in this process, as fans tend to feverishly support place-based teams that reflect a specific locale and its unique cultural nuances.

imagined community being something like Red Sox Nation where disparate peoples across the globe share interests, information, and norms tied together by a common point of reference; see, Anderson, 1991; Hobsbawm, 1990). This example is interesting because it denotes the obvious existence of global forces (ability to access Red Sox media anywhere) while communicating the cultural resonance of a particular locality (Boston) and its attendant racial and class identities, social norms, and lived experiences (see, for example, Klein, 2000).

However, these American examples are somewhat limited in what they can tell us about such forces on a global scale. While technological innovations and global media play an obvious role, much can be said about the cultural meanings and emotive potential of sport to break down international borders and encourage transnational sport-related commerce through an appeal to the nation and national identity. As ideas, products, people, and organizations rapidly navigate the globe, then, it would seem inevitable that countries would eventually begin to look the same, espouse the same ideas and values, and exist under the same political and economic logics (reflecting the homogenization thesis). While some of these changes have begun to occur (shopping malls, theme parks, and restaurants, for example, can be difficult to distinguish from one developed economy to another), there remains a great deal of cultural diversity that represents both the potential for **commodification** (turning something into a product for sale on the market) and a refutation of the powerful forces of (corporate) globalization.

One could argue that since WWII, baseball in Japan has been played very much the same as it has in the Unites States. However, others might note the particular manner in which the game is played, aspects of performance that are more valued than others, and the differences in food, music, dress, and behavior that accompany the game atmosphere reflect the broader social and cultural differences that permeate and give meaning to the game in these varying contexts. As a refutation to the global homogenization thesis, these differences embody powerful representations of national identity. Thus, in addition to the political and economic structures of nations, sport functions to constitute the nation through, "a cultural formation, a feeling of belonging, and a shared heritage" (Hardt & Negri, 2000, p. 336). The intense emotional bonds and nationalistic expressions of England's Barmy Army (supporters of England's cricket club) or Korea's Red Devils (supporters of the Korea Republic national football team) are just two examples of organized sport fans that closely relate the meanings, success, and identity of sporting teams with that of the nation. In terms of representing the nation and developing individual national identities through sport, Hobsbawm (1990, p. 143) notes that:

> What has made sport so uniquely effective a medium for inculcating national feelings, at all events for males, is the ease with which even the least political or public individuals can identify with the nation as symbolized by young persons excelling at what practically every man wants, or at one time in life has wanted to be good at. The imagined commu-

Commodification

Essentially the process through which a cultural form is turned into a product to be sold on the market. For example sport, in and of itself, is a cultural practice that has developed over time and throughout history, and reflects the people/civilizations that created/played/altered it to meet their social needs. Many of us still play sport just for fun, but the meanings we attach to it are heavily influenced by our consumption (purchase, patronage) of the sports we love. In the twentieth century, many popular sports became professionalized and pulled into the imperatives of the market. Thus, sport became a means through which to generate capital (profit) in the rapidly developing entertainment economy.

nity of millions seems more real as a team of eleven named people. The individual, even the one who only cheers, becomes a symbol of his nation himself.

Of course, this quote must also be applied to female spectators/athletes, as women have increasingly become regular consumers of sport and have long represented nations themselves in sporting competition. In this regard, Brownell (2008) recounts the historical significance of China's female athletes in the Olympics; promoted as representatives of the strength, virility, and progressive ideologies of the nation amidst dominant global perceptions of China as "the sick man of East Asia" (p. 102). Depending on the popularity of a sporting team and its historical legacy within a given nation, people identify and align themselves with it as one of the most important "badges of membership" within the nation and the imagined community in which they exist and find commonalities (Hobsbawm & Ranger, 1983). On a similar level of global significance, soccer also represents a key site where sporting competition facilitates the development of communities of supporters and intense national rivalries.

As a truly global game, soccer matches bring together local (Fulham vs. Liverpool in the FA Premier League), and global (Korea vs. Japan in the World Cup) competition in spaces where cultural values are made salient and can incite passionate fan support, rivalries, and sometimes violence. The recent Australian open match between Novak Djokovic (Serbian defending champion) and Amer Delic (born in Bosnia but playing for the U.S.) in January 2009 erupted in violence between Bosnian and Serbian supporters immediately following Djokovic's victory (Tallentire, 2009). While we often see the excitement and camaraderie of sporting competition between nations, in some cases, the intense emotional ties of fans with sporting figures and their local roots can sometimes facilitate negative perceptions and violent consequences. In addition to the obvious and unfortunate acts of violence, the way that local sporting traditions are remembered and reproduced sometimes causes controversy.

In this sense, fans' attachment and loyalty to particular teams, cultural meanings, and values have been leveraged by corporations to increase brand recognition within countries and sports deemed to represent untapped markets for TNCs. At the same time, due to the passion and allegiances of consumers to particular sporting forms, teams, and players (Giulianotti, 2002; Lewis, 2001)—concomitant with the strong national, regional, or local ties they espouse—it is often assumed that sport acts as a key site of resistance to these global forces (Rowe, 2003). One interesting example was Adidas' entrance into the New Zealand market by appropriating a traditional dance called the "haka" (performed by the New Zealand All-Blacks rugby team before matches) in an advertisement depicting rugby, the haka, and stereotypical images of

© Rui Araujo/fotolia

Soccer is the world's most popular game and nearly every country on earth supports a team that attempts to compete in the World Cup.

ancient Maori warriors to authenticate the brand (Jackson & Hokowhitu, 2002). Local leaders and scholars subsequently criticized the company for exploiting part of an ancient cultural heritage purely for capital gain (see also, Scherer & Jackson, 2007). The extent to which local cultural uniqueness is discovered, commodified, and mass produced can sometimes be disheartening to those whose culture appears to have been trivialized to sell products.

Depending on how you conceptualize what is truly local, it has become nearly impossible to find a unique cultural form that has not, in one way or another, been appropriated, commodified, marketed, and/or mass-produced for commercial purposes. Given the realities of our presence in the global age however, perhaps it is not as important to lament and fight against the loss of perceived locality, but rather to ensure responsible and inclusive global processes, especially when matters of commercializing local culture is involved. This is particularly important for sport managers involved in marketing campaigns, sponsorship deals, or advertising that plays upon aspects of culture to legitimize and popularize sport products or services. If done responsibly and with an informed understanding, cultural references can have an extremely powerful emotive commercial purpose while avoiding stereotypical representations or offensive exploitation; of course this also depends on the credibility and reputation of the company. With this in mind, the third concept of **global hybridity** offers another way of viewing processes of globalization and arguably a more positive and fluid outlook concerning the global-local debate.

Global Hybridity

Global Hybridity_____

Essentially a mixture of both homogenization and heterogenization. The hybridity thesis acknowledges that the relationship between local and global forces is much too complex to easily categorize. As such, this theory suggests that a better way to understand globalization is to view it as a global-local nexus, characterized by a complex and ever-changing dynamic between change and continuity, difference and sameness, universality and particularity. As such, global sporting events reflect markers of both local elements (nationalities, cultures, style of play) and global prerogatives (media broadcasting, revenue generation, and marketing).

A hybrid is essentially a mixture of two or more component parts that results in a new sum product. Certainly, sport and its accompanying structures, processes, and outcomes cannot be easily categorized as either local or global in nature. As such, they represent a key site for engaging the complex and ever-changing tensions between change and continuity, difference and sameness, universality and particularity, as experienced by diverse people in local settings across the globe (Robertson, 1995; Robins, 1997). Understanding how people receive and engage with cultural forms and products emanating from the global-local nexus is a key issue at hand for anyone working in the global sport marketplace. As such, the local particularities of any sporting form and its ancillary productions must be understood as a, "fluid and relational space, constituted only in and through its relation to the global" and vice versa (Robins, 1991, p. 35). In this sense, an English Premier League (EPL) team like Manchester United, represents locally unique aspects of the broader British culture and more specific peculiarities of Manchester city and its social, cultural, and sporting history. However, it also espouses and is regarded as one of the most Americanized EPL teams due to its corporate sport model; negotiating sponsorship contracts with American companies like Nike, Pepsi Co., and Anheuser Busch, mirroring the "American-style, brand-led media business" in areas of advertising, marketing, and sponsorship, and making promotional tours of the U.S. (Manchester United, 2002; see also, Hill & Vincent, 2006).

Ironically, when Malcolm Glazer (an American businessman and owner of the Tampa Bay Buccaneers) purchased a controlling stake in the United in May 2005 (valued at approximately 1.5 billion dollars American), local fans protested the action with explicit anti-American demonstrations against Glazer and the perceived American values he represented (Brown, 2007; Hill & Vincent, 2006).

Despite the already Americanized business model under which the United operated, for local fans, the idea of an American actually owning the team conjured up the unique place-based memories, values, and traditions that continue to shape the collective experience of being a local Manchester fan. Such emotions are germane to nearly all sporting teams in some degree across the world, and represent the most salient form of opposition to perceived infractions from the corporate-sport model. It is in these common and increasingly complex tensions between global and local forces that Robertson's (1995) notion of **glocalization** well theorizes the relationship arising from both cultural and commercial forces; both being relational and complimentary to each other in various situations. In other words, the **glocal** represents a continuum between these forces, or rather, "the interpenetration of the global and the local, resulting in unique outcomes in different geographic areas" (Andrews & Ritzer, 2007, p.135; see also, Ram, 2007). Nevertheless, while some scholars envision local forces as having a real impact on the structure and processes of global commerce, it is questioned whether the modifications of global companies to meet the cultural tastes and preferences of a local market is truly evidence of the local's power. A simple and common example of this is McDonald's attempts to cater to their customers in foreign markets through themed restaurants or by offering renditions of local fare: "Kosher Mcnuggets" in Tel Aviv, "kiwiburger" in New Zealand, non-beef "Mcpatties" in India, "McSushi" in Japan, and so forth (see, Watson, 1997). While some may see the local impact of these decisions, others note the overarching logics of the corporation and the principles guiding organizational adaptation and change (Ritzer, 1998, 2008; see also, Amis, 2005). In other words, while the organization may adapt to local markets by offering specialized menu items that mimic local cultural cuisine, the management logics and operational processes remain the same globally.

Before relating this to sport, and sticking with the McDonald's theme, a helpful concept is Ritzer's (1998, 2008) notion of **McDonaldization**; the process through which the principles of the fast food chain are coming to dominate more and more sectors of American society and the world. Important to note here is that it is an overall business philosophy and four key operational principles (see Table 4.3) that Ritzer envisions as central to the McDonaldization thesis and not the actual product itself (burgers and fries). Further, like many other ideas presented in this chapter, McDonaldization is a theory (a way of interpreting and making sense of something) created by Ritzer that can be applied to other social phenomena, and is not endorsed by or affiliated with McDonald's in any way.

Stemming from the rational production processes of **Fordism** (assembly line manufacturing of Model T Ford cars in the early 20th century), the principles of McDonaldization are reflective of the dominant governing logics of

TABLE 4.3

Basic Principles of McDonaldization

Calculability	Emphasizes the quantitative aspects of products (portion size, cost) and services (time it takes to get the product) over their quality. Value is thus measured in things like portion size and quick delivery of the product. For workers in a McDonaldized system, the lack of variation in the product means they are forced to focus on how quickly tasks can be accomplished (i.e., a lot of work, quickly, for low pay).
Predictability	The assurance that products and services will be the same over time and in any location. The lack of significant change means consumers know exactly what to expect when entering a McDonald's, Wal-Mart, or Starbucks, for example.
Control	Both customers and workers are controlled by systems of rational management. For example, uncomfortable seating and drive-through windows encourage customers to eat quickly and leave or buy their food and drive away. Workers are trained to do a limited number of routine tasks in a precise way; technology controlling the bulk of the labor process leaving behind the mundane service tasks, food preparation, and cleaning.
Efficiency	The optimum method for getting from one point to another. In McDonald's or any other institution, this involves a pre-designed process to achieve a desired end result (getting fast food, an insurance quote, or paying for groceries, for example) as quickly as possible (instant consumer gratification).

American business and industry; increasingly seen in sporting organizations across the world. Further, while these processes represent the global forces we have been discussing, the existence of local particularity is embodied by cultural difference; something that has become highly valued for its ability to distinguish product offerings and create emotive meanings to entice consumers (Silk & Andrews, 2001). In practical terms, effectively managing and balancing the cultural production of local difference ethically through the logics of global free market capitalism is not an easy task. Just imagine you are the acting director of marketing and promotions for the NBA in Australia. Following the established business model of the company, how do you capitalize on the essence of the NBA's American authenticity while appealing to the nuances of Australian cultural sensibilities in an accurate and effective manner? As one example of this complexity, a recent KFC commercial in Australia created a stir in the U.S. media after spreading via the Internet (the advertisement was only intended to be seen in Australia). In it, a Caucasian man is surrounded by West Indies supporters during an Australian cricket match and offers them fried chicken to quiet them down. Demonstrating the challenges of marketing cultural meanings, the advertisement was perceived to be quite offensive in the U.S. for its insinuation of racial stereotypes, but largely innocuous in an Australian context (see "KFC accused," 2010). As such, successfully navigating such contradictions begins with an understanding of the political and cultural economies developed in the late 20th century and their implications for global sport organizations. After a brief discussion of the post-industrial shift in the mode of production, two case studies (Nike and News Corporation) will be discussed in relation to the contemporary structure and experience of globally interconnected TNCs.

The Global Sporting Goods Trade: Post-industrialism, Transnational Corporations, and the Rise of Global Branding and Sponsorship

It is a world of industrialism and its longstanding imagery that we are leaving behind—the modern factories in an urban setting, the heavy machinery and the ever-present noise, along with the massed ranks of workers in overalls. In its place, we are told that we have entered a *postindustrial era;* one that is characterized by information technologies and networked offices rather than by coal or steam power and sprawling workshops (Allen, 1996, p. 534).

After World War II, rising labor costs (due to the increased standard of living in developed economies), increased production costs (due to the OPEC oil crises), and growing global competition caused countries like the U.S. and U.K. to shift from "dirty" (producing tangible goods in factory settings) to "clean" technologies like information, services, and entertainment (Allen, 1996). Within this new digital economy, the production of "things" became outsourced to developing or underdeveloped economies where labor was cheap, labor laws were weak or nonexistent, and free trade agreements favored large corporations. With manufacturing occurring in other countries, TNCs could focus their attention on the intangible aspects of consumer goods (design, marketing, advertising, and branding). In this sense, the **post-industrial** shift to **cultural (symbolic) production** at the developed economic core, and mass industrial (material) manufacture at the developing economic peripheries, exemplifies the current state of global sport commerce and international trade. As one of the most telling examples of this, Nike was extremely successful shifting from material to **symbolic production** to become a leader in the athletic footwear and apparel industry (Willigan, 1992). To be sure, CEO Phil Knight once stated that

> For years we thought of ourselves as a production-oriented company, meaning we put all our emphasis on designing and manufacturing the product. But now we understand that the most important thing we do is market the product. We've come around to saying that Nike is a marketing-oriented company, and the product is our most important marketing tool (Willigan, 1992, pp. 93–94).

These developments are further reflected in the gradual decreased production of footwear in the U.S., concomitant to the ever-ballooning expenditures on media, advertising, and marketing campaigns. The amount spent on developing the product's **cultural capital** (attaching symbolic meaning and brand identity via marketing and branding initiatives) also positively correlates with the overall return in bottom-line sales relative to other market competitors. For convenience, the extent of Nike's global interconnectedness can be divided

Cultural (Symbolic) Production

A related process to commodification that involves the inscribing of meaning to a particular product. During the industrial revolution, in order to differentiate one product from another, proprietors of a company would advertise the positive attributes of their product over their competitors. With increasing technologies, sophistication in advertising and marketing, and a decreasing industrial base after World War II, branded corporations turned to cultural meanings to attach symbolic value to their products. For example, while two athletic shoes may be made in the same overseas factory, the symbol inscribed on it denotes a greater value than just the cost to produce it. The cultural meaning and symbolism established by marketing/advertising initiatives bestows the product with greater value for consumers.

generally into two categories along the production process: raw materials, manufacturing, and transportation on one side, and design, marketing, and branding on the other. Countries like Indonesia, China, Thailand, and South Korea are amongst the many developing economies involved in **global commodity chains** in which the production process in various locales is minutely divided, routinized, and highly regulated to maximize profit (Klein, 1999; Korzeniewicz, 1994). Some scholars are critical of companies like Nike, arguing that the conditions of outsourced manufacturing processes represent the "dark side of flexible production" in which low-wage workers are exploited and local governments and contractors are manipulated into accepting contractual terms that, once entered into, maintain economic stagnancy and dependence (Harrison, 1994; Klein, 1999; Korzeniewicz, 1994). Further, once the resources (raw materials and labor) in a particular country become too expensive, corporations often quickly relocate to less developed economies that will accept lower wages and trade agreements favoring the company. Nevertheless, Nike has continued to deflect global criticism and protest about human rights abuses and unfair labor agreements with public relations campaigns assuring its efforts at improving working conditions and promoting social and environmental justice. In the 2008 annual report, Nike President and CEO Mark Parker stated that

> We're very focused on creating products that reduce their environmental impact and showcase sustainable innovation. We're committed to helping improve working conditions across the industry's supply chain. And we continue to invest in our communities. . . . Every day we see how social and environmental change can promote innovation and growth in our business and in the world (www.nikebiz.com).

The difficulty of operating with a prescient sense of corporate social responsibility (CSR) while remaining competitive in a complex and saturated global market is aptly reflected in the case of Nike. It could be argued that since 99 percent of total product manufacturing takes place outside the U.S., Nike has made good business decisions, benefitting from strategic outsourcing and flexible production (enabling greater focus on promoting the product), but is not responsible for the conditions of production directly affected by foreign contractors. In fiscal 2008 for example, Nike's contracted suppliers manufactured the following percentages of total Nike footwear: China 36 percent, Vietnam 33 percent, Indonesia 21 percent, and Thailand 9 percent (www.nikebiz.com). Within these primary contractual arrangements, further contracts are negotiated independently in as many as 34 other countries, including, but not limited to, Malaysia, Turkey, Sri Lanka, Honduras, Mexico, Taiwan, Israel, Cambodia, India, and Bangladesh.

While Nike profits from these arrangements, it is hotly contested whether the individual contractors are liable, or whether Nike, and other companies like them, should play a greater role in alleviating poor working conditions likely caused by contractual pressures and unregulated worker zones in individual countries (Frenkel, 2001; Klein, 1999). While the purpose of this chapter is not to delineate where responsibility begins or ends, this example demonstrates the tremendously complex nature of international business and trade when tangible products like sporting goods are involved. In this sense, it could be argued that advanced economies like those of the U.S. and U.K. are nearly inconducive to the production of goods when faced with the realities of global market competition. The question is, given the current economic and political model in developed nations, as the economy in countries like China and India, for example, continue to mature and catch up to Western nations, where will product manufacturing move next, and how long will this process remain sustainable? Further, what can be done in the immediate interim to protect worker rights and encourage a more egalitarian arrangement of production while keeping in mind the need for corporations to remain competitive in the global marketplace?

Despite such uncertainties on the side of material production, Nike has been extremely successful in producing symbolic value through commercial advertisements and marketing campaigns. Realizing that that they could not treat the "entire world as a single, undifferentiated entity, thereby selling the same things in the same way everywhere" (Andrews, 2008, p. 3) as Multinational Corporate Structures (MNCs) once attempted to do, Nike has adapted to local market specificities and established itself as the prototypical TNC (see Table 4.4).

The rise of Transnational Corporations (TNCs) can be attributed generally to this desire to operate globally, in as many foreign markets as possible, and with the capability of being culturally resonant (fitting in with local peculiarities) and horizontally integrated (a flexible chain of command that permits local adaptations). In many ways, sport has played a key part in this process due to the expressions of cultural differentiation that tie a particular sport, team, or athlete to the local histories, values, and shared traditions of the nation, region, or community.

As previously discussed, Rowe's (2003) notion of sport repudiating global forces (part of the global heterogenization thesis) corroborates the driving logic behind TNC's need to adapt and modify their market strategies using local

TABLE 4.4

Global Corporate Structures

Multinational Corporations (MNCs)	Entities that can be identified with a particular country/nation but operate some production processes abroad, seeking to move into external markets.
Transnational Corporations (TNCs)	Entities dissociated from a specific home country/nation. They insert themselves and their products into the local cultures of the markets they seek to penetrate.

sporting cultures to gain entry. Denoting the commercial viability of sport in the global market, Andrews (2008) notes that:

> Transnational brand strategies use locally resonant sport practices, teams, spectacles, and celebrities as a means of engaging local consumers and markets. This is because the dominant sporting culture of a nation represents a compelling cultural shorthand for the nation itself. Sport clearly exerts considerable influence upon the hearts, minds, and spending habits of the public (pp. 4–5).

It is thus no wonder that brand corporations representing all manner of products and services look to sport as a way to generate visibility, affiliation, and loyalty for their brand from the globally diverse consumer marketplace. Everything from Ford, Visa, and Pepsi, to Home Depot and Gatorade can be immersed within the sporting landscape; their proponents finding different ways to use sport to differentiate themselves from market competitors and establish credibility with consumers.

Global Sport Media: Mega-Events and Mass Entertainment Spectacles

To this degree, this final section will draw together the cultural nuances of sport and commercial sport properties with the modes of mass mediation and corporate branding just alluded to. Encompassing a substantial portion of sport-related commerce, media entities (television, radio, newspaper, Internet) play a vital role as the mediums through which products, people, events, and ideas are disseminated nationally and globally. In the case of Nike or with any other brand corporation, popular media platforms represent the means through which effective communication with target markets is achieved and sustained. Furthermore, media conglomerates have become branded entities in and of themselves, and represent formidable actors in the global dissemination of sport productions. One such company, News Corporation, represents one of the most aggressive media properties using sport as a primary source of broadcasting content across the globe. In the United States, big name media formats like Fox, MySpace, FX, and the *New York Post* are among the most recognizable holdings of the company. However, such entities represent only a fraction in scale and scope of the media giant's global portfolio. News Corporation reaches three quarters of the world's population across six continents, in more than 100 countries and 30 languages, employing 64,000 workers in film, TV, cable, satellite, newspapers, magazines, books, and digital media ("News Corporation," 2008). In regard to sport, then, a central philosophy of CEO Rupert Murdoch is that sport generates unparalleled viewer loyalty in all markets across the globe:

> Sport absolutely overpowers film and everything else in the entertainment genre. . . . Football, of all sports, is number one. . . . Sport will

remain very important and we will be investing in and acquiring long-term rights. . . . We have the long-term rights in most countries to major sporting events and we will be doing in Asia what we intend to do elsewhere in the world, that is, *use sports as a battering ram* and a lead offering in all our pay television operations (Rupert Murdoch, 1996 speech at News Corporation's annual meeting, Adelaide, Australia, Quoted in Milliken, 1996, p. 28, *emphasis added*).

Thus, some of News Corporation's most viable sport related networks include Fox Sports, Fox Soccer Channel, Big Ten Network, SPEED, and the FUEL TV in the U.S. and Sky Sports, Sky Italia, and Premier AG in Europe and STAR in Asia. Fox Sports alone holds contracted broadcasting rights for the NFL, MLB, BCS, and NASCAR; this is not to mention the other media formats that regularly feature sport content as a leading source in product offerings.

Given the global scale and scope of News Corporation, it is a useful example to consider the complexities involved in leveraging sport as a commodified and consumable product. As noted by Rowe (2003), "there is no one in the media world who has a greater commitment to the commercial exploitation of sport than Murdoch" (p. 191). With an expressed interest in expanding globally by continually penetrating new markets, sometimes with ruthless tactics of business competition (Grainger & Andrews, 2005), some scholars, critical of capitalist globalization, question the methods and outcomes of News Corporation's insatiable quest to secure a controlling stake in global media platforms. Nevertheless, on the other side of the debate, some see corporations like News Corporation as leaders in a global pursuit of enhanced choices and freedoms for consumers previously cut off from the global flow of media and entertainment. As world economies continue to advance in sophistication to rival the West (most notably China and India as they advance through their own industrial revolutions), early penetration of such markets by TNCs arguably represent a necessary and unavoidable step to continually increase profits. Such sentiments were expressed by Rupert Murdoch in the 2008 annual report:

> . . . we are seeing the creation of a global middle class of more than two billion people who are well educated, well remunerated and increasingly sophisticated in their choices . . . they will be increasingly hungry for better sources of news and entertainment. And we are in a strong position to provide it (News Corporation, 2008, p. 15).

No matter where one stands as to the ethics of global expansionism, the fact that an American/European based TNC is aggressively seeking to control the means through which newly developed foreign economies access digital information and entertainment must be considered. Returning to an earlier point about "operating in the language of the local" and catering products and services toward diverse local cultures, News Corporation has been one of the most successful media conglomerates in this regard (Dirlik, 1996; Silk &

Andrews, 2001). Such a sensibility extends from Murdoch's own experiences with global expansion:

> You would be very wrong to forget that what people want to watch in their own country is basically local programming, local language, local culture . . . I learned that many years ago in Australia, when I was loading up . . . with good American programs and we'd get beat with second-rate Australian ones (quoted in Schmidt, 2001, p. 79).

In this sense, Murdoch's expressed proclivity to use sport as a battering ram to infiltrate new markets by first providing greater mediated access to local sports extends from this logic. Once obtaining all media broadcasting rights and/or purchasing sport franchises/properties to reduce rights fees in a particular market, the introduction of pay-per-view services and cable/satellite fees take the place of basic programming access (Andrews, 2003). Thus, it may be surmised that media conglomerates operating in foreign economies are only tangentially concerned with local economic development because it may eventually affect their bottom line and ROI. As both the Nike and News Corporation examples attest, the global sport marketplace is fraught with complex situations and difficult decisions. The need for culturally aware and socially conscious marketers and managers has never been more urgent to develop new solutions for global challenges; balancing a drive for profit with practices of corporate social responsibility (see, Thomas, Schermerhorn, & Dienhart, 2004; Gustafsson, 2003). It is with such sensibilities that the next generation of sport managers and marketers has the opportunity to positively impact the communities in which they labor. With rapidly advancing technologies and the uncertainties of global economics and politics, new solutions will be needed to provide equitable access and local investment while maintaining a global competitive perspective.

Conclusion

As sport has increasingly become a defining feature of cultural practice, it has also morphed into a multi-billion dollar entertainment economy, forging partnerships and driving supply and demand in countless mediums of global commerce from large (major sponsorships and media contracts) to small (merchandise and concessions). As a result, while there are many opportunities to work in a sport organization, there are countless opportunities to work in companies that profit from or do business with sport entities. For example, during major sporting events, large quantities of select merchandise are transported to meet market demands, and someone has to coordinate these activities. Within one particular company, these duties are executed by the managing director for the promotion and distribution of sporting goods merchandise to large retail outlets across the U.S. and Europe. When big events like the Super Bowl, NBA finals, or World Cup happen, this individual travels to the host city (or the city of the team favored to win) to coordinate the rapid production and distribution of time-sensitive sporting goods apparel. For example, when it looked like

TABLE 4.5

Examples of Global Sport-Related Organizations/Careers

Amateur Athletics/ Governing Bodies	1. **Olympic**—Recognized sport federations/positions in coordination, management, and promotion of Olympic competition and development around the world. For example, the *Ministry of Sports and Physical Education in Cameroon* or the *Korean Olympic Committee and Sports Council.* 2. **Collegiate**—*Athletic Directors and Assistants/Compliance Commissioners/Managers of equipment, facilities, fund raising, etc.* 3. **Non-Governmental Organizations (NGOs)**—Often closely related to some Olympic organizations. For example, the *European Non-Governmental Sports Organisation (ENGSO).* 4. **Government sanctioned Sport Commissions**—President Obama recently instituted the "The White House Office of Olympic, Paralympic and Youth Sport" for example. 5. **Convention and Visitor's Bureaus (CVBs)**—Place-based leadership positions in convention sales and marketing, communications/Event managers and coordinators/ tourism promotion. *For example, the Paris Convention & Visitor's Bureau.* 6. **Youth sport organizations**—High school sports administration/Amateur Athletic Union (AAU).
Corporate Management/ Marketing	1. **Corporate Sponsorship**—Various positions dealing with partnership marketing, brand management, and development of effective synergies with large corporations and sport. 2. **Advertising and Marketing**—In every country where sport is commercially produced and consumed, there exists ample need for the management of advertising and marketing campaigns for leagues, teams, official sponsors, products, and services. *For example, Tiger Sports Marketing (TSM) in India, specializing in the development of Golf in the country.* 3. **Professional Services**—Sport organizations also need support in the form of financial, legal, and information technology services to maintain efficient and profitable operations. *For example, IT service managers, accountants, legal counsel, corporate auditors, etc.*
Sport Media	1. **Electronic and Digital Media**—Maintenance and development of websites, online communications, and new media to reach target consumers. *For example, www.guardian.co.uk is a leading online news source for global sport information in the UK.* 2. **Broadcast & Print**—*Broadcasters, journalists, editors, researchers,* and others involved in the production and dissemination of sport information products. *For example, FoxSports broadcasting and ESPN network and magazine in the U.S., or SportzBlitz sports publisher in Australia.*
Facilities/Events	1. **Arena/Stadium Management**—Whether a professional team owns its arena or not, they often outsource the maintenance of the facility and event operations to a professional company. In developed economies, large leisure settings like a pro stadium require significant and complex organizational management in a number of areas including *merchandise, concessions, premium services, and housekeeping.* 2. **Event/Facility Development**—Creating, managing, and promoting events and leveraging the use of space within a facility to maximize profit and customer satisfaction. *Directors, coordinators, and managers of annual events or high profile games like the Rose Bowl or UEFA Champions League Final, for example.*
Sporting Goods/ Consumer Products	1. **Product Promotion & Distribution**—Management positions dealing with contractual sales and point of distribution/coordination and supply chain management on the retail end. 2. **Product Marketing/Advertising**—Positions in marketing and developing advertising campaigns for individual products, brands, or retail outlets.

*Note: This chart is by no means comprehensive and is intended to provide merely a glimpse into the potential fields of global sport commerce. Further, each example represents a general description of organizations and careers that exist in varied iterations across the globe. Outside the U.S. and Europe in particular, the development of sport organizations, governing bodies, commercial properties, and professional entities will likely continue to proliferate as we continue to experience an intensified global interconnectedness through new technologies. Thus, combining principles of western style sport management with a heightened perspective of global issues in culture and commerce will enhance one's marketability abroad.

Pittsburgh was going to prevail in Super Bowl XLIII, the managing director was responsible for assessing local demand and predicting quantities of Super Bowl merchandise with Steelers insignia to be sold in select retail outlets. While not working in the conventional sense of sport management, this position requires diverse knowledge of a wide range of sports, consumer behavior, and management of supply and demand.

This example brings up an important point because it is likely within the processes of cultural and symbolic production (marketing, advertising, branding, sponsorship, etc.), rather than something like personnel or property management, that many sport managers may find themselves in the contemporary global sport marketplace. In this regard, it is important when seeking employment within sport organizations to also look beyond sport at companies and positions that deal indirectly with sport as a means to leverage the visibility and power of their brand. In other words, while there are opportunities to work directly with a team or sport organization in management, marketing, sponsorship, or promotion and sales, there are also many prospects in "non-sport" settings that deal with sport properties through various modes of partnership. This broad view of sport-related occupations becomes even more pronounced when considering the increasingly global interconnectedness of sport organizations, MNCs and TNCs as previously discussed. Thus, a working knowledge of the global, national, and local intricacies of sport culture and commerce will be a valuable asset in successfully navigating a career path within a multitude of global companies.

Without question the global sport marketplace is extremely complex and diverse. This chapter has attempted to provide an introduction to global processes, networks, and flows of interconnected activity as they relate to sporting organizations and the promotional armatures of global corporations. There are numerous theories through which to interpret global sporting phenomena (heterogenization, homogenization, hybridization, and so forth), and that can be used to explicate the production of sport as a significant propellant in the development of global networks, commerce, and trade. With rapidly changing communication technologies and media formats, shifting political and economic priorities within countries, and global financial crises and cultural conflicts, the institutions of sport and sport-related companies face significant challenges, but also unique opportunities. Certainly, the globally ubiquitous popularity of sport has not diminished amidst such commotion, but it is up to the next generation of internationally informed and culturally aware sport management professionals to ensure its continued viability in a responsible and effective manner.

CHAPTER 4

Interview

Colin Blount—Visa Europe
Vice President
Partnership Marketing

Colin Blount joined Visa Europe in 1989, and has held a variety of posts including Head of Network Infrastructure for Visa Europe and CEMEA regions, Head of Member Connectivity, Head of Office Systems and Head of Technical Projects. He has also managed a number of important Visa EU and Visa International projects such as IARS, VSAT and the development of the Operation Centre Basingstoke (OCB).

Until 2001 he held the post of Head of Virtual Visa Programmes where key responsibilities were to develop and maintain technology standards and specifications, programme & service management, and new technology MIS. From then, the Management of Visa's activities towards the Athens 2004 and Torino 2006 Olympic and Paralympic Games provided the platform for his current role.

Mr. Blount joined Visa from National Westminster Bank, where for two years he was involved with mainframe systems design, planning, and hardware installation. Previously, he was employed by Shell Expo on the Tern Project from 1984–1987 where he was responsible for Document Control Migration from manual to computerised function.

Mr. Blount is a former Associate of the Institute of Wood Science, and from 1976–1984 was involved in the sales of timber products.

Q: What steps did you take to get into your current position? What was your career path?

A: From Timber Technology, to Oil industry, to Computing, to Banking, to Visa! Within Visa, IT, Project management, managing Olympic Projects, managing Sponsorship properties, expanding to Partnership Marketing!

No planned steps, just things I find interesting/exciting and being in the right place.

Q: What role does knowledge of sport management and/or marketing play in gaining entrance and achieving success in your field?

A: As a generalist, I would describe my field as People and Project Management, which can apply to any discipline.

Sports Marketing provides a healthy mix of challenge, opportunity and excitement.

Q: What are you looking for in new hires to your specific organization or similar ones? More specifically, positions in marketing or management that deal with sport entities?

A: As an organisation we work to a set of defined competencies, which we seek in all employees:

- Focused on Customers
- Focused on Results
- Commitment to Quality
- Leading and Working with Others
- Integrity and Accountability
- Effective in different markets and cultures

In addition to these I would be seeking flexibility and a fit with the team, alongside any role specific skill or knowledge sets.

Q: Could you give me a general sense of the global scale and scope of Visa's business operations? (maybe just basic examples of the global reach of the organization).

A: Visa is owned by 16,400 Financial Institutions who issue 1.7 billion Visa cards which are accepted at 30 million merchant outlets in 170 countries. These currently generate 55 billion transactions per annum with a US $ value of 4.3 trillion.

Q: In what ways have rapid changes in the "global age" (evolving technologies in communication, information, and travel for example) affected your external market environment? How has the company responded to these challenges?

A: As market leader, Visa plays a key role in identifying, responding to, and leading change. In recent years we have move from offline to online authorizations, chip technology on cards, secure Internet payments, and contactless technology.

Q: What are some of the sport-related business partnerships Visa Europe has, and in what ways have they affected the success and visibility of the organization?

A: Visa has sponsored the Olympic Games since 1986 and this has been the global flagship property. This partnership has been instrumental in establishing strong brand values and adding some interest to a low interest business sector. We have now added FIFA to the global portfolio, which further strengthens our global positioning. Local markets have exercised other sporting partnerships: e.g., NFL in USA, The Argentine Rugby Team, all of which have raised the profile in key markets.

Q: It has been said that sports fans have an unparalleled devotion to their nation when it comes to international sporting contests like the Olympics or World Cup. In your branding and promotional efforts, how do you leverage the cultural nuances of national difference to generate appeal and visibility for Visa?

A: I would agree with that statement and it is always challenging to take something so massive and make it relevant to an individual. Use of appropriate imagery can make a national statement and selection of local ambassadorial talent (e.g., Team Visa is effective).

Q: What sports or sporting events are of interest for Visa to become involved with and why? How do you determine what sport-related partnerships will be viable?

A: We have the two global partnerships that provide the foundation for all other sporting partnerships. As a pretty ubiquitous brand we focus less on visibility but more on brand health and the ability to drive a positive return on investment.

Q: What specific strategies do you employ in trying to appeal to the broadest market demographic possible? In what ways has sport facilitated this?

A: Our sporting partnerships provide us with a broad demographic so the main challenge is to ensure they are used effectively, the right message at the right time.

Q: What are the biggest challenges/issues/trends you face in the near future in general; but more specifically in regard to your sport marketing and promotional initiatives?

A: • The Banking crisis and public perceptions
  • Achieving and proving a real ROI on our investments
  • Rights holders diluting their assets
  • Maintaining a long as well as a short term view

Q: In response to the global and local sport partnerships you mentioned, how much autonomy is given to brand directors in local markets to select and pursue sport partnerships within various locales?

A: No autonomy, more working partnerships. We are driven by business needs and if there is a local need that requires an enhancement to an existing property or sourcing something new, then we agree and proceed. Additional funding typically would come from local budgets.

Q: It seems likely that Visa has found it more effective to maintain brand health through large-scale sport promotions like the Olympics rather than local partnerships such as the Argentine Rugby team, for example? Whether this is accurate or not, could you explain how both global and local partnerships strengthen the position of the brand, how they are different, and how a consistent message and identity is maintained between them?

A: Again, it depends on local business needs. The Argentina Rugby Team ran alongside our global sponsorship of the Rugby World Cup, and enhanced that partnership locally. It is of course a valuable brand building partnership for the Argentine market. As a general rule the global partnerships would feature in the brand messaging reinforce our position as a global brand but there are occasions when it is tactically necessary to tactically build the brand locally.

Q: What advice would you give to a burgeoning sport manager/marketer intent on working in a capacity that requires international and global sensitivities?

Q: Be patient, culturally aware, and sensitive to local needs. Do the research so that you can argue your case from a factual rather than emotional position—individuals have strong preferences, which may not reflect market preferences. Don't forget to enjoy it—it's a privilege to work in this environment!

Study Questions

1. How has advanced technology affected the production and dissemination of sport?
2. Is the homogenization thesis still a relevant way to think about global process of interconnectivity and interdependency? Why or why not?
3. In what ways is sport production considered to be the same globally?
4. How does the heterogenization thesis inform your perspective concerning the role of sport in foregrounding national difference?
5. If working in a sport organization or targeting key markets outside of your home nation, why is an understanding of cultural difference so important?
6. Name three sport related examples of global hybridity?
7. In what ways are the principles of McDonaldization (calculability, predictability, rational control, and efficiency) evidenced in the production of sporting events, products, or services?
8. Drawing upon the concept of symbolic production, explain why Nike is one of the most successful sporting goods companies in the world?

9. In what ways has sport been so integral to the success of TNCs?

10. Other than Nike and News Corporation, what TNCs have leveraged sport to enter new markets and increase global resonance?

11. Drawing from the three global theories discussed, which one most closely resembles News Corporation's global strategy? Why?

12. In what ways can TNCs invest in the nations in which they operate while simultaneously benefiting from knowledge of local cultural sensibilities and market trends?

Learning Activities

1. As noted in the example of Nike, the production of sporting goods involves a complex system of global commodity chains that link nations and laborers in countries all across the world. In order to enhance profitability, most brand corporations invest more time and money into the intangible processes of symbolic production (marketing, branding, and advertising) while cutting costs in the tangible aspects of production (raw materials, manufacturing, distribution). Imagine you just inherited enough money to launch your own footwear and apparel company and are in the early phases of developing your brand identity and marketing plan, and identifying where production and distribution will occur. *First, decide where to place greater emphasis by assigning a number to each of the five areas below out of ten total points. Then, justify your decisions by developing a strategic plan for operations in each area, including a description of who, what, where, how, and why for each phase of the process.*

   A. Product Design—The ideas and technologies behind the development of new product lines. In order to remain competitive, it is vital to continue creating new, higher quality products to keep consumers wanting more.

   B. Branding/Marketing—Knowledge creation. Cutting edge branding/marketing campaigns are not cheap but in order to compete with the major players, it is impossible to develop a sustainable and profitable global or national market without attaching symbolic value to entice consumers and justify increased cost.

   C. Raw Materials—Quality of materials that will compose your product. Cheaper materials will net more short-term profit, but may also deter consumers on account of poor durability/comfort.

   D. Labor/Manufacturing—Outsourcing all material labor to poor developing economies is proven to cut costs and increase profitability, but how will this effect brand reputation, visibility, and corporate social responsibility? (For example, choose either, Sri Lanka (.5), India (1), China (1.5), Korea (2), Japan (2.5), France (3), U.K. (3.5), or the U.S. (4).

   E. Distribution/Transportation—The development of strong networks and efficient routes to transport raw materials and finished products to their destinations can affect supply and demand.

   For example, we could assume that Nike would look something like this . . .

   Product design—3
   Branding/Marketing—4
   Raw Materials—1.5
   Labor/Manufacturing—.5
   Distribution/Transportation—1

2. Stemming from our discussion of TNCs and the importance of sport in media broadcasting, marketing, and branding initiatives for all manner of products, leagues, and teams around the world, the process of attaching symbolic (cultural) meaning cannot be understated. In this regard, many large corporations hire global advertising agencies (Wieden & Kennedy, for example) to develop new marketing campaigns to enhance the visibility, reputation, or strength of their brand. Using the Wieden & Kennedy website (http://www.wk.com/#/) as a source for commercials, identify the ways in which sport is used to engage different national markets for their clients—Nike, Electronic Arts, Coca-Cola, Starbucks, Converse, etc. Focusing on one in particular, how would you approach the development of a similar advertising campaign if you were:

   A. The Senior Director of Marketing for the professional soccer club Monaco in the French League? (http://www.asm-fc.com/uk/)

   B. An Assistant Director of Marketing & Communications for the United States Olympic Committee (USOC)? (www.usoc.org)

   C. An Assistant Marketing Director for HSBC Private Bank? (http://www.theworldsprivatebank.com/en/)

References

Albrow, M. (1996). *The global age: State and society beyond modernity.* Stanford: Stanford University Press.

Allen, J. (1996). Post-industrialism/post-Fordism. In S. Hall, D. Held, D. Hubert, & K. Thompson (Eds.), *Modernity: An introduction to modern societies* (pp. 533–563). Oxford: Blackwell.

Alms, R. (1994, November 1). Globe trotters: NBA takes a world view of marketing. *Dallas Morning News,* pp. 1D.

Amis, J. (2003). "Good things come to those who wait": The strategic management of image and reputation at Guinness. *European Sport Management Quarterly, 3,* 189–214.

Amis, J. (2005). Beyond sport: Imaging and re-imaging a global brand. In M. Silk, D. Andrews & C. Cole (Eds.), *Corporate nationalisms: Sport, cultural identity & transnational marketing* (pp. 143–165). Oxford: Berg.

Amis, J., & Cornwell, T.B. (2005). *Global sport sponsorship.* Oxford: Berg.

Amis, J., Mower, R.L., & Silk, M. (2009). (Michael) Power, gendered subjectivities & filmic representation: Brand strategy and Guinness' Critical Assignment in Africa. In L. Wenner, & S. Jackson, (Eds.), *Sport, beer and gender: Promotional culture and contemporary social life* (pp. 97–120). New York: Peter Lang Publishers.

Amis, J., & Silk, M. (2005, August). Transnational organization and symbolic production: Creating and managing a global brand strategy. Paper presented at *Academy of Management* meetings, Honolulu, HI.

Anderson, B. (1991). *Imagined communities: Reflections on the origins and spread of nationalism.* London: Verso.

Andrews, D.L. (2003). The global sport media economy: News Corporation, entertainment cultures, and vertical integration. In D. Rowe (Ed.), *A reader in sport, culture and the media.* Buckingham, UK: Open University Press.

Andrews, D.L. (2006). Disneyization, Debord, and the integrated NBA spectacle. *Social Semiotics, 16*(1), 89–102.

Andrews, D.L. (2008, Spring/Summer). Nike nations. *Brown Journal of World Affairs, XIV*(2), 1–13.

Andrews, D.L. (2008). [Various networks of global connectivity]. Unpublished raw data.

Andrews, D.L., & Ritzer, G. (2007). The grobal in the sporting glocal. *Global Networks, 7*(2), 113–153.

Brown, A. (2007). "Not for sale": The destruction and reformation of football communities in the Glazer takeover of Manchester United. *Soccer & Society, 8*(4), 614–615.

Brownell, S. (2008). *Beijing's games: what the Olympics mean to China.* Lanham, MD: Rowman & Littlefield Publishers.

Caldwell, M.L. (2004). Domesticating the French fry: McDonald's and consumerism in Moscow. *Journal of Consumer Culture, 4*(1), 5–26.

Castells, M. (1997). *The rise of the network society.* Oxford: Blackwell.

Cochrane, A., & Pain, K. (2000). A globalizing society? In D. Held (Ed.), *A globalizing world? Culture, economics, politics* (pp. 5–46). London: Routledge.

Collins, T., & Vamplew, W. (2002). *Mud, sweat and beers: a cultural history of sport and alcohol.* London: Berg Publishers.

Comte, E. (1993, June 7). How high can David Stern jump? *Forbes, 42.*

Dirlik, A. (1996). The global in the local. In R. Wilson & W. Dissanayake (Eds.), *Global local: Cultural production and the transnational imaginary* (pp. 21–45). Durham: Duke University Press.

Dunning, E. (1999). *Sport Matters: Sociological studies of sport, violence and civilization.* London: Routledge.

Frenkel, S.J. (2001) 'Globalization, athletic footwear commodity chains and employment relations in China'. *Organization Studies, 22:* 531–562.

Giulianotti, R. (2002). Supporters, followers, fans, and flaneurs: A taxonomy of spectator identities in football. *Journal of Sport & Social Issues, 26*(1), 25–46.

Guibernau, M., & Goldblatt, D. (2000). Identity and nation. In K. Woodward (Ed.), *Questioning identity: Gender, class, nation.* London: Routledge/The Open University.

Grainger, A., & Andrews, D.L. (2005). Resisting Rupert through sporting rituals? The transnational media corporation and global-local sport cultures. *International Journal of Sport Management and Marketing, 1*(1–2), 3–16.

Gustafsson, C. (2003). New values, morality, and strategic ethics. In H. Mintzberg, J. Lampel, J.B. Quinn & S. Ghoshal (Eds.), *The strategy process: Concepts, contexts, cases* (4th edition) (pp. 295–299). Upper Saddle River, NJ: Prentice Hall.

Hall, S. (1992). The west and the rest: Discourse and power. In S. Hall & B. Gieben (Eds.), *Formations of modernity* (pp. 275–320). Cambridge: Polity Press.

Hardt, M., & Negri, A. (2000). *Empire.* Cambridge, MA: Harvard University Press.

Harrison, B. (1994, September 22). The dark side of flexible production. *National Productivity Review, 13*(4), 479–501.

Harvey, D. (1989). *The condition of postmodernity: An enquiry into the origins of cultural change.* Oxford: Blackwell.

Held, D., McGrew, A., Goldblatt, D., & Perraton, J. (1999). *Global transformations: Politics, economics and culture.* Stanford, CA: Stanford University Press.

Hill, J.S., & Vincent, J. (2006). Globalisation and sports branding: The case of Manchester United. *International Journal of Sports Marketing and Sponsorship* (May), 213–230.

Hobsbawm, E.J. (1990). *Nations and nationalism since 1870: Programme, myth, reality* (p. 143). Cambridge: Cambridge University Press.

Hobsbawm, E.J., & Ranger, T. (1983). *The invention of tradition.* Cambridge: Cambridge University Press.

Holt, R. J. (1989). *Sport and the British: A modern history.* Oxford: Clarendon Press.

Jackson, S. J., & Hokowhitu, B. (2002). Sport, tribes, and technology: The New Zealand All Blacks Haka and the politics of identity. *Journal of Sport & Social Issues, 26*(2), 125–139.

Jameson, F. (1991). *Postmodernism, or, the cultural logic of late capitalism.* Durham: Duke University Press.

KFC accused of racism over Australian advertisement. (2010, January). *Guardian.co.uk.* Retrieved from http://www.guardian.co.uk/business/2010/jan/06/kfc-advertisement-accused-of-racism

Klein, N. (1999). *No logo: Taking aim at the brand bullies.* New York: Picador.

Klein, A. (2000). Latinizing Fenway Park: A cultural critique of the Boston Red Sox, their fans, and the media. *Sociology of Sport Journal, 17,* 403–422.

Kobe Bryant tops NBA jersey sales in China. (2008, August). Brandweek. Retrieved from http://www.brandweek.com/bw/content_display/news-and-features/retail-restaurants/e3idfed28cc72bd8cb6ac411101179c14e5

Korzeniewicz, M. (1994). Commodity chains and marketing strategies: Nike and the global athletic footwear industry. In G. Gereffi & M. Korzeniewicz (Eds.), *Commodity chains and global capitalism* (pp. 247–265). Westport: Greenwood Press.

Kuisel, R.F. (2003). Debating Americanization: The case of France. In U. Beck, N. Sznaider, and R. Winter (Eds.), *Global America? The cultural consequences of globalization.* Liverpool: Liverpool University Press.

Lee, F.L. (2009, March). Negotiating sporting nationalism: debating fan behavior in "China vs. Japan" in the 2004 Asian Cup Final in Hong Kong. *Soccer & Society, 10*(2), pp. 192–209.

Lewis, M. (2001). Franchise relocation and fan allegiance. *Journal of Sport & Social Issues, 25*(1), 6–19.

Maguire, J., Jarvie, G., Mansfield, L., & Bradley, J. (2002). *Sport worlds: A sociological perspective.* Champaign, IL: Human Kinetics.

Manchester United expands its global reach. (2002, September). Forbes.com. Retrieved from http://www.forbes.com/2002/09/30/0930manchester.html

Mandel, E. (1975). *Late capitalism.* London: NLB, Atlantic Highlands Humanities Press.

McGrew, A. (1992). A global society? In S. Hall, D. Held, & A. McGrew (Eds.), *Modernity and its futures* (pp. 61–116). Cambridge: Polity Press.

McLuhan, M., & Powers, B.R. (1989). *The global village: Transformations in world life and media in the 21st century.* New York: Oxford University Press.

Miller, T., Lawrence, G., McKay, J., & Rowe, D. (2001). *Globalization and sport.* London: Sage.

Milliken, R. (1996, October 16). Sports is Murdoch's 'battering ram' for pay TV. *The Independent,* p. 28.

Moor, L. (2007). *The Rise of brands.* London: Berg Publishers.

Morley, D., & Robins, K. (1995). *Spaces of identity: Global media, electronic landscapes and cultural boundaries.* London: Routledge.

NBA China games to reach 209 countries. (2007, October). NBA.com. Retrieved from http://www.nba.com/news/china_games_071016.html

News Corporation Annual Report. (2008). Adelaide, Australia. Retrieved from http://www.newscorp.com/AR2008 Flash/NC_AR_Editorial_2008.pdf

Pieterse, J. N. (2004). *Globalization and culture: Global mélange.* Lanham: Rowman and Littlefield.

Ram, U. (2007). Liquid identities: Mecca Cola versus Coca-Cola. *European Journal of Cultural Studies, 10*(4), 465–84.

Ritzer, G. (1998). *The McDonaldization thesis: Explorations and extensions.* London: Sage.

Ritzer, G. (2008). *The McDonaldization of society 5.* Los Angeles, CA: Pine Forge Press.

Robertson, R. (1995). Glocalization: Time-space and homogeneity-heterogeneity. In M. Featherstone, S. Lash, & R. Robertson (Eds.), *Global modernities* (pp. 25–44). London: Sage.

Robins, K. (1991). Tradition and translation: National culture in its global context. In J. Corner & S. Harvey (Eds.), *Enterprise and heritage: Crosscurrents of national culture* (pp. 21–44). London: Routledge.

Robins, K. (1997). What in the world's going on? In P. Du Gay (Ed.), *Production of culture/cultures of production* (p. 28). London: The Open University.

Rowe, D. (2003). Sport and the repudiation of the global. *International Review for the Sociology of Sport, 38*(3), 281–294.

Scherer, J., & Jackson, S.J. (2007). Sports advertising, cultural production and corporate nationalism at the global-local nexus: Branding the New Zealand All Blacks. *Sport in Society, 10*(2), pp. 268–284.

Schmidt, R. (2001, June). Murdoch reaches for the sky. *Brill's Content,* pp. 74–79, 126–129.

Silk, M. & Andrews, D. (2001). Beyond a Boundary: Sport, transnational advertising, and the reimaging of national culture, *Journal of Sport & Social Issues, 25,* 2.

Tallentire, M. (2009, January 23). Violence erupts between Serbs and Bosnians after Djokovic's win. Retrieved from http://www.guardian.co.uk/sport/2009/jan/23/australian-open-violence-djokovic

Thomas, T., Schermerhorn, J.R. & Dienhart, J.W. (2004) Strategic leadership of ethical behavior in business. *Academy of Management Executive, 18*(2), 56–68.

Tomlinson, J. (1991). *Cultural Imperialism: A Critical Introduction.* Baltimore: Johns Hopkins University Press.

Tomlinson, J. (1999). *Globalization and culture.* Cambridge: Polity Press.

Turner, B.S. (2003). McDonaldization: Linearity and liquidity in consumer cultures. *American Behavioral Scientist, 47*(2), 137–153.

Watson, J. L. (1997). Transnationalism, localization, and fast foods in East Asia. In J.L. Watson (Ed.), *Golden arches east: McDonald's in East Asia* (pp. 1–38). Cambridge, MA: Harvard University Press.

Willigan, G. E. (1992, July/August). High performance marketing: An interview with Nike's Phil Knight. *Harvard Business Review,* 91–101.

Suggested Readings

Appadurai, A. (1996). *Modernity at large: Cultural dimensions of globalization.* University of Minnesota Press.

Barnier, A. (2001). *Sport, nationalism, and globalization: European and North American perspectives.* Albany, NY: SUNY Press.

Dirlik, A. (1996). The global in the local. In R. Wilson & W. Dissanayake (Eds.), *Global local: Cultural production and the transnational imaginary* (pp. 21–45). Durham: Duke University Press.

Donnelly, P. (1996). The local and the global: Globalization in the sociology of sport. *Journal of Sport & Social Issues, 20*(3), 239-257.

Maguire, J.A. (1999). *Global sport: Identities, societies, civilization.* Cambridge: Polity Press.

Ritzer, G. (2004). *The globalization of nothing.* Thousand Oaks: Pine Forge Press.

Rowe, D. (1996). The global love-match: Sport and television. *Media, Culture & Society, 18*(4), 565–582.

Silk, M. (2002). "Bangsa Malaysia": Global sport, the city and the mediated refurbishment of local identities. *Media, Culture & Society, 24*(6), 775–794.

Silk, M.L., & Andrews, D.L. (2005). The spatial logics of global sponsorship: Corporate capital, cola wars and cricket. In J. Amis & T.B. Cornwell (Eds.), *Global sport sponsorship* (pp. 67–88). Oxford: Berg.

Sklair, L. (2006). Capitalist globalization: Fatal flaws and necessity for alternatives. *The Brown Journal of World Affairs, XIII*(1), 29–37.

Stabile, C.A. (2000). Nike, social responsibility, and the hidden abode of production. *Critical Studies in Media Communication, 17*(2), 186–204.

Tomlinson, A. (1996). Olympic spectacle: Opening ceremonies and some paradoxes of globalization. *Media, Culture & Society, 18*(4), 583–602.

Ethics and Ethical Decision Making

Jan Boxill and Richard M. Southall • *The University of North Carolina at Chapel Hill*

After reading this chapter, you will be able to:

- Critically analyze an argument;
- Produce, articulate, and defend reasons for a given position and respond to objections raised to this position;
- Understand various ethical theories and how they apply to the sport-management industry and society;
- Given a specific issue, demonstrate the ability to supply reasons in favor of a specific resolution consistent with positions on other ethical issues.

KEY TERMS

A Duty
A Right
Distributive
Ethics
Good/Bad
Justice
Morality
Right/Wrong
Virtue

Introduction

In preparing to be future sport managers, students will probably not be able to resolve every issue they confront to their satisfaction, but they should at least gain a greater understanding of how to analyze issues, how they affect society, and how to best approach such issues in a manner that demonstrates respect for individual differences and similarities. Whether you become a coach, athletic director, league administrator, park-district supervisor, fitness-club manager, or professional sport organization marketer, you will need a solid understanding of ethics in order to recognize your decisions' ethical implications.

What Ethics Is

At its core, **ethics** is the study of value. Value, in this sense, covers everything from a preference for wine over beer, to the value one places on fundamental relationships with friends and family. The ultimate aim of studying ethics is to help answer the question, "What should I do?" in situations in which this question arises. Developing a "satisfactory" answer is ethics' central function.

Why is ethics important? A person's decisions and actions affect everyone with whom they interact. Therefore, decisions and actions affect families, organizations, communities, countries, and, ultimately, the world.

What Ethics Is Not

It is important to differentiate ethics from other modes of thinking or justifications for decisions and actions. Ethics is not religion, culture, or the law. However, all of these "others" also play a role in our decision making.

- **Religion:** Religious questions deal with the nature of spirituality, and are culturally dependent. There are at least 300 different religious-belief systems, and even if a specific religious instruction were received from "on high," the decision whether to follow the instruction would still require a value judgment.
- **Society and Culture:** Social and cultural questions deal with customs, traditions and taboos of a society, culture, or group, and these vary significantly from one to another. Sometimes social/cultural/group customs have ethical implications, but they are not themselves the basis for ethical reasoning.
- **The Law:** Legal questions deal with societal rules of behavior that have been codified as "a law" in a particular society. Particular law or laws may or may not have an ethical basis. Laws often emerge out of social conventions, so what is "legal or illegal" may or may not be a matter of ethics.

It is important for future sport managers to remember that ethical questions involve evaluating human behavior toward people or other creatures. Ethical principles converge across cultures and groups, and give direction for how we "ought" to behave.

We are discussing no small matter, but how we ought to live.

—Socrates

Well, then it's not cheating, is it? If nobody finds out? Yeah, it would be like finding a gray area. In motor sports, we work in the gray areas a lot. You're trying to find where the holes are in the rule book.

—IRL and NASCAR driver, Danica Patrick (who later apologized and said her comments were meant to be a joke)

Ethics_____
The study of value, very broadly construed. Ethics examines the nature of right and wrong, duty, obligation, freedom, and virtue. It is sometimes referred to as the philosophy of morality, or how people should act. Moral philosophy then is the attempt to achieve a systematic understanding of the nature of morality.

A Four-Part Ethical-Reasoning Model

Ethical reasoning utilizes a similar structure as all reasoning. First and foremost ethical reasoning involves constructing and evaluating reasons. This is typically not easy as there is no simple ethical recipe. While there is not a specific algorithm, in order to practice ethical reasoning it is important to formulate a framework, which provides a context from which to examine specific situations and to evaluate possible courses of action. One such framework is comprised of four interrelated components, which can serve to guide ethical reasoning:

1. **Description**
2. **Analysis**
3. **Vision** and
4. **Strategy**.

This guide to ethical decision making provides a structure from which to examine an existing situation and develop new insights.

1. **Description:** "What is reality?" is a basic human question that most often (especially among students enrolled in an introductory sport-management course) elicits the following response: "You have to be kidding!" While answering such a fundamental question may be difficult—if not impossible—gathering facts (i.e., who, what, when, where) about a specific situation, and evaluating and interpreting these "facts" is something managers do every day. While our individual perspective limits our ability to "objectively" analyze a given situation, we can somewhat mitigate our subjectivity by attempting to openly and transparently compare our gathered facts.
2. **Analysis:** Analysis involves openly examining and asking questions about our facts. It involves scrutinizing such facts' origins and proposed reasons for their existence. While such analysis is crucial, it is often complex, and may not offer a single satisfactory explanation.
3. **Vision/Goal:** This component looks at a person's ideals, or how they think things "ought to be" or should exist. Determining what should exist requires a person to refer to goals and established principles. It involves asking the question, "What is the best way things could turn out?"
4. **Strategies/Means:** Strategies provide a roadmap to get from how things are to how they ought to be. This step also involves asking if proposed strategies can be ethically justified. It also involves determining available tools and potential costs. It is probable that what may be the "right thing to do" may conflict with other identified goals.

Using this four-part model, managers will realize that ethical disagreements may be based on factual, analytical, existential, or strategic differences. Ethical reasoning allows us to go beyond simply reacting to systematically and analytically making ethical decisions. Such decision making utilizes the same basic structure as does all reasoning. Whenever we "think," our point of view is based on assumptions. In addition, our thinking has implications and consequences.

Ethical disagreements can arise based upon factual, analytical, existential, or strategic differences.

In all reasoning, we use ideas and theories to interpret data, facts, and experiences in order to answer questions, solve problems, and resolve issues. The process of ethical reasoning and ethical decision making must include the idea of impartiality, and assumes that each of us is a conscientious moral agent, which means—as much as possible—an ethical thinker must be impartial and listen, and must gain facts before acting.

Obstacles to Ethical Decision Making

There are at least four main obstacles to ethical decision making. Although there are others, the following obstacles provide a point of reference from which to gain a more precise understanding regarding what is meant by ethical decision making:

1. Confusing ethics with religion, culture and the law;
2. Difficulty in gathering facts;
3. Lack of moral courage; and
4. Existence of "ethics pretenders."

As previously mentioned, ethics is not religion, culture, or the law. While each may play a role in ethical decision making, they are not the basis for ethical reasoning.

As everyone—from crime-scene investigators (CSI) to sport marketers—knows, gathering facts is often not easy. In addition, uncovered "facts" may turn out to be unreliable, since facts often reflect the complexity of reality. Human prejudice can also interfere in determining facts. Every person operates from a set of assumptions and perspectives, and has different agendas and points of view. Emotions often play a role and can cloud "objectivity." All of these factors affect how facts are viewed.

There are some remedies for these potential obstacles. Responsible moral thinking involves attempting to see things as they are, not as we want them to be. While "objectivity" is a fundamental philosophical question, in order to engage in ethical reasoning, we must attempt to adopt (as much as possible) an "objective point of view." This requires a person not assuming their point of view is the **only** one, or that it is inherently the "**right**" one. It is crucial to attempt to "see" other perspectives and understand other people's assumptions. Acceptance of diversity is a must. (It should be noted that acceptance of diversity is not the same as **moral relativism**, which will be discussed later.)

Homogeneity (also known as *groupthink* or *cultural myopia*) is an obstacle to gathering objective facts and analyzing reality. People of similar backgrounds, ethnicities, and cultures are unlikely to easily see other perspectives. While group-thinkers may believe they are being "objective," this is often an illusion. Unless a person is aware of their limitations and is willing to adjust their perspective and view an alternate reality, such cultural or ethical myopia cannot be overcome.

Lack of Moral Courage

Many ethicists (especially Deontologists—See the box on moral courage) contend every person, regardless of background, culture, or ethnicity, "knows" right from wrong. Sometimes the issue is a person simply lacks the *moral courage* to do the "right thing," and act to prevent or correct a wrong. Opportunities for ethical action are plentiful, but so are reasons not to act. For example: A part-time concession worker at a Major League Baseball (MLB) ballpark who sees a fellow employee steal a t-shirt from a merchandise kiosk across the concourse may not report the theft if he is worried about being labeled a "snitch."

Not demonstrating moral courage in one's actions does not make someone a "bad" person; it means they have failed to act ethically. There are many reasons why people fail to take action based upon their values. The discussion that follows highlights five reasons for people's lack of moral courage:

1. **Discomfort:** Doing the right thing is often uncomfortable. Few like to stand up to a group, whether small or large. Suppose a classmate makes an offensive joke; how many students would say, "That's not funny; I find that offensive." Such uncomfortable events provide opportunities for sport-management students to "practice" for the real-world when acquiescence should not or may not be an option. While it may be uncomfortable, acting ethically (in accordance to one's values) sometimes requires a person to defy social conventions and deal with discomfort.

2. **Futility:** Doing the right thing is often seen as futile. Acting ethically may be viewed as a "no-win" situation. If people believe they cannot make a difference, they may feel there is no justification for doing anything.

3. **Socialization:** In many ways, athletes and sport-managers are socialized to be submissive; they are often instructed to be a "team player." Such socialization may reflect culture, gender, or social class. Although being "happy" may be a worthy outcome (See **Ethical Hedonism**), there may be far better reasons for ethical action than personal happiness. It is likely that socialization played a critical role in Major League Baseball's (MLB) recent steroid era. The lack of moral courage among many baseball players, executives, and fans resulted in what almost everyone believes is a stain on America's pastime.

4. **Bystander effect or diffusion theory:** When confronted with a situation where action is needed, people often hope or expect others will take the initiative. The greater the number of people who witness any event, the less likely any one of them will act. There have been reports of crimes being committed where

José Canseco, named in the Mitchell Report about steroid use in baseball in December of 2007, wrote in his autobiography *Juiced* that he used steroids throughout virtually his entire 17-year major league career. Canseco was the first major leaguer in history to hit 40 home runs and steal 40 bases in a season (1988).

© Gregg Newton/Gregg Newton/Corbis

BOX 5.1

Moral Courage in College Sport

In college sport, individuals who report schools for violating NCAA rules or other observed improprieties (e.g., papers being written for student-athletes or grades being changed) often find themselves ostracized by fans, their communities, and their own universities. These whistleblowers often become known through newspaper stories or court records, and sometimes are identified by university officials.

One such person is Dr. Linda Bensel-Meyers, a tenured English professor who lodged concerns about institutional misconduct by the academic services unit devoted to University of Tennessee athletes. After her allegations became public, Bensel-Meyers received death threats, her office was burglarized, and her phone line tapped. People spat on her. Air was let out of her car's tires. In 2002, she left Tennessee for Colorado. In *Breaking Faith with the College Athlete,* Bensel-Meyers described the quality of education offered to high-profile athletes as "...tantamount to institutionalized slavery."

She now works as an associate professor at the University of Denver. Her husband refused to leave, she said, so they divorced. Her two oldest sons, who were finishing high school, also stayed in Tennessee. Bensel-Meyers twice underwent operations for digestive-tract issues related to the stress caused by her coming forward.

witnesses heard cries for help from the victim but they did not call the police since they felt someone else would have made the call. In addition to potentially letting someone else take action, people often are only as ethical as the people around them. Diffusion theory (as well as socialization and discomfort) seems to explain why across the country National Football League (NFL) fans participate in and/or tolerate NFL game-day experiences that include not only cheering on one's favorite team, but what also has been described as a "culture of intoxication" (Southall and Sharp, 2006).

5. **Personal Cost:** Personal cost involves a person's ethical inaction out of fear of losing their job, their income, or "lifestyle to which they have become accustomed." While such concerns are legitimate and should be taken into account, being morally courageous may come at a high price. But, as will be discussed in Chapter 6 (Legal Aspects of Sport), while there may be costs associated with action, it is important to remember not acting also has potential costs. And as will become evident as you progress through this chapter, "ethical action is a journey, not a destination."

The Pretenders

In addition to the obstacles described above, there are several pseudo-theories that pretend to provide answers to ethical dilemmas. This section details three often-indentified "pretenders" that claim to be useful in ethical decision making: (1) Egoism, (2) Divine-Command theory, and (3) Relativism.

1. **Egoism:** Egoism can be a descriptive or normative claim. There are two distinct formulations of egoism: psychological egoism and ethical egoism. **Psychological egoism** claims everyone in fact acts out of self-interest. This is a factual claim about human nature. **Ethical egoism** is the claim that everyone ought to act out of self-interest; it is about how humans *should*

act, regardless of whether psychological egoism is a "fact." While psychological egoism may be true (i.e., people may sometime be motivated by self interest.), this does not mean people always act only on this basis. Not all human behavior can be explained by self-regarding desires. In addition, according to ethical egoism, for an action to be morally justified as necessary, it must maximize one's self-interest. However, there are many instances in which people act in ways that are not in their self-interest. For example, a soldier sacrificing his/her life by jumping on a grenade is an example of a selfless action that is not in a person's self-interest, but is viewed as moral.

2. **Divine-Command Theory:** This is a theory that **morality** is generated by a divine deity's (i.e., god[1]) commands. From this perspective, "moral" actions are those commanded by god; immoral or "wrong" actions are forbidden by god. In addition to the issue of needing to determine which "god" is making the command, for an ethicist divine-command theory raises the following dilemma:

> (A) Is something right because god commands it, or (B) does god command something because it is right. If (A), then morality is based on the deity's arbitrary will. It is conceivable a deity could order a person to do things a person previously viewed as immoral. If morality is based on the deity's will, a person would be morally required to do potentially horrible things, if so commanded. Therefore, objective claims about god's goodness are empty. If (B), while there is an independent standard from which to evaluate right and wrong, god becomes only an intermediary. This leads to the problem identified with ethics and religion.

3. **Relativism:** One way to "attack" moral standards is relativism. Relativism claims there are no "universal truths" in ethics; there are only various cultural codes. There is no measure of right and wrong other than the standards of one's society. Often, a relativist goes further and extends relativism to group and individual codes within society as well. A basic relativism argument might proceed as follows:

> *Premise 1:* Different societies or cultures have different moral codes.
> *Premise 2:* Such moral codes determine what is seen as "right" within that society or culture.
> *Therefore:* There are no objective standards that can be used to judge the relative merits of particular codes.

This argument is based upon the premise that what every person believes, must be true.

Here is another argument:

> *Premise:* A believes x, but B believes y.
> *Conclusion:* Therefore neither x nor y is true.

The mere fact that A and B disagree does not preclude there being no objective truth or no right answer.

Morality_____

Concerned with how people act and what they believe to be right or wrong. In practice it is often synonymous with ethics, but morality is also the portion of ethics concerned with interpersonal behavior.

---

[1] In ethics, it is convention to utilize a "small g" when referring to divine entities.

BOX 5.2

The Cost of Simply Standing By

Fans' NFL game-day experiences include not only cheering on one's favorite team, but also often being immersed in a "culture of intoxication" prevalent at such contests. Whether it is ritualistic tailgating or consumption of numerous alcoholic beverages during the game itself, the inextricable ties between spectators and alcohol consumption are easily identified.

On October 24, 1999 the parking lots at Giants Stadium, which opened four hours before kickoff, witnessed a Sunday game-day ritual played out at professional football stadiums across the United States: ". . . pre-game and post-game tailgate parties at which persons consume alcoholic beverages" (Sixth amended complaint and jury demand, *Verni v. Lanzaro*, 2003, pg. 7). As the afternoon turned to early evening, the New York Giants had easily beaten the New Orleans Saints 31–3, to run their record to 4-3 on the season (NFL 1999 Season Archives, n.d.). Celebratory Giants fans, among them 30-year-old Daniel R. Lanzaro of Cresskill, New Jersey, poured out of Giants Stadium to begin their journey home or to continue their celebrations at one of the local bars, such as Shakers or The Gallery, in the borough of Hasbrouck Heights in Bergen County (Sixth amended complaint).

Returning home from a family outing to pick up pumpkins for Halloween, Ronald Verni, accompanied by his wife Fazila and their two-year-old daughter Antonia, passed through Hasbrouck Heights, about five minutes from Giants Stadium, via Terrace Avenue (Crusade against DWI, 2002; Cable News Network, 2003). After purchasing and consuming at least 14 beers and an undisclosed amount of marijuana (Sixth amended complaint, 2003) while participating in pre-game tailgating and viewing the day's game at Giants Stadium, Lanzaro lost control of his 1994 Ford pickup, hit one vehicle and then collided, head-on, with the Verni family's 1999 Toyota (Coffey, 2005).

The results of the accident were horrific. Antonia, who was resuscitated by Hasbrouck Heights EMTs (emergency medical technicians), suffered a broken neck and spent the next 11 months in the hospital and in rehabilitation. The accident left the child ". . . a quadriplegic in need of round-the-clock care. Her mother went into a coma, needed reconstructive surgery on her face and had a rod inserted into her leg" (Coffey, 2005, para. 6). Antonia's father, Ronald, was unhurt in the accident.

According to a newspaper report of the accident, Hasbrouck Heights police officer Corey Lange found Lanzaro and a passenger sitting on the curb near the accident site. Both Lanzaro and the passenger had trouble standing up. When asked how much he had been drinking Lanzaro replied, "Too much" (Gaudiano, 2002, para. 2). A security guard at the hospital reported finding a marijuana "joint" in Lanzaro's pocket (Gaudiano). Lange later said that Lanzaro admitted to drinking before and during the game, and to also smoking some "pot" (Gaudiano). According to police, Lanzaro's blood alcohol level was ". . . 0.266, 2? times the legal limit of 0.10" (Gaudiano, para. 2). In August 2003, Lanzaro pled guilty to vehicular assault and was sentenced to five years in Riverfront State Prison (Coffey, 2005).

The fact that there are disagreements between what people of various cultures or societies believe or espouse in a given situation has led some ethicists to contend there can be no universal truth in ethics, no independent standard of right or wrong. Every standard is culturally bound. There are simply different cultural codes, different traditions, folkways, and so on, and that is all one needs to know. This is a position known as **Cultural Relativism.**

Faced with claims of cultural relativism, it is important to examine if there are substantive differences among fundamental belief systems or values across cultures or societies. It is important to remember that many times apparent differences arise from different belief systems (such as religions), not from fundamental values. A culinary example might make this distinction clear.

If the next time you are eating a hamburger (If you are a vegetarian, pretend you are a carnivore.), three people in succession walk up to you and express their beliefs on whether it is right or wrong to eat a cow, the disagreements among the three may be based on a number of factors. Person A says, "Eating a cow is wrong, because dead souls inhabit cows. My grandfather is dead. I do not want to eat my grandfather. Therefore, eating a hamburger is wrong." Person B says, "I know dead souls inhabit cows, but that burger smells great, and no one in my family has died yet. I am going to buy one and eat it now, while my grandfather is still alive and well. Eating a hamburger does not bother me if I do not know the soul I am eating!" Person C says, "There are no such things as dead souls. However, eating red meat is not good for a person's heart, so I think you should not eat that hamburger."

The three people's various reasons for believing it is right or wrong to eat a cow vary. Person A believes dead souls inhabit cows, so he does not eat cows in order to not eat a dead grandparent. Person B also believes dead souls inhabit cows, but is not personally offended by eating the souls of people he does not know. Meanwhile, Person C is not in favor of cannibalism, and also does not believe a dead grandparent's soul inhabits the cow. She simply does not believe that eating red meat is good for one's health.

As this vignette highlights, many factors work together to produce a society's or culture's customs. Values are only one factor. Others include religious beliefs, factual beliefs, and physical circumstances. It does not follow from the mere fact that people disagree, or have different beliefs, that there is no "objective" truth.

Different choices may not be based upon different values, but may arise from different sets of circumstances. Life often forces people to make different choices. Making a different choice from another person does not mean each person's values are different. Two college athletes may both "value" an education, but their various sports' physical, psychological, and time demands may be different. This difference may allow one student to spend more time and energy studying, therefore earning a better grade in the same course. Does each person's class grade reflect how much each valued the class or their education? Quite the contrary; both may have equally valued the course. Beyond these two individual students, it might be agreed most students value education, but circumstances may influence their access and commitment to a quality education.

Outside of sport, such values as caring for young, telling the truth, and refraining from murder are often considered "universal" values. Without truthfulness, communication would be impossible. Even in instances when it is agreed it is alright to lie, it is typically permitted only to avoid an innocent person being harmed (e.g., if a known murderer asks you if you are hiding a person upstairs in your house, in this instance it would be permissible to lie and say no).

With regard to murder, suppose there was no such prohibition. There would be no security, and society on any large scale would collapse. Groups could band together to live together and trust each other not to murder, but in order to survive they would simply be forming smaller societies that did adopt a rule against

BOX 5.3

Does Relativism Help With Budgeting? No!

Joanna Smith is the director of a youth-soccer league. Her yearly budget is provided by the local Parks and Recreation district. She must distribute this year's funds to the league's ten teams (There are an equal number of male and female teams). After fulfilling her statutory obligations—as set forth by the district—there is five thousand dollars remaining.

- How should these excess funds be disbursed?
  Joanna has a strong "belief" the funds should go to the most competitive team, which is a boys' team that won the state age-group championship the previous season. One of her assistants strongly believes the funds should go to the least competitive team, but the one whose players had an unblemished attendance record (no player missed a single practice or game) the previous season. Another assistant believes the funds should go to all the girls' teams.

- How should Joanna resolve this conflict?

- Does the fact staff members disagree mean there is no objective or agreed-upon standard from which to make a decision?
  Each sport-manager likely strongly believes their claim, but can a decision be made? If relativism is true, no decision would be possible and Joanna should simply say, "Since there is no right choice, we cannot make a decision. Nobody gets any additional money." While none of the staff's beliefs may be "wrong," that does not mean all of their beliefs are equally justified (right).

- Faced with such a dilemma, how can an ethical sport-manager make an informed decision?

- How could Joanna make a decision?
  She could start by determining whether this is a purely "practical" issue or are ethical assumptions and implications forming the basis for her decision making.

- How can these assumptions and implications be discerned?

One way is to look at the four-part ethical-reasoning model described on page 93, and use it to work through the issue.

1. In looking at the problem, Joanna and her staff should ask themselves what goal [or goals] they want to achieve? Remember, all staff members may not have the same goals, but since everyone is employed by the Parks and Recreation district, they must consider the entire league's best interests, not just one team or their own self-interest. Underlying everyone's beliefs is a common goal: they all want what is "best" for the league. This may include a goal to disburse funds "fairly." In this instance, the $5,000.00 question is: what is "fair?" Practicing ethical reasoning may not resolve the issue to everyone's satisfaction, but at least it can identify the staff-member's underlying value systems and bring disagreements out in the open.

2. Where is the league in respect to its stated goal[s]? What is the description of the situation in which the staff members find themselves? What are the facts?

3. Joanna and her staff should analyze the situation. Why are the facts as they are? What are the reasons for how they feel the way they do? What are their underlying beliefs that have shaped their positions on this particular issue?

4. How might they be able to resolve the present impasse in order to achieve the league's goal[s]?

As can be seen by breaking down the situation into its components, moral disagreements may arise within any aspect, but as the league's decision makers, Joanna and her staff must be impartial, adopt an objective point of view, listen to each other, solicit input from other league stakeholders, and offer valid reasons to support their position.

As can be seen from this real-world example, rather than helping solve sport-managers' problems, resorting to relativism does not help make a decision. It actually stifles productive discussion among staff members.

murder. Thus, there are some general moral rules that all societies will have in common because those rules are necessary for any society to exist. Cultures may differ about exceptions, but these are against a background of agreement on larger issues. So it is a mistake to overestimate the amount of differences and what they mean.

If relativism were correct, certain athletes would not have been universally criticized, condemned, and ostracized. Tiger Woods would not have lost millions of sponsorship dollars after his numerous affairs, Mark McGwire would have been voted into the MLB Hall-of-Fame on the first ballot despite his steroid usage, Marion Jones would have kept her Olympic gold medals despite her legal troubles, and Zinedine Zindane would not have been shamed by his World-Cup head butt. Relativism precludes any such criticism.

However, despite its flaws, relativism is a useful ethical concept, since it illustrates the danger of assuming all "preferences" are based on absolute, divine, or rational standards. Moral views may reflect a society's prejudices. In addition, feelings are not necessarily perceptions of truth. No one is infallible; feeling something is right does not necessarily make it right.

Within a society not everyone agrees on everything, but considered and reflective moral decision making does result in extensive agreement (i.e., reason, impartiality, discerning facts). So if we wish to utilize reason and impartial examination of facts as an independent standard for ethical decision making, relativism is not helpful.

The Contenders

Ethical Frameworks for Ethical Reasoning

There are four ethical theories often used to help in ethical decision making: (1) Consequentialism or Utilitarianism, (2) Deontology, (3) Social contract, and (4) Ethics of care. Before looking at each theoretical framework in greater detail, here are some highlights of each:

- **Utilitarianism** focuses on consequences. The right decision is the one that results in the best consequences.
- **Deontological** theories focus on duties. The right decision is one that intends to fulfill duties.
- **Social Contract** theories focus on consent or agreement. The decision is just if everyone has consented to the procedure or there is mutual agreement.
- **Ethics of care** focuses on interdependence.

A. Consequentialism (Utilitarianism)

When deliberating about what ought to be done, often the first thought involves asking, "What are the possible and likely consequences of my action?" This is a natural starting place when thinking about either moral or practical decisions. From a consequentialism perspective, people do a "good" thing when their actions result in consequences that produce the greatest balance of good over bad.

In Western philosophy, consequentialism (also referred to as Utilitarianism) is most often attributed to David Hume (1711–1776), Jeremy Bentham (1748–1832), and John Stuart Mill (1806–1873). For a consequentialist, happiness is the only thing people value for its own sake; therefore, happiness is the sole measure of value. Mill contended the principle of utility or greatest happiness principle is the foundation of morals. This principle can be stated as follows:

Actions are right in proportion as they tend to promote happiness; wrong, as they tend to produce the reverse.

Happiness (more or less) equals pleasure or the absence of pain. For example, suppose someone asks:

QUESTION: Why are you going to college?
ANSWER: To get an education.

QUESTION: Why do you want an education?
ANSWER: To get a good job.

QUESTION: Why do you want a good job?
ANSWER: Because this will promote my happiness.

It is important to note this example makes no distinctions about what constitutes or qualifies as "happiness."

Let us look at another example. Suppose you are a student and your non-student friends want to go out to a party:

FRIENDS: Come out to party.
STUDENT: I have to study.

FRIENDS: Partying is much more pleasurable than studying.
STUDENT: Yes, I agree going out with you will produce much more pleasure.

FRIENDS: Then you should come out with us; after all, what produces the greater amount of pleasure over pain is the right thing to do. Clearly partying is more pleasurable than studying.
STUDENT: But I will learn more from studying.

FRIENDS: Ignorance is bliss. You will have much more pleasure and be more content if you just party.
STUDENT: Well, if the right thing to do is that which produces the greatest amount of pleasure, then I should party. So let's party!!!

The "let's party!" ethos is really more accurately described as **simple hedonism** (a search for short-term physical pleasure). Pleasure, in utilitarianism, should not be confused with instant gratification, or with sensations or simple contentment, although at times a happy person may be content. As a rational human being, short-term physical contentment cannot be the only thing desired.

So what kind and whose pleasures are to be considered? It would seem logical to a human being that intellectual pleasures are superior to short-term physical pleasures, since even an oyster can experience simple physical pleasure. According to this line of thought, intellect, which separates humans from other animals, must be a superior pleasure.

Humans are progressive beings with capacities and faculties more elevated than animal appetites. Humans are not static beings. Such faculties include reasoning, intellect, imagination, aestheticism, productivity, and morality. Humans have higher aspirations than animals, so "goodness" cannot simply involve discussions of quantities of physical pleasure or sensations. In addition, the length and duration of any pleasure should be taken into account. Pleasures come in different durations and kinds. Based on these factors, some pleasures are more desirable than others. It is important to note a pleasure's quality cannot be determined simply by quantity. Superiority in quality outweighs quantity. While this may be difficult to determine, a pleasure that involves and employs the "higher faculties" is deemed to be of higher quality and to be given higher preference.

Unfortunately, for students who want to party with their friends and ignore their education, Hume, Bentham and Mill did not contend "ignorance was bliss." Ignorance was not "good." In their belief system, a longer-term, intellectual pleasure is better than a short-term physical one.

But since people are all equal, no person's happiness counts more than any other's. Thus the standard is not the agent's own happiness but all concerned. The moral agent must be strictly impartial, a disinterested and benevolent spectator. This requires one to recognize the effects or consequences of decisions. Such recognition becomes crucial for leaders, managers, advisers, and anyone making decisions for others.

Sport managers must make numerous decisions about resource allocation, marketing strategies, alcohol management, security and staffing issues. These decisions are often based upon anticipated consequences. Contingency planning in event management makes use of utilitarianism, since it involves asking the question, "What if?" Sport managers attempt to minimize unwanted (bad) consequences and maximize desirable (good) intended consequences. Therefore, utilitarianism or consequentialism are not only ethical theories, but they are also potential management tools. The theories help sport managers develop, plan, and organize their management strategies to meet their consumers' wants, needs and desires.

In summary, for utilitarianism, good actions are those that have the best consequences. A good action produces the greatest balance of happiness over unhappiness, where each person's welfare or happiness is equally important, not just the agent's, but all concerned.

While this is a popular theory, there are some difficulties with the theory.

- Is happiness the only good?
- How do we define happiness?
- Is "goodness" determined by utility, or do we think that some things are "right" irrespective of consequences?
- Just because something satisfies a greater number of people, does that fact make it right?

- Would a "good "action still be "good" if it contradicts some of our most deeply held beliefs, or if it just seems "wrong" to us?
- Would we be willing to sacrifice someone, or even ourselves, for the "good" of the whole?

In addition to the many questions utilitarianism seems to raise, from a practical standpoint, the theory is somewhat dependent on a person knowing all the facts and being able to calculate all the consequences prior to acting. (Such calculation is known as **hedonistic calculus**.) While obviously thinking rationally about the possible or likely consequences of one's actions makes a great deal of sense, it may be impossible for a person to know all the facts and determine who will be affected by their actions. Clearly, considering consequences is an important element of ethical decision-making, but looking only at consequences may not be enough.

B. Deontology

While utilitarianism focuses on the consequences of an action, deontological theories focus on the motives, obligations, or duties that lead to actions. These motives must be analyzed independent of anticipated consequences. Deontologists claim an action is morally wrong, not because of its consequences, but because the action *a priori* (i.e., *A priori* knowledge or justification is independent of experience) involves a moral violation. The philosopher most associated with Deontology is Immanuel Kant (1724–1804). While often difficult to assess, his ethical ideas have greatly contributed to Western ethical thought.

For Kant there are three important concepts: "The Good Will," duty, and reason.

- **The Good Will:** The only thing that is good, without qualification, is a good will. The Good Will is intrinsically good, but not because of what it affects or accomplishes. Its value is wholly self-contained and utterly independent of its external relations.
- **Duty:** Kant distinguishes (1) actions done from the motive of duty and (2) actions done in conformity with duty. An act is praiseworthy not for self-interested reasons, nor as a result of natural inclinations, but only if done from duty. The moral value of an action can only reside in a formal principle or "maxim," which is the general commitment to act out of reverence for universal moral law. For Kant, acting in this manner is a rational person's duty.
- **Reason:** If there is a universal moral law, it must be the same for all rational agents. The only thing all possible rational agents share is reason. So, universal moral law must be discoverable by practical reason. Therefore, right actions are those that practical reason would will as universal law.

What is the moral law discoverable by reason? Morality can be summarized in an ultimate universal principle of moral law, from which all duties and obligations are derived. This principle is **The Categorical Imperative**. The Categorical

Imperative summarizes a procedure for determining whether an act is morally permissible.

> *Act only on that maxim through which you can at the same time* ***will*** *it should become a universal law.*

Though expressed as a simple sentence, The Categorical Imperative requires further explanation to better understand and apply its principles.

There are several steps in constructing and analyzing The Categorical Imperative. The process involves a series of statements. As we work through the various sentences, remember to keep the various definitions in mind.

- A **maxim** is a principle of action.
- An **imperative** is a command usually stated in terms of "ought" statements. Kant distinguishes between two kinds of imperatives: hypothetical and categorical.
- A **hypothetical imperative** depends on a desire, and contains conditions. If one wants to earn a college degree, then classes must be successfully completed. This imperative depends on the desire to receive a college degree. If there is no such desire, then one is released from this imperative. However, imagine if morality was based only on hypothetical imperatives. A person could easily be released from the imperative if they so desired. But morality imposes a duty to do certain things, which leads to a system of categorical imperatives.
- **The Categorical Imperative** is a command without limiting conditions. A rational being cannot escape this imperative. Desires, inclinations, preferences, and emotions are irrelevant to such a command. Categorical imperatives are a result of reason. A rational moral agent's conduct is guided by universal laws, so categorical "oughts" are binding simply because moral agents are rational.

A Duty_____

An obligation one has to act or refrain from acting. A duty often occurs in response to another person's right.

Kant believed every time people perform an action, they act from a maxim, even though they may not be able to articulate or know that maxim before they choose to act. However, by such action, a person prescribes a maxim. For example, if a person chooses to lie in a certain situation, the maxim would be, it is always right for someone to lie in the same or similar situation.

One of the most important elements of The Categorical Imperative is the requirement that rules or duties apply universally to everyone. No one can make an exception for themselves or their situation. The Categorical Imperative must be applied to everyone; it cannot lead to contradictory conclusions.

An example Kant discussed is promise-keeping. Suppose after graduation a student lands a job as an inside sales representative for a National Basketball Association (NBA) team. Despite the initial excitement and desire to do a great job, after a few weeks the employee begins having trouble maintaining his outbound call volume (inside sales reps must make a specified number of calls to identified prospects). In a panic he decides to start calling fax-machine numbers he found by searching the Internet. The employee promises himself he will stop making the fake calls when he has collected sufficient referrals. After all, he thinks, "Nobody is being hurt. I'm still doing my job!"

After thinking about this situation, some questions might come to mind:

- What is the action's maxim?
- In this situation, what would be The Categorical Imperative?
- Is it universally permissible to CHEAT?

While the employee might rationalize cheating because it will help him keep his job this month, cheating cannot be The Categorical Imperative, since it cannot be a universal law. It would lead to a contradiction—the sales manager could never trust the employee.

> *One might think the Golden Rule satisfies the Categorical Imperative. The Golden Rule is certainly a good principle, but it is not a duty, since it depends on individual preferences.*

Kant divides the universe into persons and things. Things are non-rational entities of any kind. Persons are autonomous rational agents. In all actions there are ends and means. Kant maintains every rational being exists as an end in him or herself, not merely as a means to an arbitrary end.

> *The practical imperative that follows from the categorial imperative is: Act so that you always treat humanity—whether in your own person or in that of any other—never simply as a means, but always at the same time as an end in itself.*

This practical imperative requires respecting persons as autonomous human beings with rights and dignity, not treating people as things or objects to be "used" to achieve an end. Basically people should not be treated as things; to do so would fail to respect the most important aspects of being a rational being: autonomy and dignity.

According to Kant, we should look at our intentions, not at how much misery and happiness an act is likely to produce. Our intentions are what matter. According to The Categorical Imperative, we must insure our contemplated act will not treat anyone as mere means to an end, but will treat all people as ends in themselves.

Treating someone as mere means involves using them in a scheme of action to which they could not consent. Kant noted we do use each other in reciprocal or cooperative ways (e.g., NBA ticket-sales representatives sell game-tickets to clients and are paid a commission). But, treating a person as a mere means might involve the customer not agreeing to buy the ticket, but the sales representative tricking them into releasing their credit card number and not delivering the tickets. Successful false promising (not delivering the tickets) depends on deceiving the person to whom the promise has been made, about the real maxim. (It has already been noted that this cannot be universalized.)

A person who promises falsely (lies) treats the acceptor of the promise as a prop, or as a thing, not as a person. According to the Categorical Imperative, this makes lying wrong.

Standard ways of using others as mere means includes deceiving them and/or coercing them. If one is coerced, there is no consent. According to deontology, acts done following maxims that require deception or coercion of others are wrong. They are not only wrong, but also unjust. For Kant, duties of justice are the most important of our duties. When we fail in these duties, we have used others as mere means. But respecting persons and not treating them as things requires respecting them as rational persons with their own maxims.

Kantian ethics then differs from utilitarian ethics. Deontological theory looks at the intentions and duties that underlie the action. Consequentialism looks at an action's consequences. With all the facts, information and knowledge of the ultimate consequences, a consequentialist can—after the fact—access an action's moral worth. But as noted above, such "Monday-morning quarterbacking" is a daunting task, unlimited in scope, often imprecise, and leaves out a person's intentions. Kant's ethics are more limited in scope in assessing intentions. However, it must be remembered that deontology does not allow people to simply claim their intentions were "good" and then do whatever they want. It is not enough to say, "I did not intend for anyone to get hurt!" A person's intentions reflect the reasonably anticipated immediate results of an action. Provided *real* intentions use no other as a mere means, we do nothing unjust.

Elements of consequentialist and deontological ethics are often used in combination to make ethical decisions and develop policies. This dual usage can be seen in social-contract theory.

C. Social-Contract Theories

A social-contract theory adopts the thesis that society is fundamentally a set of tacit or explicit agreements, and our individual obligations (as members of society) follow from these agreements. If people are bound by such agreements, it makes sense to "learn" what constitutes such agreements, and how—and under what conditions—they may be discovered.

The moral philosopher who provides a modern interpretation of social-contract theory is the 20th century ethicist John Rawls (1921–2002). Rawls' ethical framework expands upon Thomas Hobbes' (1588–1679) formulation of social-contract theory outlined in his book *Leviathan*. Rawls draws upon Kantian Ethics and synthesizes, to some extent, Mill's ideal utilitarianism. However, as can be seen by examining social-contract theory, Rawls is not a utilitarian. He uses fundamental contractual concepts to determine what we (as members of society) owe one another and how we should structure our social institutions to reflect our contractual/moral commitments.

Rawls uses an analytical device—called the hypothetical situation—to discover structural principles that members of society agree should be included in social institutions. Using reason and the concept of an "ideal observer" (conceptually similar to the *reasonable person* discussed in Chaper 6, Legal Aspects of Sport), such principles can be established. An ideal observer basically is one who views the world from a "moral and objective point of view." What that requires is that we start from an "original position," a hypothetical position similar to what often has been referred to as a "state of nature." In a state of nature, everyone is rational, relatively equal, and self-interested. There are no civil laws and no government to keep people in check.

But to truly operate from an objective point of view, people must ignore the happenstances of their lives, their particular talents, inclinations, social status, and all other "accidental" features of their lives. In a state of nature, people operate as free and rational persons with all factors of inequality eliminated from their thinking. They do not know whether they will be rich or poor, healthy or sickly, advantaged or disadvantaged. They do not know their ethnicity or their gender. They operate from behind a "veil of ignorance."

Under this veil people do know that everyone is rationally self-interested but mutually disinterested. To be rationally self-interested means everyone is interested in promoting their own goods and advantages. This "natural" mutual-disinterest tempers self-interest because no one is envious of another, or seeking to gain at another's expense. Thus everyone is "rational" enough to simply not be self-interested. With these attributes, from behind this veil and in this hypothetical original position, everyone bargains fairly and in good faith.

However, under the veil no one knows what societal role they will occupy once the veil is lifted. Once the veil is lifted and people take their places, although they may not all be happy with the situation, they cannot complain their "station in society" is unjust. From a social-contract perspective, all principles of justice are set forth from the original state of nature. According to Rawls, the following two principles are fair and constitute the principles of justice.

1. **The Equal Liberty Principle.** Each person has an equal right to the most extensive liberty compatible with a similar liberty for others.
2. **The Difference Principle.** Social and economic inequalities are permissible and to be arranged so they are both:
   * reasonably expected to be to everyone's advantage (in particular the least advantaged), and
   * any offices or positions are open to all under conditions of fair equality of opportunity.

The first principle takes priority so no individual can be used to promote another person's advantage. If the difference principle conflicts with the liberty principle, the liberty principle takes precedence except in cases of extreme scarcity. This priority ordering of the principles removes one of the difficulties of utilitarianism by acknowledging Kant's practical imperative. Thus you cannot have someone disadvantaged to promote someone else's advantage, or use others for the good of the whole. This removes the notion of the tyranny of the majority, and prohibits the persecution of minorities.

What Rawls has done is analyze a **virtue** of social institutions—**justice**. Justice can be termed as both retributive (reactive, after the fact, i.e., "An eye for an eye") or **distributive** (proactive, people are owed equal respect). While justice is only one element of a "good" society, it is a foundational virtue. In addition, there is a distinction between justice and fairness. The distinction is that in any situation involving justice, a moral agent must participate. On the other hand, in situations involving fairness, a moral person can decline to participate. Reconciling this distinction, Rawls identifies the element fundamental to both—**reciprocity**, which is logically contained in both the Golden Rule and The Categorical Imperative.

In any society while we are all different, we all have similar capacities and desire for "goods." There is, however, one primary good: self-respect. There are other goods, such as rights, liberties, capacities, health, and intelligence. As rationally self-interested beings, we all desire to develop these goods, but we cannot develop them without the help of others. Furthermore, we cannot do everything we might like to do, as time and other constraints limit our abilities. In addition, since we cannot go it alone, we must reciprocate and complement one another; we become complete through our interactions with others. In this way, according to Rawls, all members of society achieve self-respect and mutual respect.

A basketball team is a great illustration of reciprocity. On the court, a basketball team is comprised of five players. Each player has a different role, which often requires different talents or attributes. In order for the team to achieve success, each player must successfully execute her role. In addition, no one player can succeed (win) without the others. No one can go it alone. Even Michael Jordan needed quality players on his team to win championships! Thus, to develop ourselves, we need teammates. By recognizing the value of teamwork, each player comes to respect each other and themselves as part of the team process.

Team members agree to assume various roles in order for the team to successfully function. Once they all agree various roles are needed, then it is a matter of finding which role best suits each player. Though each role may not lead to the same individual glory, players understand that if the strengths of the individuals were different, they would play different roles. It is through such selfless reciprocity that individuals become free and equal, rationally self-interested, mutually disinterested, and achieve self-respect and mutual respect.

In making decisions and policies for others, using the thought experiment of the veil of ignorance provides a powerful tool to recognize the implications (consequences) of our decisions and what is meant by the moral equality of persons, which is fundamental to deontology. Interestingly, Rawls' formulation of social-contract theory integrates deontology and consequentialism. This

Virtue_____

A trait that contributes to something's being good in some way. Virtue may be referred to as "righteous conduct." As a plural, "virtues" refers to character traits such as courage, wisdom, self-control, justice, loyalty, and compassion.

Justice_____

Often seen as synonymous with fairness, is the application of ethics to the structure of society. Justice is commonly divided into two areas: retributive and distributive.

Distributive_____

Retributive justice is concerned with correcting societal imbalances; distributive justice is concerned with the fair allocation of societal benefits and burdens.

integration is evident in the U.S. Constitution. As a useful ethical decision-making tool, social-contract theory has been described as being the "best" of both deontology and consequentialism.

D. Ethics of Care

While Rawls developed a theory that sought to bring together justice and fairness, his contribution often goes unnoticed today. In Western society many people are concerned about rights, as of course they should be, but rights do not often encapsulate all moral situations. However, research conducted on moral development has shown the concept of "human rights" to be essential and necessary in solving moral dilemmas. The theorist most associated with this perspective is American psychologist Lawrence Kohlberg (1927–1987), who was greatly influenced by Swiss psychologist Jean Piaget (1896–1980).

Carol Gilligan (1936–) added to this humanistic ethical perspective by providing a missing "voice"—an **ethics of care**. Gilligan's fundamental breakthrough was to include a female viewpoint, since both Kohlberg and Piaget's perspectives were singularly male—dismissing females as being deficient in morality. When Kohlberg presented moral dilemmas applicable to both female and male subjects, he contended females ethical reasoning capabilities were generally lower than males, and they tended to revert to a lower stage of conventional moral maturity. Gilligan examined this research and conducted her own, and asserted there are at least two different ideologies from which to analyze moral dilemmas: **ethics of rights** and ethics of care.

Ethics of rights emphasizes separation, detachment, and independence, and is predicated on equality or fairness, and rights. The self, as a moral agent, stands as a figure against a ground of social relationships, judging conflicting claims of self and others against a standard of equality. Objective detachment is seen as a hallmark of moral maturity. Within ethics of rights, the fundamental question is, "What is just?"

On the other hand, ethics of care emphasizes attachment, inclusion, interdependence, and differences in need predicated on equity, responsibility and compassion. This perspective recognizes that dependence on others is essential. From this perspective, objective detachment is a moral problem. Within ethics of care, the fundamental question is, "How do we respond?"

It should be noted that these two ethics are cross-cutting perspectives that do not negate one another, but focus attention on a situation's different dimensions. From the ethics-of-care perspective, relationships are not all reducible to rights; rights are individualistic in nature. For example, the moral dimensions of a family or team are not reducible to the rights of each individuals involved. There is an interdependence that cannot be explained in terms of individual rights. This interdependence cannot be ignored when making moral decisions.

Again using the basketball team analogy, differences and the roles played depend on individual differences, but the "team" does not just consist of individual roles. The team is comprised of the interdependence of these roles. Most are all familiar with the slogan: "There is no 'I' in team." This slogan does not deny the existence of the each team member as an individual (as an "I"), but recognizes the fundamental interdependence of the individuals who fill the various roles on the team. Another way to say this is, "The whole is greater than the sum of the individual parts." No coach, sport manager, or player would deny each individual has rights, but ethical decision making does not stop at identifying each person's individual rights. Both rights and care must be considered.

This complimentarity can be illustrated by looking at the ambiguous figure, which you may be familiar with from a Psychology class.

- What do you see first in this picture?
- Is the woman old or young?
- Can you see both at the same time?
- If you refocus, can you see one, then another?

If you have trouble seeing the other figure in the picture, someone may need to "show" you how to "see" the alternate reality. This is similar to the perspectives of ethics or rights and ethics of care. You can only see one at a time and may have trouble understanding the other.

Just as in the ambiguous figure, people do articulate concerns about "justice" and "caring" in discussing a moral dilemma, and people tend to focus their attention on one set of concerns, while often (and even unintentionally) minimally representing or recognizing another perspective. Research has revealed an association between a person's moral orientation and their gender. Initially, when discussing a moral dilemma, men tend to focus on justice, while women more often focus on care. But if one takes it further and asks each group to consider other solutions to the dilemma, both groups are able to determine alternatives. Interestingly, after such deliberation, when groups are asked which perspective is their "final" preferable, there is no clear gender division. What this shows is within the process of discussing a moral dilemma—in order to arrive at a possible (best) solution, diversity is important. Without diversity of perspective, people may focus on only one perspective and lose ability to see the proverbial "big picture"!

Conclusion

The process of ethical decision making is not easy, but can be "learned" by studying ethical theories. However, even when you have learned ethical frameworks, applying these frameworks and acting ethically requires practice and being willing to apply your ethical decision-making skills in the real world of sport management! Ethical issues arise often when a sport-manager least expects them, but just as athletes practice for the upcoming big game, ethical sport managers can prepare to respond to an ethical dilemma in accordance with their values.

In your career there will be many opportunities for ethical action. There will also be plenty of obstacles or excuses to acting consistent with your values. While there is no algorithm or recipe to follow, this chapter has highlighted several useful guidelines. Similar to other management tools, ethical reasoning involves contemplation and systematic introspection. If you desire to be a conscientious and ethical sport manager you will be required to make choices. If you are—at your core—a "moral" person, it is hoped this chapter's ethical frameworks have provided you with guidance about how you can make decisions. A conscientious moral sport manager should be impartial (not making exceptions for your actions), consistent, a good listener, and (as much as possible) an objective fact-gatherer.

As was discussed, it is helpful to utilize some interrelated components in ethical decision making:

- **Goal/Vision:** What is the goal you want to achieve? How should things be?
- **Social Reality:** What is the description of how things are? Gather facts, information.
- **Analysis:** Why are things the way they are? What assumptions contribute to this reality?
- **Strategies/Means:** How do we get from where we are to our goal: how things ought to be?

There are often obstacles to ethical decision making, which include gathering facts, lack of moral courage, and relativism. This chapter outlined several ethical frameworks and concepts worthy of investigation by future sport managers:

- **Consequentialism/Utilitarianism** [Hume, Bentham, and Mill]: Focuses on the consequences of an action.
- **Deontology** [Kant]: Focus on motives and sense of duty that lead to an action.
- **The Categorical Imperative:** Always act so that your maxim can become universal law; this requires universalizability.
- **Kingdom of Ends:** Never treat people purely as means, but always as ends in themselves: treat people with dignity and respect.
- **Social-Contract Theory** [Rawls]: Society is ultimately based upon a set of agreements derived from a hypothetical objective point of view. Such agreements involve reciprocity, respect & complementarity.

- **Ethics of Care** [Gilligan]: Contrasted often with ethics of rights, which emphasizes detachment and independence of "atom" people who are in conflict. Ethics of Care emphasizes attachment, interdependence, responsibility, and compassion.

Below are some final thoughts. These are not intended as rules that must be followed, but simply some words to consider during this course and beyond. As many sport managers have discovered, we are all continually contributing to the writing of the sport-management ethics manual:

- Do not let immoral or nonmoral purposes and goals block your moral vision.
- Scrutinize your motives.
- Be "careful" and thoughtful in your deliberations about your actions.
- No one is infallible.
- Each of us has a different point of view and agenda. However, remember, respect for diversity is not the same as succumbing to cultural or ethical relativism.
- Examine your perspectives.
- Do not assume your point of view is the correct one.
- Adopt an objective point of view.
- Take others into account and respect their interests.
- Try to imagine what others propose to do as if it were a rule for everyone.
- Listen to others.
- Talk to others.
- Reflect on actual and hypothetical cases.
- Be impartial. Do not make an exception of yourself.
- Be consistent—apply principles consistently to yourself and others.
- Get the facts straight.
- Listen to your conscience.
- Take into consideration virtues, duties, and consequences
- Develop strength of will.
- Have self-respect.
- Think for yourself.
- Have integrity.
- Have moral courage.
- Recognize that inaction often may be worse than action.

Remember that there are lots of opportunities for ethical action; so, too, there will be many obstacles. Ethical action and ethical decision making are not easy, but can be learned and practiced so they become part of your sport-manager tool box. Finally, in recognition of philosophers, ethicists, and sport managers who have come before, remember acting ethically is a journey, not a destination.

Interview

Dr. Jon Ericson
Professor of Rhetoric and Communications Studies
Drake University

Dr. Jon Ericson is an Ellis and Nelle Levitt Professor of Rhetoric and Communications Studies (Emeritus) and former Provost at Drake University. He is the founder of The Drake Group, a national organization working to end the academic corruption in college sport. In 2001 Dr. Ericson was named an Ethics Fellow by the Institute for International Sport.

Editor's Note: At the co-editor's request, Dr. Ericson agreed to supply an "interview" for this book. In contrast to many of this text's interviews, Dr. Ericson's comments allow us to not only examine a well-known college-sport "critic's" view of today's big-time college sport landscape, but to also analyze how and why a person may come to question the status quo and arrive at an ethical position contrary to the views of many sport-management students and college sport "fans." In addition, his commentary allows students to see how an individual's ethical position also sheds light on an adopted sociological perspective (See Chapter 2).

Our initial discussion with Dr. Ericson began with this exchange:

Q: What was the catalyst for your founding The Drake Group?"

A: I didn't do it because of ethics; I did it because I was angry.

Q: What caused you to become angry?

A: I saw the academic records of athletes.

Q: Why did the academic records make you angry?

After a lengthy phone conversation, which touched on numerous subjects related to college sport, Dr. Ericson finally suggested he forward a written response for inclusion in this book. His essay highlights the internal discussion in which an individual must engage when grappling with an ethical dilemma. His comments are much different than the other chapters' "interviews." You may have to "look up" (This was the term for what is now called "google.") some of his terms and individuals to whom he refers. But, that is not such a bad thing sometimes.

Veritas.

Alas, my colleagues were persistent and too quick for me. They kept digging and asking not so much about me but why do most people not confront the things they see that are wrong in sports? "Ask them," I said. Then again, you did ask, "Why me?"

The short answer is that I do not know. And any answer is fraught with the reality that we tend to provide reasons for our action after the fact, or as a writer once said, we tend to make ourselves the heroes of our own stories.

In *Lest Innocent Blood Be Shed: The Story of the Village of Le Chambon and How Goodness Happened There,* Philip Hallie paints a picture of what it means to face making a choice:

> When Andre Trocme said good-bye to his children, he did not know if he would ever see them again. The Maquis around LeChambon were getting more numerous and more violent, and so were the German troops and the Gestapo. Those days were full of disappearances and sudden death. But he was calm, almost joyous, not only in order to keep his family from knowing terror but because for a long time he had been hoping for a test, a hard test. His warmth, the speed of his intelligence, the vigor of his pain-wracked body that could work efficiently with only a few hours of sleep, and his luck had kept death away from him and his family and had brought admiration and love to them. Moreover, he had been efficient: he had created a rescue machine made of poor people who had enough problems of their own to keep them fully occupied. But he did not know whether he could be helpful under great pain and under the immediate threat of death. Now he would find out. He was like an eager chemist watching the results of one last acid test that would tell him if the substance before him was, indeed, gold. The substance before him was himself.

I am no Andre Trocme. Nor, you say, is college sports the Gestapo. Let Harry Stein take it from here:

> I'd asked if he [tortured by the Gestapo] was surprised the guy betrayed the group [French Resistance]. No, he said, he wasn't really surprised by anyone's behavior during that desperate period. Not by those who showed character and courage, nor those who ended up actively supporting the Germans, nor by the majority who merely stayed quiet and kept their heads down. "Even the kids in my high school," he said, "I could have predicted beforehand how almost every one of them would act. It wasn't so different from how they'd always been before."

Stein then brings it home:

> At the time it seemed a stunning thought: that by our routine behaviors and seemingly banal choices, we reveal what we're ultimately made of. But of course it is absolutely so. It is by the incidental test, day by day and hour by hour, that we establish what we are about; and, indeed, how we will respond when most severely tested.

What does all of this have to do with the corruption in college sports? For me, everything. My confronting and publicly identifying the corruption meant facing a choice. The corruption in college sports was a test: to see the substance in me.

Corruption in sports then is but another of those tests, some seemingly banal—beginning class on time; some with consequences—grade inflation—that professors face every day. Seeing academic records that by the most elastic of measures betrayed my university and my profession provided a good test.

You asked why I chose to be involved. The best I can do is say fear—at least partly fear. For years, I wearied of those who were full of advice for those who held offices for which they were once responsible. Former United States Senators telling Senators how to fix the Senate. I didn't want to be part of the "Could'a, Would'a, Should'a" club.

You ask, what is moral courage? In terms of addressing the problems in college sports, two examples may help. It takes no great courage to complain about the costs of big-time college athletics. Oh, it would appear that taking on the monster is "David and Goliath" with sticks and stones heading their way—a few nasty emails maybe but little harm done. In fact, some will see such critics as heroes. But selecting money over academic corruption as their cause leaves open the charge that they can be bought. Fighting for money means taking on the commercialized college sports industry; fighting for academic integrity requires a faculty member to take on your colleagues. When it comes to courage, it is no contest. A friend Kevin Braig wrote "that to inspire others, you have to put yourself at the center of the issue" and to make the point he forwarded Theodore White's comment that "to go against the dominant thinking of your friends, of most of the people you see every day, is perhaps the most difficult act of heroism you can have." This is why "disclosure" (The public disclosure of fraudulent academic records of college athletes. Dr. Ericson disclosed such records at Drake University.–Eds.) is the most difficult—but necessary—solution for the academic corruption in college sports: It requires a faculty member to have the courage to go against colleagues who are collaborators in the corruption.

Why do a few get involved when "the majority merely stay quiet and keep their heads down?" People become professors to be scholars not warriors. It is a full-time job. Years later now, I am still asked whether it (founding The Drake Group and disclosing the fraudulent academic records at Drake University) was worth it. For me, "Oh my, yes." It was so damned much fun. Hannah Arendt wrote that the Greeks knew something we overlook. They made the forum, not the marketplace the center of society because the polis provided the opportunity to satisfy an inherent need to perform. Satisfying this need is a key to happiness. It worked for me. Lectures are performances yes, but no lecture comes close to stepping onto the public stage and saying "Bring it on; make my day." Why did I get involved? Because it was fun.

You asked what advice I might have for undergraduate sport-management students. I have given it. This is your field of study; other students are just "fans;" you are and will be closest to the problems. That gives you a particular and special opportunity to measure yourself. What could be more fun than that?

Veritas.

("Veritas," indeed, Dr. Ericson.—The Co-Editors)

Study Questions

1. Identify the four ethical frameworks discussed in this chapter. What are some of the theories' basic elements?
2. Discuss the fundamental differences between deontology and consequentialism?
3. Highlight how social-contract theories incorporate elements of deontology and consequentialism.
4. Name and discuss the "Pretenders" described in this chapter.
5. List and discuss the obstacles to moral behavior identified in this chapter. Use these obstacles to analyze the death from an inebriated fan at Giants Stadium. Highlight the obstacles that contributed to the situation.

Learning Activities

1. Go to a sport website or daily newspaper section and find a news item that involves an ethical issue. Utilizing one or more ethical framework from this chapter, analyze the situation and make an ethical judgment.
2. Which ethical framework do you find most appealing? List as many reasons why you made your choice.

As a manager, you must deal with the inside sales representative discussed on pages 106–107. What action would you take? What theory or theories would you use to justify your action?

References

Cable News Network. (2003, October 13). *Lawsuit targets NFL*. Retrieved April 27, 2005, from http://cnnstudentnews.cnn.com/TRANSCRIPTS/0310/13/ltm.14.html

Coffey, W. (2005, January 29). Wasted innocence. *nydaily news.com* Retrieved April 12, 2005, from http://www.nydailynews.com/sports/

Gaudiano, N. (2002). Crusade against DWI. North Jersey Media Group Inc. Retrieved September 28, 2004, from http://www.hhpd.com/forms/CrusadeagainstDWI.pdf

Hobbes, T. (1651). *Leviathan, the matter, forme and power of a common wealth ecclesiasticall and Civil* (Chapters 17–31). Retrieved January 22, 2010, from http://www.earlymoderntexts.com/pdf/hobbes2.pdf

NFL 1999 Season Archives (n.d.). 1999 NFL scores and schedules. Retrieved September 28, 2004, from http://home.earthlink.net/~ob1gui/nflsbar/nflsch99.htm

Sixth amended complaint and jury demand, Verni v. Lanzaro, Docket No. BER-L-10488-00 (Superior Ct. N.J. Law Div. Bergen County, Oct. 16, 2003).

Southall, R. M., & Sharp, L. A. (2006). The National Football League and its "culture of intoxication:" A negligent marketing analysis of Verni v. Lanzaro. *Journal of Legal Aspects of Sport, 16*(1), 101–127.

Verni v. Lanzaro and Stevens, No. L-10488 (Superior Court of New Jersey, Law Division: Bergen County, January 20, 2005)

Suggested Sources

These suggested readings provide basic background material to better understand the field of ethics, or simply make for interesting reading:

Blackburn, S. (2009). *Ethics: A very short introduction*. New York: Oxford University Press.

Byers, W. (1995). *Unsportsmanlike conduct: Exploiting college athletes.* Ann Arbor, MI: The University of Michigan Press.

Eitzen, D.S. (1988b). Ethical problems in American sport. *Journal of Sport and Social Issues, 12*(1), 17-30.

Funk, G.D. (1992). *Major violations: The unbalanced priorities in athletics and academics.* Champaign, IL: Leisure Press.

Putler, D.S., & Wolfe, R.A. (1999). Perceptions of intercollegiate athletic programs: Priorities and tradeoffs. *Sociology of Sport Journal, 16,* 301–325.

Sack, A.L., & Staurowsky, E.J. (1998). *College athletes for hire: The evolution and legacy of the NCAA's amateur myth.* Westport, CT: Praeger Publishers.

Sperber, M. (1990). *College sports inc.: The athletic department vs the university.* New York: Henry Holt.

Zimbalist, A. S. (1999). *Unpaid professionals: Commercialism and conflict in big-time college sports.* Princeton, New Jersey: Princeton University Press.

Legal Aspects of Sport

Linda A. Sharp, J.D.[1] • *University of Northern Colorado*

After reading this chapter, you will be able to:

- Understand the necessity of becoming knowledgeable about legal concepts to be a better sport manager;
- Define and understand the legal theory of negligence, its elements, defenses, and some important applications;
- Define and understand the important elements of a contract;
- Understand how constitutional law applies to sport management.

---

[1] Some material in this chapter is compiled and adapted in part from Chapters 1, 7, and 16 in *Sport Law: A Managerial Approach,* by Linda Sharp, Anita Moorman, and Cathryn Claussen. Copyright © 2007. Scottsdale, AZ: Holcomb Hathaway, Publishers. Used with permission.

KEY TERMS

Constitutional Law

Contract Law

Negligence Law

> *Sports law is an amalgamation of many legal disciplines, ranging from antitrust to tax law. These disciplines are applied to facts arising from sports contexts and are supplemented by case law nuances and a growing body of state and federal statutes specifically applicable to sports. Sports law, with its wide variety of legal aspects, probably encompasses more areas of law than any other discipline. Sports law is also a dynamic field of the law with new issues arising on an almost daily basis due to court decisions, new legislation and regulations*
>
> —Dean Robert Garberinio (1994)

Introduction

You have recently been hired as your town's youth soccer league administrator. As you begin your first day on the job you are overwhelmed by how many of your responsibilities have legal implications:

- How do you ensure your coaches are competent and "fit" to work with young athletes?
- What emergency medical care is available for participants?
- What policies and procedures do you implement to make sure unruly fans do not pose a danger to game officials, other fans, or players?
- How do you properly maintain equipment and the playing fields?
- What provisions should be included in your contract with the vendor who will provide food and beverages at games?
- What levels of insurance are necessary?

Whether you become a coach, high-school or college athletic director, sport league administrator, park district supervisor, fitness club manager, sport organization marketer, or Commissioner of the National Football League (NFL), you will need to understand your job's legal aspects.

As you read your daily newspaper's online website, note how many pages are devoted to issues other than box scores and game stories. Whereas casual sports fans used to only be exposed to on-field results, numerous media outlets now analyze and discuss sport's legal aspects. Numerous stories on Entertainment and Sports Programming Network (ESPN) deal with legal issues. In fact, new sports programs such as ESPN's *Outside the Lines* often detail how the law impacts the sport industry. Popular media's focus on sport law has resulted in fans being more informed regarding legal issues and judicial decisions.

It is imperative that as a future sport manager, you recognize not only the United States' legal system, but also the law's applicability to sport and recreation settings. In addition, all sport management students must understand that our country's "open door" philosophy of hearing disputes may sometimes lead to abuses of the system. Fundamentally, our legal system operates under

Sport facilities and events provide numerous areas of potential litigation.

the premise that all citizens should have nearly unfettered access to formal legal adjudication of disputes. This philosophy is fine when people use the system only to bring meritorious claims. However, as Taylor, Jr., and Thomas (2003) noted, "Americans will sue each other at the slightest provocation" (p. 44). To some observers, our country's judicial system allows seemingly "nonsensical" lawsuits to be filed. However, so long as such claims have an underlying legal theory, such suits can be filed.

For example, a California cheerleading coach was sued by a student who alleged his failure to make the squad resulted from the coach changing his high score. The student's family sought damages and the coach's dismissal, alleging the coach sabotaged the student's cheerleading chances (Taylor, Jr., & Thomas, 2003). Another peculiar lawsuit involved a volunteer youth league baseball coach who was sued by a player's father after the team's winless season. The suit alleged the coach's incompetence cost the team a trip to an out-of-state tournament. Other frivolous suits have involved innocuous situations in which a coach benched a player during a critical hockey game, two baton twirlers were cut from a high school majorette program, and an athlete was placed on a junior varsity instead of a varsity team (Asquith, 2002)

What does this mean for prospective sport or recreation managers? In order to avoid lawsuits or adequately address lawsuits—whether meritorious or not—future managers need to learn as much about the law as possible. Lawsuits are time-consuming and expensive, regardless of whether a judgment is ever rendered against an individual or organization. Therefore, this chapter will seek to help you understand the law and use it as a tool to help prevent litigation or lessen its consequences.

In preparing for a sport or recreation industry career, students also need to utilize the law as a guide to draft better organizational policies and procedures. Better policies and procedures make such organizations safer and more hospitable environments for internal (employees) and external (clients, customers, athletes) constituencies. The law is, of course, only the starting point for having an ethical organization but we need to use the law well to have a firm foundation in building a well run and ethical sport organization. (See Chapter 5–Ethics and Ethical Decision Making.)

This chapter is intended to serve as an introduction to legal theory in order for sport managers to function effectively. Because of space limitations, the emphasis will primarily focus upon **negligence law**, contract law, and constitutional law, with a brief mention made of other pertinent topics. Since the law is continually evolving, it is critical sport managers consistently update their sport-law knowledge.

Negligence Law

A part of tort law dealing with unintentional conduct that falls below a standard established by law for the protection of others against unreasonable risk of harm.

Negligence

Negligence is conduct that "falls below the standard established by law for the protection of others against unreasonable risk of harm" [Restatement (Second) Torts §282]. Negligence is an **unintentional tort** (a civil wrong other than a breach of contract) so it is at the other end of the "intent spectrum" from **intentional torts** such as battery and assault. In a negligence action, the defendant (the party alleged to have committed the wrongdoing) has allegedly acted in an unreasonable fashion, but did not *intend* to commit the act or to cause harm. In most negligence cases, the plaintiff alleges the defendant acted in a careless or inadvertent fashion; however, this conduct is far removed from conduct in which a defendant intended to commit the act and to cause harm. Such intentional acts by a defendant often lead to **punitive damages** being awarded [an award of punitive damages goes beyond **compensatory** (actual) damages sustained by a party. Punitive damages try to deter such conduct from happening again.]

In order for a plaintiff to successfully proceed with a negligence cause of action, four elements must all co-exist. These elements are: (1) duty; (2) breach of duty; (3) causation; and (4) damages. Each of these elements will be discussed below.

Duty

The first element necessary for a successful negligence case is **duty**, which means that the defendant must have some obligation, imposed by law, to protect the plaintiff (the party who commences the lawsuit) from unreasonable risk. Duty is a question of law for the court to ascertain and is a foundational issue. The legal concept of duty is based on policy considerations that lead courts to determine a particular plaintiff is entitled to protection. Fundamentally, absent duty, there is no cause of action for negligence.

In most of this chapter's cases, the duty of care is quite evident. Some examples of a duty of care are between K-12 teacher/coach and student-athlete, or facility owner and spectator. In a K-12 setting, the duty arises based on the concept of *in loco parentis* (in the place of the parents). Schools have custodial and tutelary responsibilities for the minors in their care. The duty between facility owner and spectator arises based on the facility owner selling the spectator a ticket.

Breach of Duty

There is a **breach of duty** if the defendant has failed to meet the required **standard of care**. The court ascertains the standard of care by asking this question, "What would a reasonably prudent person have been expected to do in the same or similar circumstances?" The law of negligence is closely tied to factual circumstances. There can be no breach of duty in the abstract; whether a breach of duty exists is always relative to particular circumstances.

To assist in this determination, courts have developed an objective standard, the **reasonably prudent person**. This hypothetical person is the legal standard to which an actual defendant is held. If a defendant's actions are consistent with those of the reasonably prudent person, then the defendant has not breached the duty of care; thus, element number two of the cause of action is not met. However, if the defendant's actions fall below what would have been expected of the reasonably prudent person, then the defendant has breached the duty of care.

If the defendant possesses knowledge that is superior to an ordinary person, then the defendant is accountable for care that would be reasonable in light of such special skills, knowledge, or training. Thus, a coach with a master's degree in physical education, who has coached for 10 years, and who has special certifications pertinent to coaching will be held to a standard of care based on that special skill and knowledge.

Since jury members most likely do not have the expertise to ascertain the standard of care on their own, how do they decide what the reasonably prudent person should have been expected to do in a particular context? In an attempt to convince the jury of the applicable standard of care in a particular circumstance, the parties to a lawsuit use expert witnesses. In many cases, the plaintiff's expert witnesses may disagree with expert witnesses called by the defendant. It is up to the jury to decide which expert(s) to believe, since such belief is a question of fact, which is within the jury's purview.

Causation

The third element of a negligence cause of action is **causation**, which involves whether there is a "causal connection" between the breach of duty and the resulting injury. This is known as "proximate cause" which encompasses the notion of causation in fact and the policy question of whether a court should hold someone accountable for an injury based on the notion of **foreseeability**.

The presence of wet floors can breach the duty of care owed. If an injury were to occur as a result of the floor, the injured party may sue for damages.

Causation looks at whether a particular outcome would have occurred even if the breach of duty had not occurred. The concept is that if something would have occurred anyway, then the breach of duty cannot be said to have caused the outcome.

In addressing causation, courts also look to the question of proximate causation, which goes to the issue of whether the defendant should be legally responsible for the injury, even if there was causation in fact. This issue is primarily a question of law for a court to address, and often relates to the question of foreseeability. This means that courts often decide that the scope of liability should only extend to those risks that are foreseeable.

Damages

Damages, the final element of negligence, means that some actual loss or damage must have been sustained as a result of the breach of duty. The threat of future harm is not sufficient damage. In a negligence case, successful plaintiffs typically are awarded compensatory damages, which are designed to compensate the victim for such things as medical bills, lost wages, and pain and suffering. However, as was noted earlier, in cases where the defendant may have acted intentionally, the court may also award punitive damages to punish the defendant and send a message that this type of behavior will not be tolerated.

Defenses against Negligence

The defendant's first strategy is always to argue that one or more of the elements of the cause of action have not been established. Once cause-of-action elements have been established, the question becomes whether the defendant, in whole or in part, can avoid liability. The most common negligence defenses are discussed below.

Statute of Limitations

The defense that a cause of action has not been filed in a timely fashion is known as the **statute of limitations**. This defense is procedural, not substantive. This means that, regardless of the merits of the plaintiff's case, the cause of action may be dismissed if the complaint has not been filed in a timely manner. Each state has legislation that provides the time period for bringing a certain cause of action. If the action is not brought within that designated time period, usually the action will be dismissed.

Act of God

Act of God as a defense means that a person has no liability when an unforeseeable natural disaster resulted in injury to the plaintiff; the defendant's negligence did not cause the injury. There are two aspects to this defense that must co-exist. First, there must truly be an Act of God (i.e., some natural disaster like a storm, lightning, earthquake, flood, or hurricane) that caused the injury. Second, this Act of God must be unforeseeable. If it is foreseeable the defendant may still have liability since the defendant did not act reasonably in protecting participants from the disaster.

Contributory and Comparative Negligence

As previously discussed the hypothetical reasonably prudent person concept sets the standard in determining whether the defendant breached the duty of care. With **contributory negligence**, the question involves whether the plaintiff acted in a manner expected of a reasonably prudent plaintiff. We use the reasonably prudent plaintiff hypothetical to determine what the plaintiff should have done in a particular circumstance to protect his/her own safety. If the plaintiff's conduct falls below the standard of care, then the plaintiff is said to be **contributorily negligent**. If a court uses **contributory negligence**, any unreasonable conduct by the plaintiff precludes the plaintiff from recovering any damages.

The rule of contributory negligence is rather harsh, since any negligence by the plaintiff completely bars recovery. Therefore, most states have adopted the rule of **comparative negligence**. Utilizing this rule, the court compares any negligence by the plaintiff to the degree of negligence by the defendant. The court typically then allocates potential damages based upon the degree to which the plaintiff's negligence contributed to the action.

Assumption of Risk

Assumption of risk is the defense that is most prevalently discussed in terms of physical activity and sport. Assumption of risk is frequently discussed as either being primary or secondary, and these distinctions are important.

Primary

Primary assumption of risk means that a plaintiff understands and voluntarily agrees to accept an activity's **inherent risks**. If a plaintiff is "coerced" into attempting an activity, there is no assumption of risk. The inherent risks of an activity are obvious and necessary to its being conducted. For instance, baseball-game participants expect that baseballs may be thrown or hit at a high velocity, or that players may slide into a base while an opponent is trying to make a play. With primary assumption of risk, the defendant has no duty of care toward the plaintiff, since the plaintiff agrees to assume or accept risks that are common to that activity. The plaintiff is not agreeing, however, to accept risks that are beyond those inherent in the activity. In other words, the plaintiff does not assume the risk of the negligence on the part of a coach or instructor. Let's look at this concept in conjunction with a particular activity—skydiving.

When landing in a field at the end of a jump, a skydiver breaks his ankle. This injury is an inherent risk of skydiving, since some impact with the ground is both obvious and necessary for the activity. There is no way to land without risk; sometimes the force of landing may cause a broken or sprained ankle. Likewise, perhaps the wind came up suddenly after the jump was made and the skydiver was injured because he could not avoid a tree. This is another inherent risk that must be assumed by a skydiver.

However, what if the skydiver is killed because neither of his parachutes opened? Is the parachute's failure an inherent risk? Is this failure an obvious and necessary risk of the activity? The answer to both questions is "No" because the parachute not opening was caused by the negligence of the person who packed the chute or by the chute's malfunction. In either case, these are not risks assumed by the skydiver; they are risks beyond what the skydiver reasonably anticipated when he began the jump. In this scenario, there is no primary assumption of risk. The concept that the negligence of instructors is not an inherent risk of an activity is an important one.

Secondary

Secondary assumption of risk means a plaintiff deliberately chose to encounter a known risk and in doing so acted unreasonably. In many jurisdictions, the concept of secondary assumption of risk is subsumed within the concept of comparative negligence, discussed above. The underlying notion of secondary assumption of risk is the same as comparative negligence (i.e., the plaintiff acted unreasonably in behaving as he did).

Common Liability Issues Regarding Participants

Lack of Supervision

Many liability concerns relating to participant injuries occur because of supervision failures. Proper supervision means the persons entrusted with this responsibility are competent to oversee the participants (**quality of supervision**) and there are sufficient supervisors to fulfill the duty of care (**quantity of supervision**). The obligation to supervise does not mean there is a duty of instruction, but it does mean supervisors must be able to recognize and prevent or stop dangerous behaviors.

Quality of Supervision

The issue of quality of supervision addresses a supervisor's competence. Even if the supervisor-to-participant ratio is one-to-one, supervision may be inadequate if the supervisor does not have the competence or training to identify, prevent or intervene when dangerous behavior occurs. Possession of a heart beat and a warm body is not the equivalent of competent supervision; a supervisor must know enough about the activity in question to identify danger.

Quantity of Supervision

Supervision quantity involves determining whether there are sufficient competent supervisors relative to the number of participants, in other words, whether the ratio of supervisors to participants is reasonable.

Whether the ratio is proper is a question that cannot be answered in the abstract. There is no "magic number" for all occasions. The quantity of supervision is activity-specific. Obviously, an activity such as gymnastics presents more risk than table tennis. This would suggest a lower supervisor-to-gymnast ratio than with table tennis players. The age and maturity of the participants must also be considered. Generally, youthful participants require more supervisors. Also, if a particular group has shown a propensity to engage in rowdy behavior, this must be taken into consideration when determining the number of supervisors. If participants have physical or mental disabilities that make them more prone to injury, more supervisors will be necessary. In addition, there may sometimes be concerns with the facility/area in which an activity takes place. For example, more supervisors are necessary if participants are dispersed or because of facility/area configuration supervisors cannot maintain visual contact with all participants.

Supervisory plans should take into account all of the aforementioned principles. Further, supervisory plans should delineate not just the number of supervisors, but also the specific area of supervision. Designating specific supervision areas is necessary because, otherwise, supervisors may tend to cluster and talk with each other, leaving certain areas without supervisory coverage.

All of the above factors should be considered when making quantity of supervision decisions. Remember, the essential question remains, "What number of competent supervisors is reasonable in that setting, at that time?"

Getty Images

Activities such as gymnastics present greater risks for participants, and therefore require a greater number of supervisors, than many other sports.

Improper Instruction or Training

The question of proper instruction or training in the context of physical activity/sport has more severe liability concerns than in other educational contexts. If a coach fails to act reasonably when teaching a physical skill, serious consequences may ensue, including severe physical injury or death. The following discussion focuses on a number of critical instruction/training issues.

Adequacy of Instruction

In order for instruction to be deemed adequate, it must be suitable for the intended audience. The language used must be understandable to participants, based on their age and familiarity with the activity. Also, since verbal instruction of physical skills is often accompanied by physical demonstration, these elements must be congruent. If participants are relatively young and immature, important instructional concepts will need to be repeated more frequently than with a more mature audience. Also, minors tend to comprehend presented material very literally, so certain departures from instruction may be foreseeable.

Instructors/coaches should always follow training practices that have been widely accepted by activity experts. Courts will give great deference to the standards developed by persons or organizations that have expert knowledge about the activity. Caution should be utilized when developing drills or methods that vary from widely-accepted practices. Even though a certain method may appear to make sense, it should be widely endorsed before being implemented. Coaches and instructors should always attend professional workshops/seminars to ensure they are implementing the most current accepted practices.

Proper Skill Progression

In many cases, a culminating activity should not be attempted unless proper lead-up activities have been presented and practiced. Physical skills are often taught sequentially in order that a participant is properly prepared to engage in the culminating activity.

Dissemination of Safety Rules and Warnings

Part of learning any activity involves "knowing" what aspects are potentially dangerous. During instruction or training, safety rules and procedures should be discussed and reinforced on a frequent basis. The reason for safety rules should also be shared with participants. Every practice session should have some time devoted to safety rules/warnings pertinent to each activity. Participants should be consistently warned about an activity's risks and the adverse consequences of not following safety rules.

Mismatch

Obviously, competitive situations will almost always pit opponents who are not exactly equal in size, strength, or competency. But, in some cases, it is not reasonably prudent to allow competition between those who are so vastly different in size, strength or competency, since this could foreseeably result in injury beyond what is accepted as inherent to the activity. Often, a league or governing body may adopt formal guidelines to address such disparities. For example, youth-football age and/or weight restrictions are attempts to reasonably even the playing field. In some cases, participants may be equal in terms of size but there is a vast skill differential that makes it imprudent to match up particular opponents.

Safe Use of Equipment

Part of instructing or coaching an activity is providing necessary, proper and safe equipment. Since the courts do not view lack of funds as a legal defense, if participants cannot afford or be provided such equipment, the activity should not be continued. However, providing "necessary equipment" does not mean the essential equipment supplied must be "state-of-the-art." It means such essential equipment should reasonably meet participants' needs.

Protective equipment must be in good condition and fit properly. For example, a football helmet that is structurally sound but falls over a player's eyes does not meet the criterion of acceptable equipment. In addition, players should be taught how to properly fit equipment and how to inspect equipment prior to each use. Proper instruction in equipment use should also be given. Finally, if equipment is utilized in a nontraditional manner, information about how to use the equipment in that context should be provided.

Emergency Medical Care

Two major issues are associated with the provisions of emergency medical care to participants: (1) making sure that qualified personnel are available to render emergency first aid and CPR, and (2) ensuring that there is a protocol to get outside medical personnel to the site as quickly as possible.

Transportation

Transportation of participants is a critical function, which when assumed by an organization, must be provided in a reasonably safe manner. There are four primary issues related to transportation: (1) selection of competent drivers, (2) proper training of drivers, (3) selection of a safe mode of travel, and (4) proper maintenance of vehicles.

As has just been discussed, negligence is the failure to exercise the standard of care that a reasonably prudent person would have exercised in a similar situation. It is important for future sport managers to know and understand the elements of negligence and practice appropriate risk-management to prevent or mitigate individual or organizational exposure.

Overview of Contract Law

Knowing and applying **contract law** basics is an excellent vehicle by which organizations can gain managerial and operational benefits. Most contracts of any complexity are negotiated over a lengthy time period and there are usually multiple drafts before the final contract is signed. This provides adequate time

Contract Law_____
A promise or set of promises enforced by courts, which establish a duty to perform between parties.

for each party to reflect upon the potential agreement and consult with an attorney in order to arrive at a document that will best serve their interests.

Essentially, contract law is concerned with clarifying and enforcing all parties' wills in determining agreements. Courts are concerned with trying to give effect to each party's intent; courts do not try to rewrite contracts to make a better document for the parties or to make sure that each party has negotiated the best deal possible.

Any contract should be drafted from a **worst-case scenario** perspective. Contracts are simply reflections of human relationships and—as with all relationships—sometimes they may deteriorate. Consider the hiring of a college coach. When a coach is hired, generally everyone is ecstatic about the prospect of new "program" leadership. The last thing most people think about is the partnership's dissolution. However, coaching contracts are frequently breached, either by the college that wants the program to go in a "new direction" or by the coach who seeks the proverbial "greener pastures." Therefore, the coaching contract must be written with this reality in mind. The contract should be drafted to protect the interests of your organization in the event the contract is terminated by either party.

Formation of a Contract

"A **contract** is a promise or set of promises, for breach of which the law gives a remedy, or the performance of which the law in some way recognizes a duty" [Restatement (Second) Contracts, 1981, §1]. There are four fundamental aspects to the formation of a contract: (1) **Agreement**—offer and acceptance; (2) **Consideration**; (3) **Capacity**; and (4) **Legality**.

The formation of a contract begins with an **offer**, which is a conditional promise made to do or to refrain from doing something. For example, a person (**offeror**) may offer to sell a certain piece of fitness equipment for $400. This communicates the terms of the offer; one now knows the price of the equipment.

If a party agrees to the terms as stated, **acceptance** has been given. A promise is provided by the **offeree** to pay $400 when the equipment is delivered. If one does not mirror the offer with acceptance then the offeror is presented with a **counteroffer**. For example, if a potential buyer responded that she is only willing to pay $300 for the equipment, the initial offer has been rejected in favor of a counteroffer at $300.

Consideration involves the exchange of value. Even though there has been an exchange of promises (agreement) there can be no contract until there is an exchange of value (e.g., one party gives up something of value in exchange for the other party's value). Often, consideration takes the form of Y giving X money for a promise to do or provide something. Though there must be an exchange, the exchanged items do not need to be of equal value.

It is important to remember that if one promises to "pay" another person $100, and asks for nothing in exchange, there is no contract. All that has occurred is an unenforceable promise to make a gift of $100. However, if one agrees to pay $100 for a tennis racquet that is barely serviceable, there is consideration. Further, courts do not generally inquire as to whether the consideration was too little or too much. Since, as discussed above, a basic premise of contract law is to allow private parties to engage in transactions of their own making; courts will not generally intervene to stop a "bad deal" from taking place. Paying $100 for a much-abused racquet may be a bad choice; however, if the involved parties do so of their own volition and without any misrepresentations about the condition of the racquet, then the contract will be upheld. Sometimes people may make good deals and other times they may make bad deals; it is not the courts' prerogative to be intermediaries in consummated deals, only to ascertain if the law was followed.

Capacity means the parties to the contract are legally competent to enter into a contractual relationship. For example, minors are usually not bound by contracts, since the law makes a presumption that a minor lacks the legal competence (capacity) to enter into contracts. Thus, if a minor signs a contract, it is generally voidable at the option of the minor, that is, a minor can set aside any legal obligations stemming from that contract. There may be other circumstances affecting competence. For example, mental incompetence or intoxication may also result in a lack of capacity.

Legality means that, to be enforceable, the subject matter of the contract must not violate state or federal law. Since a contract that violates the law is—by definition—illegal, it is unenforceable. For example, since in most states it is illegal to bet on college sports, any gambling contract involving college sport betting would not be enforceable.

Contract Remedies

When one party fails to perform essential aspects of a contract, it is termed a **breach of contract**. Sometimes the breach may be remediable, but often the contract is terminated and the nonbreaching party is awarded damages as a result of the breach. In a contract case, a court is not attempting to punish the party that breached the contract; it is simply trying to compensate the innocent party for the loss of the bargain. Essentially, contract damages are designed to put the nonbreaching parties in the position they would have been if the contract had been performed as promised [Restatement (Second) Contracts, 1981, §347].

Compensatory Damages

In most contract cases, the nonbreaching party can be compensated for the loss of the bargain through monetary or compensatory damages. These damages arise directly from the loss of the bargain.

For example, let's assume a sporting-goods store agrees to sell X a football helmet for $125. X agrees to buy the helmet for that price, but the store then refuses to sell X the promised good. Not only is the store is in breach of the contract, but X still needs to obtain a helmet. Seeking a helmet, X goes to the two other stores in the area that sell that model of helmet and finds that Store A is selling the helmet for $135 and Store B is selling the helmet for $150. In this case X can collect damages from the first store. Let's examine what damages X can recover.

First, the general rule in a breach of a sales contract is the buyer can recover an amount equal to the difference between the contract and market price. In this case, however, there are two market prices, $135 and $150, for the same item. So can X recover $25 ($150 market price from Store B-$125 contract price) or only $10 ($135 market price from Store A-$125 contract price)? Assuming the item is identical, X's damages are limited to $10. According to the principle of **mitigation of damages**, a nonbreaching party must act reasonably to lessen the consequences of the breach. In this case, X must choose to buy the item for the lesser price of $135 ($10 damages). This obligation to reduce the damages, if possible, is not absolute. X does not have to get bids on this helmet from every vendor in the United States, just to deal with the vendors usually dealt with regarding this type of equipment.

The principle of mitigation of damages applies to all types of contracts, but may be more difficult to implement than in a sales-contract scenario. For example, if a university breaches its employment contract with a coach, the coach is obligated to mitigate damages by accepting a comparable offer of employment if offered by another university. The coach, however, would not have to accept employment that was inferior in compensation, level of competition, geographic location, and so on, just to lessen the damages; that would not be expected as a part of the duty to mitigate.

Specific Performance

In certain rare circumstances, monetary damages will not suffice because the object of the contract is unique. If an item is truly unique no matter what a breaching party pays, money damages will not compensate for the loss of the bargain because the item cannot be purchased on the open market. For example, if the owner of a uniform worn by Babe Ruth in a particular game against the Cleveland Indians agrees to sell the uniform for $30,000—and then later breaches the contract—**specific performance** is the appropriate remedy. This will force the breaching party to fulfill the terms of the contract (i.e., sell the jersey for $30,000).

This remedy cannot be used with personal-services contracts, however. If Kobe Bryant wanted to breach his employment contract with the *Los Angeles Lakers,* the franchise could not force Kobe to play by arguing specific performance (his playing) was necessary. Courts will not force someone to compete against his will, though they would likely prevent Bryant from playing for another National Basketball Association (NBA) team. Even if Bryant could be forced to play for the Lakers, it would be difficult to ascertain if his performance was of his highest ability.

Liquidated Damages and Penalty Provisions

Sometimes the amount of damages that should be paid cannot be exactly determined. Although contract damages cannot be mere speculation, sometimes parties do have to approximate the anticipated amount of sustained damages. For example, employment contracts often contain such an approximated provision because the parties cannot determine exact damages resulting from the breach. Therefore, when negotiating the contract, parties agree to a **liquidated damages** provision that establishes a reasonable approximation of damages. Care must be taken in drafting the liquidated damages provision because courts do not uphold **penalty provisions** that do not bear a reasonable relationship to damages to be sustained and are simply punishing a party for breaching a contract. Courts will not uphold such provisions, nor will they award **punitive damages**, unless there is some fraudulent behavior.

Constitutional Law

Though negligence and contract law are likely to be applicable in many sport management settings, **Constitutional Law** may be applied more often in specific sport industry segments. Some potential constitutional law issues that may arise include:

Constitutional Law_____
The underlying document of the U.S. government, which sets forth limits on governmental power.

- Does a public school district have the right to implement a random drug-testing policy for its athletes?
- Can a public school coach refuse to allow an athlete to miss practice in order to attend religious worship services?
- What are the limits on free speech that a public university may impose upon one of its coaches?
- If a college player at a state university is suspended from some games due to a disciplinary matter, does the player have a right to have an attorney present at the disciplinary hearing?

The United States **Constitution** sets forth our federal government's basic principles and sets up the limits of governmental power versus individual rights. Essentially, constitutional law provides the framework within which our government can restrict citizens' personal autonomy.

For a plaintiff to make a case that one or more of his/her constitutional rights have been violated, the defendant must be a **state actor**. A state actor is defined as an entity that is directly an arm of the federal, state, or local government, or given authority to act on behalf of the government. Therefore, a constitutional claim cannot be made against a private person or entity (though other areas of law may apply). For example, if a person who owns a private fitness club attempts to fire an employee for negative statements made while on the job, that employee cannot claim the owner violated his First Amendment rights of free speech. The defendant in this case is a private individual—not a state actor—so no constitutional claim can be made.

First Amendment Claims

The **First Amendment** to the Constitution outlines a number of concepts that are foundational to our society. For example, the First Amendment contains both the **Establishment Clause** and the **Free Exercise Clause**. These clauses both deal with religion. The Establishment Clause protects citizens from government's trying to establish a "state" religion; the underlying sentiment is the government should remain neutral on religious matters. The Free Exercise Clause protects our rights to choose and follow our individual religious beliefs.

First amendment disputes involving the intersection of religion and sport might include the degree to which prayer may be permitted as a prelude to a public school football contest, whether a coach at a public university or school may lead his team in prayer before a game, whether a Jewish student (who attends a public high school) may be prevented from wearing a yarmulke when playing basketball, whether a public school sport team nicknamed "Devils" must be forced to change its name, and whether a person who wore a pentagram pendant honoring her religious beliefs can be forced to take it off in order to attend a public school basketball game.

The First Amendment also has a **Freedom of Expression Clause**, which protects expressive activity (like wearing a "protest" armband or certain styles of dress) and speech. Relative to sport participants, such disputes center on whether the self-expression was valuable communication under the First Amendment and what interest the state actor (school or university) had in limiting the speech or expressive activity. In employment situations, the courts look at whether the employee is speaking on a matter of public concern, and balance such public concern against whether the employer's business would be adversely affected by the speech. As an examination of case law reveals, courts frequently utilize balancing tests in constitutional law decisions.

Fourth Amendment Claims

The **Fourth Amendment**, which protects against unreasonable searches and seizures, is often used to assert that drug-testing protocols implemented by public schools or universities to test athletes are unconstitutional. In such cases, a balancing test is also used. Essentially, an individual's privacy expectation and the degree of intrusion posed by the test are balanced against governmental interest in conducting the test. In the case of *Vernonia School District 47J v. Acton* (1995), the United States Supreme Court upheld a random drug-testing policy implemented by a public school district to test its high school athletes. The Court characterized the degree of intrusion in the test as minimal and found the athletes had diminished privacy expectations. On the other side of the balance, the school district had an important interest in stopping drug use, which had reached epidemic proportions among its high school athletes.

Fifth and Fourteenth Amendment Claims

The **Fifth and Fourteenth Amendments** set forth that a **state actor** must provide fair treatment in any governmental decision that affects a person's life, liberty, or property. This is the concept of **due process**. However, before a due-process claim is heard on its merits, the plaintiff has to establish three points: (1) the defendant is a state actor; (2) the plaintiff is a "person"; and (3) the defendant somehow infringed upon a life, liberty, or property interest.

For example, let's look at a situation in which a state university football player has been suspended for a few games for allegedly breaking a team disciplinary rule. The player claims his due process rights were violated because he did not have a fair hearing during which to contest the allegations against him. However, before a court will actually deal with these claims, it will determine whether the plaintiff has established the three points above. In this case there is state action, since the defendant is a state university. However, while the plaintiff is a person, the question is whether the plaintiff has an affected property interest (life or liberty is not at stake here). In such instances, the courts have held sport participation alone is not a property interest. So, unless the university stripped the athlete of a current grant-in-aid (GIA), the plaintiff cannot continue with his case, since he does not have a property interest involved. An interesting Texas Supreme Court case on this point is *NCAA v. Yeo* (2005).

Other Areas of Sport Law

There are many other areas of law relevant to the sport industry and being a sport manager. As you continue your sport management education you will take courses that focus on specific sport industry functional areas. Such courses may include concentrated study in sport marketing, facility management, event management, sport finance, sport economics, and sport sales and sponsorship. In addition, you will undoubtedly take a sport law course, in which you will examine in greater detail a number of legal theories and representative legal issues. See Table 6.1 for a listing of such issues.

Courtesy Mark Nagel

The Raiders have been involved in numerous lawsuits regarding their 1982 move to Los Angeles and their return to the Oakland Alameda County Coliseum in 1995.

TABLE 6.1

Legal Theory	Representative Legal Issue
Antitrust Law	Relocation of a professional sport franchise
Employment Law—Wrongful Discharge	Employee fired without cause
Negligent Misrepresentation	Erroneous information in employment reference
Tortious Interference with Contractual Relations	Recruiting away employee with existing contract
Title VII (a federal statute)	Discrimination in employment on the basis of race or sex Sexual harassment in the workplace
Equal Pay Act (a federal statute)	Unequal compensation of male v. female coaches
Vicarious Liability	Is the employer liable for the negligence of the employee?
Fair Labor Standards Act (a federal statute)	Working conditions issue relating to wages and hours
Workers' Compensation (state statutes)	Employer liability for injuries to employees
National Labor Relations Act (a federal statute)	Collective bargaining and professional teams
Uniform Athlete Agents Act (adopted by a number of states)	Regulation of sports agents
Title IX (a federal statute)	Gender equity issues relating to high school and college athletics
Americans with Disabilities Act (a federal statute)	Sport facility accessibility for the disabled
Products Liability	Liability for defective sports equipment
Waivers	Can a whitewater rafting company excuse itself from its own negligence?
Intentional Tort (assault & battery)	Participant violence
Trademark and Copyright Law	Rights to intellectual property like team logos or products
Tax Law	Should the NCAA be entitled to nonprofit status?

Conclusion

In conclusion, this chapter has been a brief introduction to the wide spectrum of sport law. Sport law is woven into every aspect of managerial practice in the sport industry. While this chapter was only a brief discussion of fundamental issues pertaining to negligence law, contracts and constitutional law, it has provided a glimpse into the legal aspects of sport and recreation. As you will learn as you continue your sport management education, there are many areas of the law relevant to the sport and recreation industries. Hopefully, your future sport law class will provide essential information for your sport industry managerial career.

CHAPTER

Interview

INTERVIEW 6.1

Scott Bearby

Associate General Counsel/Managing Director of Legal Affairs National Collegiate Athletic Association; Adjunct professor of law at Indiana University School of Law.

This interview was conducted and the transcript provided by Lori Braa (PhD student in the sport administration program at the University of Northern Colorado). Ms. Braa has extensive experience in the administration of intercollegiate athletics, including employment at the National Collegiate Athletic Association (NCAA).

Education
Undergraduate degree from the University of Notre Dame; J.D. from Indiana University.

Career
Joining the NCAA as in-house counsel in 1999, Bearby has served as associate general counsel/managing director of legal affairs since December 2001. He serves as primary counsel for the Men's and Women's Division I Basketball Championships, and also works primarily with NCAA contract and rights issues, including traditional media, new media, marketing, licensing and promotional rights, and championship-related agreements. He also serves as counsel on intellectual property matters and on the NCAA's crisis assessment team. Bearby advises the NCAA on the creation of subsidiary entities and asset acquisitions. He is an officer in the NCAA's limited liability companies that house the NIT tournament assets, eligibility center services, college football officiating, and March Madness intellectual property.

Q: How did you get into the industry? What was your career path?

A: After graduation, I worked for a small firm in litigation and then moved over to business litigation and business transactions. At the time partnership was offered to me, I looked at what I wanted to do long-term and thought about using my skill set as counsel in higher education and/or as an educator. The NCAA needed a business and intellectual property counsel, so I was attracted to that position. I also have been able to fulfill my desire to teach as an adjunct professor teaching sport law.

Q: What are you looking for in new hires, beyond a law degree, if you were hiring at the NCAA?

139

A: The NCAA has four practicing lawyers, so turnover is infrequent. Our legal staff all had previous legal experience (at least 5 years). The legal department does have an intern program. In those candidates, we look for their relevant experience within college athletics, either as an athlete or as a volunteer within the athletic department. We also look for their enthusiasm in expressing how they would maximize the unique opportunity to be a law clerk at the NCAA national office.

Within the national office (and college athletics generally), there are many people with law degrees who are using that education and legal experience outside of the practice of law. There are J.D.s in virtually every department, including enforcement/infractions, compliance, and governance. Today, many conference commissioners and athletic directors have J.D.s, and that number continues to increase.

Q: What are the biggest challenges and issues in college sport, from your role as a lawyer, for the near future and beyond?

A: In all of our legislation, policy decisions, and business transactions, the NCAA and our membership need to remain consistent in upholding the principle of amateurism as we define it and not as external entities perceive it to be.

More specific to my practice is the need to stay aware of advancements in technology and new media that influence how the competitions are played and consumed. The law struggles to keep pace with these advancements in addressing issues with regard to social media whether it is a podcast, blogs, Twitter or other forms of communication.

Q: If you had a message to future athletic administrators, from your experience and your expertise as a lawyer, what would it be?

A: Be creative in your job search. Look for the law firms who represent clients that are behind the scenes in the athletic space, including sponsors, stadium vendors, and operators. By gaining experience and connections in that environment, you are going to be much more marketable to a professional sports property, an athletic department, or another sports entity if that is your eventual goal.

Working in sports as a lawyer definitely can create opportunities to attend events and meet interesting people. However, those privileges should not be the primary reason for seeking a career in that space. One has to have a passion for what the client does and to help the client achieve its goals, but counsel must be grounded in reasonable interpretations of the law.

Study Questions

1. What are the elements of negligence? Define and discuss each.
2. What is the difference between primary assumption of the risk and secondary assumption of the risk?
3. Discuss a number of aspects of competent instruction or training. Give examples of poor instruction in a sport or physical activity of your choice.
4. Explain the concepts of agreement, consideration, capacity, and legality in the formation of contracts.
5. What is the usual remedy in breach of contract actions? When can you use the remedy of specific performance?
6. What is the principle of mitigation of damages?
7. What is the concept of state action? Why is it crucial to any constitutional law claim?
8. What three fundamental aspects must a plaintiff establish before a court will hear a due process claim on its merits?

Learning Activities

1. Read *USA Today's* daily sports pages or visit its sport web pages for a week and identify disputes related to sport law. How many different kinds of legal issues can you identify?
2. Read the following scenario and then answer the questions relating to this example of a case based in negligence.

> Robert Smith is the manager of Fitness World, a corporation that owns a small health and fitness facility. The facility has a weight room, a gymnasium, and a running track. Aerobics classes are offered at this facility. Smith has decided to begin a karate program.
>
> In an effort to more quickly generate and collect class fees, Smith advertises that classes will begin one month from today. He also begins to search for a karate instructor. Unfortunately, qualified karate instructors are in short supply. As the day for the first class approaches, Mr. Smith hires Ron Jones to serve as a karate instructor. Mr. Jones, although an imposing physical specimen and a former weightlifting champion, has virtually no martial arts training. In college, he took one judo class, but has never formally or informally studied karate. Against this backdrop, the karate class begins with Jones as the instructor.
>
> After about twenty hours of instruction (at Mr. Jones' direction) students engaged in a "free fight" situation. In one of the matches Mr. Jones directed John Jackson, a novice whose only experience in karate was the twenty hours of Fitness World class instruction, to spar with Tommy Tough, an advanced student of karate who held a Brown Belt. During the course of this "free fight," Jackson was kicked in the head by Tough and sustained severe injuries. During the course of this "free fight," Jones was talking with another Fitness World employee and was not—in any way—supervising the Jackson-Tough duo.
>
> There are a number of very credible experts in the field of karate who will testify that it is a recognized principle of good practice among karate instructors not to permit a student with minimal training to engage in a "free fight" situation.

Questions

1. Mr. Jackson has indicated he intends to file suit against Jones and Smith in regard to the foregoing incident. Discuss the elements of negligence and then discuss the allegations of negligence that Jackson's attorney would use as the basis of the suit. Based on the given facts, **present and explain as many possible** bases of negligence as you can identify.
2. What defenses are available to Jones and Smith in regard to each allegation of negligence? Discuss the applicability of each to the facts at hand.

References

Asquith, C. (2002, November 11). Sue the coach! *Sports Illustrated,* 21.

Garberinio, R. P. (1994). So you want to be a sports lawyer, or is it a player agent, player representative, sports agent, contract advisor, or contract representative? *Villanova Sports & Entertainment Law Forum, 1,*11.

National Collegiate Athletic Ass'n v. Yeo, 171 S.W.3d 863 (Tex. 2005).

Restatement (Second) Contracts (1981).

Restatement (Second) Torts (1965).

Taylor, S., Jr., & Thomas, E. (2003, December 15). Civil wars. *Newsweek, 142,* 42–53.

Vernonia Sch. Dist. 47J v. Acton, 115 S. Ct. 2386 (1995).

CHAPTER 7

Strategic Management

Deborah A. Yow • *North Carolina State*[1]
William W. Bowden • *Strategic Management Consultants*

After reading this chapter, you will be able to:

- List and discuss the management functions common to most organizations and enterprises;
- Compare and contrast sport-business enterprises, including intercollegiate athletics departments, to other kinds of business organizations;
- Identify expected positive organizational outcomes from systematic and strategic planning;
- Explain the importance of developing a strategic plan;
- Examine the University of Maryland Strategic Plan case study in order to identify the scope, sequence, and results of strategic planning;
- Identify the University of Maryland athletics "Mission Statement and Guiding Principles" document's role as a resource in developing the department's strategic plan;
- Delineate the use of a performed S.W.O.T. analysis as an integral element in the development of a strategic plan.

[1] At the time she authored this chapter, Deborah Yow was at the University of Maryland.

KEY TERM

SWOT Analysis

The future doesn't just happen—it's shaped by decisions.

—Paul Tagliabue

Introduction

In order to manage a sport enterprise, it is important to first understand a sport enterprise's unique organizational profile. Similar to other businesses, professional sport franchises and college athletic departments involve management functions such as staffing, payroll, purchasing, contracts, planning, budgeting and finance, marketing, and other functions. However, many sport organizations are also uniquely structured enterprises that utilize specialized processes. This is especially true of intercollegiate athletics programs that (1) are departments within an institution of higher education, (2) depend on unique funding formulas, (3) require specialized facilities and support staff, (4) have multi-dimensional missions, and (5) function within a large and varied stakeholder context. As a result, sport enterprises usually require a specialized management model.

While this chapter examines the strategic-planning process utilizing the structure and operation of a National Collegiate Athletic Association (NCAA) Football Bowl Subdivision (FBS) athletic department, as sport-management students continue their education, they would be well advised to closely examine the unique aspects of a wide variety of sport organizations and various industry segments. Such examination is common practice among today's successful sport managers. While this chapter utilizes a single case-study in order to highlight elements of strategic management, students who wish to work in sport should analyze a variety of professional-sport franchises, sport-marketing firms, hospitality and event-management companies, and so on, to better prepare themselves for a sport-management career. Learning and practicing such strategic analysis on a consistent basis will help students to bridge the gap between theory and real-world practice.

A NCAA FBS athletic-department's organizational chart reflects its specialized management model. Many athletic departments' organizational charts delineate similar functional areas. Figure 7.1 contains the University of Maryland athletics department basic organizational structure. You will notice each department member has a direct report above the name. This organizational structure is designed to allow information to flow from the bottom of the organization to the top with little crossover between different functional areas. Other organizations may allow more functional-area interaction without the information needing to flow to "higher" organizational levels. For additional information on the University of Maryland's Intercollegiate Athletics, see Appendix I and Appendix II at the end of this chapter.

Though the chart details Maryland's athletic department structure, it does not include the University of Maryland's overall reporting structure. In most cases, an athletic director will report to a university vice-president for student affairs, a president, or a chancellor. Despite

The University of Maryland Athletic Department has utilized strategic management decisions to improve the quality of its teams and its overall financial performance.

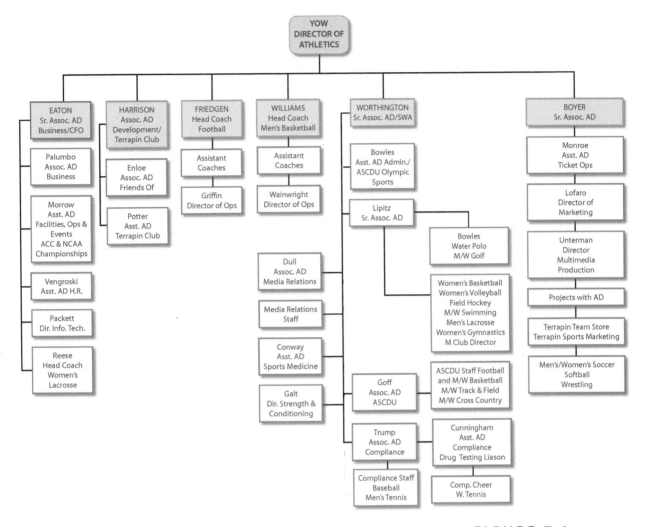

FIGURE 7.1

University of Maryland ICA Organization Chart.

the athletic department reporting to higher administration, some observers of "big-time" college athletics perceive the athletic department as being a "separate" entity with a distinct mission and operating guidelines from the rest of the academic units on campus. A long-standing and compelling debate continues on many college campuses regarding the scope and purpose of athletics programs. The fundamental questions typically asked include:

1. Are athletic departments primarily education programs?
2. Or, are they businesses unrelated to universities' educational mission?
3. Are athletic departments in the entertainment business?
4. Are the increasing financial and human resources necessary to sustain a major athletic program compatible with universities' educational mission? and
5. What exactly are athletic departments and what are their authentic missions?

While each of these questions must be asked and openly discussed by athletic-department members at all NCAA institutions, this is especially true at the NCAA Division I level. Due to increased economic pressures, the intensity with which these questions are being asked by the media, members of Congress, and the general public continues to increase.

Recognizing college sport's disparate nature, throughout this chapter an athletic department will be referred to an enterprise, a word that—in its generic sense—can embrace any or all of the organizational elements discussed.

The Function of Management

The function of management is continually addressed in myriad articles, books, and Internet entries. The basic functions are generally understood to be mission-casting, planning, staffing, goal-setting, assessing, controlling, spurring innovation, optimizing productivity, and integrating an organization's goals and operations. Drucker (1994) postulated three essential management tasks, which, by their scope and nature, serve as the foundation for an enterprise's effective functioning:

1. Establishing the specific purpose and mission of the entity,
2. Optimizing employee productivity consistent with the organization's mission and purpose, and
3. Managing the enterprise's social impacts and responsibilities.

These functions are not performed in isolation, but rather coexist and coalesce into "getting things done through and with people."

Chelladurai (2005) outlined four management functions:

1. Planning,
2. Organizing,
3. Leading, and
4. Evaluating.

Consistent with Drucker and Chelladurai's management descriptions, this chapter will highlight management functions focused on planning, organizing, and evaluating. One step in this management process involves formalizing mission statements, goals, and objectives; determining and insuring efficiency; minimizing problems; and facilitating employee efficiency.

As was discussed in Chapter 9—Sport-Sales and Revenue Generation—it is critical all organizational members are aware of and understand the organization's overriding philosophy and mission. As part of continuously reviewing and re-articulating the organization's philosophy and mission, members will periodically conduct an organizational analysis. This analysis is often termed a **SWOT** (Strengths, Weaknesses, Opportunities, and Threats) **analysis**. Awareness of an organization's SWOT assists in developing overall long-term goals consistent with the organization's espoused philosophy and mission.

SWOT Analysis_____

A strategic-planning tool used to evaluate an organization's Strengths, Weaknesses, Opportunities, and Threats.

BOX 7.1

What Is a SWOT Analysis?

A SWOT Analysis is a strategic-planning tool used to evaluate an organization's (as well as specific objectives an organization wishes to achieve) Strengths, Weaknesses, Opportunities, and Threats. This process involves identifying favorable and unfavorable internal and external factors specific to the organization and its goals and objectives.

In order to conduct a SWOT analysis, desired goals and objectives must also be identified. A SWOT analysis is utilized in the strategic-planning process and often incorporated into the strategic-planning model.

- **Strengths:** Positive *internal* organizational attributes helpful to the organization in achieving objectives.
- **Weaknesses:** *Internal* organizational attributes detrimental to the organization or objectives.
- **Opportunities:** *External* conditions helpful to the organization achieving objectives.
- **Threats:** *External* conditions which could damage the organization and prevent achieving objectives.

Identification of SWOTs is an essential first step in the strategic-planning process, because subsequent steps are often derived from uncovered information.

An organization's mission statement should succinctly and articulately express the organization's core beliefs and values. In the best of all possible worlds, it should reflect "the way we do things around here." In other words, the mission statement should reflect the organizational culture. (See Chapter 2: Socio-Cultural Aspects of Sport.) If organizational members know and "buy into" the espoused philosophy, values, and mission, long-term goal development is much more likely to occur. Such goals are broad, qualitative statements, designed to provide general direction to an organization.

Measurable benchmarks of performance are often referred to as organizational objectives. Objectives are quantifiable, and are often short-term in nature (e.g., each month, season, quarter, or year). Objectives are, however, tied to specific goals. In other words, objectives are methods of measuring the achievement of goals. Quite often goals and objectives are used interchangeably. However, while the semantics is not crucial, the ability to measure the stated goal or objective is paramount.

Once objectives have been delineated, a manager is responsible for development of specific tactics—how-to-steps—that provide a scope and sequence to perform the necessary critical steps to achieve the objectives. Tactical development includes identifying the critical tasks necessary to achieve objectives. In many managerial settings critical-task analysis involves developing checklists and determining in which order tasks must be completed. It does no good to develop tasks if they are not arranged in the proper sequence. In addition to developing specific tasks, explicit identified roles must be assigned. In order to get things done through people, the people must know and accept their roles. Development of organizational units/functional-areas and specific member's roles within these areas/units is critically important. This process is often referred to as the organizing function. Just as objectives must be measurable, so, too, roles must be explicitly outlined and expected observable and measurable behaviors should be outlined.

Finally, management involves an ongoing evaluation of all elements of the strategic management processes outlined above. The organization's mission and philosophy must inform all steps in the process. When problems occur, organizational members must understand and refer to the organization's overarching philosophy. A franchise or program's success is measured not only on the playing field or court, but also at the box office, concession stands, and merchandise store. If members of the organization do not know or believe in the organization's overall mission, it becomes much more likely that deviations from the established rules will occur when short-term problems arise. The remainder of this chapter will highlight the strategic-planning process and will outline strategic planning in sport management.

The Importance of the Strategic-Planning Process and an Explicit Strategic Plan in Sport Management

An added consideration in the management of sport enterprises, particularly in intercollegiate athletics, is the elevated stress level that often permeates the organization (Humphrey, Yow, and Bowden, 2000). Such stress may result from the highly competitive nature of college sport and the close public scrutiny that accompanies many decisions in sport management. In addition, it has been contended such stress reflects the existence of competing institutional logics (See Chapter 2: Socio-Cultural Aspects of Sport) within big-time college sport.

This chapter's essential topic is *strategic* management in a sport-industry setting. Through the use of a case-study approach, this chapter will outline the development of a comprehensive and detailed strategic plan as the basis for the strategic management of a college athletic department.

Just as a thoroughly-researched and well-developed game plan is the foundation of a winning athletic team, an appropriate and comprehensive strategic plan is the foundation for effective organizational decision-making. While in this chapter we focus primarily on the strategic planning process and the generation of a strategic plan document for an intercollegiate athletic department, the strategic-management principles and perspectives outlined above are applicable to any sport business.

A strategic plan is essential for a sport organization's success. Sound strategic planning will result in the following strategic-management outcomes:

1. A multi-year written plan to which most organizational members are committed.
2. A sense of organizational enthusiasm.
3. A specific set of measurable objectives that provide direction and guidance to the entire organization.
4. Clear job duties and responsibilities.
5. The ability of organizational leaders to pursue management functions essential for organizational success.

6. Clear staff member improvement guidelines.
7. The ability to measure (both annually and at the end of their careers) the growth and contributions of all staff members.
8. An in-place and understood written strategic plan will better insure leadership continuity and increased institutional memory, and effectively guide the organization's continued growth and development.

Planning and goal-setting are fundamental to any successful sport organization. This is especially true for sport organizations in challenging economic times. With competition for resources growing at daunting rates, and pressures to win at all-time highs, the need for strategic planning in sport organizations has increased over the last decade. A 2002 study by Yow and Bowden that examined the relationship between the use of the planning process and an athletic department's effectiveness found the following:

• Comprehensive, better-funded, and generally respected athletic programs were more frequently engaged in formal planning than other athletic programs;
• Departmental effectiveness was increased by the presence of written annual and long-range plans, when those plans were followed and executed carefully;
• The lack of a written plan (annual and/or long-range) hindered the ability of the athletic program to generate consistent support, achieve desired program and service levels, and maintain its image among its numerous publics.

Yow and Bowden (2002) concluded systematic and careful planning contribute to college athletics departments (1) making the most effective use of resources and (2) consistently ranking nationally in such core evaluative criteria as competitive results, academic outcomes, student-athlete welfare, facilities enhancement, fund-raising, and financial stability.

Sport executives and administrators are asked to make many decisions every day. There are, however, decisions that can fundamentally and significantly impact an organization's future culture, direction, and stability. Since previous research indicates planning is an important element in the execution of successful management decisions, it is important to understand the planning process.

What Is Planning?

Planning can be defined as a managerial activity that involves (1) analyzing the environment, (2) setting objectives, (3) deciding on specific actions and timelines needed to reach the objectives, and (4) providing feedback on results. This process should be distinguished from the plan itself. The strategic plan is the published document containing the intended results achieved through the planning process. The strategic plan is a guidebook to what has been agreed to and how it will be accomplished. Planning is a continuous process for strategic management. A sport organization benefits from the planning process because this systematic, continuing process allows an organization to regularly:

• Assess the organization's market position and current state. This involves performing a comprehensive Strengths, Weaknesses, Opportunities, and Threats (SWOT) analysis (see Text Box);

- Establish goals, objectives, priorities, and strategies to be completed within specified timeframes; this allows for regular organization assessments and can help motivate staff to work together to achieve specific, measurable and shared objectives;
- Achieve greater staff commitment and teamwork aimed at meeting challenges presented by the dynamic sport industry;
- Allocate resources, determine priorities, and make appropriate decisions to ensure future stability and success.

When conducting a SWOT analysis, any possible aspect of the organization should be evaluated. In some cases, a detailed SWOT analysis might take considerable time to complete. An example of one aspect of a SWOT Analysis for the University of Maryland Department of Intercollegiate Athletics is the consideration for the physical location of the university. The University of Maryland is located in College Park, Maryland, a city within 15 miles of Washington, D.C. The urban environment can be both a strength and weakness. Certainly, being located so close to Washington, D.C. (as well as Baltimore, Maryland) might be attractive for many potential students, athletes, coaches, and athletic department personnel. Those looking for a campus located within a large metropolitan area would find the University of Maryland attractive. However, the presence of a large city nearby campus may be a negative to some potential attendees or employees. The Washington, D.C. metropolitan area has traffic problems and, relative to many other areas of the United States, is an expensive place to live.

The location of the campus offers some unique opportunities for the University of Maryland athletic department. There are millions of people and thousands of businesses within driving distance. The opportunity to sell tickets and sponsorships is readily available. In additions, there are multiple media organizations in close proximity to the University of Maryland campus. Competitive athletic department events will likely attract exposure from numerous media outlets. However, the large metropolitan area can also become a threat. Since there are so many "other" things to do in the area, the University of Maryland must compete with other entities to attract fans and generate media attention.

A SWOT analysis for an athletic department would not only incorporate location, but would also investigate current players, coaches and staff, facilities, past accomplishments and athletic department history, and numerous other areas. Once the SWOT analysis is complete, the athletic department would be in a better position to determine what strategies to implement to achieve success.

Unless planning leads to improved performance, it is not worthwhile. A sport organization that wishes to remain viable and prosperous in a changing environ-

The University of Maryland is located only 15 miles from Washington, DC, which presents opportunities and threats.

Shutterstock, Inc.

ment must continuously and creatively plan. Otherwise, it will simply blindly react to its immediate environment. For this reason, though a formal written SWOT analysis may be completed once a year or once every two years, organizations should have the ability to conduct an "unofficial" SWOT analysis, as the various aspects of an organization and the environment it operates in can change quickly.

The Strategic-Planning Process

While there are many different ways in which a sport business can tackle the strategic-planning process, a systematic and thoughtful approach is necessary. Indeed, the *process* is as important as the plan itself, because the process is an opportunity for organization-wide input, deliberation, and review. It is crucial those who will execute the plan are involved in the plan's construction. The strategic-planning process is capable of creating authentic attitudinal change among personnel, as well as increasing productivity (Boyer, 2009; Yow, Migliore, Bowden, Stevens, and Loudon, 2000). The strategic-planning process involves:

1. Defining a department's purpose or reason for being.
2. Analyzing the environment, assessing strengths and weaknesses, and making assumptions.
3. Prescribing written, specific and measurable objectives that contribute to the organization's purpose.
4. Developing strategies for how to use available resources to meet objectives.
5. Developing operational plans to meet objectives, including plans for all organizational members.
6. Setting up control and evaluation procedures to determine if performance is keeping pace with attainment of objectives consistent with the organization's mission.

The six steps of the strategic-planning process are important because they require a sport organization to consider and respond to essential questions. Each process step requires the people at various organizational levels to discuss, study, deliberate and negotiate. The process also fosters a planning mentality throughout the organization. Completion of the six steps results in a strategic plan that specifies:

- Why the organization exists,
- What it is trying to accomplish,
- How resources will be utilized to accomplish objectives and fulfill its mission, and
- How outcome evaluation will be executed.

(Note: The application of this planning process to college sport is discussed in Yow, et al., 2000)

CASE STUDY

Transforming Maryland Athletics
2009–2014

Moving from general philosophies, components, and principles in the strategic-planning process and the strategic-plan document, this section presents a case-study that demonstrates the strategic-planning process.

In 2008, the University of Maryland completed and adopted a comprehensive, campus-wide, 10-year strategic plan entitled, *Transforming Maryland: Higher Expectations*. In September of 2008, as one of the University's most visible units and activity centers, the University of Maryland Department of Intercollegiate Athletics, also embarked on a comprehensive strategic-planning process. The intent was to ensure confluence with the University's 10-year strategic plan, while also outlining and prioritizing departmental goals, objectives, and strategies specific to Intercollegiate Athletics (ICA) for the next five years.

The primary aim of the ICA strategic-planning process was to focus on core evaluative areas including:

1. Branding, Partnerships and Outreach;
2. Competitive Excellence;
3. Compliance Education and Culture;
4. Facility Enhancement;
5. Financial Stability; and
6. Student-Athlete Well-Being, Academic Performance, and Personal Development.

In order to study and set the ICA five-year goals and strategies for each core area, strategic-planning committees (comprised of internal and external constituents) were formed. Since effective strategic planning must be an inclusive process, committee representation included athletes, coaches, ICA administrators, donors and ticket holders; University Athletics Council members; as well as students, faculty, staff, and alumni. (Note: Committees and areas of focus are included as an addendum at the end of this chapter.)

The strategic-planning process for ICA included the six distinct steps discussed earlier in this chapter. The first stage also included a comprehensive analysis of the department's current strengths, weaknesses, opportunities, and threats. Each of the 27 intercollegiate athletic teams, and 13 administrative units (See Addendum or University of Maryland Athletic Department website), as well as the Student Athlete Advisory Committee (S.A.A.C.), completed a SWOT analysis. The 41 individual analyses were consolidated into a comprehensive ICA SWOT assessment, which was utilized by all strategic-planning committees in developing the department's goals, strategies and timelines.

The second stage of the ICA strategic-planning process was development of specific, challenging, measurable, attainable, realistic, and timely goal-statements by each sport team, administrative unit, and the S.A.A.C. These 41 goal-statements were consolidated and considered by each strategic-planning committee in developing over-arching ICA goals, strategies, and timelines for the next five years.

The third stage of the strategic-planning process was each strategic-planning committee constructing key ICA goals, objectives, strategies, and timelines for the next five years in each core area. These goals, objectives, strategies, and timelines were identified as priority evaluative criteria to measure ICA progress from 2009–2014. (Note: A complete list of developed objectives and timelines can be found on the University of Maryland Athletic Department website—www.umterps.com. Click on the "Strategic Plan" link.)

During this ICA strategic-planning process, each of the six strategic planning committees, as well as the entire ICA staff, reviewed the department's "Mission Statement and Guiding Principles" that had been drafted by the department and adopted by the University Athletics Council in 2000. This "Mission Statement and Guiding Principles" document was used to help guide formulation of appropriate departmental goals, objectives, and strategies. This step reflected the department and all stakeholders' recommitment to the department's core mission and principles. (Note: This document can be found in this chapter's addendum.)

The ICA goals and strategies identified in the Strategic Plan were conveyed to the appropriate coaches and administrative units for implementation and completion.

Throughout the strategic plan's lifetime (2009–2014), the department will conduct regular assessments of goal attainment and update the plan, as warranted by changes in the organizational environment.

In addition, developed goals, objectives, strategies, and timelines will be utilized in ICA employees' annual Performance Review and Development (PRD), as appropriate. All ICA personnel are expected to work collaboratively, while basing their respective decision-making, prioritization and goal-setting toward meeting the departmental goals identified in Transforming Maryland Athletics: 2009–2014. This 42-page, plenary strategic-plan document can be viewed at the website www.umterps.com and by clicking on "Strategic Plan."

This document contains many additional elements of the department's SWOT analysis, including specific strengths developed (e.g., new basketball arena, capable of generating necessary revenue streams), and identified threats (e.g., presence of competitors in the urban location). Students are encouraged to download and critically examine the document and utilize it as a template for future strategic planning.

(Contributing materially and substantially to the development of the Maryland ICA Strategic Plan and to the content of this chapter was Mr. Christopher Boyer, Senior Associate Director of Athletics, The University of Maryland.)

Conclusion

We have established learning objectives for this chapter, reviewed the parameters and components of the function of management, and explored the importance of the strategic-planning process as an integral component of strategic management.

The unique nature of the sport industry requires sport organizations—if they wish to remain competitive—to systematically and strategically plan for their futures. Adopting a strategic-planning culture best positions a sport organization to achieve success.

On an individual level, sport management students need to engage in the same strategic-planning process. In each of this textbook's chapters there is information that can be used to develop your own strategic plan for a successful sport-management career. Additional, focused coursework in areas such as sport-law, marketing, sales, and facility management will provide additional opportunities to continually formulate a well-constructed strategic plan. As you contemplate the basic components presented in this chapter, take time to examine and reexamine the addendum items.

APPENDIX I

University of Maryland

ICA MISSION STATEMENT AND GUIDING PRINCIPLES

It is the mission of the Department of Intercollegiate Athletics to provide our student athletes excellent opportunities to participate in an intercollegiate athletics experience of the highest quality, with the result that their athletics experience becomes an integral and valued component of their total educational experience at the University.

In achieving this mission the Department of Intercollegiate Athletics will embrace these guiding principles:

- To develop and maintain a highly competitive and sound athletic program—reaching a standard of achievement in athletics consistent with our purposes as a University and the excellence of our institution.
- To promote character development, leadership qualities, sportsmanship, and academic excellence in our student athletes.
- To employ coaches and staff members who exhibit high standards of integrity and ethical behavior, including good sportsmanship and a desire to assist student athletes in reaching their academic potential.
- To contribute to the enhancement of institutional morale and esprit de corps among students, faculty, and staff—while providing alumni and friends a means by which they can identify with the University for mutually beneficial purposes.
- To recruit student athletes who are capable of success in the University's academic program and to provide academic support and student development opportunities that will effectively assist student athletes to reach their potential.
- To function responsibly and with accountability in all its initiatives, programs, and operations, which includes providing equal treatment and opportunity for student athletes, coaches, and staff, in employment and in all athletic department programs and activities as required by law and University policy.
- To maintain fiscal and operational integrity by balancing budgets and carrying out sound management practices.
- To provide consistently excellent customer service.
- To comply carefully with institutional, conference, and NCAA regulations.
- To ensure ethnic and gender diversity among its coaches, staff, and student athletes, consistent with the University's educational mission.

APPENDIX II

STRATEGIC PLANNING COMMITTEES AND THE FOCUS AREAS

I. Branding, Partnerships and Outreach
A. Marketing and Sponsorships
B. Media Relations
C. Development
D. "Friends Of" Groups
E. Game Atmosphere
F. Ticket Services
G. Video Services

II. Competitive Excellence
A. Recruiting Expectations
B. Scheduling Policies
C. Coaching Standards
D. Financial and Athletic Aid
E. Strength and Conditioning
F. Director's Cup Expectations

III. Compliance Education and Culture
A. Title IX Compliance
B. Representatives of Athletics Interest
C. Admissions/Eligibility
D. Drug Testing
E. Student-Athlete Code of Conduct
F. NCAA Certification
G. Agents
H. Staff Education and Orientation

IV. Facility Enhancement
A. Capital Projects
B. ICA Facilities Master Plan
C. Competition Venues
D. Indoor Training Facilities
E. Practice Facilities
F. Facility Scheduling
G. ICA Offices
H. Information Technology
I. Parking
J. Sustainability
K. Championship Hosting

V. Financial Stability
A. Operational Budgets
B. Aid Budgets (Terrapin Club)
C. Cost Containment
D. Revenue Growth
E. Reserve Growth
F. Personnel Retention

VI. Student-Athlete Well-Being, Academic Performance, and Personal Development
A. Academic Support/Career Development
B. Academic Excellence (Graduation Rates, APR, GSR, GPA)
C. Individual Admits
D. Student Life (Housing, Campus Safety, Dining Services)
E. Athletic Training and Sports Medicine
F. Student Athlete Advisory Committee
G. CHAMPS/Life Skills
H. M Club

Interview

INTERVIEW 7.1

Martina K. Ballen
Senior Associate Athletic Director of Athletics for
Business and Finance
The University of North Carolina at Chapel Hill

Q: Could you describe your career path from undergraduate student to your current position?

A: I received a Bachelor of Science in Business Administration from UNC–Chapel Hill. I worked a couple of years for the Federal U.S. District Courts as a Deputy Clerk. I then returned to school and earned an MBA from Wake Forest University and was hired by a bank as a credit analyst. After one year, I was assigned to Chapel Hill as a commercial loan officer to manage the main office branch on Franklin Street. I was later hired by the UNC Department of Athletics as Director of Finance. Over the years, my title and levels of responsibility have expanded to my current role of Senior Associate Athletic Director for Business and Finance.

Q: What are the most pressing issues currently facing college athletics?

A: Compensation and Facilities are the most important issues we face. Adjusting to the rapid growth in compensation for the coaches of our revenue sports, as well as

implementing significant facility upgrades is difficult while at the same time trying to continue to fund a broad-based sports program. Despite allocating major resources to these growing areas, it is becoming increasingly difficult to keep up with demand.

Q: Are there specific job skills sport-management students should look to develop while still in school?

A: I think that a lot of sport-management students tend to shy away from the finance side of the business. Understanding and managing finances in sports is essential to understanding how an athletic department or sport-related business operates. Taking business and finance classes are vitally important.

Q: What publications do you regularly read to stay apprised of sport-business events?

A: *The Sports Business Journal* and *Athletic Business.*

Q: Would you recommend students pursue graduate school? If so, when should they pursue a graduate degree and what area of study would you recommend?

A: Definitely! It is competitive for young people to get into this business. Anything that would give them an advantage is a must! If the focus is finance, marketing, fundraising or management, I would definitely recommend a MBA.

Q: Is there a certain business area in college sport you see emerging in importance in the near future?

A: I think that the Internet has emerged as a critical area of importance. Athletic programs are beginning to understand the full range of opportunities available on-line.

Q: Can you describe or share strategic management or strategic planning situations in which you have participated.

A: Over the years, I have been involved in numerous strategic planning/financial planning processes for the UNC Athletic department. Through these efforts, we focused on our mission and core values and determined what we would need to do to continue our commitment to meeting Title IX guidelines and funding scholarships for a broad-based athletic program, while maintaining competitive budgets for football and men's and women's basketball. Through our financial planning process, we identified areas where we could generate additional revenue, as well as areas where we could reduce or eliminate costs.

Study Questions

1. What are the functions of management?
2. What are the unique characteristics of the sports/athletics enterprises that set them apart from other organizations?
3. What are the needs and the benefits of strategic planning within sports enterprises?
4. Discuss the scope, content, and expected outcomes of the case study strategic plan. Include the philosophical bases, perceived need, and expected outcomes for the development of such a plan.
5. Using the Maryland "Mission Statement and Guiding Principles" document, explain how such a document might be helpful in developing a strategic plan within any organization.
6. Explain how an organizational chart for a sport enterprise might indicate the essence of its strategic plan.
7. Are there ways that a SWOT analysis can contribute to the preparation of a strategic plan? How?
8. Outline the organization, processes, and expected outcomes of a strategic plan that you would develop for a sports enterprise, including a flow chart depicting the components of the plan.
9. Evaluate the six-step formula for developing a strategic plan.
10. Critique and make recommended revisions or enhancements to the case study's structure of six committees and the areas of focus of each committee.

References

Boyer, C. (2009). *Strategic planning in intercollegiate athletics.* Chapel Hill, NC: University of North Carolina, Guest lecture, EXSS 740—Administration of Sport.

Chelladurai, P. (2005). *Managing organizations for sport and physical activity: A systems perspective* (2nd ed.). Scottsdale, AZ: Holcomb Hathaway, Publishers.

Drucker, P.F. (1994). *Management.* New York: Harper and Row Publishers.

Humphrey, J.A., Yow, D.A., Bowden, W.W., (2000). *Stress in college athletics: Causes, consequences, coping.* New York: The Haworth Press.

Transforming Maryland Athletics: 2009–2014 (Strategic Plan Document) (2009). College Park, MD: University of Maryland Department of Intercollegiate Athletics.

Yow, D.A., Migliore, R.H., Bowden, W.W., Stevens, R.E., & Loudon, D.L. (2000). *Strategic planning for collegiate athletics.* Binghamton, NY: The Haworth Press.

Yow, D.A., and Bowden, W.W. (2002). A survey of NCAA Division I athletic programs in regard to their planning procedures. Unpublished manuscript.

Sport Marketing

Matthew J. Bernthal • *University of South Carolina*

After reading this chapter, you will be able to:

- Properly define marketing and sport marketing;
- Appreciate that successful marketing begins with understanding the customer;
- Recognize the role of marketing in sport;
- Understand segmentation and positioning;
- Appreciate the importance of branding and positioning;
- Identify the key components of a marketing plan.

KEY TERMS

Sport Marketing

Relationship Marketing

Market Segmentation

Fan Identification

Positioning

> *"The aim of marketing is to know and understand the customer so well the product or service fits him and sells itself.*
>
> —Peter F. Drucker, Management Expert

> *"This may seem simple, but you need to give customers what they want, not what you think they want. And, if you do this, people will keep coming back."*
>
> —John Ilhan, Founder, Crazy John's Phones

> *"In the marketplace, there is much advertising that talks about a product or service, but often there is no engagement of the customer. As marketers, if we choose to not talk with the customer, or if we talk at the customer and do not engage them in our marketing efforts, the customer will likely tune out and not engage with our products. They have the final word. At Ringling Bros. and Barnum & Bailey, our product is experiential and beginning with our product development, in our marketing, and after they enjoy their experience at The Greatest Show On Earth, we strive to incorporate the customer in the experience from the moment we enter their consideration set."*
>
> —Dan Donoway, Former Vice President–Marketing, Ringling Bros. and Barnum & Bailey

Introduction

Sport is big business. In today's marketplace, this statement appears somewhat obvious. Entertainment and Sports Programming Network (ESPN) paid $8.8 billion for the rights to broadcast Monday Night Football and the National Football League (NFL) Draft from 2006–2013. CBS paid $6.2 billion for the rights to broadcast the National Collegiate Athletic Association (NCAA) Division I Men's Basketball Tournament from 2003 through 2014. Electronic Arts pays Tiger Woods $7.5 million per year to endorse its Tiger Woods PGA Tour video game, while TLC Laser Eye Centers pays him a "mere" $3 million per year to endorse their laser eye surgery centers. Reliant Energy has contracted to spend $300 million over 32 years for the naming rights to the Houston Texans stadium. Sport fans spend large amounts of their resources, both money and time, on the "consumption" of their favorite athletes and teams. On average, over 17,000 fans pack National Hockey League (NHL) and National Basketball Association (NBA) arenas for each game, while it is not unusual for over 100,000 fans to fill a stadium to watch a college football game.

New product offerings, from mixed martial arts events to professional bass fishing events and everything in between, have expanded the options available to sport spectators. It seems that if there is a sport event to be held and/or broadcast, there is a market for it. Identifying that market, reaching it, and convincing the consumers that comprise it to spend their money on the sport product is the job of sport marketers.

So, what exactly is sport marketing and what is the main characteristic of successful sport marketers? The answer is surprisingly simple. When most students beginning an introductory sport marketing class are asked to define sport marketing in their own terms, the two words that are most typically used are advertising and sales. That is, sport marketing is viewed, rather logically, as the advertising and selling of sport products. This view of marketing is rather typical, yet somewhat narrow. Indeed, good sport marketers must wield many tools successfully, including advertising, personal selling, pricing and public relations. However, at its foundation, successful sport marketing is bigger than the instruments that fill the marketer's toolbox. Consider the following questions:

One of the goals of sport marketers is to determine the best methods to utilize to attract customers.

- How does a marketer of a poorly performing baseball team drawing poor attendance design pricing packages and communication strategies that lead more consumers to attend more games?
- How does a marketer of a professional bass fishing event convince consumers to pack a 15,000 seat arena simply to watch fish being weighed?
- How does an NHL hockey team in the southern United States develop a fan base when the vast majority of people in its market have had little, if any, exposure to the game of hockey?
- How does a sport team maximize sponsorship sales and sponsor satisfaction?

The answers to these and similar questions must begin with the central component to successful marketing, *understanding the customer*. Successful marketers of any product, including sport, understand that they must think like their customers think, and understand their customers' wants, needs, and dislikes. A marketer of the losing baseball team understands that even losing teams can satisfy a consumer's desire for an affordable family outing, and as a result develop advertisements that appeal to the consumer's desire to spend quality time with family and construct family pricing packages that communicate value to the consumer. Through an understanding of sport consumers, a successful sport marketer would realize that when it comes to attending sport events, females are generally less motivated by winning than are men, leading to an allocation of a higher percentage of the advertising budget to media vehicles that reach women. The marketer of the professional bass fishing tournament will understand that one primary motivation drawing spectators to this event is the desire to view and purchase products and learn successful techniques used by the professionals. This leads the marketer to develop and market a product exposition along with the weigh-in where consumers can view and purchase the latest and greatest in fishing tackle as well as learn techniques from clinics given by those fishing in the tournament. A marketer of an NHL team in the southern United States determines that to strengthen long-term attendance, a comfort with and appreciation for the sport of hockey must be developed. This leads to marketing strategies such as developing and promoting in-line skating hockey leagues, providing team-branded in-line hockey equipment to physical education programs at schools within the market, and the like. In advertisements, the marketer emphasizes attributes of the game of hockey (e.g., hard-hitting checks and the general physical nature of the game) that are likely to be as appreciated by the "typical" southern fan as they are by the "typical" northern fan. The sponsorship marketer knows that in order to maximize sponsorship sales, sponsorship packages must be tailored to meet the specific business needs of various potential sponsors. Through researching and talking with potential sponsors, this marketer will develop sponsorship packages that focus on increasing brand awareness for one, sampling new products to consumers for another, and for yet another, allowing the sponsor to entertain potential clients and reward valuable employees through hospitality at the event(s).

This chapter began with quotes from Peter Drucker, John Ilhan, and Dan Donoway, none of whom work in sport marketing. So why do they lead this chapter? For the sole reason that successful marketing in any industry begins and ends with what these three individuals and others like them recognize: understanding and satisfying customer wants and needs. It matters not whether the product is Ilhan's cell phones, Donoway's Ringling Bros. and Barnum & Bailey Circus, a sport event, or a sporting good. A focus on the customer, from product development on, is paramount. Chuck Steedman, Fenway Sports Group Executive VP, illustrated this when he commented about determining which concerts to hold in the Boston Red Sox' Fenway Park: "While I'd like to have Megadeth play Fenway, it doesn't appeal to our season-ticket holders" (Coast to Coast, 2009, p. 29). As sport marketers, it does not necessarily matter how we would like to see our product advertised or how much we might be willing to pay for it. What matters is designing advertisements and establishing prices (among other things) that will appeal to our customers. Through thoroughly understanding them, our marketing avoids the pitfall of so many unsuccessful and/or inefficient marketers: "throwing ideas against a wall and seeing if they stick." By being in touch with customers, good marketers have a much better understanding of the marketing strategies that are likely to stick, as well as the ones that are likely to fail.

Definitions of Marketing and Sport Marketing

Considering the prior discussion, it should come as no surprise that when definitions of marketing and sport marketing are examined, there is a central component common to each: the customer. The American Marketing Association (AMA) defines **marketing** as "the activity, set of institutions, and processes for creating, communicating, delivering, and exchanging offerings that have value for customers, clients, partners, and society at large" (Definition, 2009). While many definitions of sport marketing exist, the vast majority share this focus on the customer either directly or indirectly. Shank defines sport marketing as "the specific application of marketing principles and processes to sport products and to the marketing of non-sport products through association with sports" (Shank, 2009, p. 3). While not directly mentioning the customer, one needs only to look at the AMA definition of marketing itself to see that "applying marketing principles and processes to sport products" means creating, communicating, and delivering value to sport customers and managing sport-customer relationships. Schwarz and Hunter define sport marketing as "a process of developing and implementing activities related to the production, pricing, distribution, promotion and publicizing of a sport product" (Schwarz & Hunter, 2008, p. 14). This definition directly incorporates what are commonly referred to as the "4 P's" of marketing: product, price, place (distribution), and promotion. An understanding of the customer, however, is paramount when developing an attractive product, pricing it to sell, and distributing and promoting it effectively. Other definitions of sport marketing focus a bit more directly on the consumer. Fullerton (2007, p. 3) defines sport marketing as "the proactive efforts that are designed to influence consumer preferences for a variety of sport products and services." Mullin, Hardy, and Sutton (2007, p. 11) put an even greater focus on the consumer by defining sport marketing as "all activities designed to meet the needs and wants of sport consumers through exchange processes." With its simplicity and its focus on the consumer first and last, this definition is one that students of sport marketing would be wise to adopt.

Sport Marketing_____

All activities designed to meet the needs and wants of sport consumers through exchange processes.

Market Segmentation

While successful sport marketing centers on meeting the needs and wants of sport consumers, it is clear that not all sport consumers want and need similar things from their sport products. Through market segmentation, sport marketers determine which groups of consumers provide the greatest sales and marketing opportunities (Shank, 2009). **Market segmentation** can be defined as the process of dividing large, unlike groups of consumers into smaller, more defined groups of people who share similar characteristics (Mullin, Hardy, & Sutton 2000). By grouping consumers into relatively homogeneous groups, marketers can increase their efficiency and success through the knowledge that consumers with similar wants and needs will respond similarly to specific marketing efforts. A market is segmented utilizing bases of segmentation. While numerous bases of segmentation exist, the most common are demographics, psychographics, benefits, geographics, and geodemographics.

Market Segmentation_____

The process of dividing large, unlike groups of consumers into smaller, more defined groups of people who share similar characteristics.

Demographics include such common variables as gender, age, family size, income, and ethnicity. Since such variables are so easily understood and available (one can obtain the demographic breakdown of a geographic market from any number of sources), they tend to be one of the most common ways a market is segmented. As an example of demographics, consider the efforts many sport properties have engaged in to reach females. Many collegiate athletic departments as well as NFL teams offer "classes" designed to teach women the basics of football. At these classes the women learn rules, basic strategies, and meet coaches and players. The obvious hope is that the more women learn about the game, the more likely they are to become fans of it and, of course, by extension, consumers of the home team. In attempting to connect with more women, some Major League Baseball (MLB) teams have had wine-tastings at the ballpark. Yet others have featured their players with their own families in team advertisements in the hope that showcasing the players as "good family men" will resonate with women. As another example, MLB has attempted to develop a connection with young girls by partnering with Mattel to create and market MLB Barbie, complete with uniforms of some of the more popular MLB teams.

Other uses of demographic segmentation can be seen with virtually every sport property. For example, many teams have gameday promotions that target a specific age group (e.g., dollar beer night for a minor league team in a college town, autograph night to target children, etc.). A fitness center might offer special classes designed specifically to appeal to senior citizens, and a daycare to help attract those consumers with young children. A golf tournament might attempt to reach the Latino market through airing Spanish language advertisements that feature players that this market can easily identify with.

BOX 8.1

Miami PGA Tour Event Will Be First to Air Ad in Spanish

The CA Championship this week will become the first domestic PGA Tour event to air a Spanish language television commercial, as the Miami tournament looks to tap the buying power of South Florida's Hispanic Population.

The Spanish-language spot, as well as an English-language version, is narrated by Camilo Villegas, a native of Colombia. Villegas attended the University of Florida and has been a crowd favorite at the Miami event since finishing second in 2006.

"There aren't any tour players who live in Dade or Broward counties that are competing on tour," said tournament director Eddie Carbone. "So Camilo's kind of our adopted son with the various Latin communities and especially the Colombian community."

There are more than 2 million residents of Hispanic or Latino descent in South Florida, according to the most recent U.S. Census data, or about 40 percent of the total population.

Starting this week, the spots will run on English and Spanish-language affiliates through barters or ad time donated by stations. Ads will be tagged with the tourney's Website, the station logo and/or the station's charity.

The tournament is also planning a Spanish-language print and retail campaign.

Other PGA Tour events have run Spanish-language radio ads or bought outdoor advertising, said tour officials, but the CA Championship is the first domestic event to film a PSA in a language other than English. Professional women's events have run Spanish-and Korean-language advertising in recent years, the LPGA said.

The CA championship, a World Golf Championship event, is set for March 12–15 at Doral Golf Resort in Miami.

Psychographics is another basis of segmentation. **Psychographics** can essentially be described as lifestyles, or activities, interests, and opinions (**AIO Dimensions**) (Wells & Tigert, 1971). Psychographics involves segmenting on activities such as what a consumer does for a living, what they do for fun, what types of media they utilize most often, their political opinions, their religious beliefs, the social causes that they support, and the like. If marketers can understand their consumers at this level, they will better be able to predict their product preferences and tailor marketing efforts to appeal to them. An example of psychographic segmentation can be seen in the Oklahoma City Blazers' promotion geared toward attracting those involved in an agricultural lifestyle or otherwise interested in agricultural activities. The Blazers, an American League Hockey team, sought this psychographic segment through its Future Farmers of America (FFA) promotion. Members of FFA, an agricultural youth organization, sold tickets to a game as a fund-raiser. The Blazers allowed the FFA to keep $5 for every $10 ticket sold. Further, those FFA members attending the game had the opportunity to win one of four farm animals (a cow, a lamb, a goat, and a pig) being given away as prizes. This promotion was a creative way for the Blazers to attract this psychographic segment. It also allowed the Blazers to provide value to one of their sponsors, American Farmers and Ranchers Mutual Insurance ("FFA," 2008).

As another example of psychographic segmentation, many sport teams are marketing to Christians with Christian-themed events. Third Coast Sports, in fact, is a Nashville company that provides religious themed promotions to sport teams. Such promotions are now common in both minor and major leagues and across a spectrum of sports over the entire country. A typical promotion might have a team give away Bibles and religious figure (e.g., Noah, Goliath) bobbleheads to attending fans, entertain the fans pre- and/or post-game with a Christian rock band, and have the players play in specially made jerseys with names of books of the Bible and corresponding verse numbers on the back instead of the players last names and regular numbers. These types of psychographic promotions have become extraordinarily successful in attracting large numbers of new consumers to ballgames. For example, the Nashville Sounds, a AAA minor league baseball team, report that their "faith nights" attract attendance that is 59 percent higher than their average (St. John, 2006).

As a final example of psychographic segmentation, consider an example provided through the Women's National Basketball Association (WNBA). Some teams in the WNBA, such as the Sacramento Monarchs, the Miami Sol, and the Los Angeles Sparks, have aggressively pursued the lesbian market through fairly visible means such as pep rallies at lesbian bars and Gay Pride nights at select games. In reaching out to this segment, such teams also place advertisements in lesbian publications and set up promotional booths at Gay Pride events (Weir, 2001).

A third common method of segmentation is **benefit segmentation**. Benefit segmentation is based on the realization that different consumers may seek different benefits from the same product. As an example outside of sports, think of a brand such as Excedrin pain reliever. One might find it surprising that Extra Strength Excedrin has the same exact ingredients as Excedrin Migraine. Why would the makers of Excedrin, Bristol-Myers Squibb, market a brand extension that has the exact same ingredients as one of their existing brands? They understand that there is a segment of consumers that has a specific need from their product: relief from debilitating migraine headaches. They knew that clearly communicating that their product could provide this benefit by creating a brand extension that marketed it as such would increase their overall sales as opposed to if they had continued to market only Extra Strength Excedrin. In other words, consumers see Excedrin Migraine as specifically designed for relief of migraine pain, and not the same as any other pain reliever, not even Extra Strength Excedrin (and now you know better!). Successful sport marketers learn from companies like this and recognize that their product can often fulfill a variety of benefits sought by a variety of market segments. For example, through research, suppose a sponsorship salesperson for a spectator arena finds that a potential sponsor is having trouble with high rates of employee turnover. This salesperson might then make the connection that this potential sponsor could benefit from entertaining valuable employees in a luxury suite, and emphasize such a benefit in a sales presentation. On the other hand, this same salesperson discovers that another potential sponsor is seeking more brand awareness in the community, so arena signage is highlighted in a sponsorship presentation pitched to that potential sponsor.

As another example of benefit segmentation, think about the marketing of youth sports. Often, parents and children are seeking very different benefits from participation in youth sports. When communicating with parents, a marketer trying to increase participation in a local youth soccer league, for example, might emphasize the parent-sought benefits that youth soccer provides: it is relatively inexpensive, it emphasizes participation, it is safe, a child does not have to have a great deal of initial skill to begin playing, and it provides great exercise and an "energy-drain" from children participating. On the other hand, imagine the same marketer making a presentation to young children only (i.e., without their parents) in a school assembly. It is highly unlikely that the marketer would focus on benefits such as safety, inexpensiveness, or how soccer can help the children "drain energy" so they will be easier for their parents to manage. Rather, the marketer would be wise to simply focus on the benefits more likely to be sought by children, such as fun, more time spent with friends, camaraderie through outside events such as trips for pizza after the game, and the like.

Benefit segmentation is ubiquitous in the sporting good market. Many sporting good product categories base their segmentation primarily on this basis. Golf balls are segmented based on whether a player is seeking more spin (for the benefit of better control around the green) or less spin (the benefit of better control off of the tee), a softer or harder feel, a higher trajectory or lower trajectory, and the like. Tennis racquets are marketed to various specific benefit-seeking segments: players seeking more control, those seeking more power, those seeking a racquet that is particularly suited to net play, etc. Sport apparel is marketed toward consumers seeking clothing that wicks sweat away from the body during athletic participation, those seeking clothing that blocks wind, those seeking clothing that improves aerodynamics, those wanting more "fashionable" sport apparel, and the like.

A fourth basis of segmentation is **geographic segmentation**. This involves creating market segments that are based on geographic location. Marketing to different geographic segments often necessitates different marketing strategies for each. This could be due to geographic differences in things such as weather, culture, and demographics. For example, sporting good retail outlets such as Golf Warehouse might have several different geographic segments, and treat each differently in relation to marketing strategies such as pricing and promotion. In a northern state, for example, prices for Golf Warehouse's clubs would likely fluctuate much more during the course of a year than they would in a state such as Florida. The reason is that demand for golf clubs in Florida remains relatively consistent throughout the year due to the warm weather, while demand for clubs in northern states drops during the long winter months, simply because consumers are less likely to buy clubs when they know they will not be playing for a while. How can a retailer like Golf Warehouse adjust to this drop in demand in northern states? Through strategies such as price promotions (e.g., sales) and non-price promotions (e.g., buy a set of clubs and get a free putter and four free rounds at a local golf course). Strategies such as these help the retailer keep sales much more stable throughout the course of the year than they would be otherwise. The greater demand for golf equipment in general in Florida versus a northern state such as Minnesota would also likely lead to a retailer such as Golf Warehouse investing in more locations in Florida.

Cultural differences in geographic locations can also affect marketing considerations. Some might argue, for example, that our earlier example of the WNBA actively targeting the lesbian segment might be a more risky strategy in a market in the "Deep South" than in markets such as Los Angeles and Sacramento. Those who hold this view would likely do so because they perceive a stronger cultural acceptance of homosexuality in many West Coast markets than Southeastern markets.

A final basis of segmentation that is commonly used in sport marketing is **geodemographic segmentation**. Geodemographic segmentation is so named because it reflects a synergy of geographic and demographic targeting. It also builds in psychographics, however. It is based on the simple notion that people tend to live around other people that are similar to themselves. What does this mean for marketers? It means that if a marketer can demographically and psychographically identify the type of person that is a likely consumer of their product, they can be located and marketed to with relative efficiency.

One of the pioneers of geodemographic segmentation is Nielsen Claritas. Nielsen markets what is called the PRIZM system, which defines every U.S. household in terms of 66 demographically and psychographically distinct segments called "clusters" (PRIZM, 2010). Think back to our marketer of youth soccer. It is likely that he or she can envision their typical target segments.

Perhaps one segment sounds something like this: "Upscale, suburban, married couples with children-that's the skinny on Kids & Cul-de-Sacs, an enviable lifestyle of large families in recently built subdivisions. With a high rate of Hispanic and Asian Americans, this segment is a refuge for college-educated, white-collar professionals with administrative jobs and upper-middle-class incomes. Their nexus of education, affluence and children translates into large outlays for child-centered products and services" (Lifestyle, 2010, p. 2). Kids & Cul-de-Sacs is one of the 66 PRIZM clusters, and its description certainly sounds like a demographic and psychographic profile of a likely target for youth sports. Once our youth soccer marketer has identified Kid's & Cul-de-Sacs as a likely consumer of his or her product, things become easier. Direct mail pieces, for example, can be targeted to zip codes that have been identified as having high numbers of Kids & Cul-de-Sac households. From the PRIZM data, the marketer can learn which magazines and newspapers these likely consumers read, and which television shows they watch, information that can help in placing advertisements for the youth soccer league.

Geodemographic systems such as PRIZM can also assist in new business feasibility or location analysis. For example, if Gold's Gym were scouting several markets in which to locate a new facility, what kind of market segments do you think the company would look for in the various proposed locations? One segment likely to be consumers of Gold's Gym is Young Influentials. This cluster, according to Nielsen, "reflects the fading glow of acquisitive yuppiedom. Today, the segment is a common address for young, middle-class singles and couples who are more preoccupied with balancing work and leisure pursuits. Having recently left college dorms, they now live in apartment complexes surrounded by ball fields, health clubs and casual-dining restaurants" (PRIZM NE Segments, 2010, p. 2). One consideration for Gold's Gym, then, when deciding among the various proposed locations, would be the relative numbers of likely consumers (e.g., Young Influentials and other PRIZM clusters who are reasonable targets for Gold's Gym) within a reasonable drive time of the various locations.

PRIZM and systems like it are widely used by major sport marketers such as the National Association for Stock Car Auto Racing (NASCAR), and major live entertainment marketers such as Feld Entertainment. Acquiring such data obviously costs money. However, geodemographic systems such as PRIZM help these marketers locate likely consumer segments for their products and reach these segments much more effectively and efficiently.

The Interconnectedness of Segmentation Bases

It is important to realize that while it is expedient to discuss each of the bases of segmentation in isolation, they rarely operate independently from one another. It does little good for a marketer, for example, to target children aged 7–12 without understanding and appealing to the psychographics of this segment. The Miami Heat, for example, actively targeted children through several strategies based on such knowledge. Understanding the media habits of children, the Heat placed advertisements on Cartoon Network and Nickelodeon. Understanding that children appreciate and identify with superstar players, these ads featured not only Heat stars but stars from opposing teams. Understanding that a common activity of children is "pestering" their parents, the Heat pitched six-packs of tickets directly to children in these spots, essentially enticing children to market these packages to their parents (Ad Spotlight, 2004).

As another example of the interconnectedness of segmentation bases, imagine that the United States Tennis Association (USTA) attempts to increase both young adult single and senior citizen participation in its adult leagues across the country through a direct mail promotional piece and a television advertising campaign. Young adult singles and senior citizens are simply two demographic segments. However, should the USTA market the leagues to both segments using the exact same message? Based on their *psychographics,* these two *demographic* segments might be attracted to league play because of very different *benefits.* For example, young adult singles might be convinced to try league play because of the social opportunities it affords, while senior citizens might place more emphasis on the health and psychological benefits that come from staying physically active. Ideally, marketing communications geared toward each segment would then reflect this.

Relationship Marketing

An increasingly common concept embraced by sport marketers is referred to as **relationship marketing**. Relationship marketing is defined as marketing with the conscious aim to develop and manage long-term and/or trusting relationships with customers, distributors, suppliers, or other parties in the marketing environment (Dictionary, 2009). Within the sport industry, marketers have become increasingly aware that to consistently succeed over the long-term, satisfactory relationships with consumers must be created and *sustained.* It matters not whether the consumers are fans, sponsors, league participants, retail customers of a sporting goods store, members of a fitness center, or some other type of sport consumer. The bottom line is that sustained, satisfactory relationships with customers are paramount. To illustrate a main reason why, consider the concept of the lifetime value of a customer. **Lifetime customer value** represents the value, in dollars, that one customer is worth to a particular company. Let's imagine that you spend an average of $5 per week at McDonald's, and have since the age of 10. That means that since you were 10 years old, you've spent an average of $260 per year at McDonald's. That's probably not a stretch! If McDonald's can keep this relationship with you as a customer for the remainder of your life expectancy, they will have had you as a customer for 67 years (the average life expectancy in the U.S. is approximately 77 years). This means that you are worth $17,420 to McDonald's in direct revenue over the course of your life. For McDonald's, it certainly pays to keep you as a customer by delivering a satisfactory product and customer service, providing incentive to return,

Relationship Marketing___
Marketing with the conscious aim to develop and manage long-term and/or trusting relationships with customers, distributors, suppliers, or other parties in the marketing environment.

and simply making you feel valued as a customer! Sport marketers should approach their customers with the same mindset. How much is each individual fan, sponsor, fitness center member, and so on worth to the marketers of those products? Not the dollar value of an individual game ticket, a single event sponsorship, or the price of a year's membership at a fitness center. Rather, they are worth what they would have spent on the product over a reasonable lifetime as a customer. Viewing them as such will generally lead to increased efforts at customer satisfaction (e.g., putting on exciting, well-run events) and effective relationship marketing programs.

A relationship-marketing program generally consists of one or both of two primary strategies: financial bonding and social bonding. In general, **bonding** refers to the creation of a unified commitment that holds those in the relationship together (Fullerton, 2007). **Financial bonding** involves the provision of financial incentives to your customers in order to encourage a continuing customer relationship, while **social bonding** involves providing social or psychological incentives that encourage a continuing relationship. Consider a hypothetical local public golf course in Central Florida (a highly competitive market with many public courses) that decides to implement a relationship-marketing program in order to build long-term relationships (and thus revenue!) with players. The course, Baytree, establishes the free Baytree Buff program and collects basic information from those who join. Such information includes contact information, demographics such as gender, age, marital status, presence of children in the household, birthday, anniversary, and other information such as favorite restaurants (from a list of partnering restaurants). This information is used to create a database that serves as a tool to implement the program. A simplified version of the Baytree Buff program might look like that shown in Table 8.1.

With this program, Baytree is well on its way to developing sustained, valued relationships with local players, and gains a competitive advantage over the many competing courses in its market that are not aware of the value of relationship marketing.

Relationship marketing programs can be constructed in any number of ways, limited only by the marketer's creativity and/or resources. They may be based primarily on social bonding, financial bonding, or (as in our Baytree example) both. Many are relatively simple. Dick's Sporting Goods, for instance, has a simple financial bonding program called ScoreCard Rewards. Shoppers sign-up for the program and receive a barcoded ScoreCard that they present to the cashier every time they purchase something at Dick's. One point is earned for every dollar spent. Every time the customer accumulates 300 points, they are mailed a $10 gift certificate to Dick's. Dick's regularly mails members added incentives to reach the 300 points, such as a coupon for 100 or even 200 ScoreCard points with the customer's next purchase at Dick's. This encourages shoppers to visit Dick's more often, and make more purchases at Dick's than they otherwise might. The regular mailings also simply keep Dick's Sporting Goods top-of-mind with members.

TABLE 8.1

Relationship Marketing Program for Baytree Golf Club

Strategy	Goal	Type of Bonding
One round of free golf for every five rounds played	• Encourage more rounds played by each customer than they might have otherwise • Discourage play at competing courses	Financial and Social
Play at least once every month and at least 18 times for the year and receive unlimited play during one week of the following summer	• Encourage consistent play throughout the year • Discourage play at competing courses • Reward increases course usage during the slow summer season, enhancing atmosphere and ancillary revenue (food/beverage, clubhouse merchandise)	Financial
Members are invited to annual party at clubhouse	• Social gathering for members, thanking them for their patronage	Social
Course partners with local restaurants to provide gift certificates to members on their birthdays. Certificate is mailed to members by the course with a birthday card. In exchange, each participating restaurant receives a hole sponsorship (name on tee box sign).	• Regular reminder to members that Baytree appreciates them • Provides opportunity for creating relationships/partnering with local businesses	Social and Financial
Baytree Buff League: Members form two-person teams for Friday afternoon 9-hole competitions. Teams pay flat yearly fee amounting to a per-9-hole rate heavily discounted from the regular rate.	• Encourage social activity, friendships, and competition among players in the context of Baytree • Encourage regular play at Baytree • Increase ancillary revenue	Social and Financial

Sport teams in various leagues regularly employ relationship-marketing programs to help build **fan identification**. Fan identification is defined as the personal commitment and emotional involvement customers have with a sport organization (Sutton, McDonald, Milne, & Cimperman, 1997). Think of a sport team that you are very passionate about. Perhaps you consider yourself a die-hard fan of the Boston Red Sox. You would be considered to have "high identification" with that team. The reasons sport marketers want high fan identification are relatively obvious. Such fans generally attend more games, support the team through good seasons and bad, and buy and wear/display more team merchandise. Through helping fans feel a sense of belonging and staying actively involved with a franchise, relationship-marketing programs strengthen two factors identified by Sutton et al. (1997) as antecedents of fan identification, affiliation, and activity. Such programs help fans build a sense of connection with

Fan Identification_____

The personal commitment and emotional involvement customers have with a sport organization.

the team and stay actively involved with the team. The San Diego Padres have one program called the Frequent Friar Club. Members earn points for games attended and receive rewards dependent upon how many points they earn through the course of a season. Rewards range from free gourmet coffee all the way to the opportunity to take batting practice at PETCO Field. Members also receive other benefits that are not dependent upon how many games they attend (e.g., free movie pass, ticket discounts, etc.). Such programs, combined with other bonding strategies (e.g., a strong presence on social networking sites such as Facebook) increase the likelihood of teams generating high identification with a core group of fans. Many professional teams place such importance on relationship marketing, in fact, that they have job positions devoted to the construction and management of these programs. These types of positions are likely to expand greatly in the next 10 years.

Sport marketers also value the establishment of strong, sustained relationships with sponsors, engaging in strategies to help sponsors feel valued and connected to the sport property (team, event, etc.). In fact, the word "partner" is increasingly used in place of the word sponsor, as partner suggests a two-way, mutually beneficial relationship between sport property and sponsor. That is, sport properties develop relationships with sponsors through caring about each sponsor's needs, and tailoring sponsorship packages to fit these needs, as briefly described earlier in this chapter. They also develop relationships with sponsors by providing each with **fulfillment audits**, post-sponsorship reports that illustrate and highlight how the sport property fulfilled their corporate needs. For example, a sponsor might sponsor a sport event primarily to entertain valued clients (and prospective clients) in a large, catered, hospitality tent provided as part of their sponsorship package. The sport property that recognizes the value of a sustained relationship with this sponsor would be wise to provide them with a fulfillment audit that contained (among other things) pictures, and perhaps even video, of the valued and prospective clients enjoying themselves in the hospitality area. In short, sport marketers develop sustained relationships with sponsors by *caring about their business needs, developing sponsorship plans to satisfy these needs, and showing them, post-event, how these needs were satisfied.*

Branding and Positioning

Another extremely important aspect of sport marketing is branding and the related concept of positioning. Schwarz and Hunter (2008) nicely define a **brand** as a name, term, design, symbol, or feature that identifies one sport product as being different from another; the mixture of attributes can be tangible or intangible, are usually symbolized in a trademark, and if managed properly, create value and influence. Related to this value and influence, having a strong sport brand helps that brand create what is termed **brand equity**. Brand equity is the marketplace value that a brand contributes to a product (Shank, 2009). To illustrate, think of consumers wishing to purchase a few new t-shirts in which to work out. They go to the apparel section in their local department store and find a three pack of generic t-shirts and a three pack of Nike t-shirts. The package of generic shirts costs $12, while the package of Nike t-shirts costs $39.99. Do you think some of these consumers would purchase the more expensive Nike t-shirts? Now add in the information that the shirts are exactly the same, except for a small Nike swoosh in the upper right corner of the Nike t-shirts. Do you still think that many consumers would purchase the more expensive Nike shirts? The answer to each question is an absolute yes! The value of the Nike brand, in the visual representation of the name and the logo and all of the perceptions (e.g., "fashionable," "reliable quality," etc.) that go with it, adds significant value to the products on which it is placed. Quite simply, significant value resides in the Nike name and swoosh.

Other powerful brands having strong brand equity exist across the sport product spectrum. Others in the sporting good and apparel arena include brands such as Adidas, Reebok, and relative newcomer Under Armour. The NFL as a league has strong brand equity, as do a number of individual teams within the league (e.g., Dallas Cowboys, Pittsburgh Steelers). University athletic programs can benefit from strong brand equity, as evidenced by brands such as the University of Texas Longhorns, the University of Florida Gators, and the like. In these cases, winning certainly helps, but also important are the strong and valued brand symbols themselves (the Cowboy's star, the University of Florida's popular gator head logo, etc.). Gold's Gym is a fitness center that benefits from the strong brand equity it has created. Many athletes benefit, in the form of product endorsement revenue, from creating (often with the help of their agents) strong brand equity, with themselves as the brand. The New York Yankees have such extraordinary brand equity that because of the power of their brand, they decided against selling naming rights to their new stadium and thus bypassed the revenue that would have resulted. Yankees COO Lonn Trost said "You would not rename the White House and you would not rename Grant's Tomb or the Grand Canyon. We will not rename Yankee Stadium" (Trost, 2008). Such a statement is a powerful testament to the brand equity that team enjoys.

Brands that have high brand equity are usually well-positioned. **Positioning** is essentially establishing a brand's image in the minds of consumers. It may be thought of as establishing a brand's "personality." Many things contribute to a brand's positioning, such as the brand name, logo, colors (team colors, for example), price, and advertisements, to name but a few. To illustrate positioning, think back to the XFL, a professional football league created by World Wrestling Entertainment (WWE) head Vince McMahon. While the league folded after its inaugural 2001 season, it provides a clear example of the concept of positioning. The WWE was in charge of branding for the league and for each of the league's individual teams, and did many things in an attempt to position the brand as a differentiated alternative to the NFL. First, the name of the league itself, XFL, was part of a positioning attempt. The letter X represents specific meaning to many in our society: extreme, edgy, hardcore, violence, sex. Therefore, it's use next to the "FL" communicated to consumers that this meaning was part of the XFL's personality. Second, team names were chosen in an

Positioning_____
Establishing a brand's image in the minds of consumers.

effort to build on this personality. Teams had names such as the Rage, Demons, Hitmen, Outlaws, Maniax, and Xtreme (note the use of the letter X in the spelling of the latter two). Third, team logos were chosen to build on this personality as well. For example, the Orlando Rage's logo represented an enraged, red, hulking-like figure, while the Los Angeles Xtreme's logo represented what appeared to be a ninja throwing star.

Fourth, the football used by the XFL itself was designed to contribute to the positioning of the league in that its colors were black and red as opposed to the traditional brown. Much like the letter X represents meaning in our culture, so do colors. Dependent upon the context of their use, black and red in combination can communicate meaning such as powerful, fast, violent, and fearsome. Fifth, the league created rules in order to position themselves as a more fun and "extreme" league as compared to the NFL. For example, players were allowed to place nicknames on the back of their jerseys in place of their last names. A game rule allowed no fair catches on punts (potentially leading to violent hits). Another required only one foot in bounds on catches. Halftimes were only ten minutes long, ostensibly to keep the pace of the entire event experience from lagging. Finally, microphone and camera use during the broadcasts attempted to position the league as more extreme than the NFL. Microphones were placed in a myriad of places (e.g., huddles, locker rooms, coaches) to provide the television viewer with new and unique access to the game that they had not experienced before. Cameras were placed in numerous positions to provide the viewer with new viewing angles. There are numerous reasons postulated as to why the XFL did not survive past its first year of play, and one primary reason relates to positioning. It might be hypothesized that fans saw too much of the WWE (WWF at the time) "sport-entertainment" personality in the XFL, and simply did not desire this personality for their professional football. In other words, it might be contended that while the XFL successfully differentiated its image from that of the NFL, it did a poor job predicting the extent to which fans desired to consume that image within the sport of football.

The concept of positioning is important not only for professional leagues and teams, but for many types of sport products, whether they be collegiate athletic programs, sport equipment brands, access facilities such as fitness centers, spectator facilities, or athletes themselves. In a fundraising letter sent to alumni by Valparaiso University's (VU) athletic department, VU distinguished their athletics by contrasting it to some of the rather unsavory news emanating from other college programs at the time (e.g., recruiting scandals, academic scandals, etc.). Their letter attempts to position the VU athletic program in the minds of readers as a "clean," "upstanding" program that will make alumni proud . . . and is thus deserving of their financial support.

When one thinks of the golf equipment market, what words come to mind when thinking of the Titleist brand and the Nike brand? When thinking of the Titleist brand, a consumer is likely to think of words such as "tradition," "quality," and perhaps "conservative." Such attributes are fostered by Titleist's marketing communication and branding, from its endorsers to the classic script font in which its brand name is written. When thinking of the Nike brand, one might think of words such as "modern," "youthful," "cutting edge," or even "Tiger Woods." Such a brand personality is carefully crafted by Nike to differentiate itself from brands such as Titleist.

Individual athletes also represent brands and are positioned. The Ladies Professional Golf Association (LPGA), for example, has increasingly positioned its athletes as fashionable and sexy (Show, 2009a), highlighting its young and attractive "celebrity" players such as Natalie Gulbis and Paula Creamer in its marketing. In so doing, it hopes to attract more and younger viewers who may be only casual fans of golf. An agent marketing Dennis Rodman in the twilight of his NBA career might have found success marketing him to teams struggling in attendance by positioning him as an entertaining, flamboyant, "character" who could provide somewhat of a boost to ticket sales and media attention.

External Contingencies

It is important to understand that sport marketers do not operate in a vacuum. The environment in which they operate contains many factors beyond their control. These factors, which can be termed **external contingencies**, include the economy, technology, competition, physical environment, cultural and social trends, the political and legal environment, and demographics (Shank, 2009). Such contingencies can present both opportunities and threats to sport marketers as they develop strategies to market their products. To illustrate the necessity of sport marketers' attention to these factors, consider the economy and technology in brief detail.

The state of the economy affects both the amount of money consumers have to spend on sport products, as well as their willingness to spend the money that they do have. This applies to both individual consumer spending on sport products, as well as corporate spending on sponsorship. As an example of this, the U.S. economy experienced an economic downturn beginning in late 2008. The stock market plunged, unemployment rose, and wages for those employed stagnated. Further, people were bombarded on a daily basis with media messages reminding them how bad the economy was. This resulted in an economic climate that had individual consumers more hesitant to spend their money on non-necessities, and corporations less willing to allocate tight dollars to sport sponsorship. One obvious way this affected marketing strategy was in pricing. In down economies, sport marketers must pay particular attention to their pricing strategies and must often adjust prices to meet reduced demand. This may mean ticket price reductions, special ticket promotions, or simply avoiding ticket price increases in a down economy. The NFL, for example, introduced a limited number of lower-priced tickets ($500) to the 2009 Super Bowl in response to the poor economy. Further, and perhaps more illustrative, most NFL teams kept ticket prices the same for the 2009 season in response to the down economy. Eighteen NFL teams held prices steady, while three teams reduced prices. Much of this pricing strategy can be attributed to the poor economy (Team Marketing Report, 2009b). For example, Chicago Bears Senior Director of Sales and Marketing said his team's decision to keep ticket prices flat was a "good decision in a tough economic environment" (Team Marketing Report, 2009b). The economy contributed to teams in other leagues following suit. For example, in Major League Baseball, while only six teams held prices steady or increased less than one percent over the 2008 season, a full ten teams actually reduced ticket prices, with several teams also offering cheaper concession options (Team Marketing Report, 2009a). Further, twelve MLB teams had a lower Fan Cost Index (FCI) for 2009 versus 2008. The FCI represents the average price for a family of four to attend a sport event, and includes four averaged-priced tickets (for two adults and two children), four hot dogs, four small soft drinks, two small beers, two programs, two hats, and parking. The average FCI for the four major U.S. professional leagues is provided in Table 8.2.

As noted, the economy can also affect sponsors' ability and willingness to sponsor sport events. Growth of sport sponsorship in 2009 was forecasted to be the slowest in seven years due to cutbacks driven by the poor economy (Sessa, 2009). Further, a major industry survey found that 51 percent of those companies surveyed said that their sponsorship spending would decrease in 2009, and another 36 percent said their spending would remain relatively unchanged (Klayman, 2009). In this same survey, 47 percent of companies even reported that they would be seeking to get out of current sponsorship deals. It is quite clear that in poor economies, sponsors become hesitant to sign new deals because of economic uncertainties, as well as because of fears that consumers will see the spending as wasteful at a time when the sponsors may, for example, be laying off workers. This can affect sport marketers in a number of ways. Realizing that sponsorship revenue might suffer in poor economic times, wise sport marketers pay particular attention to the investigation of new revenue streams. For example, the NBA recently reversed a long-standing (1991) ban on courtside advertising by liquor brands in an attempt to increase revenue during the current poor economy (Lombardo & Lefton, 2009). Poor economic conditions also present a challenge to the sport marketer with regard to sponsorship sales. In economic downturns, sport marketers must increasingly seek to put together sponsorship proposals that directly address the specific needs of each individual potential sponsor and must

TABLE 8.2

2009 Fan Cost Index for NFL, MLB, NBA, NHL

League	Average Ticket Price	FCI
NFL	$74.99	$412.64
MLB	$26.64	$196.99
NBA	$49.47	$291.93
NHL	$49.66	$288.23

Source: Team Marketing Report, Chicago, IL.

be particularly cognizant about sponsorship pricing. In addition, they must seek improved leveraging opportunities for their sponsors. **Leveraging** (also termed **activation**) refers to the utilization of various marketing strategies to improve sponsor value. For example, donut retailer Krispy Kreme utilized sport sponsorship as part of its marketing strategy during expansion into the U.S Midwest. One team they sponsored was the Kansas City Royals. To leverage this sponsorship, Krispy Kreme gave away one dozen donuts to all attendees at every Royals' game for each game in which the Royals had twelve or more hits. This allowed Krispy Kreme to leverage its association with the Royals into heightened brand awareness and increased sampling of its product in the Kansas City market.

Technology is another external contingency that has had significant recent impact on sport marketing strategy. For example, mobile phones have now become much more than phones. Relatively new mobile devices such as the Apple iPhone allow for Web browsing and offer multimedia (e.g., streaming video) capabilities. Where beneficial, sport marketers look to such technology with an eye to how it can help them better market their product. The Green Bay Packers, for example, have m.packers.com, a web-site for fans using mobile devices. The site provides a display of information from the team's main web-site, packers.com, that is suited for mobile devices. The Packers, like many other sport teams, also take advantage of mobile technology to keep in touch with their fans through mobile alerts such as text messages on team news, ticket promotions, and the like sent to fans who subscribe to the service. The NHL is utilizing mobile technology to offer the NHL Bundle to Canadian fans with mobile devices. For $8 per month, the NHL Bundle offers live and delayed game broadcasts, original video programming, and live radio play-by-play of NHL games. The NFL also offers live mobile broadcasts of games televised over the NFL Network (Mickle, 2009). Twitter allows teams to stay connected with fans by sending short messages, called "tweets," to fans via texting, instant message, or the Web. Such technology allows leagues and teams to stay in virtual constant contact with fans, increasing fan identification as well as the success of promotions that can be broadcast through such a medium.

Advances in video and broadcast technology have allowed sport marketers to offer enhanced products and enjoyment to fans. The Dallas Cowboys recently installed a $40 million high definition video board in their new $1.15 billion stadium in Arlington, Texas. The board is four-sided, with a 160' wide and 71' high feet screen for fans on both sides of the stadium, and a 50' wide and 28' high screen for fans in both end zones. Such boards offer fans enhanced views of the action and replays, and offer increased value to sponsors through enhanced messaging opportunities. Sports broadcaster ESPN continues to blaze trails through the use of technology, recently announcing that it will soon begin a new channel to broadcast sport events in 3-D.

Opportunities for sport marketers made possible through advancing technology are certainly not limited to mobile devices or video and broadcast technology. Yet another strategy increasingly used by sport organizations combines technology with another external contingency, cultural and social trends. Specifically, many sport organizations are taking advantage of social media (the

Dallas Cowboys Video Board

various means by which people communicate via the Internet), and in particular of the increasing popularity of social networking. It is now common for teams to create a presence on social networking sites such as Facebook and MySpace, and many are also creating their own official fan social network Web sites. Major League Soccer's Houston Dynamo, for example created MyDynamo.net. The Minnesota Vikings have WeAreVikingsFans.com. Both independent sites such as Facebook as well as team-operated sites help teams build fan identification through connecting and involving the fan with the team and other fans. These sites accomplish this in a number of ways. Fans can communicate through message boards (e.g., the "Wall" in Facebook) and blogs, find other fans in their geographic location with which to connect, post pictures and videos, and view pictures and videos from other fans. Many of the team-operated sites allow fans to create and invite other fans into their own "communities within the community" centered on a common interest such as a favorite player or team history. Team-operated sites also allow fans to build their personal fan profile for others to see (e.g., name, favorite players, favorite memories, etc.). Not only do such sites help teams build fan identification and community, but also through the process of joining such sites, fans provide the team with information that can be used to target future marketing messages.

With regard to all external contingencies and the role that they play in shaping marketing strategy, the key lesson for sport marketers is to always pay close attention to all that is happening in the environment (cultural environment, technological environment, competitive environment, etc.) in which they operate. Such attention will illuminate both marketing threats and opportunities that less attentive sport marketers will, at their own peril, miss. Attention without action, however, does little. Marketers must respond creatively to their external environment. As a brief example, recall the surge of U.S. gasoline prices in 2007–2008. Understanding the "pain at the pump" consumers were experiencing, creative sport marketers took advantage, turning this economic threat into an opportunity. Callaway Golf, for example, gave away gift cards worth $100 in free gas with the purchase of certain drivers (Ramde, 2008). For fans buying 2008–2009 season tickets, the New Jersey Nets offered 10 percent of the purchase price back in the form of free gas. While not offering a price promotion, the Detroit Pistons utilized the gas price surge as a public relations tool, having Pistons players pump $20 of free gas per car during a one-and-a-half hour period at one local gas station. In each case, these organizations attended to a happening in the external environment and utilized it to their advantage.

The Marketing Plan

The formal blueprint that marketers follow in the execution of their marketing strategy is called a **marketing plan**. Formulating a marketing plan guides the sport marketer in developing a strategic plan that increases the probability that the product will find success in the marketplace. The plan includes a SWOT (a firm's Strengths, Weaknesses, Opportunities, and Threats) analysis, intended target markets, and resulting strategies for promotion, pricing, and distribution. A marketing plan will also often include performance objectives, such as goals for a percentage increase in event attendance over the prior year, quarterly sales objectives, brand awareness objectives, and the like.

To illustrate the basics of a marketing plan, consider a plan for a February Philadelphia stop for the event "Monster Jam," a monster truck competition sanctioned by the U.S. Hot Rod Association (see Box 8.2). A brief summary of selected strategies of the marketing plan for the Monster Jam show is provided here. Not all strategies in the actual plan are presented, nor is every detail provided about the strategies that are presented. The summary is simply intended to give the reader a glimpse of the content of an actual marketing plan.

Marketing plans vary widely in their detail and thoroughness. For example, an expansion of the Monster Jam plan above might provide additional demographic and psychographic detail about the target markets, including income levels, areas of geographic concentration, other activities they are interested in, types of media that they consume, and the like. This can provide insight into how to reach the targets with various marketing messages. It might also include budgetary information such as the amount allocated to each media outlet (e.g., radio station, television station). However, the idea behind each plan is the same. The process of formulating the plan is an exercise that assists marketers in thinking strategically about how to best market their product, and the resultant plan essentially acts as a marketing "recipe" to follow. A marketing plan does not guarantee success, but it certainly increases its probability.

Conclusion

Sport marketing is a fascinating and growing industry. It is impossible to fully describe or even briefly discuss everything that sport marketing entails in one chapter. The purpose of this chapter, rather, has been to highlight and emphasize the foundation upon which sport marketing, and indeed all of marketing, is built: understanding and satisfying customer wants and needs. In doing so, we have introduced the key related topics of sport marketing, market segmentation, relationship marketing, branding and positioning, external contingencies, and the marketing plan. There are many interesting and important aspects of sport marketing that have not been either directly addressed or addressed in great detail here. For example, there is much more to learn about pricing, sponsorship, public relations, advertising, and marketing research, to name but a few. There are indeed a myriad of tools in the marketer's toolbox, and the person who is an expert at using each has yet to be found. However, if in using each one of the tools of the trade, the marketer keeps the customer front and center, his or her chances for success increase exponentially.

BOX 8.2

Strengths/Opportunities

- Ticket prices remain very affordable at $27, $22, and $5 for children;
- The Philadelphia market is focused on football, but it is unlikely the Eagles will be in the playoffs and thus take focus away from show promotion or consumer's disposable income allocated to entertainment.

Weaknesses/Threats

- The show has been in the market for several years and is thus in need of fresh marketing ideas;
- The marketing budget has not increased over the last two years;
- No big names;
- Normally snowy and cold weather which hurts possibilities of doing a PR event outside.

Target Audience

- Primary target market: Males 18–44
- Secondary target market: Children 6–11

Ticket Prices

- Adult: $27, $22
- Child: $5
- Discounts: Group Tickets for 20+ people $14 per ticket
- Boy Scouts 12 or older: $13
- Early Bird purchases: $22, $17
- Adult coupon: $22, $17

Promotion

Radio

- WMMR (rock), WXTU (country)
  —WWMR sponsors a truck
  —WWMR runs ride to work/school in a monster truck with the morning show promo
  —15 :10 (10 second) advertisements
  —Hourly Monster Jam on-air promotions during weekend of event
  —Advertisements on WWMR.com
  —Live mentions by on-air personalities
- For the following stations, seek to provide tickets in exchange for on-air ticket giveaways, on-air mentions, website inclusion, email blasts, and distribution of Monster Jam promotional material at station events:

WJSE, WJBR, WMGK, WSTW, WZZO, WTHK, WPST, WRDW, WIOQ

Outdoor Advertising

- Ads on 60 bus backs on suburban bus routes
- 12 Billboards

Internet

- Monster Jam logo and web page link on every partnering radio station website
- E-mail blasts in early December to database lists, including Tony Hawk Boom Boom HuckJam, WWE, Motocross, Incubus, Linkin Park, Beastie Boys, prior Monster Jam shows, American Idols Live, Van Morrison, Red Hot Chili Peppers, Barenaked Ladies, Panic at the Disco, Wachovia Complex Cyber Club
- A presence on MySpace, Facebook, and Friendster will be created to help reach the younger crowd
- Sixers, Flyers, Phantoms, and Kixx to send discount e-mail to members promoting Monster Jam

Television

- KYW-TV 3 (CBS)
  —The Early Show (M–F, 5 am–7 am)
- WPVI-TV 6 (ABC)
  —TGIF (Friday during news 5 pm–6:30 pm)
  —Fast Forward (last Saturday of each month)
  —Visions (Saturday at 7:30 pm)
- WCAU-TV 10 (NBC)
  —10! Show (M–F, 10 am–11 am)
- WTXF-TV 29 (FOX)
  —Good Day Philadelphia (Weekdays 5 am–9 am)
- Comcast SportsNet
  —Daily News Live

Partnerships

- Wendy's
  —Tray liners in-store mid-through-late December
- Bally's Total Fitness
  —Prominently displayed promotional information at front desk of all area locations
  —Promotional offer and show information in all Bally print advertising
  —"Bally Total Fitness Discount" to Monster Jam displayed on Ballytotalfitness.com with direct link to purchase tickets
  —Monster Jam information included in Bally's e-blast

CHAPTER 8

Interview

Eric Nichols
Director of Marketing
University of South Carolina Gamecock Athletics

Eric Nichols was named director of marketing for the University of South Carolina athletics department in June 2008. Nichols oversees all aspects of athletics' marketing and serves as the marketing liaison to the athletics ticket office, Web site and video production, as well as Gamecock Sports Properties, Barnes and Noble merchandising, university licensing and communications, and Global Spectrum. Nichols came to USC following a successful stint at Vanderbilt University, where he served as the athletic department's Director of Marketing and Promotions since January of 2004. He has a bachelor's and a master's degree from the University of Tennessee–Martin.

Q: Describe your career path.

A: I began my athletic administration career as a student assistant women's volleyball coach at the University of Tennessee at Martin (UTM). From there I was offered a graduate assistantship and earned my MBA from UTM. After a brief six-month stint with Nike, I went back to college administration as a facilities assistant at Vanderbilt University in 1998. I was promoted to Direc-

tor of Game and Event Management in 2000 and later switched gears and became the Director of Online Services with the primary responsibility of managing the official athletics website. In 2004, I was promoted to Director of Marketing where I served until I took a similar position at the University of South Carolina in 2008.

Q: Describe what you consider to be one of the most valuable learning experiences that you have encountered during your career and how that experience has contributed to your success and/or made you a better sport marketer.

A: I did not know at the time how valuable the information would be, but during college I had a professor stress how important it would be to "study your profession." He encouraged me to continue to learn and soak up as much knowledge as possible through trade journals, networking, and professional organizations. I have taken that advice to heart and passionately seek to learn anything that might give me an advantage to doing my job better.

183

Q: In general, what do you see as the two most important determinants of successful marketing and why?

A: Listen and create buzz. The audience is ever-changing and without really listening to your audience customer failure is a certainty. We must always be adaptable. The creation of buzz stems from the method by which consumers communicate now. Word-of-mouth has become more prevalent than ever due to the explosion of social media. Therefore, one must have a great story or product or event with which to gain attention. Also, a good product just so happens to be the most important attribute to retaining a customer.

Q: What do you believe to be the biggest challenges faced by the sport-marketing industry in the near future?

A: At the time of this question I would undoubtedly say the economy. But even after the economy recovers, I expect buying habits to change a bit and people might become a little tighter with discretionary income. Secondly, learning how the new fans—kids—are consuming our products. Fewer kids are having the ability to enjoy sports like they might have in the past due to escalating prices. However, television, iPhones, cell phones, et cetera have made the ability to be "a fan" more

possible than ever without ever setting foot inside a venue. Communicating with and motivating this group will be an important task.

Q: As Director of Marketing for Gamecock Athletics, what are the primary things you look for in new hires?

A: I'll credit Rick Pitino for this one—a PHD—Poor, Hungry, and Driven. But in all honesty, the perception of our business is vastly different from the reality, and having the hunger to work long days and nights while also being driven to get better is what I would like to have on my staff. Oh, and you have to be creative too.

Q: What is your advice to students considering a career in sport marketing?

A: Start now. Whether it is two hours a week or two hundred, students have to begin now. With the stiff competition for these jobs, displaying an understanding of what it takes and having a reference in the business is critical. And finally, when you get your foot in the door, do not blow it! Figure out how you can help the department, and help them better than anyone they have ever had in their office.

Study Questions

1. This chapter has defined good sport marketing as being customer-focused. Explain what this means and provide an example of a sport marketer (can be an individual, franchise, league, etc.) that you believe has a strong customer focus.
2. Give an example of a sport marketer who you believe has a relatively weak customer focus and has suffered because of it.
3. Describe what is meant by fan identification. What are the various reasons that we want highly identified fans?
4. What businesses do you frequent outside of the sport industry that use relationship-marketing strategies? Do you believe you have spent more money with some of these businesses than you otherwise would have due to these marketing efforts?
5. Describe the concept of lifetime value.
6. A key to successful sport marketing is staying tuned in to external contingencies (competition, technology, social/cultural trends, etc.). This chapter has very briefly illustrated the external contingencies of the economy and technology. What are some examples of how other external contingencies can affect the strategies of sport marketers?

7. What are the major components of a marketing plan?
8. What are the major bases of market segmentation?
9. What is meant by positioning? What are some sport brands that you believe position themselves well? What are some sport brands that you believe could be positioned better?
10. What is included in the Fan Cost Index (FCI), and what is the average FCI for the NFL, NBA, MLB, and NHL? How have these FCIs changed over the past five years?

Learning Activities

1. You are the marketing director for a minor league hockey team in a city of your choice. Using each of the bases of segmentation discussed in this chapter, identify five distinct market segments that you will target. Develop ten game day promotions (autograph night, discount beverage night, etc.), with each segment that you have identified being targeted by at least two of them. Try to be creative with your promotions. Now, develop other marketing strategies that you might use to target each of your five segments. Your strategies should include, but not be limited to, advertising and pricing.
2. You work in marketing for a Major League Baseball team. You have been charged with developing a relationship-marketing program for the team, a program which will increase fans' involvement with the team throughout the year. What might your relationship-marketing program look like? Be sure to include elements of both social bonding and financial bonding.

References

Ad Spotlight (2004). Ad spotlight. Team Meeting Report, February, p. 6.

Coast to Coast (2009, December 22–28). Coast to coast. *Street and Smith's SportsBusiness Journal,* p. 29.

Definition. (2009). Definition of marketing. *MarketingPower.com.* Retrieved on April 5, 2009 from http://www.marketing power.com/AboutAMA/Pages/DefinitionofMarketing.aspx

Dictionary. (2009). *MarketingPower.com.* Retrieved on April 5, 2009 from http://www.marketingpower.com/_layouts/ Dictionary.aspx?dLetter=R

FFA. (2008, January 14). FFA fundraiser night at the Blazers. *Business Wire.* Retrieved on January 4, 2009 from http://www.businesswire.com/portal/site/google/index.jsp?ndmViewId=news_view&newsId=20080114006248& newsLang=en

Fullerton, S. (2007). *Sports marketing.* New York, NY: McGraw Hill.

Klayman, B. (2009, October 28). Over half of firms to cut sponsorship spend: Study. Retrieved on November 3, 2009 from http://www.reuters.com/article/idUSTRE52969320090310

Lifestyle. (2010). Lifestyle and Behavior Segmentation: Nielsen PRIZM. Retrieved on January 7, 2010 from http:// enus.nielsen.com/etc/medialib/nielsen_dotcom/en_us/documents/pdf/fact_sheets.Par.69269.File.dat/PRIZM_US_ SS_n8006.pdf

Lombardo, J. & Lefton, T. (2009, January 19-25). NBA cans ban on liquor ads. *Street & Smith's SportsBusiness Journal,* pp. 1, 26.

Mickle, T. (2009, February 2–8). Bell to offer live NHL content in Canada. *Street and Smith's SportsBusiness Journal,* p. 3.

Mullin, B., Hardy, S., & Sutton, W. (2007). *Sport marketing* (3rd ed.). Champaign, IL: Human Kinetics.

PRIZM. (2010). PRIZM: Overview. Retrieved January 7, 2010 from http://en-us.nielsen.com/tab/product_families/nielsen_claritas/prizm

PRIZM NE Segments (2010). PRIZM NE Segments. Retrieved January 7, 2010 from http://www.tetrad.com/pub/documents/pnesegments.pdf.

Ramde, D. (2008, June 8). Companies offering free gas to attract business. *USA Today*. Retrieved on June 8, 2008, from http://www.usatoday.com/money/economy/2008-06-08-2344632439_x.htm

Schwarz, E. & Hunter, J. (2008). *Advanced theory and practice in sport marketing*. Oxford, UK: Butterworth-Heinemann.

Sessa, D. (2009, January 26). *Sport sponsorship growth to be slowest in 7 years, report says*. Retrieved on January 28, 2009 from http://www.sponsorship.com/About-IEG/IEG-In-The-News/Sports-Sponsorship-Growth-to-Be-Slowest-in-7-Years.aspx

Shank, M. (2009). *Sports marketing: A strategic perspective* (4th ed.). Upper Saddle River, NJ: Prentice Hall.

Show, J. (2009a, February 2–8). A call to be more hospitable. *Street and Smith's SportsBusiness Journal,* pp. 1, 13–14.

Show, J. (2009b, February 2–8). Miami PGA Tour event will be first to air ad in Spanish. *Street and Smith's SportsBusiness Journal,* p. 27.

St. John, W. (2006, June 2). Sports and salvation on faith night at the stadium. *New York Times*. Retrieved January 6, 2010 from http://www.nytimes.com/2006/06/02/sports/02faith.html

Sutton, W., McDonald, M., Milne, G., & Cimperman, J. (1997). Creating and fostering fan identification in professional sports. *Sport Marketing Quarterly, 6*(1), 15–22.

Team Marketing Report (2009a). Team marketing research. *Team Marketing Report,* April, 6–7.

Team Marketing Report (2009b). Team marketing research. *Team Marketing Report,* September, 8–9.

Trost, L. (2008, December 22–28). They said it. *Street and Smith's SportsBusiness Journal,* p. 29.

Weir, T. (2001, July 24). WNBA explores lesbian fan base. *USA Today*. Retrieved January 6, 2010 from http://www.usatoday.com/sports/basketba/wnba/stories/2001-07-23-lesbian-fans.htm

Wells, W., & Tigert, D. (1971). Activities, interests, and opinions. *Journal of Advertising Research, 11,* 127–135.

Suggested Sources

Street and Smith's SportsBusiness Journal—www.sportsbusinessjournal.com

Team Marketing Report—www.teammarketing.com

American Marketing Association—www.marketingpower.com

Sport Marketing Quarterly, Morgantown, WV: Fitness Information Technology.

Duffy, N. & Hooper, J. (2003). *Passion branding: Harnessing the power of emotions to build strong brands*. West Sussex, England: John Wiley and Sons, Inc.

Ries, A. and Ries, L. (1998). *The 22 immutable laws of branding: How to build a product or service into a world-class brand*. New York, NY: HarperCollins.

Ries, A. and Trout, J. (1993). *The 22 immutable laws of marketing: Violate them at your own risk*. New York, NY: HarperCollins.

Sport-Sales and Revenue Generation

Richard M. Southall • *The University of North Carolina at Chapel Hill*
Ronald J. Dick • *Duquesne University*

After reading this chapter, you will be able to:

- Describe how consultative selling differs from traditional selling;
- Articulate how consultative selling creates an impact;
- Demonstrate how to use the bridging-the-gap sales process;
- Highlight how to keep good relationships and help clients make investment decisions;
- Understand how to establish business credibility;
- List some rules that help influence buying decisions;
- Apply these influence rules to the sport-sales setting;
- Demonstrate the ability to analyze customer needs; and
- Outline the process of recommending solutions and gaining commitment.

KEY TERMS

80/20 Rule	Prospecting
Base Salary Plus Commission	Reciprocity
	Referral
Closes for the Next Step	Relationship Marketing
Closing	ROI
Commitment and Consistency	Social Proof
	Sport Sponsorship
Liking	Telemarketing/ Teleselling
Override	

Introduction

The United States is a capitalistic, sales-driven society, and the sport industry is particularly capitalistic. If you can sell, you have a high likelihood of being able to procure a sport job and position yourself to advance rapidly. Completing an undergraduate sport-management program—even one that requires a sport-industry internship—does not guarantee an entry-level employment position. However, the easiest way to insure a career in the sport industry, regardless of undergraduate major or advanced graduate studies, is through sales. Many people in sport start off in sales and then transition to other areas, such as public relations, finance, advertising, marketing, promotions, production, research and development, or human resources. Some sport organizations require all of their employees to complete a sale-training program so they better understand the sales process. Since sales are the lifeblood of the sport industry, most sport organizations want all of their employees to "always be selling." Many sport industry Chief Executive Officers (CEOs) and Chief Financial Officers (CFOs) "sold" at some point in their careers. John Spoelstra, former President of the New Jersey Nets and recognized leader in sport marketing, believes the CEO or President of a sport organization should demonstrate the importance of sport-sales by remaining actively involved with the sales department (Spoelstra, 1997). The ability to sell is especially important in sport marketing, because sales and marketing are inter-related. The transition from sales to marketing is often seamless. If you can sell, you can most likely execute a marketing plan.

What Is Selling?

There is no truer business statement than "nothing happens until we sell something." If you want to work in sport, you need to recognize and embrace the importance and art of selling. Sport ticket-sales are the life-blood of the sport industry. All functional areas or departments in a sport organization must work with the sales department because ticket revenue is the bedrock upon which all sport revenue depends. Without ticket sales, the value of sponsorship and media contracts significantly decreases. In addition, revenues from parking, concessions and licensed merchandise cannot be realized unless customers attend events. Though sales are critical to success, many do not understand what successful selling actually entails. Selling is not simply a transaction where money is exchanged for a product or service. Rather, selling is an artistic endeavor and a scientific process that *satisfies customers' wants, needs, and desires.*

Courtesy Mark Nagel

Though tickets for sport events are sold at the box office, most of the "selling" occurs long before the customer visits a facility.

- In the sport industry, revenue generation through sales and associated activities is critically important. Any sport-management student truly interested in a sport career should have an understanding of the revenue-generation (sales) process, and what a salesperson actually does. In sport—or any industry—a salesperson: Finds and develops new clients.

- Builds relationships (customer loyalty) by developing goodwill.
- Maintains client contact and continually satisfies current clients' wants, needs and desires.
- Solves problems and provides service for customers.
- Provides formal and informal marketing-research data.

The Sales-Training Process

Sport-management students who want to become sport-sales consultants must learn sales-process fundamentals and apply these principles in a variety of experiential settings. In recent years, there have been a number of sport-industry practitioners who have criticized sport-management professors and programs for not offering sales as part of their curriculums (Dolich, 2004; Helyar, 2006). In response to such criticism, some sport-management scholars (Irwin, Southall, & Sutton, 2007; McKelvey & Southall, 2008; Southall & Dick, in press; Southall, Dick, & Van Stone, 2008) have proposed sport-sales training programs based upon the following components:

1. **Philosophy Agreement**—Ensure individual philosophical agreement with an organization's mission and goals.
2. **Product**—Develop fundamental product knowledge. Become an expert on the organization's products and services.
3. **Prospect**—Learn and apply basic prospecting principles in order to develop a consistent prospect database.
4. **Practice**—Begin the process of practicing and refining sales fundamentals under a sales professional's direction and guidance.
5. **Performance**—Bridge the gap between theory and practice by combining real-world selling with ongoing analysis and refinement of sales strategies.

Irwin et al. (2007) coined the phrase "Pentagon of Sport-Sales Training" to describe this process and developed a schematic representation to provide a roadmap to sport-sales success (see Fig. 9.1.).

Aware that the fastest track to a sport-industry job is through sales, Southall and Dick (in press) provided empirical evidence that participating in a metadiscrete experiential sales-training program can improve sport-management students' chances of landing a job in the highly competitive sport industry. This chapter is designed to provide an introduction to the fundamental components of the sales process and an opportunity to gain insight into methods that sport organizations use to generate revenue. Students are strongly encouraged to take this information and apply it to real-world settings prior to completing their degree.

As part of your preparation for a sport-management career, you will undoubtedly take concentrated coursework in such areas as sport law, sport marketing, sport finance, and sport facility/event management. In addition, it is

FIGURE 9.1
Pentagon of Sport-Sales Training

Irwin et al. (2007). *Pentagon of Sport Sales Training: A 21st Century Sport Sales Training Model.*

a great idea to take a course that focuses on the sales process, even if that course is not offered as part of the standard sport-management curriculum.

The Sales Process

While there may be variations, the sales process usually consists of the following:

1. Ensuring philosophical agreement.
2. Developing and organizing prospects.
3. Adopting a Sales-Consultant Approach.
4. Opening the Sale.
5. Conducting the Analysis.
6. Reaching an agreement. Obtaining purchase consent and following-up with the client.
7. Value-adding and obtaining personal introductions.

Step 1—Ensuring Philosophical Agreement

Insuring philosophical agreement involves learning, understanding and internalizing an organization's sales culture and sales philosophy. A sales organization's culture reflects its physical, emotional, and developmental environment. Reflecting this environment, a sales philosophy is an organization's strategic approach to selling. A firm's sales philosophy is continually revised and modified based upon consumer feedback and sales-success levels.

An organization's sales philosophy and culture are derived from—and must be consistent with—the organization's dominant institutional logic, organizational culture, and philosophy. These elements are reflected in organizations' developed mission statements and goals, as well as its organizational artifacts, rituals, habits, and reality view. All facets of an organization's strategic marketing plan, including such marketing-mix elements as sponsorship partnerships, advertising strategies, and promotional contests should be consistent with the sport organization's overall institutional logic and organizational culture.

For instance, many beer companies would willingly agree to **sponsorship** partnerships, develop advertising campaigns, and integrate promotions in conjunction with college-sport events. However, many universities decline to pursue extensive alcohol sponsorships, allow such advertising, or engage in beer-company sponsored promotions since that would conflict with their core educational philosophy. But, as has become more apparent in the past few years, some athletic-departments and universities seem to have no issue with such activities.

These concepts and issues, as well as fundamental elements of ethics, are discussed in Chapter 2: Socio-cultural Aspects of Sport and Chapter 7: Ethics. While engaging in undergraduate studies, when interviewing for a first sport-industry job, and throughout a sport-industry career, it is crucial to identify and articulate an individual ethical belief system. Interviewing with various sport organizations should include analysis of each sport organization's institutional logic and organizational culture.

An organization's sales culture manifests itself in its selling environment, which include such independent and interdependent factors as the sales manager, sales room, sales-peer group, and the organization's overall view of the sales function. Examining and evaluating a selling environment involves investigating:

* Staff performance expectations
* Experience levels of sales managers,
* Sales training and technologies utilized, and
* Product or services (including the public's perception and demand) (Irwin et al., 2007).

An organization's sales culture and selling environment may affect and be affected by dramatic ideological, political, and/or organizational shifts, depending upon the organization's success or failure:

* Hiring or laying off sales staff,
* Adding or eliminating discounts,
* Leveraging or courting behaviors,
* Adding or eliminating ticket plan options,
* Early payment incentives or payment plans,
* Adding or eliminating promotional nights and giveaway items,
* Adding to or cutting group-sales inventory, and
* Implementing or cutting back on sales contests and other performance incentives.

For instance, in 1991 the National Basketball Association (NBA) established rules restricting its teams from selling TV-visible hard liquor signage. However, changing cultural norms and a slumping economy caused the NBA to rescind those rules in 1999. Though franchises were able to sell those previously restricted advertisements, not every team elected to implement hard liquor sales as part of their sponsorship sales philosophy.

While sport-management students may not have developed their own coherent and consistent sales philosophy, the process can be enhanced by studying traditional sales philosophies, *best practices,* and new segmentation or technological approaches. Some common sport-industry sales philosophies are listed in Table 9.1. While not an exhaustive list, four of the five philosophies emphasize sales persons' roles prior to and after a sale. In addition, four philosophies stress "customer satisfaction" and the need for sales staff to fulfill customer expectations. It is also no surprise all five sales philosophies highlight the importance of personal interaction in the sales process.

Once a sales consultant understands and is comfortable with an organization's sales philosophy, he/she can more comfortably begin the sales process. The next step involves developing and organizing sales prospects.

TABLE 9.1

Common Sport-Industry Sales Philosophies

Sales Philosophy	Summary
Sun Tzu–Art of War Adaptation	Relationship selling based upon being prepared and anticipating customer needs and interests—win-win thinking (Michaelson & Michaelson, 2004).
Prize Inside	An up-front approach to benefit-based selling based upon the premise that every consumer wants to know their prize—how do they benefit from or what do they get from the sale (Godin, 2004)?
The Customer Comes Second	Sales staff needs must be satisfied before those of the customer (Rosenbluth, 1992).
Consumer-Behavior Driven	Sales success involves identifying and understanding potential consumers, and creating personal relationships in order to persuade customers (McCormack, 1996).
Eduselling	Educating and partnering with customers before, during, and after the sale leads to purchase satisfaction and long-term customer retention (Sutton, Lachowetz, & Clark, 2000).

Adapted from Irwin et al. (2007). *Pentagon of Sport Sales Training: A 21st Century Sport Sales Training Model.*

Step 2—Developing and Organizing Prospects

Prospecting is the process of finding people (also known as "leads") who have the desire and means to purchase a product or service. It is the first step in customer development and directly affects revenue-generation potential. The goal of prospecting is to efficiently determine if a specific individual is actually a "prospect." If a person truly has neither the desire nor the ability to invest in the product or service being offered, there is really no reason to make a presentation. A "real" prospect has wants, needs, and desires that can be satisfied by a product or service, and the ability to act to satisfy these wants, needs, and desires. A sales consultant's job involves uncovering how her product or service can most effectively satisfy these identified wants, needs and desires. The prospecting process involves determining how best to uncover, generate and develop qualified leads.

Prospecting_____
Searching for and creating new customers.

Effective prospecting involves generating a significant amount of prospect volume. The more qualified prospects to whom you speak, the more sales will eventually result. A general rule of thumb is that each 50–100 new contacts will lead to 10 sales presentations, which will lead to 2–3 sales. Certainly, this ratio can be improved if the prospects' characteristics identify them as more likely to purchase the product or service the salesperson has to offer. However, while enhancing the likelihood of sales success through better analysis may be possible, it is still important for students to remember: "To make one sale, multiple prospects must be contacted." The high contacted-prospects-to-sales ratio is the most daunting part of sales. It often discourages some students from pursuing a career in sport sales since even a successful sales consultant will experience continual "failure." The best sport analogy that puts the importance of prospecting into its proper perspective is to remember that a major-league baseball player who gets a hit three out of 10 times at bat will likely be enshrined in the Hall of Fame. What is sometimes forgotten is that a great hitter also "fails" to get a hit seven out of 10 at bats. Within this context, it is important sport-management students recognize SALES SUCCESS can be greatly increased through more efficient prospecting, but the process is still time intensive and not foolproof.

Effective prospecting typically involves:

- Gathering all relevant contact information (including best method of contact)
- Developing and maintaining prospect and contact history
- Developing a systematic follow-up system (Contact software can help with this)
- Maintaining a high level of professionalism
- Consistently sustaining contact with the prospect, even when a sale is not proposed (A rule of thumb is 4–7 contacts are necessary before a sale is finalized) and even after a sale is executed.
- Ask for the sale—ABC (Always Be Closing)

The key to effective revenue generation is consistent, professional contact over time. Keep talking to new, qualified prospects and sales will eventually follow!

Sport-Sales Prospecting Sources

Prospecting Lists Provided by Management

There are different techniques to utilize when speaking with prospects identified from lists provided by management. (Note: These techniques are spelled out in greater depth later in this chapter. See #3, Adopting a Sales Consultancy Approach and #5, Conducting an Analysis.) Most prospects will have different reasons why they are looking to invest or why they should potentially invest. It is the sales-consultant's responsibility to uncover these reasons so that appropriate sales proposals can be developed. Some examples of prospecting lists provided by management include:

- Canceled season ticket holders
- Canceled partial-plan holders
- Single-game ticket purchasers
- Current customers (partial-plan purchasers)
- Direct mail/structured campaign lists
- *Ticketmaster* lists
- Chamber of Commerce database
- Targeted business lists
- Group sales lists
- School lists
- Church lists

Personal Prospect-Lead Sources

A successful sport-sales consultant will be able to capitalize on the provided lead or prospecting sources discussed. However, the overall results depend on effectively uncovering each prospective client's needs, wants and desires. To achieve greater success, it is important on each call to ask appropriate questions to qualify prospects (determine their wants, needs, and desires—e.g., are they interested in purchasing season tickets for personal or business use, are they a "fan" or more interested in utilizing the ticket for entertaining clients), and ask for their business on each call (this is expanded upon in the section "Closing for the next step" later in this chapter).

As a future sport-sales consultant you must develop a game plan for generating quality leads, over and above those provided by management. Below are a few suggestions of additional ideas for generating quality prospect leads:

- Association lists (i.e., sales and marketing executives, Rotary and Lions Clubs, labor unions, doctors' associations, financial groups, alumni associations, communication associations)
- Business publications
- Newspapers
- Networking groups (Facebook, MySpace, Twitter, etc.)

- Friends/family
- Contacts from previous jobs
- Word of mouth
- Driving by new buildings/New companies/Company relocations
- Customized seminars (in-person or online)
- Telephone book

It is important to remember the likelihood of sales success increases as potential prospects generated from these lists are segmented by their propensity to purchase. This involves asking questions in order to gauge the level and intensity of wants, needs, and desires, and the ability of prospects to act to satisfy these needs. By engaging in this qualification process and gathering as much information before and during initial contact, sales consultants can improve their efficiency and enhance potential sales success.

Brainstorm Activity: Can you identify additional prospecting sources? Can you list 3 to 5 names of actual prospects for several categories listed above?

Step 3—Adopting a Sales-Consultant Approach

As has just been discussed, a salesperson must eliminate the fear of failure, since it is a part of the sales process. Sales consultants must always remember that since prospects do not know them well, potential refusals to purchase are not personal rejections. If potential clients do not buy, they are not rejecting a sales-consultant's recommendation; they are simply declining the recommended product or service because it is not perceived to be a good fit for them at that time. The product or service just does not satisfy their wants, needs, and desires. The fear of rejection is the single most important obstacle a sales consultant must overcome.

Sell Like a Medical Doctor: The sales consultant should do the following: Examine, diagnose, and prescribe. The mutual trust and agreement between a sales person and client, must be similar to that of a doctor and patient.

In order to become a successful sales consultant, it helps to study and adopt characteristics of successful sales people. This may involve examining the way sales consultants dress, as well as their posture, outward behaviors, and public-speaking habits. In addition, a future sales consultant must understand the fundamental elements of consultative selling.

BOX 9.1

Social Networking

Social Networking (SN) sites, such as Twitter, Facebook, MySpace, and Linkedin, have emerged as powerful tools for organizations to connect with current and prospective customers. They are unique in their ability to allow for an immediate and meaningful connection that provides an opportunity to exchange information between sport organizations and fans. Social networking sites appeal to marketers due to their minimal cost and flexibility. Further, contacting consumers via social networking sites has become socially acceptable and considered a less invasive method of contact by consumers than conventional methods such a personal sales call or e-mail. If properly managed, sites can be used to engage fans in conversations about an organization's brand, thereby creating a community that shares common interests.

One example of a professional sport organization effectively using both Facebook and Twitter as an integral part of their sales and marketing programs is the Chicago Blackhawks. The Blackhawks utilize each platform (see Table 9.2) in a unique way to promote the organization and connect with fans. The use of these two social networking sites enables the organization to connect with customers which leads to increased levels of fan involvement and team loyalty. Though social networking is still being studied, there is no doubt that it has tremendous potential as a brand-building tool.

The Internet and social networking sites' open access format provides positives and potential negatives.

Organizations need to control the flow of information on social networking sites in order to protect their brand. One concern that has arisen for every major professional sport franchise as well as numerous Division-I athletic departments is the presence of unofficial "official" Facebook pages. Many sport organizations now employ at least one staff member who researches the location of websites claiming to be "officially" associated with the organization. Sport organizations can lose credibility if unauthorized content and commentary is falsely distributed to customers under a website claiming to be the team or athletic department.

Sport organizations should also have a clear policy regarding the proper use of SN sites and the nature of posts via any platform by players, coaches, and other members of the organization. Inappropriate posts should be handled in the same manner as other behavioral issues. Further, it may be appropriate for organizations to begin to write clauses into contracts regarding the proper use of social networking sites by players, coaches, and staff. This is even more important given the newly enacted league policies (e.g., NFL and NBA) forbidding the use of Twitter by coaches and athletes just prior to, during, and immediately following games. Though social networking's future specific use and impact is unknown, every sport organization must recognize it is already an important marketing tool, and its impact will likely continue to grow in the future.

TABLE 9.2

Facebook	Twitter
• Official team content, such as: Blackhawk's blog, photos, and video	• Up-to-date information regarding team including play-by-play of game in progress, injury, trade, and scouting reports
• Link to mobile marketing campaigns, Twitter site, and official team website	• Answers to fan questions and trivia
• Dialogue between fans through posts on the team's wall and fan photos	• Updated team event calendar
• Updates on team events, promotions and player signings	• Events for fans, such as viewing parties for those who are unable to attend games.
• Updates on other organizations of interest to fans	• Up-to-date information on other organizations or events that may be of interest to fans, such as: USA v. Canada in Men's Hockey, 2010 Vancouver Olympics, play-by-play, where to watch and listen to game

> *Sales-Consultant's Golden Rule: Sell with the honesty, integrity, caring, understanding, empathy, and thoughtfulness that your client expects. "Care" about your client and present information in an organized and logical fashion.*

What Is Consultative Selling?

In transactional (i.e., traditional) selling, products and services are often sold as commodities. When you go into a car dealership to buy a car, you will often be exposed to transactional selling. Since each car dealership sells a product that usually can be bought at a nearby competing dealership, a car-salesperson most often attempts to use such selling strategies as high pressure and/or deception in order to make a sale. The salesperson pushes a certain kind of car and tries not to let a visitor leave without feeling awkward about failing to purchase. The primary determinant of selling cars is often believed to be price; therefore, whoever can come up with the "best" price is the one who will likely make the sale. In such traditional commodity-selling the emphasis is on price, features, and terms of the sale. Typically, "hard" selling techniques are used.

Such techniques are not only unethical, but they may also be fraudulent. One example of such techniques is called the "bait and switch." It involves advertising a product or service (the bait) at an extremely low "bargain" price in order to attract prospects. Then, after a prospect has had his hopes raised that his wants, needs, and desires will be met, the salesperson reveals that while the advertised product/service is not available, a more-expensive, but more valuable, substitute product of service is available (the switch). The goal of the bait-and-switch is to convince a prospect to purchase the switch in order to mitigate the disappointment over not getting the bait, or as a way to recover sunk costs (e.g., transportation, time, money, etc.) expended trying to obtain the bait.

The essence of consultative selling involves a shift in focus from the product to the people involved. In consultative selling the emphasis is on the process of:

- Building high-trust relationships with prospects;
- Developing respect between the prospect and salesperson;
- Uncovering prospects' WANTS, NEEDS, and DESIRES;
- Discovering the impact of these wants, needs, and desires on prospects;
- Positioning the product not as a commodity, but as a solution to these wants, needs, and desires.

By understanding and applying these principles, consultative salespeople distinguish themselves from others. While applying these elements will not guarantee a successful sport-industry career, a salesperson's chance of achieving success is greatly enhanced.

What Makes Consultative Selling Different?

Think of the term "salesperson," and write down five adjectives that come to mind. Are most of them negative? If so, this demonstrates negative experiences with salespeople who had a lack of understanding of consultative selling. As a future sport-sales consultant, it is likely some prospects may initially have these same negative perceptions. This negative stereotype is why there is such a need for the consultative approach in sport sales.

As sport organizations continue to re-evaluate their sales strategies, consultative selling continues to be viewed as a more professional and effective approach. Not only do consultative salespeople have a higher success ratio, but consultative selling is also seen as an ethical way of doing business (See Chapter 7: Ethics). While this introduction to consultative sales will not be sufficient training to "make" you a professional sport-sales consultant, it will provide an overview of the knowledge, skills, and attitude necessary to close more orders and generate more revenue for a sport organization, while earning more money and maintaining your self-respect.

Sport-sales consultants "bridge the gap" between sport organizations and prospective customers, by helping prospects identify their individual wants, needs and desires, and make an informed buying decision. Traditional salespeople typically compete primarily on price and try to charm prospects out of their money for short-term financial gains. Consultative selling creates a systematic and strategic problem-solving process.

While the specific order of these listed steps may vary, and they may sometimes occur simultaneously, some initial steps in the consultative sales process are commonly identified as including:

- Conducting market and prospect research (e.g., Prospecting),
- Planning your calls (e.g., writing a script),
- Meeting clients,
- Generating interest,
- Listening to prospects' wants, needs, and desires, and
- Establishing credibility.

Once these initial steps have occurred, consultative selling involves continually analyzing a prospect's wants, needs, and desires in order to develop and present them with possible solutions. Once these solutions have been presented it is often necessary to justify associated costs.

The final phase of consultative sales consists of gaining prospects' agreement that the presented solutions meet their expressed and emerging needs, facilitating the investment (helping them buy), and following up to make sure they are satisfied. While transactional salespeople mistakenly believe the sale is the end of the relationship, in consultative selling it is merely the beginning. Servicing the client is critical to long-term consultative success. Transactional salespeople fail to interact with new and existing clients until it is time to seek a new sale. This often creates animosity between the client and the organization, since the client perceives the relationship as one-sided, in which the sport organization views them as simply a consumer to be sold.

It is important to make sure to remember a couple of consultative-selling points:

- Consultants form partnerships and relationships with prospects, while traditional sales people treat prospects only as commodities or consumers;
- Consultative selling is an art form that is shaped by a person's individual personality. Many factors, including such things as—assertiveness, responsiveness and human instincts—shape one's consultation style and determine how each consultant relates and reacts to each consulting situation. A consultant's attitude and mindset are directly associated with how she will be perceived and accepted by clients, and affect how successful the process is for all involved.

Consultative Sales Skills

One of the most important skills in consultative selling is listening! Sport-sales consultant productivity is enhanced by listening to and understanding a prospect's needs before offering a solution. The initial step in developing a fruitful relationship is to establish trust. In traditional selling, the focus on price often causes the prospect to become tense and distrustful, fearful the salesman is trying to "get my money." As an example, think of yourself as the customer. How much better would you feel if the person to whom you were speaking made an effort to get to know you as a person, rather than viewing you simply as a nameless, faceless commodity?

In addition to building rapport with their clients, sales consultants avoid the following traps that reduce effectiveness and lead to sales "burnout." Transactional salespeople are often ineffective, because they:

- are driven to get an order at all costs
- often resort to deceptive sales tactics
- are not empathic to prospects' expressed concerns
- create a win/lose environment, and
- believe they must "change people's minds."

Sales consultants are most productive when they:

- are "driven" to satisfy prospects' needs and assist their buying decisions through conducting an analysis of the prospects' wants, needs, and desires;
- tell prospects the truth;
- develop genuine and relaxed relationships; and
- create win/win partnerships.

It is important to remember that in consultative selling if telling the truth results in no sale being consummated, it is "better" to have a reputation in the marketplace for being honest in business relationships than to make a sale no matter how it is accomplished (Note: This point forms the basis for Chapter 7: Ethics). A reputation for being honest can result in later sales to prospects once their situation changes and can often result in the "failed" prospect conveying the sales consultant's honesty to other prospects (through personal introductions) who may be more likely to invest in the product or service being offered.

Table 9.3 summarizes key terms that differentiate traditional selling from consultative selling.

Step 4—Opening the Sale—Presenting

The heart of the sale is presenting. Presenting deals with participation, proofing, visuals aids, persuasive communication, demonstration, and dramatization.

A sales presentation allows the consultant to show the prospect why a product or service is the best solution or how it satisfies their wants, needs and desires. The presentation must be planned, practiced, rehearsed, and reviewed constantly.

TABLE 9.3

Transactional Selling Jargon	Consultative Selling Terms
Sell or Sold	Help, Assist, Acquire
Tickets	Seats, Packages
Authorization Form, Contract	Paperwork, Agreement Form
Cost or Price	Investment, Amount
Deal	Opportunity
Problem	Challenge
Pitch	Presentation, Demonstration
Objection	Area of Concern, Request for Additional Information
Customer	Client
Appointment	Visit
Seat Location	Sightline, View
Buy or Pay	Own, Invest
Referral	Personal Introduction
Cheaper	Economical

Opening

Much of sales success involves capitalizing on a good first impression. However, it is important to remember a good first impression is not all there is to selling. If a sales consultant has done his/her job, at the completion of a consultative-sales presentation, a prospect should logically want to purchase. An easy example of the sales consultant process involves drawing a large "T" on a piece of paper and listing all the reasons to invest on the left side of the page, and reasons not to on the right side. A consultant conducts this cost-benefit analysis with a prospect while asking for verbal input. When the exercise is completed, if there are more reasons to own, "investing" in the product or service makes logical sense. After conducting such an analysis, clients have "ownership" in their decision, since they "know" they participated in the decision by logically analyzing their available options.

Greeting and Introduction—Building Rapport

The confidence and tone projected in the opening are critically important. The opening is more than just saying hello, it is the opportunity to establish who you are, your agenda, and why your prospect should allow you to present your product or service.

Some fundamental points related to the opening include:

- Be energetic and enthusiastic; you may have only about 30 seconds to convey your initial point.
- A simple good morning or good afternoon is a good way to start. If you know the prospect's first name, use it. Saying a person's name personalizes the encounter and indicates to the prospect the salesperson is thinking of the potential client as a person rather than merely a potential sale. Next, say your name, as well as the organization's, and ask them how they are doing today. Wait for an answer. Respond appropriately. This response may involve more than just saying, "That's good."
- Find areas of mutual interest
- Show empathy—How are they feeling? Ask yourself the following question, "How do I think they want to be treated?"
- Ask questions and allow the prospect to answer while you listen intently.
- Provide feedback (e.g., restating their supplied answers) to show you have listened and heard what they have said.

It is important to remember these fundamental elements set the tone for the entire presentation and develop rapport with the prospect. If you are a confident and friendly person, show it. If you are happy, smile. Smiling is contagious, both in person and over the phone. The cliché "Smile and the whole world smiles with you" is also true!

Agenda, Objective, and Purpose

After being courteous and friendly and building rapport, it is important to clearly identify the purpose of the presentation. In short, tell prospects what is in it for them. Why should they listen to or set aside some of their valuable time? This portion of the presentation is, literally, a matter of seconds. There is no reason to hide the presentation's purpose from the prospect. If—through proper prospecting—it has been determined a prospect has wants, needs, and desires that can be satisfied by the proposed product or service, the purpose of the call is self-evident.

Presenting the Product

Presenting the product is the part of the presentation that allows knowledgeable and well-prepared sales consultants to "shine." It is the part that displays their expertise and product knowledge and allows them to gain complete control of the conversation. In addition, through the needs analysis or qualifying questions it is also the area that allows consultants to tailor their product benefits to meet the clients' needs.

Consultative selling allows for identification and evaluation of prospects' needs and development of strategies to address both short and long-term needs, wants and desires. Based on information collected during the prospecting stage, a consultant should be in a position to deliver a logical presentation with recommendations to the prospect. Choosing the correct presentation to satisfy the prospect's wants, needs, and desires does not happen by accident. The chosen presentation is the culmination of professional preparation. Consultants who have internalized a logical sales philosophy are earnestly interested in helping prospects make decisions that are "right" for them. Being knowledgeable about the available products or plans, the consultant will more likely pick the one appropriate for the situation. Based upon solid market research, including prospects' demographic, psychographic and socio-economic information, consultants can contextualize prospects' needs, wants, and desires and offer appropriate products or services.

Step 5—Conducting an Analysis

Handling clients' concerns is challenging because it puts consultants in tough situations that may—because of different viewpoints—involve escalating tensions. For clients to change their minds they often have to agree with the consultant and abandon previously expressed concerns and lower constructed defense mechanisms. Doing so may be perceived as dangerous or put the client in a vulnerable psychological position. If the sales consultant has provided logical reasons for a client to invest in the product or service and satisfy expressed wants, needs and desires, a "sale" should follow.

However, prior to or during the sales process, there are several mistakes that can sidetrack the sales process. These mistakes include:

1. Lack of product knowledge.
2. Wasting time—Be polite, but get to the point of the meeting.
3. Poor planning—We do not plan to fail, we fail to plan.

4. Pushiness—Phrases like "How can I help?" or "What can we do?" help the client understand you are concerned for their position (This concept will be covered in depth in the "rules of influence" section under the heading of "**Liking**").

5. Not dependable—Do what you say you will do.

6. Too optimistic or unrealistic expectations. The customer will see right through unobtainable benefits.

7. Unprofessional conduct—Being critical of competitors, using foul language, or dressing inappropriately can potentially prevent a sale from occurring.

Liking_____

A person's feeling of affect on or preference for another person.

Hearing and Addressing Concerns

Hearing and addressing a prospect's concerns, does not mean a consultant must attempt to overcome these concerns. However, it is important to shift the prospect's focus from the negative concern to a positive and collaborative problem-solving approach to addressing the concern while finding a way to still satisfy the prospect's wants, needs, and desires. In addition, this process must be undertaken while still maintaining a respectful and friendly relationship.

The following are five concepts that can assist a sales consultant in addressing client concerns:

1. **Presence**
   - Maintain your presence and project concern and confidence without appearing rejected.
   - Let the client articulate their concern without interrupting, showing hostility or demonstrating you have taken their concern as a personal rejection.
   - Welcome their feedback and encourage them to fully express their opinion.

2. **Empathy** (identifying with and understanding another's situation, feelings, and motives)
   - Demonstrating and articulating empathy for expressed concerns in order to keep lines of communication open.
   - Let the client know in a proper tone that you understand and are open to their point of view. Empathy does not mean you agree, but it does mean you are willing to listen and explore their concerns.

3. **Questioning**
   - Most concerns are expressed in vague and broad language. Most often they are not specifically articulated.
   - A sales consultant must actively listen and ask clients to repeat or redefine vague concerns.
   - Based upon this focused restatement of concerns, a consultant must ask targeted questions in order to uncover specific and often "real" concerns.
   - Specific questions to uncover clients' real concerns are questions focused on the "why." (e.g., "Is there any particular reason why you would not be interested in a season ticket package right now?")

4. **Position Your Idea or Solution**
   - Once you narrow the concern with a "why" question, address your client's real concerns.
   - Sometimes effective positioning can be accomplished through using testimonials from other clients' who had similar concerns and discussing how those concerns were addressed. An example of this may be that a season-ticket prospect expressed a concern that she would not be able to attend all the home games on the schedule. The sales consultant could discuss how these concerns have been addressed for other clients through their investing in specific partial ticket plans and also taking advantage of ticket-resale programs the sport organization offers.

5. **Check**
   - Once you have offered a solution to the concern, you should not assume your effort has satisfied the client. Check to see how your client feels about your response. Conducting this check will help to:
   - Prevent assuming the client's concern has been satisfied;
   - Measure the state of the relationship;
   - Move onto the next point;
   - Develop a climate conducive to achieving agreement.

This five-step process of openly addressing expressed concerns provides a framework consistent with a consultative sales approach. In addition to these steps, the following rules of influence allow sales consultants to effectively and ethically collaborate with prospects to "get to the yes" and satisfy their expressed wants, needs, and desires.

Techniques to Alleviate and Mitigate Client Concerns

In his books *Influence: Science and Practice* (2008) and *Influence: The Psychology of Persuasion* (2006), Robert Cialdini describes several effective methods for positively influencing people's behaviors. Understanding the methods discussed in Cialdini's books and employing *influence judo*—influencing without appearing to influence—allows sales consultants to decrease the likelihood of client concerns arising, and—if they do—mitigate their intensity.

Cialdini's Rules of Influence include:

1. **Reciprocation.** Potential customers will try to repay, in kind, what you have provided that is of value to them. In other words, provide reasons why the prospect should feel obligated to repay you and your franchise/client by making a buying decision. These reasons may be tangible or intangible benefits. Reciprocation motivators can include a free gift, an exclusive t-shirt, a preferred customer party, a chance to rub elbows with celebrities, public recognition associated with their purchase, something that will develop a sense of belonging, or appealing to their sense of purpose.

Free give-away items for the first 10,000 fans arriving at a home game is one example of **reciprocity**. Another example is providing an opportunity for suite owners to attend exclusive practice sessions or gain access to hospitality events during which they can meet players and celebrities. Reciprocity is designed to satisfy clients' psychological or emotional wants, needs and desires they may perceive–as the effective *MasterCard* advertising campaign has expressed–as being "priceless."

2. **Commitment and Consistency.** Once clients have made an investment decision, they will encounter personal and interpersonal pressures to behave in a manner consistent with that commitment. By clearly articulating and summarizing the rationale for their decision, a sales consultant allows this commitment to be made. Once people believe they have made a "correct and wise investment," they will most likely follow through on this decision and are also predisposed toward future similar decisions. In other words, if a fan has made a decision to invest in a season-ticket package and has to put down a non-refundable deposit, the client is much more likely to follow through and pay off the outstanding balance.

3. **Social Proof.** In a given situation, clients view a behavior as correct to the degree they see others performing it. To insure prospects see purchasing a ticket as a correct behavior, they need to be shown/told that others have made this choice and it has paid off for them. If their neighbor, friend, or business associate has purchased, they are likely to do the same.

4. **Liking.** People prefer to say yes to the requests of people they know and/or like. It is important to *not* alienate your prospect by being too demanding or pushy. Remember, the choice to purchase is theirs, not yours. Addressing concerns to accelerate the sales process is important, but you should not be too pushy.

5. **Authority.** Purchasers tend to follow the dictates of "genuine authorities" because such individuals usually possess high levels of knowledge, wisdom, and power. (See p. 195 textbox: Sell Like a Medical Doctor.) Customers recognize and appreciate a professional sales consultant who has developed a high level of product knowledge and possesses confidence in a product or service. It is important for sales consultants to know their product's strengths and weaknesses. When selling, be realistic about the product or service and sell to its strengths, but also openly admit any deficiencies and proceed.

6. **Scarcity.** Any product seems more valuable to prospects when the product is less available. Limited-product availability is useful to a sales consultant, especially if the scarcity is a result of high demand (see social proof.). Make sure prospects feel they will join an elite group by making the investment. Make them feel valued. Scarcity is related to the first rule (reciprocity). If not every fan can obtain access to a certain club lounge, concourse, or seating section, then these items' perceived values often increases. If there are only 100 tickets available to a given game, but there are more than 100 fans waiting to purchase tickets, the demand (and perceived value) of those tickets to the general public will increase. *StubHub* or other resale entities are a reaction to this basic concept of "supply and demand."

Reciprocity_____

A mutual exchange, a return in kind. People react positively and feel obligated to repay others for favorable treatments received.

Commitment and Consistency_____

A person making a decision, will experience pressure from others and themselves to behave consistently with that decision. Depending on a person's past actions, they will be predisposed to making future decisions consistent with those past actions.

Social Proof_____

People will do things they see other people are doing. Assuming other people possess more knowledge about the situation, they deem the others' behavior as appropriate or better informed.

Step 6—Reaching Agreement

Closing_____
Reaching a sales agreement with a client.

Every professional sales consultant may have different thoughts regarding how to reach an agreement with a client. Reaching agreement or **closing** is simply getting a client to make an investment decision. The following section addresses some misconceptions about reaching agreement and provides some thoughts regarding how to evaluate sales success.

One of the most common misconceptions is that "closing" only means getting a "Yes." Sometimes, consultants feel that if they do a good job presenting their product or service there is really no need to close; the product should sell itself. The following statements exemplify this mistake:

- If I can get the prospect positive about the presentation, I can close a call without a decision.
- When a customer says 'I'm interested,' there is no reason to push further.
- I cannot close on the first call; it is simply an information-gathering call.

Close for the Next Step—On Every Call or Presentation

Closes for the next step____
Asking for a client's business or requesting referral information.

Regardless of the sales-process stage, it is important that a sales consultant always **closes for the next step**. Closing for the next step involves always asking for a client's business. Sales consultants who ask for a client's business are both setting up the next step (gaining agreement) and also closing for the next step (getting an investment and obtaining personal introductions).

In order to close for the next step, a sales consultant must be able to ask effective closing questions during each conversation with a prospective client. When envisioning a "close," it may be helpful to visualize the last few minutes leading up to asking for the business. In addition, by effectively and proactively listening to a prospect, in some circumstances a sales consultant may be able to ask for a client's business shortly after first meeting the prospect.

If a consultant always closes for the next step, clients are conditioned to invest. Taking this step is based upon assuming every prospect is going to invest. Making this assumption makes consultants more confident in their presentation and closing abilities. In today's sport industry, one of the most important habits is to become accustomed to and comfortable asking for a prospect's credit card number. Asking for a client's credit card number allows the client to understand that making the investment will be a simple process, expedites the investment, and allows the client to visualize their owning the product or service. While it is crucial to always close for the next step, not all closes will occur on the first call or at the conclusion of the first presentation. Many closes occur after multiple calls or presentations. Most successful multiple-call closes are the result of effective listen-

Successful sales consultants help bring enthusiastic crowds to sport events.

Shutterstock, Inc.

ing, strong communication skills, and diligent follow-up. If it is inappropriate to immediately ask for a prospect's business, begin to set a timeline during which small closing steps can be completed (This is called "setting the table.") that will culminate in asking for the client's business.

Pre-closing Questions

In order to ask for business at the appropriate time, a sales consultant needs to know exactly what their clients want and how their specific needs, wants, and desires can be met. Specific and pre-planned pre-closing questions prevent useless rambling and long-winded explanations. Furthermore, customers like to feel they have an active part in choosing a seat location, partial package, and so on.

Consider the following Pre-closing Questions (PQ) that might be asked of a ticket prospect:

- Is it more important to you to be closer to the action or closer to the center section?
- How will you be investing in these seats?
- Is it more important for you to see certain teams or is day-of-the-week more important?
- How many games would you like to come to?
- What is your time frame for getting these tickets?
- If it is up to you, would you purchase these seats?
- If your budget is approved, will you purchase these seats?

In addition to utilizing pre-closing questions, another pre-closing technique is to simply quit talking and allow the prospect to think about their investment. In other words, "Silence Can Be Golden!" Silent moments in a telephone conversation or when the client is sitting in the venue in the actual seat being discussed, seeing their name on the stadia scoreboard or *Jumbotron,* allows the prospect to visualize their being at the game. This contemplative time can be positive. Therefore, sales consultants must recognize it is not always necessary to fill every conversation or presentation with verbiage. Sometimes it is most effective to let the game experience speak for itself. (Letting the game experience sell itself is exemplified in the saying, "Let the steak's sizzle [the sound of a steak makes when it is placed on a grill] sell the beef.")

Reaching Agreement requires the following:

1. Enthusiasm.
2. Planning sales calls and presentations.
3. Knowing the prospect's wants, needs, and desires.
4. Giving a professional presentation.
5. Utilizing a trial close and pre-close questioning.
6. Sensing the client's real concern(s).
7. Addressing and solving these concerns.
8. Reminding the client of the product or service's benefits.
9. Asking for the order and then being silent.
10. Never burning a bridge.

At the completion of the sales process the customer's logical conclusion should be to buy. A purchase decision allows for potential clients to develop "ownership" in the decision-making, because they feel they participated in the decision. If a client truly wants, needs, or desires the product or service being offered, at the conclusion of the sales process they should invest.

Trial Close

Often, a trial close involves asking a prospect a series of "Yes/No" questions. These answers provide the consultant with client feedback. When asking these questions the consultant must be comfortable with silence, since the prospect may take time to think about the answers. Some examples of trial close questions might be:

- Does that sound good to you?
- Is this seat location good for you?
- Does this make sense so far?
- Do you like this ticket, package, etc.?

Close—Getting an Action Commitment

There are several types of closes or closing techniques available to a sales consultant. All such techniques involve the consultant making sure a new client has agreed to the investment and is ready to take action to put the investment in motion. The list of closing statements below is not exhaustive, but provides a starting point.

Types of Sales Closes

1. **The invite close**

   After pre-close questioning and a trial close to uncover and address clients' concerns, a sales consultant has an obligation to ask new clients to initiate their investment. This step (the close) is the final element of reaching agreement.

   A close is simply asking a simple question:
   - "Why don't you give it a try" or
   - "Why don't you give us a chance?"

2. **Directive or Assumptive Close**
   - An assumptive close is initiated when a consultant moves on to the next step in the process, as if assuming an investment decision has already been made. If the client agrees to initiate the investment by agreeing to the next step, the assumption has been validated and an investment decision has occurred.
   - The following statement is an example of an assumptive close. "If you do not have any further questions, then here is the season-ticket authorization form to sign. (Form is placed in front of client and pen provided.) I will take the completed form back to the office, and deliver your tickets and your season-ticket owner gift to you tomorrow."

3. **Alternative close**
   - Since everyone wants to have a choice, the alternative close provides prospects with two choices from which to choose. To initiate this close a consultant asks the client a series of choice questions.

     For example, the client's choices may be:
     —Which ticket package—A or B—do you want?
     —Should we mail the tickets to your home or work?

4. **Order-sheet form close**
   - During an order-sheet form close, the consultant takes out a ticket order-form and begins to fill it out. Part of the process of completing the form involves asking the prospect a series of questions: "What is the correct spelling of your name? What is your address? What is today's date?"
   - While asking these questions a consultant should not look up. When a prospect provides the information in order for the form to be completed, he/she has agreed to make the investment.

5. **Authorization close**
   - Initiating an authorization close consists of opening an authorization form (e.g., season-ticket authorization form), making check marks to indicate where to sign, and pushing it in front of the client and saying, "Congratulations, you have made a great investment."

6. **"I want to think it over" close**
   This close occurs when a client says, "I would like to think it over." Clients who say this are actually saying, "No." In this situation, a sales consultant should calmly accept the "No," put their padfolio away, stand, and politely say, "Thank you for your time." While shaking the client's hand, the consultant says, "You have concerns. Can you share them with me?" The consultant then simply waits for a response.

Step 7—Obtaining Personal Introductions

For misguided or uninformed sales people "asking for a referral" is viewed as a needless hassle and of little value. On the other hand, a professional sales consultant understands the value of personal introductions. Personal introductions are instantaneous "warm leads" that are much more likely to become clients. Asking a new or existing client for the names of personal friends or business associates who would like to make the same investment (e.g., enjoy the fun and excitement of a football or basketball game, soccer match, or snowboarding competition) they just made is consistent with many of Cialdini's *rules of influence* discussed earlier.

The art of asking for personal introductions involves an ongoing individual commitment to asking prospects or clients for their assistance during all contacts. Asking for personal introductions should be done on all calls.

Referral_____
When someone gives a salesperson a sales lead (name, address, phone number, and/or e-mail to contact).

Forming a relationship with a potential client is much easier when a friend or colleague has suggested the introduction. How much easier is it to introduce one's self based upon a warm introduction through a friend or colleague?

In the sport sales context, questions that best provide personal introductions often need to include certain qualifiers to stimulate feedback. Instead of simply asking, "Could you provide me with the names of four people I could call?" asking for personal introductions may involve asking some simple qualifying questions. For example, in order to obtain some personal introductions from a season-ticket holder, a sales consultant might ask one of the following questions:

- Who might you want to sit with or near?
- Who do you know who owns tickets to one of the local sport teams?
- Who at your company is responsible for organizing outings?
- Who in your social group (church, etc.) is responsible for organizing outings?
- Who is the coach of your child's youth sport team?

As has been discussed, personal introductions are "warmer" leads, more amenable to being approached by a sales consultant than "cold" leads (e.g., names out of the telephone book). The success of a personal-introduction lead is based upon the concept of social proofing, which is that people are more inclined to behave in a certain way, in this case purchase a product or service, to the degree they observe others doing so. A personal introduction is, at its most basic, simply someone telling a friend or acquaintance, "You should do what I have done!"

Conclusion

Base salary plus commission_____
Combination of a set salary—based on a staff member's experience—and a percent of generated sales (typically between 1–5% on renewed business and 5–20% on new business).

Telemarketing/teleselling__
Marketing/sales approach that features the use of personal selling techniques in a non-face-to-face context and utilizes telecommunications technology as part of a well-planned, organized, and managed marketing program.

Sport sales is a competitive facet of the sport industry with wide ranging salaries. Typically, sport-sales consultants' compensation is a combination of a small **base salary** and **commission** on sales (typically between 1–5 percent for renewed business and 5–20 percent for new accounts). Even the most experienced sales consultants will have a commission structure built into their compensation agreement. This allows the sales consultant to makes a large amount of money or a small amount of money, depending on their performance. In some cases, professional sport franchises will have highly successful sales consultants who make as much, if not more, than many of the vice presidents of the organization.

However, entry-level sales consultants can be overwhelmed by the small "guaranteed" pay and the tremendous amount of time **telemarketing/teleselling** to potential prospects. Often, organizations know within a month or two if a recently hired and trained sales consultant will be able to assist the organization. Successful sales consultants typically receive higher commission packages as they advance within an organization. In addition, promotion to sales manager may enable a sales consultant to be paid an override for sales executed by staff members. Most sport organizations do not mind paying large commissions to their sales staff as it means revenue is being generated. A sales consultant that makes a 10 percent commission on $900,000 of sponsorship sales is earning a high income while providing a good return on investment (ROI) for the organization.

Though researching and targeting new clients is critical to the success of any sales operations, sales consultants should remember the 80/20 rule of sales. Typically, most organizations sell 80 percent of their products to 20 percent of their customer base. The "regular" customers of an organization are critical to the financial viability of the organization. It is much more expensive and time intensive to convince a non-customer to become a one-time buyer than it is to maintain a current customer's buying habits. In addition, current customers are more likely to increase their current rate of product or service consumption than a non-customer is to try the product or service one time. For these reasons, relationship marketing is an important aspect of selling. Every successful sales consultant will first ensure, and then work to enhance, the commitment from current customers prior to seeking new sales.

Today sport is both a product and a means for other businesses to sell their non-sport products. Fundamentally, the modern sport industry is predicated upon encouraging sport fans and participants to consume the sport product. This consumption is the end result of the sales process. This chapter outlined a sales-training progression and delineated the fundamental steps of the consultative sales process. As will become apparent to sport-management students, if you can sell, you have a high likelihood of being able to find a job in the sport industry. Simply stated, the easiest way to get into the sport industry is through sales.

As part of their career preparation, all sport-management students should take part in a sale-training program, so they better understand the sales process. In addition, students should recognize that selling is simply satisfying clients' wants, needs and desires. In addition, no matter what facet of the sport industry in which a sport-manager works, every sport organization member must "always be selling."

Override _____

Compensation paid to a sales manager for overseeing a sales staff. For example, if a sales manager has five employees that report to him he may receive a 1 percent bonus of the total revenue generated by the five sales-staff employees.

Return on investment (ROI)

Marketing success is measured by the following ratio: revenue generated/costs incurred.

80/20 Rule _____

Revenue-generation "rule" that 80 percent of a sport organization's revenue comes from 20 percent of its customers.

Relationship marketing ____

Integrating a business partner's wants, needs and desires with a company's strategic marketing plan in order to create and sustain a mutually beneficial relationship.

Interview

Mr. Jim Van Stone
Vice President of Ticket Sales
Washington Capital (National Hockey League)

Q: What advice would you give a graduating senior in high school that is looking to enter the sport business industry in four years?

A: You should enter the best university that will accept you as you graduate high school. You should learn and do as well as you can in ALL of you classes, especially your business courses. Get the best internship you can. You should work for your athletic department in some way, as this is an easy way to gain experience and build your network of contacts.

Q: What advice would you give a graduating senior in college who is looking to enter the sport business industry today? Is graduate school a good option? Will that change my job opportunities?

A: A graduate degree will NOT change the first job you obtain after the completion of undergraduate degree. Your first job will be in sales with or without a graduate degree. The advantage of going to graduate school after completing an undergraduate degree is that the majority of your education will be completed early in your life

and your career may benefit down the road. The disadvantage is you pay for your graduate degree tuition or accumulate more school debt and you are responsible for your health benefits.

Q: You have hired more than 100 young, recently graduated college seniors. What skills do you require and prefer?

A: The industry of sport is no different than other businesses. I look for the B and B which is the best and the brightest. I am looking for smart, mature, responsible, and hard-working employees. I want to hire a sales representative who wants to sell. Many sport executives use sales as a stepping-stone to another department within the sport industry. I am fine with that idea, but while you are in the sales department "be" in the sales department.

Q: How important is cover letter, resume, and references to a graduating senior?

A: It is very important. These three pieces of paper are a brochure of who you are, and must be well written while being free of all spelling errors.

The cover letter has to be personalized to the individual, speak to the fact it is a letter of application, list and explain experiences from the resume, discuss examples of your work ethic, thank the readers for their time, and restate an e-mail address and phone numbers.

The resume should be written in Times Roman, size 12 font, on one page with both school and home addresses, anticipated graduation date, education and experiences listed chronologically from today to past. Be sure to avoid using any "crazy" email addresses or any phone messages that are not professional.

The references should include at least three but no more than five with the name, full address, phone number and email also included. You should ask the individual to be a reference prior to submitting their name and every reference should be a non-relative. Select individuals who do the following: know who well, will definitely return a call or e-mail of a potential employer, and will provide information about you that will make the potential employer want to interview you!

An important reminder for students is to NEVER display pictures of yourself in compromising positions on your Facebook or other social media websites. If you think you "party" too much, then you probably do. Do not advertise it. There have been situations where a potential employee was rejected because of information gleaned from social-media sites.

Q: How important is an internship and networking?

A: It is important to network. Your network is not who you know, but it is who knows you. It is important to seek and obtain "quality" internships. Students constantly ask me the question, "Should I try for an internship with one of the four major teams or a minor league organization?" I would try for one of the four major league teams, especially if that is where you want to eventually be employed, but both levels can provide great educational experiences. While it is easier to go from the majors to the minors than vice versa, the down side to interning in the majors is that sometimes the intern gets pigeon-holed as the finance intern, marketing intern, or the ticket intern. Regardless of where you intern, you should try to gain experience in all departments to learn what everyone in the organization does. Acquiring this wealth of knowledge will more likely occur at the minor-league level since a minor-league organization has fewer employees.

Q: What skills have serviced you well as your career climbed from sales representative to assistant director of sales to director of sales to vice president of sales?

A: I think the skills that have served me well are as follows: being a people person, being willing to work long hours during the season and to relocate for a promotion, being firm, but fair to my staff, putting the company first, being open minded to new ideas, and being a problem-solver. In addition, the ability to be a team player, set goals, and retain a competitive desire to succeed, while adapting during good and bad times has assisted my career progression. I also think I am able to judge and cultivate talent.

Q: How important was physically relocating to the growth of your career?

A: I would never have become a vice president of sales if I had not been willing to relocate. It meant everything. By relocating, I have learned from so many different people and organizational cultures, which has enabled me to apply different philosophies to solving problems.

Q: How has the industry changed since you were first employed?

A: The following has occurred: the value of professional sport franchises has dramatically increased, the players and coaches salaries have exploded, new arenas with club boxes and suites have proliferated, sport marketing has gone global, technology has advanced and assisted the capturing of names and fan profiling, ticket prices have increased at a higher rate than inflation, secondary ticketing has become "mainstream," and the recent recession has eroded season ticket bases which has forced improvement in selling individual and group tickets.

Study Questions

1. Explain how does consultative selling differs from traditional selling.
2. List several ways in which consultative selling creates an impact.
3. List and describe the seven steps of the sales process described in this chapter.
4. Briefly describe how to keep good relationships and help clients make investment decisions.
5. List and describe the elements of the Pentagon of Sport-Sales Training.
6. Illustrate some steps a sales consultant can take to establish business credibility.
7. List and provide sport-specific examples of the rules of influence discussed in this chapter.
8. Describe some methods a sales consultant can utilize to analyze clients' needs.
9. Briefly explain the process of recommending solutions and gaining commitment.
10. Highlight at least three types of closes outlined in this chapter.
11. Illustrate the process of asking for personal introductions and utilize the appropriate rules of influence in discussing why this is a crucial step in the sales process.

Learning Activities

The following activities are designed to bridge the gap between sales theory and practice. Several of the activities require outside planning and organization and may not be feasible in an introduction to sport management course. However, these activities may be utilized as part of ongoing sport-management club activities.

1. Invite a sport-sales director of sales or vice president of sales from a local major or minor league sport organization to speak to your class or to a sport-management club on campus.
2. Contact your university's athletic director or associate athletic director for external relations (i.e. marketing) and develop a relationship in which the class develops a sales program for an Olympic-sport game. This would involve the class selling ticket inventory or developing a promotional campaign for the chosen contest.
3. For this chosen contest, each class member should develop a sales script which addresses the following product elements: who, what, where, and when in the first sentence.
4. For the chosen game or another sport product, develop a funnel of twenty (20) prospects. Prospects may be drawn from the following groups: alumni, local community members, university student-body, friends, relatives, or former ticket holders who have attended a college/university sport event.
5. Break into groups of three students and role-play the script. There are three roles- consultant, prospect, and active observer. All three students should perform each role. After each presentation, critique the presentation, offering constructive advice and suggestions for improvement.

Culminating Activity

As part of the developed sales campaign, call "real-life" prospects from developed funnel lists, or lists provided by the athletic department. If possible, calls should be made from a location in which students can be observed and possibly videotaped. Student cell phones can be used, if necessary. The time when calls are made should vary, occurring Monday–Thursday 4:30–8:30 P.M. and Saturdays 10 A.M. to 4 P.M. Students should be encouraged to participate in a two-three hour selling practicum.

References

Cialdini, R. B. (2006). *Influence: The psychology of persuasion.* New York: Harper Paperbacks.

Cialdini, R. B. (2008). *Influence: Science and practice* (5th ed.). Boston, MA: Allyn and Bacon.

Dolich, A. (2004, November). Speech at the annual meeting of Sport Marketing Association, Memphis, TN.

Godin, S. (2004). *Free prize inside.* New York: Portfolio.

Helyar, J. (2006, September 16). Failing effort: Are universities' sports-management programs a ticket to a great job? Not likely. *Wall Street Journal.*

Irwin, R. L., Southall, R. M., & Sutton, W.A. (2007). Pentagon of Sport Sales Training: A 21st Century Sport Sales Training Model. *Sport Management Education Journal, 1*(1), 18–39.

McCormack, M. (1996). On selling. West Hollywood, CA: Dove Books.

McKelvey, S., & Southall, R.M. (2008). Teaching sport sponsorship sales through experiential learning. *International Journal of Sport Management and Marketing, 4*(2–3), 225–254.

Michaelson, G.A., & Michaelson, S.W. (2004). *Sun Tzu: Strategies for selling.* New York: McGraw-Hill.

Rosenbluth, H.F. (1992). *The customer comes second.* New York: Quill/William Morrow.

Southall, R.M., Dick, R.J., & Van Stone, J. (2008). *Bridging the Gap ticket sales-training manual.* Pittsburgh, PA: Bridging the Gap, LLP.

Southall, R.M., & Dick, R.J. (in press). Assessing sport-sales training effectiveness: Development of a baseline sample. *Journal of Applied Marketing Theory.*

Spoelstra, J. (1997). *Ice to the Eskimos: How to market a product nobody wants.* New York: HarperCollins.

Sutton, W.A., Lachowetz, A., & Clark, J. (2000). Eduselling: The role of customer education in selling to corporate clients in the sales industry. *International Journal of Sports Marketing & Sponsorship, 2*(2), 145–158.

Sport Communication

Brad Schultz • *University of Mississippi*

After reading this chapter, you will be able to:

- Describe the relationship between sport, media and audience as it manifests itself in the communication process;
- Explain how sport organizations struggle to control and manage content from a communications perspective;
- Detail how changes in technology have impacted sport media relations.

> *"How did baseball develop from the sandlots to the huge stadiums? From a few hundred spectators to the millions in attendance today? My answer is: through the gigantic force of publicity. The professional sporting world was created and is being kept alive by the services extended the press."*
>
> —Connie Mack, owner and manager of Major League Baseball's
> Philadelphia Athletics (1901–1950)

Introduction

Distribution_____

How sport content reaches the sport audience. The audience itself is taking more of a role in distributing today's content.

Hall of Fame baseball owner and manager Connie Mack wrote the quoted words more than a half-century ago, but they are still just as true today. The media play an essential role in the development and growth of sport, while sport and the athletes who play are important to the media. Each entity depends on the other to assist with their consumer's economic consumption. The relationship is symbiotic; all three could exist independently, but none would achieve the same level of success without the others.

This chapter seeks to define these relationships from a communications perspective. Sport, media, and audiences have changed drastically in the past hundred years, and will likely continue to change in the future. These changes have affected the communication process' nature and methods. As technology continues to advance, communication relationships and methods will move in new directions. Certainly, students aspiring to work in the sport industry should not only remain abreast of current changes in communication, but should also try to anticipate and prepare for future changes and how those changes will impact sport operations.

Figure 10.1 displays a good way to conceptualize the communications relationship between sport, media and audiences. In a broad sense, athletes and events provide **content** for the media outlets that cover them. Large-scale events, such as the Super Bowl and World Series, as well as small-scale events, such as a city golf tournament or 5-K run, give the sport media content to fill newspaper and magazine pages, and television and radio rundowns. In turn, the media serve as the means of content and information **distribution**; getting those events (and the news related to them) disseminated to sport audiences. While the means of distribution have greatly changed since 1870, with newspapers and other print

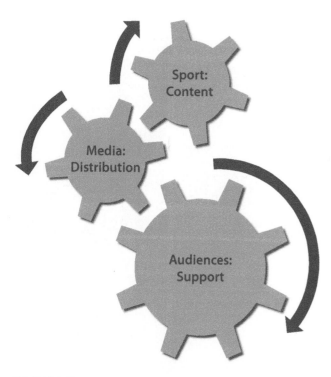

FIGURE 10.1_____

The Relationship between Sport, Media, and Audiences

sources now augmented by various broadcast and Internet outlets, the distribution of sport events to consumers continues to directly support sport organizations, teams, and athletes. Such distribution supports economic consumption through such things as the purchases of event tickets, merchandise, and ancillary items.

The meshing of gears is a good way to think of sport **representation**, because sport, media, and audiences are all interrelated, and the effect is not simply in one direction. For example, in addition to their support of sport organizations, audiences also support the media by purchasing subscriptions and pay-per-view plans and by supporting advertisers. In addition to distribution, the media also directly support the sport industry by paying rights fees to broadcast events. These interrelationships can be examined on a much closer level.

Media

Media and Audience

Media's primary role is to serve as the conduit through which sport content and information passes to the consuming public (see Figure 10.2). This has been the media's main function since sport first gained popularity with mass audiences in the late 19th century. The industrialization and urbanization of that time period created audiences large enough to support both sport organizations and the mass media. The media quickly realized their financial interests were tied to supplying information to a growing sport audience. Fueled by information supplied mainly through newspapers and magazines, interest in sport grew tremendously during this time period. As early as 1887 a national association of baseball writers noted, "All sides now realize that their interests are identical. The reporters have found . . . a source of employment. The game has found in the reporters its best ally and most powerful supporter." According to one study, the amount of news space dedicated to sport jumped from four percent in 1890 to 16 percent in 1923 (Bryant & Holt, 2006). Baseball historian Harold Seymour (1971) noted that newspapers also worked to maintain fan interest with stories of "speculation, review or gossip" about players and with "off season stories about player signings, rebuilding of teams, rule changes and trades" (p. 92).

The media role of sport information provider has not changed through the years, although dramatic changes regarding the means of distribution have occurred. Author Mike Sowell (2008)

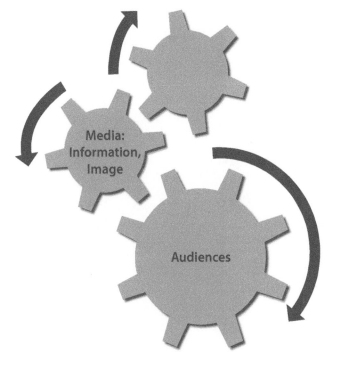

FIGURE 10.2

Information and Image: How Media Affect Audiences

suggested that national sport coverage became possible in 1849 when the telegraph was first used to cover a championship boxing match. Distribution technology has evolved from 19th century telegraph, 20th century broadcast (television and radio), and now to 21st century new-media (Internet and digital forms). New distribution methods have created two major changes to the media's information role: (1) there is much more potential information, and (2) the information is available instantaneously or nearly instantaneously in most cases. With the advent of the Internet and other broadband technologies, the amount of sport information available to consumers has increased exponentially. The sheer volume of information is almost incalculable, but a look at some of today's most popular sport's websites suggests the size of today's sport audience is staggering (Table 10.1). As new-media technologies such as podcasting, high definition television and satellite radio continue to grow, so will the amount of sport's information available to audiences.

These new-media technologies have also shrunk the sport-information **news cycle**; that is, the information that is now available to sports audiences is getting to them much more quickly. For the print media the news cycle had typically been about 24 hours, which is how long it took for information to permeate through to most audiences via this distribution channel. The cycle shortened to minutes with the coming of radio and television, and now is only a few seconds due to the availability of the Internet. These changes have had significant consequences for the print media as many companies have struggled to adapt to the new Internet environment. While *The New York Times* fell $1 billion in debt and the Tribune Company recently filed for bankruptcy, several other newspaper groups faced shutdown and liquidation (Hirschorn, 2009). Among the casualties were the *Cincinnati Post* and Denver's *Rocky Mountain News;* Seattle's *Post-Intelligencer* ended its print version and went completely online in 2009 (Macmillan, 2009).

TABLE 10.1

Most Popular Sport Websites, 2008

Rank	Site	Links to Other Sites	Daily Reach	Unique Audience (in Millions)
1	Yahoo! Sports	656,011	28.2% of global Internet users	26.0
2	ESPN	19,484	.99%	22.8
3	Fox Sports on MSN	1,886	.29%	16.0
4	NFL	7,847	.28%	15.0
5	CBS Sports	6,636	.23%	13.3

Sources: Nielsen Online, NetView (September 1, 2008–September 30, 2008); Alexa Web Traffic Rankings, December 2008.

The sport print media have been quick to transition to the Internet, which, given its ability to store large amounts of information and offer consumers the ability to interact with one another, is ideally suited for sport coverage. Magazines such as *Sports Illustrated, The Sporting News,* and *ESPN The Magazine* all have an extensive web presence. Much of the content is the same as the magazine offers in print, but is provided free on the web. That has raised some concerns about revenue, but the web versions generate money from advertising and also offer additional content that requires a subscription. Though generating revenues on the Internet is not yet completely understood, there is no doubt the Internet is the primary sport news delivery channel of the 21st century.

Though an increase in speed is certainly valuable and appreciated by consumers, it also increases the dangers of publishing rumor, speculation or information that is simply untrue, and in many cases the media has lost credibility. For example, when Kansas State fired football coach Ron Prince in 2008, the website "GoPowerCat.com" immediately released a story detailing that the new coach would be Gary Patterson of Texas Christian University. Patterson immediately denied the report, forcing the site to retract the story. According to Bob Lutz (2008, pp. 23–25) of the *Wichita Eagle,* "Sending a false story into the mainstream is our worst nightmare. But with a story this big—and everything that happens with K-State football is big—there is an urgency to be first with the news . . . we're all on point to be first with the news. That's our job. Being first. Not being wrong."

While information is an essential part of the media business, it would be wrong to say that the media serve merely as impassive channels of communication. Information does not simply come from the media like water from a faucet; rather, the media also shapes the context, form and tone of that information. Media scholars Maxwell McCombs and Donald Shaw (1972) call this **agenda-setting**—how the media exert a significant influence on public perception through their ability to filter and shape media content. According to McCombs (2002, p. 1), "Not only do people acquire factual information from the news media, readers and viewers also learn how much importance to attach to a topic on the basis of the emphasis placed on it in the news."

In a sport sense, the media present a particular **image** of sport events and athletes. This image can depend on several factors, including the economic and cultural conditions that exist at the time. For example, the 1920s were a time of great excess and achievement, and athletic heroes such as Babe Ruth, Red Grange and Jack Dempsey were lauded as heroic figures in the mainstream media. Ruth received perhaps more adulation from the media than any other sport figure, before or since. He was not only the "Babe," but "the Bambino," "the Sultan of Swat," and "the Colossus of Clout." Former teammate Harry Hooper observed of Ruth, "I saw it all from beginning to end, and sometimes I can't believe what I saw: this kid, crude, poorly educated . . . gradually transformed into the idol of American youth and a symbol of baseball the world over. I saw a man transformed from a human being into something pretty close to a god" (Connor, 1982, p. 66).

Agenda-setting_____

A theory of mass communication which suggests the media exert a significant influence on public perception through their ability to filter and shape media content.

Image_____

How sport athletes, organizations and events, and the information related to them, are portrayed in the media and presented to sport audiences.

Sportswriters like Grantland Rice, Damon Runyan, and Heywood Broun played key roles in creating the athlete's heroic mystique. Rice, who shaped the image of countless athletes once noted, "When a sportswriter stops making heroes out of athletes, it's time to get out of the business" (Inabinett, 1994, p. ix). Rice is most often remembered for naming Notre Dame's famous "Four Horsemen" in an article he wrote after the 1924 Notre Dame-Army football game. The story's opening—"Outlined against a blue-gray October sky the Four Horsemen rode again . . . " is one of the most famous lines in sportswriting history.

By contrast, the 1960s was a time of protest and anger that saw the emergence of the "anti-hero"; athletes celebrated for their flaws rather than their heroism. A younger generation of athletes like Joe Namath and Muhammad Ali rejected many of the traditional notions associated with sport, such as morality, clean living, and humility. Author Marty Ralbovsky (1971, p. 74) noted, "Why, said Ali, can't a black athlete be proud of his blackness and be called what he wishes? Why, said Namath, can't an athlete admit publicly to drinking, smoking (and) making love to beautiful women? Traditionalists answered them by removing them from the mainstream and clouding their accomplishments in controversy."

Sports became a television staple during the 1960s and 1970s, a growth that was further fueled by technological developments. Cable and satellite television dramatically increased the amount of available sport content, and the competition for sport's audiences. This ended the dominance of the three major networks (ABC, NBC, CBS) in terms of televised sport programming and opened the field to a host of new competitors. Media mogul Ted Turner began broadcasting many of his Atlanta Braves' games on Turner Broadcasting System (TNT), which was available to nearly every cable subscriber across the country. Entertainment and Sports Programming Network (ESPN) emerged in the late 1970s and made following sports a 24-hour-a-day, seven-days-a-week enterprise.

It could be argued that growth of media and competition in the 1990s and 2000s has led to a "celebrity" portrayal of athletes and sports. "This is a tabloid-crazy society," says longtime CBS sportscaster Jim Nantz. "We love nothing more than a good scandal" (as cited in Schultz, 2005, p. 15). Over the past 20 years the sport media have extensively covered scandals involving steroids, gambling, drugs, and other assorted vagaries. Nancy Kerrigan underwent intense media scrutiny in 1994 as part of one of the biggest sport's tabloid stories ever—the 1994 Olympic Ice Skating incident involving Tonya Harding. Over the course of several weeks Kerrigan's media portrayal went from victim, to heroine, to ingrate. After it was finally over she commented, "The media used me for months, then just threw me away" (Shales, 2000) (see Box 10.1).

However, despite the prevalence of media members covering the on- and off-field activities of athletes, the media's ability to exclusively shape and control the nature of sport's content has weakened in recent years. Technological developments like personal websites, Twitter accounts, Facebook pages, and blogs have created content outlets for athletes, sport organizations, and even fans. As

BOX 10.1

The coverage of the attack on Nancy Kerrigan, the subsequent role of Tonya Harding in the attack, and their competition at the 1994 Winter Olympics became a media frenzy and one of the most publicized events of the 'celebrity sports' era. Journalist Mitch Albom covered the story and said, "We basically ignored every other athlete in the Olympics. We were too busy covering Tonya and Nancy's practice sessions" (as cited in Schultz, 2005, p. 15).

Tonya Harding-Nancy Kerrigan Timeline

January 6, 1994:	During the U.S. National Figure Skating Championships in Detroit, skater Nancy Kerrigan is attacked at a practice session. Her knee is injured severely enough that she is forced to withdraw from the competition. Tonya Harding goes on to win the competition and qualify for the Winter Olympic Games.
February 1, 1994:	Harding's ex-husband Jeff Gillooly accepts a plea bargain in exchange for testimony against Harding. Gillooly admits that he and Harding bodyguard Shawn Eckhardt hired Shane Stant to attack Kerrigan. Harding does not admit complicity in the attack, but does admit to helping cover up the crime.
February 5, 1994:	The U.S. Figure Skating Association says it has "reasonable grounds" to believe that Harding was involved in the attack and initiates proceedings to have her removed from the Olympic team. Harding threatens legal action and retains her place on the team, but Kerrigan joins the team with a special exemption.
February 17, 1994:	Kerrigan and Harding are both on the ice together during practice. The session is covered by more than 700 media members.
February 23, 1994:	Kerrigan finishes second and Harding eighth at the figure skating finals at the Winter Olympics in Lillehammer, Norway. Audience interest is so high that ratings for the event are still the sixth-highest in U.S. television history.
March 16, 1994:	Harding avoids further prosecution by pleading guilty to hindering the investigation of the attack. She received three years probation, 500 hours of community service, and a $160,000 fine.
June 30, 1994:	The United States Figure Skating Federation (USFSA) strips Harding of her national championship and bans her for life from skating in USFSA events.

just one example, Twitter (a form of micro-text messaging) has now allowed athletes to more directly communicate with fans. "We're hitting (Twitter) hard," said Chris Bosh of the National Basketball Association's (NBA) Toronto Raptors. "You can put up what you're doing. Or if you have a question, you'd be surprised how much people know. You can be, like, 'I need directions to this spot.' People will tell you" (Feschuk, 2009, para. 5). As of June 2010, Bosh had Twitter connections with more than 121,000 fans, which is impressive, but is dwarfed by fellow NBA star Shaquille O'Neal who had more than 2.9 million connections. These kinds of developments have important consequences for the relationship between the media and audiences, and will be discussed later in this chapter.

Media and Sports

The media primarily support the sport industry by distributing events and games to large audiences (Figure 10.3). In the early 20th century sport events and organizations depended mainly on ticket sales for revenue. During that time, newspaper coverage helped increase audience interest, spurring higher ticket sales. When radios became common in the late 1920s and 1930s, baseball owners were worried that broadcasting games live would decrease paid attendance by giving away the product for "free." Thus, the three Major League Baseball teams in New York agreed to a ban on radio broadcasts until 1938. Later, Major League Baseball, horse racing, and boxing would make similar decisions regarding television in the 1950s.

However, baseball and other sports eventually realized that radio and television broadcasts actually increased interest, ticket sales, and profits, as the excitement of the ballpark and arena could quickly be relayed to a large audience. More people became exposed to sports through the mass media and, in turn, the interest resulted in greater attendance. As sports became more popular and more in demand by audiences, sport organizations began charging fees to television and radio stations for the rights to broadcast events. An important legal development was the passage of the Sports Broadcasting Act (SBA) of 1961. Up until that time teams were required by antitrust laws to individually negotiate their own television rights deals. The Act removed the antitrust restriction and allowed leagues to negotiate as a whole on behalf of their member teams (and distribute the money equally in a revenue-sharing plan). National Football League Commissioner Pete Rozelle was the driving force behind passage of the SBA, and the NFL immediately saw dramatic increases in its television rights fees. Today, the NFL has one of the richest rights-fees packages among all sports leagues ($17.6 billion over eight years). Rights fees for the Olympic Games have also increased dramatically since the 1960s (see Table 10.2).

The media recoup the payment of rights fees via advertising contracts. Larger audiences generate greater interest—and therefore higher payments—from potential advertisers. For example, the Super Bowl typically draws an audience of more than one hundred million viewers (in fact, the five most-watched programs in U.S. television history in terms of total audience are all Super Bowls). The cost of a 30-second Super Bowl commercial has increased from $42,000 in 1967 (Super Bowl I) to $3 million for the 2010 Super Bowl ("Super Bowl," 2010). But in general, Super Bowls are the exception rather than the rule.

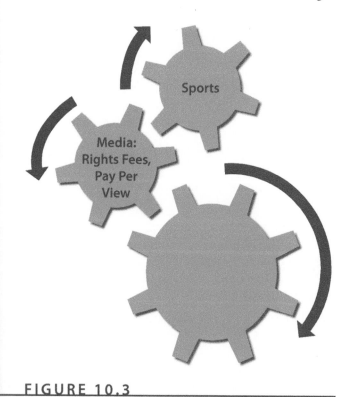

FIGURE 10.3

Rights and Fees: How the Media Affect Sports

TABLE 10.2

U.S. Olympic Rights Fees

Games	Site	Network	Rights Fees
1960 Summer	Rome	CBS	$394,000
1984 Summer	Los Angeles	ABC	$225 million
2008 Summer	Beijing	NBC	$894 million
2012 Summer	London	NBC	$1.18 billion

Source: Martzke, 2003

Television ratings for most sport events have declined sharply in the past 10 years, even for such signature events as the World Series (Sandomir, 2003). Such declines reflect the fact that, while televised sports can still attract large audiences, in general, audiences have splintered into smaller niche audiences over the past 20 years. This **fragmentation** is due largely to new media technologies which give audiences more channels and more consuming options. Thus, the 2000s have seen the rise of specialized sport channels such as the Golf Channel, Speed TV, and the Tennis Channel (not to mention channels created by the NFL, NBA, NHL, and MLB), which cater to devoted, but smaller groups of viewers.

Fragmentation
The splintering of large, mass sport audiences into smaller, niche audiences due primarily to the growth of media channels and options.

The media still pay rights fees to distribute games, but are reluctant to pay enormous sums except for events like the Olympics that can draw massive, diverse audiences. Increasingly, the media are turning to a **pay-per-view** system in which smaller audiences pay directly for the rights to access content. New technologies like digital television and radio make this possible, and the amount of pay-per-view material has increased significantly. NBC's "Triple Cast" Olympic coverage in 1992 was a precursor to today's pay-per-view model. The network offered its usual free coverage of the Barcelona Olympics during primetime hours, but also gave audiences a chance to purchase additional programming on one of its three sister networks. The plan was largely ridiculed at the time, but today almost all networks and sport leagues offer a similar plan (Payne, 2006). In addition to their free programming offered on television and radio, the NFL ("Sunday Ticket"), NBA ("Full Court"), NHL ("Center Ice") and Major League Baseball ("Extra Innings") all offer pay-per-view content on television and radio. NFL "Sunday Ticket," a program that allows subscribers access to every televised game each Sunday, is probably the most popular of the pay-per-view plans. In 2009, DirecTV signed a four-year, $4 billion deal for exclusive rights to the package (King, 2009).

The money DirecTV pays to the NFL is an example of how teams and leagues are creating new revenue opportunities. Several leagues and individual teams are also increasing revenue through the creation of their own networks and Internet sites. Two of the most prominent are the YES Network (New York Yankees) and SNY (New York Mets). The Big 10 has its own television network, and the University of Texas has plans to create its own television network in the near future. By creating networks, teams and schools can control both the content and distribution parts of the sports media process.

Sports

Sports and Media

In some instances, the goals of sports organizations and athletes are compatible. Sports and the media are dependent on audiences for revenue; sports provide the content, which the media then distribute. Audiences financially support both the media and sports entities. But there are times when the goals of the media clash with the goals of athletes and sport organizations. As noted earlier, today's media often emphasize scandal, investigation, and full disclosure. This is often in direct conflict with athletes and sport organizations, who always want to be portrayed positively. Thus, there is a constant information tug-of-war between sports and the media as both fight to capture the attention of audiences.

Athletes and sports organizations have a major advantage in this struggle: they control the content that the media need. So just as the media try to shape the style and tone of sport content, athletes, teams, and organizations do the same. One of the ways this is accomplished is through **access**, which is the degree to which the sport content providers make themselves available to the media in terms of reporting and coverage (Figure 10.4). Sport figures can usually control and shape the nature of information that gets to the public by determining how much and how often that information is released. Access to practices, games, and interview opportunities is typically controlled by the individual content provider. On the professional level, athletes usually determine for themselves how much access to allow. In some cases, teams or leagues will require access, such as during the Super Bowl or All-Star Game media day. Athletes have been punished for failing to make themselves available for league-mandated media events. But on the whole, athletes determine how much media access they will allow, and some have decided to rarely speak to the media. Duane Thomas, Steve Carlton and Albert Belle were athletes who refused *all* media access at one point in their careers. Though there are still some exam-

Access

The extent to which sport organizations, leagues, teams, and athletes make themselves available to the media in terms of coverage and reporting.

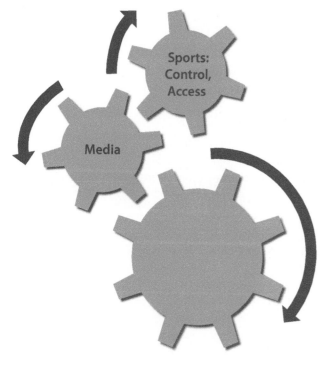

FIGURE 10.4

Control and Access: How Sports Affect the Media

ples of athletes who attempt to deflect most media attention, typically athletes will want at least some media attention as it increases the likelihood that other marketing and endorsement opportunities can be generated.

Limited access can create potential problems for the media–particularly since consumers often want to know more than just who won the game and how many points were scored. By nature, athletes and coaches are usually suspicious of the media and reluctant to provide any information that might prove to be misinterpreted, damaging, or simply embarrassing. Former Texas Tech assistant football coach Lyle Setencich summed up the attitude of many sports figures: "I don't like any of the guys giving interviews. Anything they say may be construed to be a smart-aleck type thing. If you're a football coach, that's like cancer" (Phillips, 2004, para. 6).

Because the media need content, they keep trying to get coaches and athletes to talk. This tension sometimes escalates into open hostility as the media seeks to gain access where it is not welcome. In the course of breaking a story for *Sports Illustrated* in 2009, reporter Selena Roberts flew to Miami to try to get an interview with baseball star Alex Rodriguez about his alleged use of performance-enhancing drugs. After the article was released, Rodriguez called Roberts a "stalker" who had tried to break into his home (Koster, 2009). Although Rodriguez later backed off his comments when challenged by Roberts, there have been numerous cases where athletes and the media have clashed, sometimes physically. Veteran newspaper and television reporter Bill Plaschke (2000, p. 44) observed, "Athletes are at their most vulnerable when dealing with the media. We're everywhere, and we're not looking to make friends, but front pages. With the proliferation of TV, radio and Internet reporters, pro athletes often need to be rude and pushy just to catch their breaths."

Most sports organizations, and even some athletes, have a system in place to prevent such incidents from happening. On the professional sports level, teams and organizations have a full-time **public relations** staff, which has several responsibilities. One is the production and distribution of information related to the organization and its athletes. This could take the form of a news release (timely or factual information), fact sheet (statistics and related information), quote sheet (direct comments from players, coaches, or support personnel), or media guide (a lengthy and detailed compilation of facts, quotes, pictures, and historical information). For some staff members, their sole responsibility is creating and distributing this information to the media (see Figure 10.5).

The other primary responsibility of the public relations staff concerns media access and activity. This mainly includes credentialing media members to cover games and scheduling interview access with players and coaches. Although public relations staff members try to accommodate the media as much as possible, access is ultimately decided by the individual athlete.

On the college sports level the public relations functions are usually handled by a sports information department, headed by a **sports information director** (SID). The SID is responsible for all communication with the media and the public, and access is usually much more controlled than at the professional

Public Relations_____
Methods by which sports teams, athletes, and organizations control and manipulate their access and information in regards to the media.

BOX 10.2

Major Meltdowns: Notable Athlete-Media Confrontations

Date	Incident	Result
November 19, 1977	Enraged after his Buckeyes fumbled against arch-rival Michigan, Ohio State coach Woody Hayes punched an ABC sideline cameraman.	The Big 10 put Hayes on probation for this incident, but his career ultimately was ended when he physically attacked a Clemson player near the end of the 1978 Gator Bowl. Ohio State fired Hayes immediately after the game.
April 26, 1993	Kansas City Royals manager Hal McRae trashed his entire office, throwing things off of his desk including a phone, which cut a reporter, and yelling profanities at reporters. McRae was angry at the questions reporters asked him after a 5-3 loss to Detroit.	McRae was not officially punished, but managed the Royals only one more season.
March 17, 1995	Indiana University basketball coach Bob Knight launched into a lengthy diatribe against an NCAA media liaison at a post-game news conference. The liaison had earlier suggested to the media that Knight would not be attending the session.	It is hard to pick just one incident from Knight's long career of media intimidation. For this one, the NCAA reprimanded Knight and fined the university $30,000.
June 30, 2005	As he walked on the field for a practice, Texas Rangers pitcher Kenny Rogers pushed KTVT photographer Larry Rodriguez, threw his camera to the ground and kicked it. Rodriguez was taken to a hospital.	Major league baseball fined Rogers $50,000 and suspended him for 20 games.
September 22, 2007	Oklahoma State football coach Mike Gundy went on a tirade at a post-game press conference. He verbally attacked newspaper columnist Jenni Carlson for a story she had written about one of Gundy's players.	Gundy was not officially censured, but his comments—including "I'm a man! I'm 40!"—became an instant Internet classic. The YouTube version of the incident has now received more than 1.6 million views.

Sources: *Sports Illustrated*, NBC, ESPN.

level. Because college athletes have class and outside responsibilities and do not get paid to play, SIDs work with coaches to limit their media access. Most schools have a system in place where access to players and coaches is allowed only through the SID or someone else in the sports information department. In some cases, coaches and SIDs completely prohibit access to certain athletes, most typically for younger players. These restrictions can be frustrating for media members when the story has the potential to put a player or coach in a negative light and in such instances, the media often try to circumvent official channels to get the

Ole Miss Soccer to Face Washington in NCAA First Round

OXFORD, MISS.—A sea of Red-clad Rebel fans joined the No. 25 Ole Miss women's soccer team at the Indoor Practice Facility here Monday evening as the field of 64 was announced for the NCAA Championships, and the entire place erupted upon learning that the Rebels would be headed to Portland, Ore., where they will face Washington in the first round Friday.

The program earned its first NCAA Tournament berth since 2005 and the fourth in program history, all under the direction of head coach Steve Holeman. Ole Miss also made the postseason in 2002 and 2003.

"It's an exciting day for the Ole Miss Rebels," Holeman said. "I'm especially excited for our three seniors. They have a chance to continue their career and play in the Big Dance. What a tremendous crowd we had here. I want to thank all the fans who showed up. We must have had close to 200 people celebrating that special moment with us. Now we have some work to do. It's just step one."

Ole Miss will square off against the Pac-10's Washington Huskies (11-5-4) on Friday at 4 P.M. Pacific time at the Clive Charles Soccer Complex in Portland. The winner will advance to face the winner between the No. 2 seeded host University of Portland (18-1) and Denver (17-5-1) in Sunday's second round. Both Ole Miss and Washington earned at-large bids, while Portland was the automatic qualifier from the West Coast Conference and Denver the champion of the Sun Belt.

Holeman's Rebels enter the tournament with a 14-5-2 overall record and finished third overall in the Southeastern Conference with a 7-2-2 league record. The team boasts an offense and defense that rank among the nation's statistical leaders, while piling up the fourth-most wins in a season in school history.

"This team has had a great season," Holeman said. "This bid to the NCAA tournament is well-deserved. We have a lot of big wins against the likes of Florida, Georgia, Auburn and Memphis, who are all in the tournament.

Among the catalysts for the Rebels' success this season have been the team's three senior captains—defender Mallory Coleman, All-SEC midfielder Danielle Johnson and All-SEC forward Hannah Weatherly. Coleman has helped lead a Rebel back line that has allowed only 13 goals in 20 matches, while Johnson and Weatherly have paced an offensive attack that ranks second in the SEC with 2.15 goals per game.

"This is unreal," said Coleman, a native of Clinton, Miss. "We've anticipated this day for a long time. We've had a great season with some really big wins. We've worked very hard, and as a senior there's no better way to end your season. This is by far the top moment in my career. We've had some good teams, but this team is very deserving."

Ole Miss and Washington will be meeting for the first time. In fact, the Rebel's have only faced one Pac-10 opponent in program history, suffering a 3-1 loss at Arizona State in 2001.

"We know Washington is a great program, and we're going to have to be at our very best," Holeman said. "It's been a while since Ole Miss Soccer has been out to the West Coast. I think the girls are really excited to travel. We've traveled well this year. We were the only SEC team to go undefeated on the road in league play. A lot of these girls have never been to Oregon; I've never been to Oregon. We know it's a tremendous place to play, and we're looking forward to it."

-UM-
November 9, 2009
Ole Miss Athletics Media Relations

FIGURE 10.5

A "typical" college athletic department press release. Courtesy of Ole Miss Athletics Media Relations.

information they need. An example occurred in 2006 and 2007 during coverage of an alleged rape involving members of the Duke University lacrosse team. Duke shut down access to the players and coaches involved, leaving the media to fend for themselves. "We were hampered early on by the unwillingness of the players . . . to speak with our reporters," said Melanie Sill, at the time the executive director at the Raleigh (NC) *News and Observer.* Responding to charges that media coveage of the case was biased against the players, Sill noted, "Our overall reporting was solid and on point, however . . . it intensified as we ran into obstacles. Nonetheless, we should have stated more emphatically that we had not been able to get their side of things" (Ham, 2007, para. 5-7).

The sports information department is organized much like a professional public relations department, with different staff members in charge of different aspects of media relations. For example, in 2008 the University of Texas in Austin listed 25 full-time members in its Communications/Media Relations department. The size of the sports information department typically depends on the competition level at which the school competes. A school like Texas has dozens of staff members, while a smaller Division-II or Division-III school might have only one or two full-time people (Table 10.3).

Regardless of size, much of the emphasis in today's sports information departments is shifting from printed to digital material. Traditionally, these departments would send out reams of printed press releases each week, and also produce a bulky printed media guide. Now, much of this information is sent by electronic mail or incorporated into the school's athletic web site (Figure 10.6).

For athletes who are high school age and younger, there is usually no one who controls access other than a coach or parent. Very few high schools have anything like a public relations staff or a sports information director, and as a result, media access to information regarding scores, statistics and schedules is sometimes not dependable. In terms of granting interview access to players, most high schools try to accommodate the media, but in many ways they are even more protective of athletes than at the college level. For example, while at St. Marys in Ohio, legendary high school football coach Skip Baughman forbade his players from granting any interviews during the season. Typically, the only system of access at the high school level is what the coach or athletic director will allow.

At any level—high school, college or professional—access becomes extremely limited and almost non-existent during a crisis situation. A crisis situation is any type of bad news that could damage the reputation of the athlete, team, or organization. Typically, crisis situations occur away from the playing field. Examples might include a baseball player accused of using steroids or a football player being arrested for drunk driving. During a crisis situation, media access to the involved athlete, coach, or administrator is likely to be significantly restricted. In many cases, information will be limited to an official statement released by the player or organization, or perhaps a statement from a representative such as a lawyer. Former sports broadcaster and current college educator Charlie Lambert observed, "Journalists who cover top-level sport are facing a

TABLE 10.3

University and College Sports Information Departments

The size and scope of sports information departments usually depend on the size of the school and its athletic budget. In 2008–09, the University of Texas at Austin had 22 full-time staff working in sports information; Vanderbilt University had seven, while Ohio Northern University had two.

School	Enrollment	Media-Related Staff Positions
University of Texas (Austin)	50,170	Senior Associate Athletics Director for Communications Assistant Athletics Director for Media Relations (Football) Special Assistant to Football Coach for Communications Assistant Media Director (Women's basketball and golf) Assistant Media Relations Director (Baseball) Assistant Media Relations Director (Men's Golf, Swimming/Diving, Tennis) Assistant Media Relations Director (Rowing, Softball, Volleyball) Assistant Media Relations Director (Football, Men's Track and Field/Cross Country, Texas Relays) Assistant Media Relations Director (Football) Assistant Media Relations Director (Soccer, Women's Track and Field/Cross Country) Senior Administrative Associate Senior Associate Athletics Director for Communications Manager, Media Production Services Senior Web Manager Web Manager Electronic Publishing Specialist Manager, Media Production Services Photo Manager Photographer Administrative Assistant Publications Supervisor Communications Coordinator
Vanderbilt University	12,093	Director of External Relations Media Relations Director (Football) Media Relations Director (Men's Basketball) Media Relations Director (Baseball) Media Relations Director (Women's Basketball) Director of Online Services and Promotions Editor of Commodore Nation
Ohio Northern University	3,721	Sports Information Director Assistant Sports Information Director

Sources: University of Texas; Vanderbilt University; Ohio Northern University.

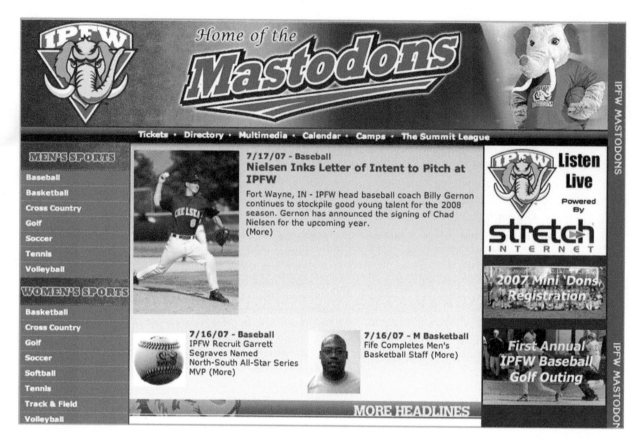

FIGURE 10.6

A "typical" college athletic department's Web page. Reprinted by permission of IPFW.

real challenge. Teams and organizations are so powerful and so wealthy that they want to control everything that is said or written about them" ("Journalism leaders," 2008, para 5).

Resistance during a crisis will not mean that the media will give up trying to get access to pertinent involved individuals. Certainly, media members will continue to look for access and sources who will adequately help them find and report needed information. In their attempt to report on the Bay Area Lab Cooperative (BALCO) steroids scandal, newspaper reporters Mark Fainaru-Wada and Lance Williams were stonewalled through official sources. "Going in, we were completely blind," said Fainaru-Wada. "No one had heard of BALCO. It was a matter of chasing as much as you could" ("Mark Fainaru-Wada . . . ," 2004, para. 4). In their three-year investigation, the reporters eventually turned to anonymous sources to uncover the story. They defied a U.S. District Court judge by refusing to identify their sources, and although they were sentenced in September 2006 to 18 months in prison, they never served any time. In his statement before the court, Fainaru-Wada said, "Throughout the BALCO affair, critics have questioned the motives of our reporting, suggesting that it has been little more than a witch hunt or an effort to profit off the big names who have been drawn into the scandal. Supporters have portrayed us as champions in the global fight against performance-enhancing drugs. For us, however, BALCO has always been an earnest and sincere effort to present the truth" ("Fainaru-Wada's statement . . . ," 2006, p. A14). In 2004, Fainaru-Wada and Williams won an Investigative Reporters and Editors award and the George Polk Award.

Given the inherent tension between reporters trying to find out information and athletes and organizations trying to control it, some communications strategies have evolved. The oldest and most traditional strategy is to stonewall, or simply refuse to give the media any comment or information. However, it is becoming increasing difficult to control information in the age of digital communication and Internet access. Information can leak from a variety of sources, including blogs, Internet bulletin boards and fan forums. Stonewalling allows others to manipulate and shape public perception, since there is no comment from the involved parties. It further suggests that those involved have "something to hide" by not talking to the media. Many of the baseball stars implicated in the recent steroid scandal tried the stonewalling strategy, which eventually damaged their credibility and their reputations.

BOX 10.3

The Bay Area Lab Cooperative (BALCO), under the direction of founder and owner Victor Conte, marketed performance-enhancing drugs to several prominent athletes, most notably in baseball and track and field. Conte pleaded guilty to providing steroids and money laundering. The work of investigative reporters Mark Fainaru-Wada and Lance Williams was instrumental in helping the BALCO investigation.

BALCO Investigation Timeline

September 3, 2003:	Local and federal authorities raid BALCO offices.
Dec. 2–3, 2004:	The *San Francisco Chronicle* publishes stories containing grand jury testimony given by Jason Giambi and Barry Bonds as part of the BALCO investigation. In it, Giambi admits to steroid use while Bonds says he may have unknowingly taken steroids.
March 23, 2006:	Fainaru-Wada and Williams publish *Game of Shadows,* a best-selling book that highlighted details of their BALCO investigation.
May 5, 2006:	Fainaru-Wada and Williams are subpoenaed to testify before a federal grand jury about how they obtained the testimony of Bonds, Giambi, and other athletes.
Sept. 21, 2006:	Judge Jeffrey White tells *San Francisco Chronicle* reporters Fainaru-Wada and Williams he will order them jailed for up to 18 months if they do not comply with his order to reveal their sources.
February 14, 2007:	The identity of the source of the illegally leaked grand jury testimony is revealed as Troy Ellerman, one of the BALCO defense attorneys. Federal authorities agree to drop their efforts to send Fainaru-Wada and Williams to prison.

Source: BALCO investigation timeline, 2007

Another potential crisis strategy is *full disclosure.* Some athletes believe that by freely giving information to the media they can save themselves the problems associated with stonewalling. In addition, an athlete or coach who is cooperative usually enjoys better media treatment and has a better public image. However, this strategy is also problematic if the athlete is not disclosing the whole truth. Former baseball star Pete Rose talked to anyone who would listen that he never bet on games involving his own team, a stance he maintained for almost 20 years. When Rose finally admitted in 2004 that he had been lying, his already tarnished reputation suffered another serious blow.

Most athletes, coaches, and organizations use a strategy somewhere in between stonewalling and full disclosure. The strategy depends on several factors, including the severity of the incident, and the past history of the athlete or organization involved. Every person involved in a crisis incident will be working with one goal in mind—to protect the image and public reputation of those at the center of the controversy.

A more recent communications strategy that has emerged is used by athletes and organizations in both crisis and non-crisis situations. New developments in media technology have given athletes and organizations much more power and control over the messages they send to audiences. Primarily, the ease and **interactivity** of the Internet makes it possible for them to bypass the mainstream media and take their messages directly to sports audiences. For example, several athletes now write their own blogs, including well-known players such as Curt Schilling and Barry Bonds. (The media-shy Bonds used his blog as the primary means of communicating with the public during the BALCO scandal and his chase of the all-time home run record).

Interactivity_____
Two-way communication that allows the audience to provide feedback and take part in the communication process. Interactivity has increased with the advent of new media such as the Internet and blogging.

A blog allows the content provider to get his or her message out without media interference, and thus take much greater control in shaping public opinion. In 2008, NBA player Jamal Crawford responded to a story in the *New York Post* from writer Marc Berman that he had criticized a teammate: "You've been around me four years, have I EVER did anything like throw a teammate under the bus? He says 'No,' so then I said, 'So why would I do it now? Why, when we're trying to build team chemistry, do something like that?' He couldn't really answer me, so I said, 'Well, now I'm going to have to write about you on my blog'" (Edwards, 2008, para. 4).

There are drawbacks to teams and athletes getting involved in blogging. With more than 112 million blogs and another 120,000 new ones created each day, there is a danger that the message will simply get lost in cyberspace. Studies suggest that most people who blog do it for personal reasons and create material that is personal and subjective, but not necessarily truthful. As a result, most audiences take blogging for what it is: opinions published to push a certain agenda. To be done well, blogs require a lot of time and constant updating. Finally, athletes run the risk of actually making these worse, or at least not making them any better. Consider the embarrassment of NFL player Chris Cooley. In September of 2008, his own blog site temporarily included a prominent picture of his male anatomy. Cooley apologized and removed the picture, but it did not help his public image.

LE 10.4

st-Watched U.S. Television Programs, All-Time

ed on ratings or percentage of television households, not total number of viewers)

k	Show or Episode	Date	Percentage of U.S. Television Households	Total Number of Viewers
	Last episode of M*A*S*H	February 28, 1983	60.2	50.2 million
	Super Bowl XVI	January 24, 1982	49.1	40 million
	Super Bowl XVII	January 30, 1983	48.6	40.5 million
	Winter Olympics (Kerrigan-Harding skating final)	February 23, 1994	48.5	45.7 million
	Super Bowl XX	January 26, 1986	48.3	41.5 million
	Super Bowl XII	January 15, 1978	47.2	34.4 million

rce: A.C. Nielsen Media

(Miller, 2008). In 2008, consumers streamed nearly five million hours of "March Madness on Demand" video and audio through CBSSports.com, up 81 percent from the previous year. "There is tremendous growth in live streaming sports," said Jason Kint, senior vice president and general manager of CBSSports.com. "It is not cannibalizing television audiences, but providing dynamic opportunity across platforms" (Miller, 2008, para 2).

Sports teams and leagues are taking advantage of these new opportunities by creating their own websites, networks and pay-per-view packages, all of which increase their revenues. The NFL's Sunday Ticket package, which enables satellite subscribers to access every televised game each Sunday, has approximately 1.5–2 million subscribers. A similar Major League Baseball subscription called Extra Innings has around 500,000 subscribers (Consoli, 2005; Gorman, 2009; King, 2009; Stewart, 2004). Content providers have learned that audiences are willing to pay hefty subscription fees (in the case of Sunday Ticket, around $250 for the full season of games) for the rights to access this material. "[All of this] builds stronger fan bases among more people who will watch more," stated Tennis Channel CEO Ken Solomon. The more you see, the more you want to see—which is why sports will continue to get stronger and stronger" (Miller, 2008, para. 4).

Audience

Audience and Media

Traditionally, the audience has been a passive consumer of sport's content. Athletes and sport organizations created the content, the media distributed it,

Some athletes also utilize Twitter to relay information to interested fans. Twitter enables athletes and coaches to "tweet" short messages to anyone who wishes to receive updated information. Many athletes and coaches have utilized Twitter, but unfortunately, the ease of distributing information can have some drawbacks. Dwight Howard sent messages to fans while he was suspended from Game 6 of the Orlando Magic's first round NBA playoff series against the Philadelphia 76ers. Though Howard received some criticism, it was nothing compared to the complaints Charlie Villanueva of the Milwaukee Bucks elicited when he used Twitter during halftime of a game in which he was playing. His coach and other members of the Milwaukee Bucks' organization were certainly not amused to hear that one of their players was thinking more about sending messages to fans than about the current game being played.

Sports and Audiences

The relationship between sports and audiences is fairly straightforward and does not require a great deal of elaboration. Across any media platform, the primary benefit sport provides to audiences is attractive and highly popular content (Figure 10.7). One could make it a chicken-and-egg argument: is there so much sport content in the media because it is popular with audiences or is it popular with audiences because there is so much of it in the media? The likely answer is that sport has a primary place in U.S. culture and its significance is reflected in the high demand for sport content across various media outlets. Author James Michener (1976, p. 355) observed that "one of the happiest relationships in American society is between sports and the media."

Historically, the demand for sport content has been met through a combination of newspapers, magazines, radio, and television. Television is ideally suited because of its ability to present the live drama of sport events to large audiences. In fact, five of the top 10 and 11 of the top 20 all-time highest rated television shows are sport events (Table 10.4).

New developments in media technology are creating new distribution systems and are dramatically increasing both the total amount of mediated sports content and the demand for it. Broadband technology now allows audiences to access sports content, including video and live game action, directly through a computer via Internet access. In its first year, ESPN360 ran 3,000 live events. According to the network, distribution has grown 41% and unique viewers and total minutes were both up nearly 400 percent

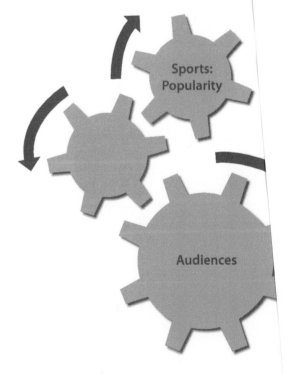

FIGURE 10.7

Popularity: How Sports Affect Audiences

and finally audiences watched, read, or listened to it. Other than niches like sports talk radio, it was a one-way communication process in which the audience had little or no input other than the decision to consume. But this relationship has changed drastically in the past 20 years, due mainly to advances in media technology. This new technology has significantly empowered sports audiences, who now have more consuming options, and have greater input into how content is presented (Figure 10.8).

Much of this new power comes from developments in broadband technologies, such as the Internet, digital television and radio, and satellite delivery. Sports fans now have access to much more information and can get it almost instantaneously, which puts pressure on the content providers to have more content choices. The number of channel options has increased tremendously and much of that space has been used to meet the increasing demand for sport content. Audiences can now customize their consumption habits by picking and choosing from a variety of content offerings.

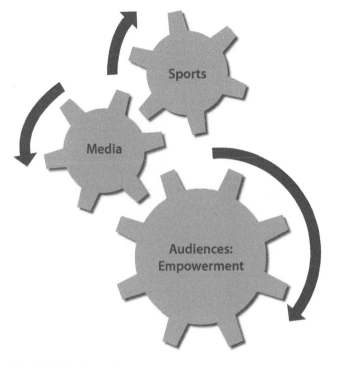

FIGURE 10.8

Empowerment: How the Media Affect Audiences

Perhaps the greatest advances are occurring on the Internet, where audiences not only have greater access, but now also have the opportunity to create and distribute their own sports content. Message boards, community fan forums and blogs allow audiences much greater control over what content they choose to consume and how they consume it. In northern Virginia, teenager Marc James started a blog as a personal homepage offering sports news. It now has grown into a sports commentary content site with more than 120,000 postings and a staff of about 40 people who publish original columns three days a week. "I think blogs are the wave of the future, because they give a voice to the ordinary fan that has an intelligent opinion, but in the past didn't have the medium to voice it," James said. "People want to hear less of what the so-called experts have to say and more of what the sports geek down the street thinks" (Bruscas, 2004, para. 5).

The opinions or ravings of a few rabid fans are not the only information getting posted to sport blogs. In some instances, audience content is directly competing with and impacting the traditional sport content providers, including the media. When former University of Alabama football coach Mike Price lost his job for allegedly going to strip clubs and participating in other sordid late-night behavior, the story was not broken in the mainstream media. The details and rumors initially surfaced on the Internet, particularly on *Tider Insider,* a website devoted to Alabama football, run by lifelong fan Rodney Orr. Dan Raley covered the story for the *Seattle Post-Intelligencer* and said, "You have to be careful about online boards. You don't want to repeat silly rumors, but *Tider Insider* had all the details way before anything was in the press" ("Internet allegation . . . ," 2003, para 5).

The Mike Price episode and other similar situations have direct consequences on the traditional sports-media-audience relationship, particularly in terms of how the media must now adjust to new competition. WJRD-TV in Tuscaloosa noticed the attention Orr was getting, and offered to bring his site to television. *Tider Insider* now includes a 30-minute weekly television show that appears on cable, DirectTV and the Dish Network in Alabama ("Meet Rodney," 2008). Perhaps the most famous of the "new breed" of Internet journalists is ESPN's Bill Simmons. Known as "The Sports Guy," Simmons began his writing career on his own website rather than by working for a newspaper or magazine. Once his unique style had attracted a large following, ESPN hired him to write columns, work as a correspondent on its *E60* television show, and interview various sport and non-sport personalities for his weekly podcasts.

Sports reporters also now regularly scour the message boards and blog sites to make sure they are not missing any important stories. "I go on [the Internet] every day," says Steve Irvine of the *Birmingham News,* "but mainly for the humor. They're clowns, basically, but you get a pulse on what the fans think. Everyone on this beat is looking at them, though" ("Internet allegation . . . ," 2003, para 8). Adds Mike Fish, a senior writer for *Sports Illustrated*'s web site, "They make our jobs harder because there's so much stuff out there [and] we have to do a massive amount of screening. There's a lot of vicious, ugly stuff" ("Internet allegation . . . ," 2003, para 6).

More media and more attention also mean that sports athletes, teams and organizations lose some ability to control their content and image. It is extremely difficult for athletes to escape the spotlight; the camera is always on, mainly because it seems as if everyone has a camera. Just as Mike Price was somewhat caught with his pants down (no pun intended), other athletes and coaches must now be aware that anything they say or do can be caught on camera and put into the public domain. In September of 2008, a cell phone video of NBA player Josh Howard was posted on YouTube. The video showed Howard making disparaging (and profane) comments about the National Anthem, which understandably created a public furor. Howard tried to initiate damage control by issuing an apology through his own blog site (as discussed earlier in this chapter), but his public image took a major hit.

Currently, there is a big debate in journalism about this audience-generated content and whether is qualifies as "real" journalism. Most of the people who write and distribute this content ignore many of the traditional journalistic values such as checking facts and citing sources, and do not even consider themselves journalists. "Blogging as it has evolved has been very different from conventional reporting," says Jane Kirtley, a professor of media ethics and law at the University of Minnesota. "Blogs are not intended to be objective. They are supposed to be opinionated, snarky and in your face—and that's not the way the mainstream media usually goes about reporting" (Hull, 2006–2007, para. 9).

However, there is no debate about blogging's impact upon today's media. Online consumption of video material rose 66 percent between 2007 and 2008, and YouTube owned a third of the 10 billion online video views in February 2008. By 2006, as many as 80 percent of the top 100 U.S. newspapers provided at least one reporter blog (Teeling, 2006). Around 55 percent of the public believes blogging will be an important aspect of journalism in the future, while 74 percent say amateur citizen reporters, not the established media outlets, will play a key role ("Zogby poll . . . ," 2007).

Conclusion

The basic framework that athletes, teams and sport organizations provide content and related information for the media to distribute to interested audiences, who financially support both entities still exists. However, there are important changes taking place within that basic framework that will have consequences for the future of the interrelationship. These changes raise several questions, the answers to which might significantly alter the accepted communication model involving sports, media and audiences.

- **What role will technology play in the future?** Emerging technologies have already influenced the sports-media-audience relationship. As technology gets more sophisticated, how will it affect communication? With a few exceptions, the mass audience of yesterday has evolved into the smaller, niche audiences of today. Communication is more targeted and more specific, meaning that audience demographics are now just as important as sheer audience size. Will future technological advances make audiences even smaller? In other words, will we soon be seeing such things as an ESPN channel dedicated specifically to 18–24-year-old male outdoorsmen who like to hunt deer with a crossbow? The sports information of the future might be tailored to a specific individual and delivered to that person via cell phone or other similar device. Technology also promises to continue increasing the amount of information available and the speed at which it is delivered. Sports organizations and the media will have to make sure they are technologically up-to-date and able to satisfy the growing demand for information.

- **Where will audience-created content lead?** The hot trend now is blogging, Twittering, message boards, and anything else that lets the audience participate in the sport-communication process. Athletes, teams, organizations and even the media have been quick to pick up on the trend and incorporate it into their communication strategies. In fact, it is almost impossible today to find an outlet that does not let the audience participate through such methods as fan contests, message boards, trivia games, and the like. What will be the next new developments in this area? Now that audiences have both the means of creating and distributing content, will that seriously threaten the traditional distribution function of the media? Will the media respond by incorporating more audience content, as WJRD-TV did with *Tider Insider?*

If audiences are more in control of content that could also cause a shift in the type of content that is distributed. Consider a relatively new company in Maryland called DigitalSports, which uses a combination of former journalists, parents and novices to cover local high school sports online. It is the kind of in-depth coverage of high school athletes, teams, and coaches not typically found in the mainstream media, but it is attracting an audience. DigitalSports gets more than 250,000 unique visitors per month. Larger, more established high school sites like Maxpreps.com get about 1.5 million visits per month (Goldfarb, 2007).

- **How will economics affect all this?** Obviously, all sports communication takes place within a larger economic context that makes all such communication possible. The media are able to distribute and shape sports content and information only to the extent that they can do so profitably. In a media era where there is increasing emphasis on the bottom line, some sport content and communication could be altered, reduced or simply eliminated. Several local television stations, including those in Wichita, Pittsburgh and Albany, have recently made major changes to the sports segments within their newscasts. WTEN in Albany, New York did away with the sports anchor and its traditional sports content. "The traditional sportscast features highlights and scoreboards from national teams that most viewers just don't care about, and those who do already know if their team won," said news director Rob Puglisi. "In the days before the Internet, before ESPN, people had to rely on their local TV sportscast for these national scores and highlights. It's just not the case anymore" (McGuire, 2005, para. 13). This might be another reason that blogging, websites, and audience-generated content are becoming increasingly popular. Such content is relatively cheap to produce and distribute, which makes it attractive for media outlets.

  The basic economic model of the sport communication system is also changing. Advertising to mass audiences through print and broadcast sources has been the main economic engine for decades, but with the breakup of the mass audience into niche audiences there are questions as to whether advertising can continue to sustain the system. Increasingly, media outlets and content providers are turning to subscriptions (such as with the NFL's Sunday Ticket) and pay-per-use plans. Advertising on the Internet is also growing and may one day exceed advertisement levels for television and newspapers. If the economic system of the future changes drastically it will have a corresponding effect on the sport-communication process.

- **Will the delicate balance of the sport communication process tip in a certain direction?** This is the big question—will technology, economics or some other factor cause one group to dominate the other among sport, the media, and audiences? Technology has empowered audience members and taken away a certain degree of power from the media. However, it is highly unlikely that consumer-driven content could one day completely replace the distribution function of the traditional media. Although much of today's online content is produced by volunteers, numerous analysts doubt they could fill the information gap that would occur if traditional media organizations completely disappeared.

It is more likely that the basic communication relationship among sports, media, and audiences will stay intact, but undergo some retooling. After all, athletes, teams, and organizations still own what drives the entire process—content and information. That fact is inescapable, no matter what the media and audiences do. Despite trends toward audience participation, the media are still the most efficient system of distributing that content and the communication related to it. The media and sports are still dependent on audiences for feedback and support. As long as those pillars remain in place, one group or another may become more powerful for a time, but the traditional relationship between sports, media and audiences will continue long into the 21st century.

Interview

Mike Lageschulte is the Director of Publications and Broadcasting at the University of Utah, where he has worked in the Sports Information department since 1995. He shares some of his thoughts on how sports information departments should handle a crisis situation:

"Handling a crisis situation needs to be a collaborative effort. The first step is to get the coaches and student-athletes involved to disclose what the problem is to the administration. Ideally, this will take place before the media gets hold of the story. As the media contact, you will often be the first person contacted about a potential legal/criminal issues. Even though you may not have the legal clearance, or in some instances be far enough along in the investigative/fact-finding process where you are ready to release details or make any lengthy statements, just being prepared for what is coming, and being able to confidently tell the media that you are aware of the situation and that it is being dealt with internally, is a major plus. When the media senses they have you scrambling, they have a tendency to become even more aggressive.

Once the administration is aware of the potential issue, you must strategize how best to deal with it publicly. Everyone who will be involved, including the president of the university, university legal advisors, the head spokesman for the university P.R. office, the A.D, and the SID, need to be a part of this process. In addition to the individuals directly involved in the incident, all of the aforementioned people will be drawn into a crisis situation. And, they all have something to contribute based upon their area of expertise. Everyone needs to be upfront with one another about what they're thinking and what they're feeling, and not be afraid to make suggestions. Then a strategy needs to be formulized as to what will be announced to the public and when, and who will do the talking.

Unlike the normal day-to-day situations that arise in athletics, it is likely that the university public relations department will want to take over handling the media in a major crisis situation. Along those lines, I think one of the best things you can do is to limit the number of people that will be talking to the media. The more streamlined your communication is, the better your chances are of getting your message across and getting the same information to everyone. And, perhaps more importantly, it limits the chances of incorrect information and/or details that you don't want to be made public getting out."

Source: Schultz, B. (2005). *Sports media: reporting, planning and producing*. Burlington, MA: Focal Press.

Study Questions and Exercises

1. Looking at some of the new communications technologies coming out on the market, which are the ones most likely to impact the sport-media-audience communication process. How do you think these might make an impact and what part of the process would they be most likely to affect?

2. If you could remove one part of the sport-media-audience communication process without harming the overall system, which part would it be and why? Is it even possible to remove one of the parts without rendering the entire system dysfunctional?

3. There has been a recent movement toward more pay-per-use and subscription models in sports content and communication. Assuming all the material currently on the Internet became pay-per-use, which of the following do you think audiences would be most willing to pay for and why?

   a. Live game action of a favorite team or player(s)

   b. Statistics and/or other factual information

   c. Interviews with athletes, players, coaches, and other sports figures

   d. Commentary or stories contributed by sportswriters

   e. Interactive sports material such as fan forums and message boards

4. Peruse some of the Internet sports sites dedicated to audience-created content (such as Fan Media Network—www.fanmedianetwork.com). Why do you think people would want to spend the time and money creating and distributing such content? Is such content merely a fad or perhaps the future of sport communication? Why or why not?

5. Consider the well-publicized steroid scandal in Major League Baseball (and all of sports, for that matter). How did MLB handle the situation in terms of protecting its image and controlling its message? What, if anything, should baseball executives have done differently?

6. You are the beat reporter for a local college football team. A star player for the team is arrested on drug charges and the school has refused all media access beyond an official statement. What are some ways you could go about getting the information you need to report the story?

References

BALCO investigation timeline. (2007, November 27). *USA Today*. From: http://www.usatoday.com/sports/balco-timeline.htm

Bruscas, A. (2004, February 24). Going blog wild: Anyone with a computer and an opinion can launch a media startup. *Seattle Post-Intelligencer*. From: http://seattlepi.nwsource.com/othersports/161835_blog24.htm

Bryant, J., & Holt, A. (2006). A historical overview of sports and media in the United States. In Raney, A. & Bryant, J. (eds.). *Handbook of Sports & Media*. Mahwah, NJ: Erlbaum.

Connor, A. (1982). *Voices from Cooperstown: Baseball's Hall of Famers tell it like it was*. New York: Collier Books.

Consoli, J. (2005, April 19). NBC, ESPN snap up NFL packages, *AdWeek*. From: http://www.allbusiness.com/marketing-advertising/4153921-1.html

Edwards, B. (2008, October 17). Jamal Crawford confronts reporter who wrote a false story about him. *Fanhouse*. From: http://nba.fanhouse.com/2008/10/17/jamal-crawford-confronts-reporter-who-wrote-a-false-story-about Fainaru-Wada's statement to the court. (2006, September 22). *San Francisco Chronicle*, A14.

Feschuk, D. (2009, February 17). Bosh, NBA all a-Twitter over latest blogging fad. *Toronto Star*. Retrieved December 27, 2009 from http://www.thestar.com/Sports/NBA/article/588483

Goldfarb, Z. (2007, December 3). Can youth sports coverage pay off online? *Washington Post*, p. D1.

Gorman, B. (2009, February 24). ESPN spending $1.1 billion for NFL rights, $300 million for MLB, $270 million for NASCAR. *Wall Street Journal*. Retrieved January 16, 2010 from http://tvbythenumbers.com/2009/02/24/espn-spending-11-billion-for-nfl-rights-300-million-for-mlb-270-million-for-nascar/13350

Ham, J. (2007, April 16). Media rehab and the Duke lacrosse case. *Carolina Journal Online*. Retrieved January 16, 2010 from http://www.carolinajournal.com/mediamangle/display_story.html?id=4011

Hirschorn, M. (2009, January-February). End times. *The Atlantic*. Retrieved January 16, 2010 from http://www.the atlantic.com/doc/200901/new-york-times

Hull, D. (2006/2007, December-January). Blogging between the lines. *American Journalism Review*. From: http://www.ajr.org/article.asp?id=4230

Inabinett, M. (1994). *Grantland Rice and his heroes: The sportswriter as mythmaker in the 1920s*. Knoxville, TN: University of Tennessee Press.

Internet allegation comes true for Alabama coach. (2003, May 6). *USC Online Journalism Review*. From: http://www.ojr.org/ojr/glaser/1052193609.php

Journalism leaders forum. (2008, January 16). 8th forum asks to explore the impact of digital on sports television. From: http://journalismleadersforum.blogspot.com/2008_01_01_archive.html

King, P. (2009, March 24). Direct TV deal is lockout insurance. *Sports Illustrated*. Retrieved January 16, 2010 from http://sportsillustrated.cnn.com/2009/writers/peter_king/03/24/meetings/index.html?eref=T1

Koster, K. (2009, February 9). Alex Rodriguez takes shot at Sports Illustrated writer Selena Roberts. *Chicago Sun-Times*. Retrieved January 16, 2010 from http://blogs.suntimes.com/sportsprose/2009/02/alex_rodriguez_takes_shots_at.html

Lutz, B. (2008, November 8). Remain calm, Wildcat land. *Wichita Eagle*. From: http://www.kansas.com/252/story/589913.html

Mack, C. (1950). *My 66 years in the big leagues*. Philadelphia: John C. Winston.

Macmillan, R. (2009, March 26). *Washington Post, New York Times* seek new cost cuts. Retrieved January 16, 2009 from http://www.reuters.com/article/idUSN2648160620090326

Mark Fainaru-Wada on the sports doping probe and protecting sources. (2004, December 17). *Columbia Journalism Review*. From: http://www.ergogenics.org/blc28.html

Martzke, R. (2003, June 6). NBC keeps rights for Olympic broadcasts through 2012. *USA Today*. From: http://www.usa today.com/sports/olympics2003-06-06-nbc_x.htm

Meet Rodney. (2008). *Tider Insider*. From: http://www.tiderinsider.com/rodney.html

McCombs, M. (2002). Agenda-setting role of the mass media in the shaping of public opinion. *Suntory and Toyota International Centres for Economics and Related Disciplines*. From: http://sticerd.lse.ac.uk/dps/extra/McCombs.pdf

McCombs, M., & Shaw, D. (1972). The agenda-setting function of mass media. *Public Opinion Quarterly, 36* (Summer), 176–187.

McGuire, M. (2005, March 23). WTEN to alter nightly sports. *Albany Times-Union*. From: http://timesunion.com/aspstories/storyprint.asp?StoryID=344447

Michener, J. (1976). *Sports in America*. New York: Random House.

Miller, S. (2008, November 24). Playing the online field. *Multichannel*. From: http://www.multichannel.com/article/CA6617210.html

Payne, M. (2006). Olympic turnaround. New York: Praeger.

Phillips, T. (2004, October 26). Texas Tech football notes. *Ft. Worth Star-Telegram*. From: http://www.dfw.com/mld/dfw/sports/colleges/10017571.htm

Plaschke, B. (2000, January-February). 'That's twice you get me. I'm gonna hit you, right now, right now!' *Columbia Journalism Review*, pp. 42–44.

Ralbovsky, M. (1971). *Super bowl*. New York: Hawthorn.

Ritter, L. (1966). *The glory of their times*. New York: Macmillan.

Sandomir, R. (2003, September 10). The decline and fall of sports ratings. *The New York Times.* Retrieved January 16, 2010 from http://www.nytimes.com/2003/09/10/sports/tv-sports-the-decline-and-fall-of-sports-ratings.html?page wanted=1

Schultz, B. (2005). *Sports media: Reporting, planning and producing.* Burlington, MA: Focal Press.

Seymour, H. (1960). *Baseball: The early years.* New York: Oxford University Press.

Seymour, H. (1971). *Baseball: The golden age.* New York: Oxford University Press.

Shales, T. (2000, September 25). Oh, the tragedy: Olympics coverage is just too sad. *Electronic Media,* 4.

Sowell, M. (2008). The birth of national sports coverage: An examination of the *New York Herald's* use of the telegraph to report America's first "championship" boxing match in 1849. *Journal of Sports Media 3*(1), 53–75.

Stewart, L. (2004, November 9). New TV deal gives NFL the night shift. *Los Angeles Times.* From: http://articles. latimes.com/2004/nov/09/sports/sp-nfltv9

Super Bowl 30 second ads to cost $3 min in 2009: Report. (2008, May 6). *Reuters.* Retrieved January 16, 2010 from http://www.reuters.com/article/idUSN0644484220080506

Teeling, E. (2006, August 1). The use of the Internet by America's newspapers. *The Bivings Report.* From: http://www.bivingsreport.com/2006/the-use-of-the-internet-by-america%E2%80%99s-newspapers/

Zogby poll: Most say bloggers, citizen reporters to play vital role in journalism's future. (2007, February 13). *Zogby International.* From: http://www.zogby.com/news/ReadNews.dbm?ID=1247

CHAPTER 11

Facility Management

Jason M. Simmons • *Sport Administration Program, University of Louisville*

After reading this chapter, you will be able to:

- Differentiate between stadiums, arenas, and special-event facilities;
- Identify key sources of revenue for a sport facility;
- Develop a comprehensive risk management plan;
- Explain various aspects of facility operations including housekeeping, maintenance, and security;
- Describe how legal requirements affect various aspects of facility management.

KEY TERMS

Alcohol Management

Americans with Disabilities Act

Arena

Clutter

Crowd Management

Festival Seating

General Admission

Out-sourcing

Personal Seat License

Qualifying the Event

Reserved Seating

Risk Management

Special-event Facility

Stadium

> *The challenge in facility management is always going to be money. It's expensive to maintain your facility. If it doesn't look nice, the less opportunity you'll have to raise revenue with it.*
>
> —Kenneth C. Scull—Stadium Manager, Papa John's Cardinal Stadium—Louisville, KY

Introduction

Modern facilities serve the purpose of providing a gathering place for fans to watch sporting events. Regardless of the facility's size or specific purpose, facility managers undertake specific functions including:

- Scheduling and booking events
- Marketing events to generate revenue
- Selling tickets to attending customers
- Developing risk management plans for attendees
- Managing crowd behavior to ensure patron safety
- Maintaining a clean environment
- Providing services and amenities to generate revenue
- Remaining aware of emerging trends in advertising and sponsorship sales
- Adhering to legislation regarding accessibility

Although many of the concepts discussed in this chapter can be applied to a variety of public assembly facilities such as gyms, convention centers, amphitheatres, and auditoriums, this chapter will focus upon stadiums and arenas used primarily for sport.

History of Sport Facilities

Since ancient times, sport facilities have served two basic functions: to provide a setting for a sport to be played and to provide large groups of spectators with a place to congregate. The use of public assembly facilities for sport can be traced back to ancient Greece and the first Olympic Games in 776 B.C.E. Olympia Stadium was built into a hillside which provided sloped seating for spectators. In 331 B.C.E, the Greeks constructed Panathenaic Stadium in Athens, a 50,000-seat facility which, following several reconstructions, was used during the first modern Olympic Games in 1896 and the 2004 Summer Games in Athens (Fried, 2010).

Much like Greeks centuries prior, the Romans were also noted for their use of multi-purpose sport facilities. One of the most famous landmarks in the world, the Roman Coliseum, was used as a sport facility following its construction in 80 A.D. Circus Maximus, an ancient Roman racetrack which could seat upwards of 300,000 spectators, featured a number of modern amenities including concessions, seat cushions, and luxury boxes (Fried, 2010). In addition, reserved seating formats resembling ticket strategies used in today's stadiums were also featured. Broken pieces of clay pottery, which were dyed to match entrances and seating sections within the facility, were distributed to spectators prior to entry (Graham & Ward, 2004).

The earliest sport facilities in the United States could hardly be considered stadiums in the contemporary context of the word. Ballparks in the 1860s were typically nothing more than a temporary fence designed to keep spectators off the field during a game. Sport facilities were not built with permanence in mind until the turn of the 20th century when Harvard University built the first steel-reinforced concrete stadium for its football team. Major League Baseball (MLB) franchises also built a number of stadiums using concrete and steel designs, including Tiger Stadium in Detroit, Comiskey Park in Chicago, and Fenway Park in Boston (Trumpbour, 2007).

Prior to the 1950s, the majority of sport facilities in the United States were privately financed by individual teams. However, as metropolitan areas on the west coast and in the southeast began to grow rapidly and the transportation industry increased its efficiency, established professional sport franchises began to investigate the potential for publicly-funded facilities. The Boston Braves moved to Milwaukee in 1953 primarily to play in a new facility. In 1958, the Brooklyn Dodgers and New York Giants moved to Los Angeles and San Francisco, respectively. The success of these teams in generating revenue in publicly-financed facilities convinced other municipalities that they could attract franchises, and convinced many teams that they needed to potentially move if their home market would not begin to pay a significant portion of their stadium expenses.

As governmental entities began to build new facilities, a sport facility construction boom began in the 1960s and 1970s. Many of the newly constructed facilities were designed to house multiple tenants, and, coinciding with a boom in automobile sales, were built in areas where large parking lots could be built around the facility. A number of publicly funded multiuse sport facilities were constructed during this time to house both baseball and football teams. Examples of these facilities included Veterans Stadium in Philadelphia (Phillies and Eagles), Three Rivers Stadium in Pittsburgh (Pirates and Steelers), and Candlestick Park in San Francisco (Giants and 49ers). Teams leased the facility from local governments, while the revenue from parking and concessions were often split between the two parties (Howard & Crompton, 2005).

In the late 1980s and early 1990s, sport franchises began to realize tremendous profits from luxury suites and club seating. The National Basketball Association's (NBA) Detroit Pistons opened The Palace at Auburn Hills in 1988 and MLB's Baltimore Orioles opened Oriole Park at Camden Yards in 1992. Each of these facilities altered the sport facility financial landscape by offering numerous luxury suites, wider concourses for concession sales, and a more pleasant entertainment experience than many other established facilities. These landmark facilities caused many other sport franchise owners to either seek a new facility or to investigate the feasibility of significantly remodeling their existing facility, often at taxpayer expense.

Franchises also began to sell more advertisements in the facility and naming rights packages became commonplace in the 1990s. Rapid expansion of franchise revenues coincided with an expiration of many of the leases initially signed in the 1960s and 1970s. Many taxpayers and government officials observed the rapid escalation of franchise revenues and player salaries and, consequently, began rejecting large subsidies for new professional sport facility construction. Though some new facilities were built with significant public dollars in the 1990s, by the latter half of the decade the trend away from large subsidies had begun. When the San Francisco Giants tried to garner public support for a new facility, they were rejected by voters four different times (Kim, 2000). Eventually, although the city and county of San Francisco helped with infrastructure improvements to the surrounding area, the Giants had to pay for the construction of AT&T Park, which opened in 2000. By 2010, most communities had emphatically rejected any notions of committing substantial dollars to future facility projects.

Types of Facilities

The term "public assembly facility" is used to describe "all public and private facilities designed to accommodate people wishing to assemble for a common purpose" (Graham & Ward, 2004, p. 3). Amphitheatres, convention centers, and auditoriums are different types of public assembly facilities commonly used for a variety of purposes. An auditorium or theatre hosting a touring musical production serves as a gathering place for patrons to watch the performance. An outdoor amphitheatre can hold thousands of congregating spectators for a summer concert. Much like these entertainment facilities, the venues used for sporting events are also considered public assembly facilities.

Arena

Indoor facilities used to host sport, entertainment, and business events; portable seating designs allow the floor area to be arranged to accommodate multiple tenants.

In sport, the most common public assembly facilities are arenas, stadiums, and special event facilities. An **arena** is an indoor, multi-purpose facility capable of hosting an assortment of sport, entertainment, and business events. Many arenas have portable seating designs that allow the floor area to be arranged to accommodate a variety of tenants. Basketball and hockey games are typically associated with arenas; however, a number of other sport and entertainment alternatives can utilize the flexibility an arena provides. Madison Square Garden is an example of an arena. The primary tenants of Madison Square Garden are the New York Knicks of the NBA, the Women's National Basketball Association's (WNBA) New York Liberty, and the New York Rangers of the National Hockey League (NHL). Aside from these three sport entities, the arena also hosts a number of other events, including boxing, college basketball, wrestling, lacrosse, tennis, and concerts.

Courtesy Mark Nagel

The Colonial Life Arena at the University of South Carolina is an example of a facility that hosts a variety of sport and entertainment events.

Stadiums are typically larger than arenas and can be either outdoors or domed. An alternative design has been to incorporate a retractable roof, allowing stadiums to capitalize on both open-air and dome elements. Facilities such as Lucas Oil Field in Indianapolis (Colts), University of Phoenix Stadium in Glendale (Cardinals), and Minute Maid Park in Houston (Astros) are examples of stadiums with retractable roof designs. Stadium use is commonly associated with football and baseball, yet a number of other sports such as soccer, tennis, lacrosse, and cricket may stage their events in these large public assembly facilities.

Aside from its primary tenants, stadiums regularly host a variety of alternative events such as concerts, conventions, and trade shows. In 2008, INVESCO Field at Mile High, home to the NFL's Denver Broncos, hosted Barack Obama's party acceptance speech at the Democratic National Convention. Detroit's Ford Field was the site of the 2009 National Collegiate Athletic Association (NCAA) men's basketball Final Four. As a sport facility manager, a primary responsibility will be to develop creative ways in which the facility can be utilized. A college football stadium, for example, is only used by its primary tenant six to eight times a year. Aside from team practices, the facility will sit empty unless the facility manager and the athletic department can develop alternative event opportunities. A full discussion on qualifying an event for a public assembly facility will be presented later in this chapter.

Many sports like horse racing, golf, and auto racing require a specialized facility to meet their needs. These single-purpose venues are known as special-event facilities. Indoor soccer fields, ice-skating rinks, bowling alleys, and softball complexes are also considered special-event facilities. Unlike arenas and stadiums, special-event facilities are built with a specific event in mind. Churchill Downs in Louisville, KY, is an example of a special-event facility built uniquely for horse racing. Much like stadiums and arenas, special-event facilities are also capable of hosting events outside of their intended purpose (Graham & Ward, 2004). For example, Churchill Downs hosted a Rolling Stones concert in 2006, the first event of its kind at the famed track.

Nationals Park, home of MLB's Washington Nationals, was one of the first professional sport facilities to incorporate "green" technology into its design.

Stadium_____
Outdoor or domed public assembly facility that hosts sport and entertainment events.

Risk Management

Risk management is the process of identifying potential risks and reducing the likelihood those risks will occur. An effective risk-management plan has three goals: (a) minimize liability and financial loss, (b) reduce insurance premiums when risk is transferred to another party, and (c) maintain a safe environment for employees and spectators (Fried, 2010).

Every activity within a sport facility carries with it the potential for risk. A spectator could trip walking down a flight of stairs or burn the roof of their

Risk Management_____
Process of identifying, assessing, and treating risks in order to reduce facility liability and ensure a safe environment for employees and spectators.

mouth while sipping hot chocolate. A foul ball may hit an unsuspecting specta- tor in the head at a baseball game. The potential for harm is everywhere in a sport facility. As a facility manager, it is impossible to anticipate or plan for every risk, regardless of the effectiveness of a risk-management plan. It is impor- tant to remember that the purpose of a risk-management plan is not to identify every possible risk, but rather to reduce the frequency of risks as well as mini- mize liability.

What exactly is risk management? Risk management is a three-step process that involves forecasting, assessing, and treating risks (Ammon, Southall, & Nagel, 2010). It is a proactive strategy aimed at reducing risk and liability, as opposed to solely reacting once a risk or crisis has occurred. When forecasting risks, the most important thing to keep in mind is communication. A facility manager is typically not involved in the day-to-day operations of every aspect of the facility. In order to develop the most comprehensive list of potential risks, a facility manager should consult with staff members from concessions, security, maintenance, housekeeping, public relations, and the box office. In addition, it would be prudent to seek advice from managers of other sport facilities to get an idea of any additional risks they may have encountered. Lastly, previous incident reports are a vital tool in identifying risks that are likely to occur in a facility.

The risks one may encounter in a sport facility are contingent on a number of factors. Weather, event type, design flaws, type of facility, and patron demo- graphics all pose the potential for harm (Ammon et al., 2010). For example, the atmosphere at an NBA playoff game is going to be much different than that at a trade show. Potential risks associated with each event are going to vary accord- ingly. Spectators at an NBA playoff game are more likely to consume alcohol and become disruptive to fans around them. Such a risk is unlikely to be an issue at trade shows, where alcohol may not even be served. Similarly, a football game played at Lambeau Field in January is going to carry different weather- related risks than a game played in Arizona in the winter. However, an outdoor Arizona venue may pose heat-related risks in the summer that would not be present in Wisconsin. Winter storms bring snow and ice, which can lead to a variety of special risks. The parking lots and streets surrounding the stadium will be slick, increasing the likelihood of an accident. Sidewalks and stadium steps will also gather ice, increasing the likelihood of a slip-and-fall incident. Each added variable presents a new set of risks. As a facility manager, one must account for each of these variables when identifying potential risks.

The second step in the risk management process is assessing the risks iden- tified during step one. A useful tool in assessing risks is a simple risk matrix that accounts for both the frequency and severity of risks (Ammon et al., 2010). Frequency refers to how often a risk is likely to occur: infrequent, moderate, or frequent. Severity refers to the loss attributed to a risk, both physical and finan- cial. Level of severity can be classified as low loss, moderate loss, and high loss. An example of a risk category matrix is presented in Table 11.1. Using the exam- ple of a National Association for Stock Car Auto Racing (NASCAR) event, one can see how the risks associated with this event fit into the risk matrix. The use

TABLE 11.1

Risk Category Matrix

	High Frequency	Moderate Frequency	Low Frequency
High Loss	None	Debris from wreckage flies into stands	Serious injury or death of spectator or driver
Moderate Loss	Excessive alcohol consumption	Spectator accident (i.e., slip and fall)	Physical altercation between spectators
Low Loss	Stadium traffic following the event	Sunburn	Fraudulent tickets

of a risk matrix allows facility managers to make better decisions regarding the treatment of these risks.

A facility manager has four options when it comes to treating risks: avoidance, assumption, transfer, and reduction. The first option, risk avoidance, should only be used for risks in which the potential for loss is high and the risk has a high frequency of occurrence. Events carrying risks that are likely to often result in physical harm and/or damage to the facility should probably be avoided (Ammon et al., 2010).

The second option for treating risks is risk assumption. A facility will be financially responsible for any risks it assumes. Therefore, a facility will only want to assume a risk if the potential for loss is minimal. For example, many sport facilities have reserved parking for sport events. Sooner or later, at least one patron is going to attempt to park in a spot assigned to somebody else. This is a risk that occurs with moderate frequency, but results in low loss for the facility. Such a risk should be assumed by the facility, as the loss is not significant enough to avoid the event all together or transfer the risk to a third party.

Risk transfer simply means transferring the financial liability of a risk to another party. Ammon (2003) suggests the risk transfer treatment be used for risks which are not severe enough, in terms of loss, to avoid completely, yet are still too great for the facility or sport organization to bear on its own. Types of risk transfer include insurance, waivers, indemnification clauses, and the use of independent contractors. Insurance is the most common form of risk transfer. Most students are probably familiar with insurance as it relates to an automobile. The risk of driving a car is not so great as to warrant avoiding the activity all together, yet the potential risks are probably too large for one to accept financial responsibility if something goes terribly wrong. The medium to utilize then, is insurance. The driving risks are transferred to another party who is willing to assume that risk. Insurance companies require regular payments in exchange for coverage. In the event of an accident, the insurance company will pay damages to the injured party, assuming the deductible has been met.

Insurance works in a similar fashion for sport facilities. The types of insurance typically available to facility managers include property, business interruption, general liability, employment practice liability, professional liability, liquor liability, and product liability (Sharp, Moorman, & Claussen, 2007).

The final type of risk treatment, risk reduction, should be used in combination with the treatments outlined above. Risk reduction is the practice of taking preventative measures to minimize risks in a facility. Reduction is a useful treatment for reducing the frequency of risks in a facility, and fewer risks also means lower insurance premiums and a safer environment for spectators and employees. Consider the example of a hockey arena. One of the risks associated with hockey is pucks flying into the stands and injuring guests. A reduction strategy the NHL utilizes to deal with this risk is the use of protective netting behind the goals. The net reduces the frequency of pucks flying into the stands, which reduces injuries associated with this risk, which in turn lowers insurance premiums and makes a safer environment for spectators at hockey games. Remember, risk reduction should not be used as an alternative to avoidance, assumption, and transfer. Instead, risk reduction should be used to complement each of these risk treatment strategies. The risk treatment matrix in Table 11.2 outlines the risk treatment option best suited for each risk category.

Revenue Sources

Increasingly, stadiums and arenas have become tools to generate additional revenue for sport organizations. When one thinks of revenue generated from a sport facility, ticket sales typically first come to mind. However, sport facilities are able to generate revenue from a variety of additional sources as well. Revenue from modern facility features such as luxury seating, naming rights, and personal seat licenses (PSL) often help underwrite new facility construction costs and major renovations. Ancillary services such as concessions, novelties, and parking also contribute to a facility's potential profits.

TABLE 11.2

Risk Treatment Matrix

	High Frequency	Moderate Frequency	Low Frequency
High Loss	Avoidance	Transfer/Avoidance and Reduction	Transfer and Reduction
Moderate Loss	Transfer and Reduction	Transfer and Reduction	Transfer/Retain and Reduction
Low Loss	Transfer/Retain and Reduction	Retain and Reduction	Retain and Reduction

Source: Ammon, Southall, & Nagel, 2010

Economic generators for a sport facility do not exist in a vacuum. Attending a sport event is about more than just watching a game; it is an experience. Food, beverages, parking, promotions, and facility cleanliness all contribute to the fan experience. A negative experience in the parking lot might affect one's decision to attend events in the future. This decision affects not only facility ticket revenue, but revenue from concessions, merchandise, and parking as well. This section will explore the primary sources of revenue for a sport facility, as well as discuss the role of the facility manager in generating additional revenue.

Outside Events

From 1998–2007, sport organizations in the United States spent $27.9 billion on stadium construction (*Sports Business Journal*, 2008). This figure includes all sport facilities built at the major, minor, and collegiate levels. Ironically however, the facilities' primary tenants will only use the venue a handful of dates out of the year. National Football League (NFL) teams usually only use their facilities 10 times each season. Even Major League Baseball stadiums, whose teams have more home games (81) than any other professional sports league in the United States, have 284 open dates per year. An additional revenue source for sport facilities comes from leasing/renting the facility to outside events such as concerts, performing arts shows, conferences, trade shows, and conventions. Not only does the facility profit from rental fees, but these events generate revenue for the facility through ancillary services such as concessions, parking, and merchandise sales, each of which will be discussed later in this chapter.

When scheduling an outside event, a facility manager must consider several things. The first involves the schedule itself. In order to maximize attendance, most events should be scheduled at a time that does not conflict with other prominent events or community activities. For example, the facility manager for the Matthew Knight Arena in Eugene, OR, will want to avoid scheduling an event on the same day and time as the "Civil War" football game between Oregon and Oregon State, as most of the community will be watching the game. Second, careful consideration must be taken to determine the risks associated with an outside event. For example, the very nature of moshing at heavy metal concerts increases the likelihood of damage to the facility and spectator injury, as seen in the later example of the AC/DC concert. Knowing the risks beforehand will allow the facility manager to develop a more comprehensive risk management plan. Finally, the facility manager must determine if the event is a match for the facility. This is known as **qualifying the event**. During this process, the facility manager must consider each of the following questions:

Qualifying the Event_____
Process of determining if an event is appropriate for a facility.

- What are the values and expectations of the event? Are they similar to the values and expectations of the facility?
- Is there room on the schedule for this event? Does the event conflict with the facility's primary tenant?
- Does the event fit the facility in terms of space requirements and specialized support (ventilation for pyrotechnics or dirt for monster trucks)?

- Does the event have a sound financial plan? Will profits from the event exceed expenses?
- What are the demands of the event (time, staffing, changeover)? Can the facility meet these demands? (Graham & Ward, 2004).

The process of qualifying the event should not be overlooked. Each event is unique and will present different challenges for a facility manager. Outside events are significant economic generators for a sport facility, however, issues with scheduling, risks, and event fit must be considered prior to booking an event.

Tickets

Ticket sales not only account for a large portion of a facility's revenue, but a significant portion of a sport organization's overall earnings as well. Manchester United grossed €324.8 million for the 2007–2008 season, 39 percent of which came from game-day revenues consisting largely of ticket sales (Houlihan et al., 2009). At the NCAA Division-IA level, ticket sales account for 27 percent of all athletic program revenue (NCAA, 2003).

Tickets are categorized as reserved, general admission, or festival/lawn seating. **Reserved seating** is used for events that require a designated ticket for each seat in the facility. Much like the system used by the Romans more than 2,000 years ago, reserved tickets will indicate the section, row, and seat a patron is assigned for a specific event. Tickets may be sold on a first-come, first-served basis. This is known as **General Admission** seating. Each patron pays a fixed price and can sit in any unoccupied seat in the facility. Lawn or hillside seating at an outdoor facility is another form of general admission ticketing known as **Festival Seating**. Floor seating in front of the stage at a concert is another type of festival seating. By nature, this type of seating carries unique risks not present in alternative ticketing formats. For example, three fans were trampled to death in front of the stage at an AC/DC concert in 1991, resulting in a trend away from festival/floor seating near the front of the stage. However, some college stadiums such as Memorial Stadium at Clemson, as well as many minor league baseball parks with berm seating in the outfield, still use hill-seating formats in designated sections of their stadiums.

Most facilities sell tickets prior to the actual event. Advanced ticket sales allow the facility manager to prepare for an event both in terms of services offered and staff required (Ammon et al., 2010; Graham & Ward, 2004). For example, larger events will necessitate the use of additional concession stands. Consequently, additional staff will be required to operate concessions services.

Naming Rights

Thirty years ago, most stadiums and arenas were usually named after important public figures, geographic regions, or in some cases, even the home team. However, most sport facilities now are named after a corporate sponsor who has paid to attach their moniker to the facility. A brief look at the sport facility

Reserved Seating
Ticketing system used for events that require a designated ticket for each seat; reserved tickets indicate the section, row, and seat a patron is assigned for a specific event.

General Admission
Tickets are sold on a first-come, first-served basis; each patron pays a fixed price and can sit in any unoccupied seat in the facility.

Festival Seating
Form of general admission ticketing in which spectators are not assigned to a specific seat, but rather a standing/seating area within a facility such as in front of the stage at a concert or outfield berm seating at a baseball game.

landscape reveals only a handful of venues which have resisted the urge to succumb to corporate sponsorship. Facilities such as Lambeau Field in Green Bay, Fenway Park in Boston, and Soldier Field in Chicago have become the exception rather than the rule. Naming rights agreements can generate considerable revenue for sport organizations, which explains why teams are so willing to name their facility after a corporate sponsor.

AT&T Park is an example of a corporate-named facility.

The New England Patriots were one of the first sport organizations to realize the potential for generating revenue through naming rights agreements. In 1971, the Patriots sold the naming rights to their stadium to Schaffer Brewing Company for $150,000. It was not until the mid-1990s however, that sport facility naming rights became popular. A distinguishing characteristic of stadium construction during this time was the diminished reliance on public funds to build new facilities (Howard & Crompton, 2005). Naming rights provided a major source of revenue for team owners looking to finance construction costs. At the end of the 20th century, sport facility naming rights sold for an average of $87 million (Greenberg, 2000). Today, corporations are willing to pay more than four times that amount in certain situations. Barclays Center and Citi Field have the largest naming rights agreements at $400 million over 20 years (Jones, 2008).

Aside from financing facility construction costs, the revenue generated from naming rights also allows teams to pay higher player contracts and add amenities to their facilities (Greenberg, 2000). The primary benefits sought from corporations in naming rights agreements are exposure and increased sales. Naming rights are a type of corporate sponsorship that allows businesses to break through the clutter of more traditional advertising and signage. A company name on the side of a sport facility is much more noticeable than a billboard next to a highway. Other benefits associated with such agreements include access to premium seating, free tickets, parking passes, and additional signage within the facility (Howard & Crompton, 2005).

Most naming rights agreements average 20–30 years in length (Fried, 2010). There are exceptions however. The Miami Dolphins recently sold the naming right to their facility to Margaritaville Brewing Company for a single season. While such naming rights deals are not the norm, Land Shark Stadium generated considerable exposure in the months leading up to the 2010 Super Bowl in Miami. Conversely, collegiate sport facilities are often named after a booster who contributed a large portion of funds for facility construction. These naming rights are usually permanent and cannot be resold later when the facility requires renovations (Howard & Crompton, 2005). To avoid this potential problem and to maximize revenues, many facilities have opted to sell the naming rights to other areas of the facility such as the playing surface, seating areas, and entryways. For example, the University of Maryland football team plays at Chevy Chase Field at Byrd Stadium. This strategy is also used at the professional level. The Arizona Cardinals sold the naming rights to the southwest, southeast, and north stadium entrances of their facility to Verizon, Budweiser, and the University of Phoenix respectively. Even the club level entrances have been tagged with the corporate monikers for Gila River and Insight (Arizona Cardinals, n.d.).

Advertising and Promotions

Naming rights are just one form of advertising available in a public-assembly facility. Additional signage within the facility can generate millions of dollars in annual revenue for a sport organization. A facility manager has the responsibility to create space for signage throughout the stadium. Signage should be strategically placed throughout the venue in locations that draw the attention of spectators. Most commonly these locations include the scoreboard, the scorer's table for basketball games, along the outfield wall and behind home plate for baseball, either directly on the ice or along the dasher boards in hockey, along the sidelines and behind the goals in soccer, and even on cup-holders and the backs of restroom stall doors.

Improvements in technology have paved the way for advancements in facility signage allowing teams to generate even more advertising income. The Miami Heat, for example, hung a large LED display called Mediamesh on the front of their arena that is used as an electronic banner for advertising (Lombardo, 2009). Similarly, the New Jersey Nets use a technology called "sky banners" to advertise in vacant seating sections around their arena. These banners cover approximately 1,000 seats and are used as a screen for advertisement projections (Muret, 2009).

Printed materials are another source of advertising in a sport facility. Businesses may purchase space in media guides, game programs, ticket backs, seating charts, and team schedules to advertise goods and services. Other businesses will sponsor fan giveaways such as water bottles, posters, and noise-makers with the team and company logos on them. Announcements and in-game promotions are additional opportunities for businesses to partner with the sport facility.

The opportunities for generating revenue through advertising are seemingly endless. However, too much signage can be a bad thing. Not only does signage tarnish the attractiveness of a stadium or arena, it also causes clutter. Advertisers seek recall and recognition when purchasing signage in a sport facility. Clutter decreases the likelihood of advertiser recall, thus reducing the value of facility advertising (Graham & Ward, 2004).

Clutter
Product of too much signage in a facility; decreases the likelihood of advertiser recall, thus diminishing the value of facility advertising.

Personal Seat License
Source of facility revenue that requires guests to pay a one-time fee for the right to purchase tickets for a specific seat.

Personal Seat Licenses

Personal Seat Licenses or Permanent Seat Licenses (PSLs) are widely used in sport facilities as a primary source of revenue for stadium construction. PSLs do not provide annual operating income like many of the sources previously discussed in this chapter. Instead, personal seat licenses require individuals to pay in advance for the right to purchase tickets to an event in the future. The revenue generated from PSLs can greatly reduce the amount of money a team owner or athletic department has to raise to build a new facility. The New York Giants sold permanent seat licenses for as much as $20,000 to help off-set the $1.6 billion construction costs of their new stadium (Kuriloff, 2008).

Aside from the upfront revenue, PSLs also represent a financial commitment from the fans. The one-time costs to own a seat means fans only own the right to buy tickets for that specific seat. They still have to purchase tickets to each game. In fact, most personal seat license agreements require fans to purchase tickets to all home games over the life of the contract (Howard & Crompton, 2005). By requiring PSL owners to purchase tickets, facility managers can estimate attendance figures with greater accuracy. For example, if a facility has sold 70,000 personal seat licenses, the facility manager can expect at least 70,000 tickets will be sold to the events. This information will allow the facility manager to better prepare in terms of proper staffing and budget projections.

PSLs are not without their disadvantages however. In most cases PSLs are permanent, but in some cases a personal seat license may expire. The Oakland Raiders encountered difficulties selling their PSLs in 1995 because they were only valid for 10 years. Facilities also run the risk of disenchanting a portion of their fan base by asking customers to essentially pay twice to attend a game. Some fans may have been season-ticket holders in the past and are now being asked to purchase a PSL for the continued right to purchase season tickets. Additionally, purchasing expensive PSLs may restrict a large portion of a team's fan base from attending games. For example, PSLs for seats along the 50-yard line at the new Cowboys Stadium in Arlington, Texas, cost upwards of $150,000 per seat! Even seats in the upper level corners come with a PSL price tag of $5,000 (Dallas Cowboys, n.d.).

Though a PSL may allow the customer to purchase seats for perpetuity, it may not be convertible to another patron. Some facilities limit the transfer of PSLs to certain family members, or may only allow a PSL to be sold one time.

Luxury Seating

One of the largest revenue sources for a sport facility is luxury seating. Luxury or premium seating typically refers to two types of seating areas: luxury suites and club seating. The popularity of luxury suites can be directly linked to the revenue they are able to produce. According to Howard and Crompton (2005), luxury suites in professional sport facilities across the country account for approximately $600,000,000 annually. Much like PSLs and naming rights, team owners are often dependent on the revenue from luxury seating to fund new stadiums. Access to these premium seats often comes with a hefty price tag. Luxury boxes for the Kentucky Derby at Churchill Downs cost $87,000 on average (Mullen, 2003). Suites at Nationals Park in Washington, D.C. cost up to $450,000 per season (Muret, 2007).

Luxury suites are usually marketed to corporations with large amounts of money to spend entertaining clients and employees. Luxury suites typically offer premium sightlines and are designed to include personal comfort amenities such as carpet, hi-definition televisions, wait service, wet bar, air temperature control, and private restrooms. However, the Palace at Auburn Hills has recently opened some luxury suites that have no direct view of the court. The suites are set up like a private club and sell exclusivity, as well as other perks like preferred parking and dining services.

The profits generated from luxury seating will vary based on amenities, location, and term length. Suites located on the 50-yard line or behind home plate are going to be considerably more expensive than suites located in the end zone or down the right field line. Prices will also vary based on the length of the contract. Luxury suites are financed on a long-term basis, typically between 5–10 years. For a facility manager, it is important that these contracts vary in length to avoid having to replace a significant portion of the facility's revenue at one time (Howard & Crompton, 2005).

Club seats are not as luxurious as a suite, but feature many of the same amenities at a lower price, while usually offering the patron a closer proximity to the on-field action. The price of club-level seats can vary dramatically depending on the seat location and services offered. Typical club seats may cost anywhere from a few hundred dollars per season to several thousand dollars for a single premium event. Legend Suite seats at the new Yankee Stadium range from $500 to $2,500 per game (Associated Press, 2008). Amenities typically reserved for club seating include padded seats, premium parking locations, wait service, gourmet food and drink items, and access to club-level bar or lounge.

Ancillary Services

In addition to the revenue generators discussed above, facility revenue can come from a number of other sources. Ancillary services such as concessions, novelties, and parking are usually reliable sources of revenue for a sport facility during an event.

Concessions

Food and beverage services are critical to a facility's success because sporting events often overlap mealtimes. Fans expect concessions to be available at sport events. If operated correctly, concession services can be a significant source of revenue for a sport facility.

The most popular concession items have typically been hotdogs, hamburgers, nachos, peanuts, cotton candy, popcorn, ice cream, and soft drinks. Alcohol sales also typically contribute significantly to the revenue generated from concessions. A trend in newer facilities has been to offer specialized or gourmet food and beverage options. Citi Field in New York offers fans a wide array of food

Courtesy Mark Nagel

Concessions are an important revenue source for sport facilities.

choices, including barbeque ribs, sushi, tacos, and fish sandwiches (Citi Field, n.d.). In addition to specialty items, research has shown customers are more likely to purchase products with familiar brand names such as Pizza Hut or Dunkin Donuts (Graham & Ward, 2004). Some facilities are now offering "all you can eat" sections to attract customers. Tickets to those sections usually allow patrons to consume as much food and drink as they want (excluding alcohol).

A facility manager can either operate concession services in-house, or hire a private contractor, which is known as **out-sourcing**. Like any choice, there are advantages and disadvantages for each. Running the food and beverage service in-house allows the facility manager to directly control the staff and the products being sold. The facility will also retain all of the profit generated from concession sales. The disadvantage is that the facility manager must assume all the risks and responsibilities of operating concession services including training staff, monitoring alcohol sales, keeping product inventory, and adhering to health and labor laws. Conversely, when out-sourcing food and beverage services, such responsibilities are shifted to a private contractor. In addition, a private contractor may have more experience and expertise in the industry, and likely has greater leverage with food and beverage suppliers. The downside of contracting out is that the facility must split the revenue from concessions with the concessionaire (Graham & Ward, 2004).

Regardless of whether food and beverage services are operated in-house or contracted out, the facility manager has the responsibility to ensure the concessions experience is positive for guests. This means making efforts to reduce the amount of time customers spend in line. Menu boards should clearly indicate products, sizes, and prices to limit questions and confusion at the counter. Simple price increments will reduce the complexity of monetary transactions for both customers and employees (Ammon et al., 2010). Customers will also expect supplementary items such as napkins, plastic ware, and condiments to be available.

Out-sourcing_____
Hiring an outside organization or private contractor to operate facility services such as concessions, security, and maintenance.

Novelties

Another source of revenue for a sport facility are souvenir products such as programs, t-shirts, hats, jerseys, pennants, foam fingers, and posters. When determining which novelty products to sell, a facility manager needs to consider the audience demographics, the past purchase history of that audience, and the potential profits garnered from each item (Graham & Ward, 2004).

Much like concessions, facility managers can either choose to operate merchandise services in-house, or contract the service to an outside party. Facility managers can sometimes maximize revenue by operating merchandise in-house; however, the risks associated with this operating arrangement must be assumed by the facility as well. Revenue from merchandise sales is directly linked to the risk and responsibilities assumed by each party. Usually, the most profitable method for the facility is the percentage-of-sales contract in which the facility staff takes a more active role in novelty operations, and pays the vendor a percentage of the total merchandise sales (Graham & Ward, 2004).

Parking

Anytime a car is driven, a place to park is needed. Fans have few alternatives when it comes to parking for an event; therefore, sport facilities are typically able to charge for the service. Most facilities charge a flat rate for parking that is collected as guests enter the lot. The Sacramento Kings charge a flat fee of $10 per vehicle for Arco Arena parking on game day (Arco Arena, n.d.). Seasonal parking passes may also be available for purchase by frequent visitors such as season-ticket holders or luxury-seating tenants.

Additional revenue can be generated from parking even if the facility itself is not in use. Parking lots are an ideal location for travelling events such as circuses, concerts, and trade shows needing a temporary venue. Facility lots/garages in downtown locations are an attractive option for companies in need of employee parking during the day. The more uses a facility manager can find for the parking lot, the more attractive it will be to companies seeking exposure through advertising and signage. A unique trend in parking lot advertising is signage placed on the concrete tire stops between spaces. Sponsors may also be willing to pay to have their company name appear on the daily parking receipt given to customers as they leave the lot (Gorman, 2003). In order to maximize revenue generated from facility parking, a facility manager must develop creative ways to utilize the parking lot, while not interfering with stadium parking on game day.

Not only is parking a source of revenue for a sport facility, it is also a service. Parking lots should be designed with convenience and accessibility in mind to minimize traffic congestion. Facility managers should also utilize parking staff and law enforcement officials to direct traffic flow before and after an event. Another parking issue facility managers need to be aware of is safety/security. Parking lots/garages should have adequate lighting and the parking surface should be well maintained. The visible presence of law enforcement officials in and around the parking area will also deter criminal activity such as theft, vandalism, and the sale of pirated merchandise (Graham & Ward 2004).

Operations

A facility's ability to generate revenue is largely dependent on the operations services it provides. The purpose of operations is to provide not only a clean environment for spectators, but a safe and comfortable one as well. The operations department has many responsibilities in a facility. These responsibilities typically include developing policies and procedures, booking and scheduling events at the facility, box office management, concessions management, purchasing, and equipment inventory. Additionally, a facility's operations department is also responsible for housekeeping, maintenance, and security. While these services are not a direct source of revenue for a public assembly facility, they may affect a customer's decision to visit a facility again in the future. This is especially true if these functions are managed poorly.

Housekeeping

It is easy to overlook housekeeping services when attending a sporting event. Housekeeping is responsible for keeping the public assembly facility clean. This includes the seating area, restrooms, suites, concourse areas, concession stands, stairways, and ramps. Patrons expect the seating area to be free from trash from the previous night's event. Any beverage spills in the concourse should be cleaned and an ample supply of toilet paper and paper towels should be available in the restrooms.

An additional housekeeping crew will be required for facility clean-up following an event, as such an endeavor requires significantly more labor than everyday housekeeping duties such as vacuuming and emptying trash cans (Graham & Ward, 2004). This is especially true in large public assembly facilities such as stadiums and arenas. As is the case with concessions and novelties, a facility manager usually has the option to operate custodial services in-house or outsource housekeeping responsibilities to a private contractor.

Custodial efforts will be aided by the strategic placement of janitorial closets throughout the facility. Housekeeping staff need space to store equipment and cleaning supplies, as well as access to a water source. At a minimum, there should be one janitorial closet on each floor of the facility. It is also recommended that each restroom contain a janitorial closet to store common restroom supplies like toilet paper, soap, and paper towels (Stotlar, 1997).

Maintenance

Car owners are all too familiar with the concept of maintenance. Vehicles require oil changes, engine tune-ups, new brakes, and replacement tires. While these minor maintenance functions are a nuisance, they serve the purpose of preventing costly repairs later.

A sport facility is no different. A facility's ability to generate revenue and provide services to its guests can be attributed to how well it is maintained. A facility maintenance staff is responsible for preventative/routine maintenance, keeping inventory of supplies and ordering new parts, maintaining repair records, minor repair work, and serving in an advisory role for major projects such as facility renovations or large equipment replacement (Fried, 2010).

An effective maintenance plan is critical to extending the life of a sport facility and its equipment/mechanical devices. Preventative maintenance should be scheduled on a daily, weekly, monthly, and yearly basis. Cyclical repairs on the other hand, such as replacing carpet every five years in a heavily trafficked area, should be planned for on a recurring basis. Breakdown maintenance is appropriate when equipment eventually stops working (Fried, 2010). As equipment breakdowns are inevitable, facility managers should have funds set aside to aid in overcoming the financial burden associated with large equipment replacement.

Another key component of any successful maintenance plan is the budget. A facility cannot be successfully maintained without funding. According to Fried (2010), at least five percent of the facility's annual expenses should be devoted to maintenance and repair work.

Security

A facility manager has a responsibility to make sure all guests are safe while attending a sporting event. The primary resource for ensuring the safety and comfort of facility patrons is security. In addition to venue guests, security serves the purpose of protecting the facility itself.

The most common security practices used to protect the public at sport facilities include bag checks upon entry, metal detectors or hand-held wands, security cameras, and turnstiles to manage crowd ingress to the facility. In addition, the labor required to effectively secure a facility has increased significantly since September 11, 2001 (Lamberth, 2003). Ancillary systems such as fire alarms, sprinklers, and emergency power are also utilized to protect the facility and its patrons. Emergency power is the most important element of a security plan during a facility evacuation. Should the facility's power fail, a generator can provide power for emergency lighting and sound systems, allowing updates and evacuation instructions to be relayed to facility guests (Sedlak & Traugott, 2002).

Security is another service that may be operated either in-house or contracted out. Contracting some or all of the security responsibilities offers a number of benefits to facility managers. First, the cost of hiring, training, and maintaining a security staff will be deferred to the private contractor. It may be cost prohibitive for a facility to employ an in-house security staff that is only needed on a limited basis. Second, inconsistencies in work availability for security personnel at sport facilities may result in high turnover rates. Having to hire and train new staff members on a regular basis will be both expensive and time-consuming for facility managers. Third, security needs will vary based on the type of event. Contractors are usually able to provide appropriate levels of security, tailored uniquely for individual events. Another benefit of contracted security is expertise. Contracted security personnel will be expertly trained and will be knowledgeable of potential risks within a sport facility. Finally, using a private contractor lessens the liability the facility must retain related to security risks (Price, 2007).

Facility security during an event often deals extensively with **crowd management** and **alcohol management**. Crowd management is a necessary security component and should be part of a facility's risk management plan. Once a crowd mobilizes or becomes violent, it is difficult, and often dangerous, to attempt to control its behavior. Crowd management, therefore, is designed primarily to supervise the crowd before it gets out of control (Fried, 2010).

An effective crowd-management plan should include four components: a well-trained staff, an ejection policy, effective communication, and signage throughout the facility (Ammon et al., 2010). Directional signs are designed to guide patrons to various locations within the facility such as emergency exits, ticket windows, restrooms, concession stands, and first aid stations. Signage is also a useful crowd management tool in guiding spectators to their seats. An ejection policy will help protect guests from violent and disruptive fans. Many times these behaviors are amplified through the consumption of alcohol.

Crowd Management_____
Strategy designed to prevent crowd from getting out of control; security, signage, and communication all serve to effectively maintain crowd control.

Alcohol Management_____
Limits the risks associated with alcohol consumption, as well as reduces facility liability regarding alcohol-related incidents.

Naturally, an ejection policy will be a vital component of an alcohol management plan as well.

Alcohol is a difficult issue for facility managers. Alcohol sales at sport events are usually a significant revenue generator. But alcohol sales often enhance disruptive behavior during the event and increase the likelihood of drunk driving once the event has concluded. An alcohol management plan will limit these risks, as well as reduce facility liability regarding alcohol-related incidents. Alcohol policies vary from facility to facility, however, recommended alcohol management practices include:

- Denying admittance to guests who visibly appear impaired;
- Prohibiting guests from bringing outside beverages or beverage containers into the facility;
- Prohibiting guests from leaving the facility with alcoholic beverages;
- Requiring a valid government ID for all alcohol purchases;
- Prohibiting the passing of alcohol to minors;
- Reserving the right to refuse service to guests who visibly appear impaired;
- Designating a cutoff point for alcohol sales (e.g., the end of the third quarter in football or basketball games);
- Limiting alcohol sales to two beers per purchase with a 20 oz. maximum container size (Hambrick, Simmons, Greenhalgh, & Brownlee, 2009).

Americans with Disabilities Act

Signed into law by President George Bush in 1990, the **Americans with Disabilities Act** (ADA) prohibits discrimination based on disability in four areas: employment, state and local government activities, places of public accommodation, and telecommunications (Department of Justice, 2005). Public Accommodation (Title III) is of particular importance to facility managers. Places of public accommodation include hotels, restaurants, movie theaters, grocery stores, gas stations, airports, parks, day care centers, and even sport and recreation facilities such as stadiums, arenas, and gyms (Sharp et al., 2007). Sport facilities are required by law to be ADA-compliant. It is the responsibility of the facility manager to ensure the facility is accessible to patrons with disabilities.

The ADA defines an individual with a disability as "a person who has a physical or mental impairment that substantially limits one or more major life activities, a person who has a history or record of such an impairment, or a person who is perceived by others as having such an impairment" (Department of Justice, 2005, p. 1). Major life activities include walking, speaking, seeing, hearing, breathing, learning, working, and the ability to care for one's self (Greenberg, 2000).

Facilities built for occupancy after January 26, 1993, must be fully compliant under the ADA (Ammon et al., 2010). The Department of Justice outlined a number of facility features that must meet ADA standards. One such feature is the seating area. At least one percent of a facility's seating area must

Americans with Disabilities Act_____

A law signed in 1990 prohibiting discrimination based on disability in employment, state and local government activities, places of public accommodation, and telecommunications; sport facilities are considered places of public accommodation and therefore must be accessible to persons with disabilities.

be wheelchair accessible and provide companion seating. Accessible seating must be available throughout the venue, including the club level and luxury suites, and should be elevated to provide unobstructed sightlines over standing spectators (Department of Justice, 1997).

Beyond the seating area, persons with disabilities should have access to the same amenities and features of the facility as able-bodied patrons. Such amenities include concession and merchandise stands, parking, and restrooms. Concession stands should have lowered counters to provide service to individuals in a wheelchair. Parking for guests with disabilities should be made available near accessible facility entrances, and restrooms should be equipped with lowered mirrors and larger stalls (Department of Justice, 1997).

Facilities occupied prior to the ADA's enactment have different regulations from newer facilities. Architectural barriers that restrict access to existing facilities must be removed if such a renovation is "readily achievable." The term "readily achievable" refers to alterations that are relatively simple and inexpensive, such as the addition of wheelchair ramps and the replacement of thick carpets which are not suitable for wheelchairs (Ammon et al., 2010).

It may not be possible to remove all barriers that restrict access to a facility. In such instances, a demonstration of "good faith" in achieving accessibility is sufficient to meet ADA standards. Mingus (2005) suggests four steps by which a facility manager can demonstrate "good faith" towards ADA compliance. The first step is a self-evaluation of the facility. A facility manager should identify areas where the facility meets or falls short of ADA compliance. The second step is the formation of an advisory council, which should include individuals with a disability, to help plan for future facility alterations. Next, a plan and timeline for improvements should be developed. The final step in "good faith" compliance is the adoption of a facility philosophy regarding ADA that welcomes people of all walks of life, including those with a disability, into the facility. What is most important is that all guests, including those with disabilities, have access to the facility and can enjoy the experience.

Conclusion

Facility management is a critical segment of the sport industry. Public assembly facilities, such as stadiums and arenas, provide significant sources of revenue for sport organizations through modern features such as luxury seating, naming rights, and personal seat licenses. Ancillary services such as concessions, merchandise, and parking are also important economic generators for a sport facility. A facility's ability to generate revenue is directly linked to the services and operational functions it provides. Housekeeping, maintenance, and security services contribute to the overall fan experience at sport and entertainment events.

Facilities pose a number of additional challenges for facility managers, including risk management and complying with the Americans with Disabilities Act. Sport facilities offer many potential dangers. A comprehensive risk management plan will help facility managers minimize the risks associated with a sport event. In addition, the amenities and services offered in a sport facility should be fully accessible to all patrons, including those with disabilities.

CHAPTER

Interview

INTERVIEW 11.1

Kenneth C. Scull
Colonel U.S. Army Retired
Stadium Manager/Assistant Athletic Director
University of Louisville—Papa John's Cardinal Stadium

I first came to Louisville in 1997 to assist in the completion and the opening of Papa John's Cardinal Stadium. Prior to that I was Deputy Athletic Director at the United States Military Academy at West Point, New York, where I supervised the athletic department from top to bottom, including facilities. I graduated from the United States Military Academy in 1969 with a degree in engineering, and served in the Infantry branch of the United States Army. I also hold master's degrees in public administration and business administration.

Currently, I am the stadium manager for Papa John's Cardinal Stadium (PJCS) at the University of Louisville. PJCS is a 42,000-seat facility used primarily for the university's football team. The stadium just completed an expansion project in 2010. The seating capacity following expansion is now approximately 55,000.

On the day of an event, the first thing I do is make sure the parking lots are open and security is in place. I also make sure everyone in the facility is on time and doing what they are supposed to be doing. If they are not, I need to make adjustments. Prepping the facility on game day is time-consuming, and involves numerous mundane tasks like putting the flags up appropriately.

The sound and video board need to be working properly. During the event, my primary function is reacting to situations that are exceptional. I also like to make sure everyone is in the right place and the employees are being courteous to our guests.

As a football facility, our primary sources of revenue are ticket sales, luxury seating, parking, and concessions. The ticketing structure is based on a donation level that creates an additional revenue stream for the athletic department. When we are not hosting a game, we create revenue by renting the facility and parking lot to events such as large high school football games, semi-professional games, and concerts. Parking from other big events such as the Kentucky Derby at Churchill Downs creates revenue as well. We also rent locations within the stadium such as the Brown and Williamson Club and the press lounge. Aside from rent, these events also generate revenue from our catering service.

The most important considerations when renting a facility are the event's promoter and the schedule. The promoter must have a financial structure that makes sense to ensure the event is profitable. If the promoter lacks a good scheme, then most likely the event will not be worth the time, effort, or risk that go into putting on an event. As far as the schedule is concerned, sequencing is critical. It usually takes a week to get ready for a concert, so events need to be sequenced accordingly. Typically, a concert cannot be held the day after a football game. Also, one needs to consider the staff required to put on an event. Large events require large numbers of people to work. If the facility is trying to do something big when another prominent event in town is occurring, there is a good chance that finding staff to work will be challenging, especially for part-time workers.

At PJCS, concessions are operated through a private contractor. The primary advantage of outsourcing concessions is that the concessionaire is the license holder for alcohol sales. The state looks to the license holder on the premises for all things related to alcohol law enforcement and dram shop laws. In addition, we do not have to hire and manage employees with a specific set of skills for a one-time event. The concessionaire has staff that works 12 months out of the year at a variety of facilities throughout the region, and is able to provide sufficient qualified personnel for our selective events. Finally, the concessionaires are experts at what they do. Their core competency is food. Ours are facilities and athletics. We do not try to be something we are not.

Security is another service we outsource, for many of the same reasons. During an event, the primary responsibilities of security are crowd management, behavior, and safety. Many of the risks in our facility are associated with alcohol consumption. We assume much of the risk for behavior related to alcohol, which sometimes becomes an issue. The event experience should be fun for everybody. Unruly fans should not be permitted to disrupt other patrons and this can become an issue with alcohol consumption. A lot of drinking goes on in the parking lot before and after an event. Any time a mixture of people who are driving and people who are drinking and not paying a lot of attention is present, risks are increased. Security also needs to be prepared to deal with emergency situations such as bad weather, bomb scares, or a variety of other threats.

The biggest challenge in the field for the near future is money. It is expensive to operate a facility. If it does not look nice, revenue opportunities decrease. Generating revenue to maintain a facility is an ongoing challenge. Another trend for the future of facility management is technology. The industry has benefited, and will continue to benefit, from advancements in technology. Technology has helped tremendously in the areas of crowd management and security. The use of computers saves time previously spent writing everything down. Tickets can be counted faster and the number of patrons in a facility can be more easily tracked now than in the past. In addition, all the systems inside the facility are computer-based so it takes fewer people to operate the facility.

One of the things I am looking for in new hires is a sense of mission that exceeds the job description. In addition, a candidate needs a variety of skills and skill sets to be successful in this field. These skills include:

- The initiative and ability to act with minimal supervision;
- Attention to detail;
- Interpersonal skills;
- Business skills including knowledge of the law as it pertains to contracts.

I would advise any student thinking about working in facility management to intern in a sport facility. Students really need to get out from behind a desk and see the scope of what it takes for a facility to function well, from taking out the trash to providing optimal customer service. Internships are the best way to gain practical experience and get a foot in the door. The value of real-life work experience should not be underestimated.

Study Questions

1. Identify and define the four treatment options of a risk management plan.
2. Why is it important for a sport facility to comply with the Americans with Disabilities Act (ADA)? Which areas of the facility must be accessible to persons with disabilities?
3. Explain the differences between reserved seating, general admission, and festival seating.
4. What are the advantages and disadvantages of operating concessions in-house? What about through a private contractor?
5. What is a personal seat license? How does a PSL generate revenue for a sport facility?
6. How do housekeeping and maintenance operations contribute to the fan experience?
7. Discuss the versatility of the parking lot in terms of generating revenue for a facility.

Learning Activities

1. Attend a sport event at your college. Rather than experiencing the game solely as a fan, pay attention to the different ways the athletic department is generating revenue through the facility. Bring a notebook and record the various revenue sources. What types of ancillary services are offered? Is corporate sponsorship or advertising present in the facility? Does the public address announcer mention athletic department sponsors during stoppages in play? Identify two areas where the facility could generate additional revenue for the athletic department.
2. Conduct an interview with a facility manager. Discuss the potential risks associated with an event at the facility. Using the information in this chapter as a reference, complete the risk category matrix below with the risks you identified with the facility manager. After completing the matrix, discuss how you would treat each of the risk categories. Identify strategies you would use to reduce the frequency and/or severity of those risks.

	High Frequency	Moderate Frequency	Low Frequency
High Loss			
Moderate Loss			
Low Loss			

References

Ammon, R. (2003). Risk management process. In D.J. Cotton, J.T. Wolohan (Eds.). *Law for recreation and sport managers* (3rd ed., pp. 296–307). Dubuque, IA: Kendall/Hunt Publishing Company.

Ammon, R., Southall, R.M., & Nagel, M.S. (2010). *Sport facility management: Organizing events and mitigating risks* (2nd ed.). Morgantown, WV: Fitness Information Technology, Inc.

Arco Arena. (n.d.). Parking. Retrieved on May 6, 2009 from http://www.arcoarena.com/ default.asp?lnopt=2&pnopt=8.

Arizona Cardinals (n.d.). University of Phoenix Stadium. Retrieved on December 17, 2009 from http://www.az cardinals.com/stadium/a-to-z-guide.html.

Associated Press. (2008). Seats behind home plate at the Yankees new stadium cost $500–$2,500. Retrieved on June 14, 2009 from http://sports.espn.go.com/mlb/news/story?id=3305979.

Citi Field. (n.d.). Citi Field: A-Z guide. Retrieved on May 14, 2009 from http://newyork.mets.mlb.com/nym/ballpark/guide.jsp.

Dallas Cowboys (n.d.). Cowboys Stadium. Retrieved on December 16, 2009 from http://www.dallascowboys.com/tickets/newStadiumMain.cfm.

Department of Justice, Civil Rights Division, Disability Rights Section. (1997). Accessible stadiums. Retrieved on April 30, 2009 from http://www.ada.gov/stadium.pdf.

Department of Justice, Civil Rights Division, Disability Rights Section. (2005). A guide to disability rights. Retrieved on April 30, 2009 from http://www.ada.gov/cguide.pdf.

Fried, G. (2010). *Managing sport facilities.* Champaign, IL: Human Kinetics.

Gorman, W. (2003). That asphalt jungle in not just for cars: Making money from your parking lot. *Facility Manager.* Retrieved on May 6, 2009 from http://www.iaam.org /Facility_manager/Pages/2003_Jan_Feb/Feature_1.htm.

Graham, P. J., & Ward, R. (2004). *Public assembly facility management: Principles and practices.* Coppell, TX: International Association of Assembly Managers.

Greenberg, M. J. (2000). *The stadium game* (2nd ed.). Milwaukee, WI: Marquette University Press.

Hambrick, M., Simmons, J., Greenhalgh, G., & Brownlee, E. (2009, March). *Grading the alcohol policies of professional sports leagues: A practical application of dram shop statues.* Paper presented at the Sport and Recreation Law Association Conference, San Antonio, TX.

Houlihan, A., Parkes, R., Hawkins, M., Hearne, S., Ashton-Jones, A., & Schmick, C. (2009). Lost in translation: Football money league. Deloitte. Retrieved on June 7, 2009 from http://www.deloitte.com/dtt/cda/doc/content/UK_SBG_DeloitteFML2009.pdf

Howard, D. R. & Crompton, J. L. (2005). *Financing sport* (2nd ed.). Morgantown, WV: Fitness Information Technology.

Jones, E. (2008, March 31). Cowboys stadium names: Jerry Jones Field? *Sports Business Digest.* Retrieved on May 4, 2009 from http://sportsbusinessdigest.com/cowboys-stadium-names-jerry-jones-field/.

Kim, R. (2000, April 12). Giants home, at last Giants home, at last. *San Francisco Chronicle.* Retrieved from http://www.sfgate.com/cgi-bin/article.cgi?f=/e/a/2000/04/12/NEWS12997.dtl.

Kuriloff, A. (2008). Giants to sell personal seat licenses for new stadium. *Bloomberg.* Retrieved on December 17, 2009 from http://www.bloomberg.com/apps/news?pid=20601079&sid =a2ID53cok6FU &refer=home.

Lamberth, C. (2003). Raised awareness: Changing trends in security at sports & entertainment facilities. *Facility Manager Magazine.* Retrieved on May 7, 2009 from http://www.iaam.org/Facility_manager/Pages/2003_Sep_Oct/Feature_1.htm.

Lombardo, J. (2009, January 12). A new sign of the times? *Sports Business Journal.* Retrieved on May 6, 2009 from http://www.sportsbusinessjournal.com/article/61109.

Mingus, M. (2005). The ADA: Does your facility demonstrate "good faith progress" towards compliance? *Facility Manager.* Retrieved on May 6, 2009 from http:// www.iaam.org/Facility_manager/Pages/2005_Apr_May/LEGAL.HTM.

Mullen, L. (2003, November 17). Churchill Downs sells out its 64 new luxury boxes. *Sports Business Journal.* Retrieved on May 3, 2009 from http://www.sportsbusinessjournal.com/ article/35138.

Muret, D. (2007, March 19). Nats consider price hike for suites. *Sports Business Journal.* Retrieved on May 4, 2009 from http://www.sportsbusinessjournal.com/article/54271.

Muret, D. (2009, April 27). Nets use projections technology for big new ads in seating bowl. *Sports Business Journal.* Retrieved on May 6, 2009 from http://www. sportsbusinessjournal.com/article/62331.

NCAA. (2003). *2002–03 NCAA revenues and expenses of Division I and II intercollegiate athletic programs report.* Indianapolis, IN: National Collegiate Athletic Association.

Price, C. L. (2007). Choosing and using contract security: Learn how to make the most of your venue's investment in "ambassadors for hire." *Venue Safety and Security Magazine.* Retrieved on April 27, 2009 from https://www.iaam.org/vss/pages/2007_summer/ feature1.htm.

Sedlak, R., & Traugott, A. (2002). Is your venue ready for an incident? *Facility Manager Magazine.* Retrieved on May 6, 2009 from http://www.iaam.org/Facility_manager/ Pages/2002_Jan_Feb/Feature_7.htm.

Sharp, L.A., Moorman, A.M., & Claussen, C.L. (2007). *Sport law: A managerial approach.* Scottsdale, AZ: Holcomb Hathaway, Publishers.

Sports Business Journal. (2008). Facilities. *Sports Business Journal.* Retrieved on April 6, 2009 from http://www.sports businessjournal.com/article/58747.

Stotlar, D.K. (1997). Operations and maintenance. In M.L. Walker & D.K. Stotlar (Eds.). *Sport facility management* (pp. 31–42). Sudbury, MA: Jones and Bartlett Publishers, Inc.

Trumpbour, R.C. (2007). *The new cathedrals: Politics and media in the history of stadium construction.* Syracuse, NY: Syracuse University Press.

Sport Finance

Matthew T. Brown • *University of South Carolina*

- Properly define basic terminology common to finance and accounting;
- Understand the importance of sound financial management practices in sport management;
- Identify and interpret basic financial statements;
- Have the ability to perform a basic analysis of an organization's financial performance;
- Properly identify five forms of financing a sport organization.

KEY TERMS

Expenses

Finance

Financial Management

Revenues

Wealth Maximization

> *Anyone who quotes profits of a baseball club is missing the point. Under generally accepted accounting principles, I can turn a $4 million profit into a $2 million loss and I could get every national accounting firm to agree with me.*
>
> —Paul Beeston, then a Toronto Blue Jays vice president, formerly president and COO of MLB, now president and CEO of the Blue Jays, 1979

> *You go through* The Sporting News *for the last 100 years, and you will find two things are always true. You never have enough pitching, and nobody ever made money.*
>
> —Former MLB players'association head Donald Fehr, 1995

Introduction

Successful sport managers have many things in common. For one, they pay attention to the current operations of their organization and monitor environmental factors that might impact operations. For example, the recession that began in December 2007 followed periods of rapid economic expansion in the 1990s and mid 2000s. While the economy was expanding, the sport industry grew. New venues were constructed, leagues were formed, and teams were added. Funding much of the sport industry's expansion was a deepening relationship with corporate America in the form of ticket and luxury suite sales as well as sponsorship and advertising packages. As the great recession began, the sport industry faced great risks because of its increased dependence on the corporate dollar. Figure 12.1 illustrates one aspect of the corporate support of the sport industry.

Two of the main sources of revenue for professional and collegiate sport organizations are advertising revenues and facility naming rights revenues (Figure 12.2). As seen in Figure 12.1, the top 10 sport advertisers spent a total of $1.6 billion in 2008. Anheuser-Busch, the largest sport advertiser at $277.4 million per year, spent 81 percent of its total 2008 advertising budget in the sport industry. While the recession did not have much impact upon 2008 sport advertising deals since most of them had been signed prior to the December 2007 economic downturn, the amount of money spent for sport advertising in 2009 decreased dramatically. The Ladies Professional Golf Association (LPGA) had to drop several tour stops in 2009 due to losses in sponsorship and advertising revenues. For 2010 the LPGA struggled to find title sponsors for 15 of its 29 events (Kreidler, 2009).

To be successful, sport managers also must pay attention to the future operations of their organization. In professional sport, labor relations often impact the operation of teams and leagues as new collective bargaining agreements

Rank	Company	2008 Sports Spending	2008 Total Ad Spending	% Sports
1	Anheuser-Busch Cos.	$277,409,224	$343,369,045	80.8%
2	AT&T Mobility, LLC	$243,316,201	$920,544,578	26.4%
3	Chevrolet Motor Division	$178,252,600	$345,996,424	51.5%
4	Sprint Nextel Corp.	$152,616,107	$553,706,585	27.6%
5	Verizon Communications Inc.	$147,938,230	$795,658,183	18.6%
6	Toyota Motor Sales Inc.	$142,516,793	$344,039,943	41.4%
7	Ford Motor Co.	$136,288,521	$384,062,300	35.5%
8	DirecTV Inc.	$130,381,457	$247,439,322	52.7%
9	McDonald's Corp.	$120,350,982	$406,973,677	29.6%
10	Visa International	$108,446,395	$241,833,562	44.8%

Source: *Sports Business Resource Guide & Fact Book 2010*

FIGURE 12.1

Top 10 Sports Advertisers (2008)

(CBAs) are negotiated. The National Football League (NFL) restructured its revenue-sharing system between team owners and players when it signed its last CBA in 2006. The change in revenue-sharing has made it harder for a few small-market teams to remain financially viable. Teams have had to look for new sources of revenue as a result. For example, the Buffalo Bills have moved one regular season and one preseason game each year to Toronto in an attempt to generate higher revenues. The National Hockey League (NHL), the most international of the North American leagues, faces financial challenges as the exchange rate between the U.S. dollar and the Canadian dollar (Loonie) fluctuates. All sport organizations faced some uncertainty though after the collapse of the financial markets in 2008.

Early in 2009, Massachusetts Senator John Kerry proposed the *TARP Taxpayer Protection Corporate Responsibility Act* after celebrity website TMZ posted a story questioning the use of taxpayer funds at the Professional Golf Association's (PGA) Northern Trust Open (Newport, 2009). The act would prevent any TARP recipient from hosting, sponsoring, or paying for entertainment events unless the company received a waiver from the Treasury Secretary ("Secretary of Golf," 2009). The TMZ story stated that Northern Trust, recipient of $1.6 billion from the Troubled Asset Relief Program (TARP), held lavish parties, fancy dinners, and concerts with famous singers. After learning of the sponsorship, Representative Barney Frank sent a letter to Northern Trust, co-signed by 17 additional congressmen, demanding that it return the $1.6 billion. Columnists from across the political spectrum joined in the criticism, including Maureen Dowd and Bill O'Reilly (Newport). Ignored in the criticism were the potential business benefits the sponsorship brought to Northern Trust, such as providing access to decision-makers in business, reaching potential new customers, and increasing the firm's visibility.

The banking industry spent $900 million on sport sponsorship rights fees in 2008 and $122.3 million on sport advertising. Of the top 10 stadium naming rights holders, four were companies operating in the financial sector (see Figure 12.2). While legislation restricting sponsorship spending has yet to pass in Congress, the impact of the earlier government outcry was damaging. Soon after the TMZ incident, Morgan Stanley, recipient of $10 billion in TARP funds, and Wells Fargo, recipient of $25 billion, announced changes to their golf sponsorships. Morgan Stanley decided to remain a sponsor of the Memorial Tournament, but company executives did not entertain clients at the event. Wells Fargo, owner of Wachovia, cut its presence at the Wachovia Championships held outside Charlotte, North Carolina (Newport, 2009).

Facility	City	Sponsor	Price	Number of Years
City Field	Queens, NY	Citibank NA	$400.0 million	20
Reliant Stadium	Houston	Reliant Energy Inc.	$310.0 million	31
FedEx Field	Landover, MD	FedEx Corp.	$205.0 million	27
Minute Maid Park	Houston	The Coca-Cola Co.	$178.0 million	28
University of Phoenix Stadium	Glendale, AZ	Apollo Group Inc.	$154.5 million	20
Bank of America Stadium	Charlotte	Bank of America	$140.0 million	20
Lincoln Financial Field	Philadelphia	Lincoln National Corp.	$139.6 million	20
Lucas Oil Stadium	Indianapolis	Lucas Oil Products	$121.5 million	20
Gillette Stadium	Foxboro, MA	Global Gillette	$120.0 million	15
Invesco Field at Mile Hile	Denver	Invesco Institutional NA	$120.0 million	20

Source: *Sports Business Resource Guide & Fact Book 2010*

FIGURE 12.2

Top 10 Stadium Naming-Rights Contracts

There are many environmental factors that affect the current and future operations of sport organizations. These pressures shape the way the sport industry has evolved and influence how it will continue to evolve. Successful sport managers understand the impact of various forces. However, the most successful sport managers also must have an understanding of the **goal of the firm**. The goal of most firms is *wealth maximization*, the maximization of the overall value of the firm or organization. To truly understand wealth maximization, sport managers must have a solid understanding of finance.

Finance

Finance is the science of fund management that incorporates concepts from accounting, statistics, and economics. Within finance, there are three distinct sectors. One has been discussed already, *financial management*, which focuses upon financial decision-making with the outcome for most organizations being wealth maximization. **The money and capital markets** sector includes securities markets like the New York Stock Exchange (NYSE) and the Chicago Mercantile Exchange. Investment banking, insurance, and mutual fund management are also in this sector. The **investments** sector includes firms like Merrill Lynch and Edward Jones. The focus of the investments sector is portfolio management. Companies help individuals and institutions invest in securities and select investment choices based upon risk and the risk tolerance of the investor.

Most working in the sport industry will not be involved with the investments sector or the money and capital markets sector. However, everyone working in sport will either be directly or indirectly impacted by the financial management of their organization. As the goal of financial management is wealth maximization, those working within financial management of a sport organization are concerned with the acquisition and use of funds to meet this goal.

For wealth maximization to occur, the finance department forecasts future revenues and plans for future costs and expenses. In sport, this may include calculating cash flow increases resulting from higher television rights fees, and determining how much the organization can enhance player payroll as a result of the forecast. The finance department also fills one portion of the control function of management. Through coordination with other departments in the organization, efficiency of operation and resource utilization can be achieved. The finance department makes investment and financing decisions while working with financial markets and investment firms when necessary. The type of debt financing used when constructing a new arena is but one example.

Although firms in the sport industry may be structured as a for-profit, not-for-profit or governmental entity, in terms of for-profit enterprises, sport has many commonalities with other types of business. Therefore, much that applies to the financial management of a sport organization is similar to the financial management of an organization in any other industry. These commonalities include value creation, or increasing the value of a firm over time, and revenue growth. However, there are areas of difference.

Wealth Maximization_____

The goal or outcome of financial management for most organizations; increasing the overall value of the firm.

Finance_____

The science of fund management that incorporates concepts from accounting, statistics, and economics.

Financial Management_____

Financial decision-making within a firm with wealth maximization being the goal for most organizations.

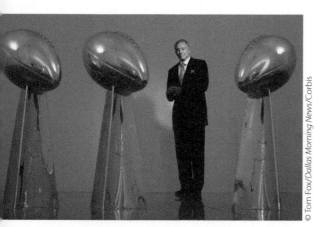

Jerry Jones has worked tirelessly to enhance the Dallas Cowboy's brand and spent extensively to win championships.

© Tom Fox/Dallas Morning News/Corbis

One major difference is the wide variety of ownership objectives within sport (Foster, Greyser, & Walsh, 2006). Typically, companies within an industry compete for wealth maximization. Owners in professional sport, however, might not be primarily interested in this goal. Rather, they may be more interested in winning championships. Or, they might be seeking celebrity status by being one of a select few professional sport-franchise owners nationwide. Another goal may be to protect a community asset. Particularly relating to winning championships, differing objectives of owners can harm the competitive balance in a league. Extremely wealthy owners with a willingness to incur losses over several seasons can create an imbalance in competition. As a result, at the beginning of a season, only a few teams may have a realistic chance of winning a championship. Leagues have reacted by implementing salary constraints, revenue sharing, and other similar mechanisms that create both competition between franchises on the field and cooperation regarding financial management of it.

Basic Finance and Accounting Concepts

To truly understand financial management and the financial operations of an organization, a sport manager needs a basic knowledge of accounting. Accounting data provides information that can be used to make decisions regarding the use of limited resources. For example, if transportation costs are expected to increase by 15 percent during the season due to a sudden increase in fuel prices, an organization needs to determine if it can absorb the increased costs within its budget. If not, the organization must determine whether alternate, cheaper forms of transportation are available or if expenses can be cut elsewhere.

Accounting data also helps an organization effectively control human and material resources. Data from sales revenues can be used to determine which intern is generating the most revenue for the organization and which intern will be hired for a full-time job at the end of a season. Finally, accounting data can be used to ensure that ownership of resources is maintained. Inventory can be tracked and equipment replacement cycles can be developed using accounting data.

Importantly for financial management, accounting data includes information regarding an organization's revenues, expenses, and debt. Revenues include money coming into an organization. Selling tickets is a common revenue-generating activity in sport. Expenses are costs incurred by the organization. Common costs in sport include wages, utilities, equipment, and transportation. **Debt** is the owing of money to others.

Revenues_____

Money coming into an organization. Selling tickets is one common example of generating revenue in sport.

Expenses_____

Costs incurred by the organization. Common costs in sport include wages, utilities, equipment, and transportation.

Accountants prepare many financial statements, but four are particularly important for use in financial management. These include budgets, income statements (or profit and loss statements), balance sheets and statements of cash flow. Each financial statement is important and each is used in slightly different ways. They are the primary source of information used to assess the financial health and performance of an organization.

Budget

Simply stated, a **budget** outlines where a business intends to spend its money and where it plans to receive revenue. It is a tool for financial planning. A budget is created based upon projections made about the future financial performance of the organization. For example, Figure 12.3 shows the 2008–2009 operating budget of the "State University's" athletic department. The department estimates that revenues will be $92.2 million over the fiscal year. Their estimate was 1.9 percent lower than the projected revenues from the 2007–2008 fiscal year due to the anticipated impacts of the recession on revenues. Further, the State University estimates a $10.3 million net operating surplus over fiscal year 2008–2009. After transfers to cover the costs of building, renovating, and maintaining facilities, the department is left with a $2.6 million increase in its current fund balance. State University has been using its surplus to fund the department's capital needs (i.e., facility renovations and improvements).

From a planning standpoint, a financial manager can use several budgets types to track his or her organization's revenues, expenses, cash, and capital expenditures. These budgets-within-budgets depict the impact of the budgeting process on overall organizational revenues, expenses, cash flows, and capital expenditures. For example, the State University's athletic department has three budgets-within-budgets. The department prepares an operating budget (Figure 12.3) revenue budget and a capital expenditure budget. During the 2008–2009 fiscal year, the department plans to transfer $7.7 million from its operating budget to its capital expenditure budget. It does not anticipate a transfer to or from its revenue (endowment and other funds) budget however. The department denotes transfers to its other budgets under the *Transfers and capital expenditures* section.

Income Statement

An **income statement** is also known also as a profit and loss (P & L) statement. The income statement measures an organization's expenditures and receipts between two specific points in time. It consists of three sections: operating, non-operating, and net income. The operating section contains the operating revenues and expenses of an organization. Operating revenues typically include proceeds from sales. In sport, this may include ticket sales, sponsorship sales, advertising income, parking revenue, concessions revenue, and merchandise revenues. Operating expenses may include salaries, selling expenses, and general

Fiscal Year 2008–2009 Operating Budget
(in thousands)

Revenues	Bugeted Amount	% of Total
Spectator Admissions		
Football	$31,570	35%
Basketball	1,895	2%
Hockey	1,857	2%
Other	229	0%
Conference Distributions		
Television (Football and Basketball)	12,660	14%
Football Bowl Games	1,747	2%
NCAA Basketball	2,612	3%
Other	400	0%
Priority Seating and other Annual Gifts	13,600	15%
Corporate Sponsorship	9,880	11%
Licensing Royalties	3,800	4%
Radio	2,100	2%
Facilities	1,870	2%
Concessions/Parking	1,860	2%
Other	937	1%
Investment Income	3,444	4%
Current Revenues	**$90,461**	**100%**
Expenses		
Salaries	$30,860	38%
Student Financial Aid	15,129	19%
Team and Game Expense	15,005	19%
Facilities	7,093	9%
Deferred Maintenance Fund Transfer	4,500	6%
Other Operating and Administrative Expenses	6,575	8%
Debt Service Transfer to Plant Fund	1,029	1%
Current Expenses	**$80,191**	**100%**
Net Operating Surplus	**$10,270**	
Transfers and Capital Expenditures		
Capital Expenditures from Current Funds		
And Transfers to Plant Fund	$(7,700)	
Transfers to Endowment Fund	—	
Net Transfers and Capital Expenditures	**$(7,700)**	
Increase (Decrease) in Current Fund Balances	**$ 2,570**	

State University (2008)

FIGURE 12.3
State University Athletic Department Budget

and administrative expenses. Stepwise, expenses are subtracted from revenues, leaving operating income, also referred to as earnings before interest, taxes, depreciation, and amortization (EBITDA). Or,

Revenues
− Expenses
_____
Operating Income (EBITDA)

The non-operating section includes non-cash expenses like depreciation and amortization expenses. Also included are interest and tax expenses. Stepwise, depreciation and amortization expenses are subtracted from operating income to leave earnings before interest and taxes (EBIT). Interest expenses are subtracted from EBIT to leave earnings before taxes (EBT). Corporate income taxes are calculated based upon the firm's EBT. Or,

Operating Income (EBITDA)
− Depreciation
− Amortization
_____
EBIT
− Interest
_____
EBT
− Income Taxes
_____

The third section is net income. Here, income taxes are subtracted from EBT to leave the increase or decrease in the organization's income over two points in time. Or,

EBT
− Income Taxes
_____
Net Income

Combined, the income statement framework is:

Revenues
− Expenses
_____
Operating Income (EBITDA)
− Depreciation
− Amortization
_____
EBIT
− Interest
_____
EBT
− Income Taxes
_____
Net Income

Figure 12.4 shows a sample income statement of the Wisconsin Ham Fighters, a professional sport franchise. From the income statement it can be seen that approximately 38 percent of the team's income comes from television

Wisconsin Ham Fighters Statements of Income
Year ended March 31, 2009

OPERATING INCOME

Ticket & Media Income

Home games (net)	$ 31,097,266
Road games	16,175,953
Television and radio	95,901,900
TOTAL TICKET AND MEDIA INCOME	**$143,884,218**

Other Operating Income

Luxury site income	$ 13,020,027
Properties income (Other League Revenue)	37,005,636
Marketing/Retail Operations (net)	44,373,516
Other—Local Media, Concessions and parking (net)	13,365,493
TOTAL OTHER OPERATING INCOME	**$107,764,672**
TOTAL OPERATING INCOME	**$251,648,890**

OPERATING EXPENSE

Player costs	$140,777,731
Game expenses (Operations/Maintenance (net))	7,816,059
General and Administrative	32,169,400
Team expenses	26,790,015
Sales and Marketing expenses	23,684,410
TOTAL OPERATING EXPENSES	**$231,237,615**
PROFIT (LOSS) FROM OPERATIONS	**$ 20,411,275**
OTHER INCOME (EXPENSE)	**$(11,355,506)**
Income before expansion revenue and provision for income taxes	9,055,769
Provision for income taxes	$ 4,973,500
NET INCOME before expansion revenue	**$ 4,082,269**

FIGURE 12.4

2009 Wisconsin Ham Fighters Income Statement

and radio revenue, or $95.9 million. An additional $37.0 million (14.7% of overall income) is transferred to the team from the league's properties' division and $16.4 million is transferred from the league to the team for the Ham Fighters' share of road game revenues. Revenue from league properties comes from the sale of licensed merchandise. Combined, approximately $149.3 million comes from the league to the Ham Fighters. This is 59.3 percent of their overall revenue in 2009.

Most of the operating expenses of the team go to player costs. During the 2009 fiscal year, player costs were $140.7 million. This was 60.9 percent of overall operating expenses.

Balance Sheet

The **balance sheet** measures the financial condition of an organization at a specific point in time. The balance sheet reflects an organization's stock, or a rough estimate of its wealth. There are three sections of a balance sheet. **Assets** indicate ownership and include items like cash, inventory, accounts receivable, land, equipment, and buildings. **Liabilities** are financial obligations and debts owed to others. Accounts payable, accrued expenses, and long-term debt are examples of liabilities. **Owners' equity** reflects the owners' investment in the company and includes retained earnings, paid-in capital, and stock held by the organization. At all times, the value of an organization's assets must equal the value of its liabilities plus owners equity. This equation is:

$$\text{Assets} = \text{Liabilities} + \text{Owners' Equity}.$$

On the balance sheet, assets and liabilities are listed in order of **liquidity** and are divided into short-term and long-term accounts.

The Ham Fighters' Balance Sheet can be seen in Figure 12.5. Assets were $302.8 million at the end of the 2009 fiscal year. Current assets, those assets that can quickly be converted into cash, totaled $44.5 million. This was 14.7 percent of total assets. The majority of the Ham Fighters' assets were investments. In total, the Ham Fighters hold $168.5 million in investments. This amounts to over half of the assets owned by the franchise (55.7%).

The total liabilities (current + long term) of the team were $66.2 million (see Figure 12.5). Within the next year, the Ham Fighters will pay $5.0 million in deferred compensation. This is a current liability. Deferred compensation owed after the current year is a long-term liability. The Ham Fighters owe players an additional $11.5 million in long-term deferred compensation. Equity was $236.6 million with a majority being retained earnings (99.7%).

Statement of Cash Flows

A statement of cash flows measures cash moving into and out of an organization. For publicly traded firms, preparing a statement of cash flows is a relatively new requirement. The Financial Accounting and Standards Board (FASB)

Wisconsin Ham Fighters Balance Sheet
Year ended March 31, 2009

ASSETS

Current Assets

Cash	$ 3,686,648
Inventories	4,227,311
Unamortized signing bonuses	15,167,782
Accounts Receivable	9,856,132
Deferred income taxes	7,536,534
Other current assets	4,033,842
TOTAL CURRENT ASSETS	**$ 44,508,250**
INVESTMENTS	$168,526,011
Property & Equipment (net)	51,492,416

Other Assets

Unamortized signing bonuses	15,495,649
Deferred income taxes	—
Other noncurrent assets	22,784,489
TOTAL OTHER ASSETS	**$ 38,280,137**
TOTAL ASSETS	**$302,806,815**

LIABILITIES AND STOCKHOLDERS' EQUITY

Current Liabilities

Current maturities of long-term liabilities (Deferred Compensation)	$ 5,022,429
Notes payable	1,016,187
Accounts payable	2,826,248
Accrued expenses	12,502,389
Accrued income taxes	—
Deferred revenues	10,251,042
TOTAL CURRENT LIABILITIES	**$ 31,618,295**

Long-Term Liabilities

Note payable	$ 8,594,002
Deferred compensation	11,516,509
Other	14,456,667
TOTAL LONG-TERM LIABILITIES	**$ 34,567,178**

Stockholders' Equity

Common stock and additional paid in capital	$ 22,670,747
Retained earnings	235,904,954
Accumulated other comprehensive income	(21,954,360)
TOTAL STOCKHOLDERS' EQUITY	**$236,621,341**
TOTAL LIABILITIES AND STOCKHOLDERS' EQUITY	**$302,806,815**

FIGURE 12.5

2009 Wisconsin Ham Fighters Balance Sheet

required companies to present a statement of cash flows in published financial statements beginning in 1987.

In sport especially, statements of cash flows are extremely important as they provide the best picture on the overall financial health of the organization. A statement of cash flows differs from income statements. This is due to the difference between a firm's cash flows and accounting activities. For example, on an income statement there are several recorded expenses, like depreciation and amortization expenses, that are non-cash expenses. While counted as expenses on the income statement they do not negatively impact cash.

Sport leagues have received several favorable rulings from the Internal Revenue Service (IRS) that have enabled team owners to create tax shelters through their franchise purchase. Additionally, the U.S. Congress has enacted laws that enable the sport franchise owner to amortize the value of the franchise when purchased over the first 15 years of ownership. Therefore, franchise owners may have large depreciation and amortization expenses entered on the income statement. As stated in the chapter's opening quote, this could turn an actual $4 million profit into a $2 million "book" loss. However, while the club has an accounting loss of $2 million, it likely will see an increase in cash flows over the same period.[1] Most sport teams can follow Generally Accepted Accounting Procedures (GAAP) and use depreciation and amortization expenses to make the income statement look like the team is losing money when in actually the team has increased its cash position from the previous year. This in part explains why throughout history owners have claimed that they are not making money.

Cash flow is the sum of net income plus non-cash expenses minus non-cash revenues, or

Cash Flow = Net Income + non-cash expenses – non-cash revenues.

Non-cash expenses include the amortization of intangibles, depreciation, and accounts payable. Non-cash revenues are items like accounts receivable and accrued revenues not yet collected.

To calculate cash flows over a period of time, several adjustments to net income are made. First, sources of cash, or cash inflows, are added to net income. Cash inflows occur when non-cash assets decrease, liabilities increase, or owners' equity increases. Next, uses of cash, or cash outflows, are deducted from net income. Cash outflows occur when non-cash assets increase, liabilities decrease, or owners' equity decreases.

Statements of cash flows are divided into three areas. The first is cash flow from operating activities. Here adjustments to net income are made which result from positive and negative cash flows related to the firm's basic operating activities. Figure 12.6 is a statement of cash flows for Under Armour®. The adjustments made related to operating activities include the addition of the organization's depreciation and amortization expenses. Further changes to accounts receivable, inventories, accounts payable, and accrued expenses are recorded in this section.

---

[1] This explains why the values of sport franchises typically increase over time. Without positive cash flows, there would be no increase in franchise value.

Under Armour, Inc., and Subsidiaries Consolidated Statements of Cash Flows

(In thousands)

	Nine Months Ended 30-Sep-09 (unaudited)
Cash flows from operating activities	
Net income	$ 31,583
Adjustments to reconcile net income to net cash provided by (used in) operating activities	
Depreciation and amortization	20,795
Unrealized foreign currency exchange rate (gains) losses	(6,135)
Stock-based compensation	7,760
Loss on disposal of property and equipment	37
Deferred income taxes	(2,441)
Changes in reserves for doubtful accounts, returns, discounts, and inventories	(1,213)
Changes in operating assets and liabilities:	
Accounts receivable	(57,728)
Inventories	28,433
Prepaid expenses and other assets	371
Accounts payable	(13,885)
Accrued expenses and other liabilities	15,093
Income taxes payable and receivable	2,987
Net cash provided by operating activities	$ 25,657
Cash flows from investing activities	
Purchase of property and equipment	$ (16,049)
Purchase of trust-owned life insurance policies	(35)
Proceeds from sales of property and equipment	—
Net cash used in investing activities	$ (16,084)
Cash flows from financing activities	
Proceeds from revolving credit facility	$ —
Payments on revolving credit facility	(25,000)
Proceeds from long-term debt	3,567
Payments on long-term debt	(5,580)
Payments on capital lease obligations	(301)
Excess tax benefits from stock-based compensation arrangements	4,266
Payments of deferred financing costs	(1,354)
Proceeds from exercise of stock options and other stock issuances	4,331
Net cash provided by (used in) financing activities	$ (20,071)
Effect of exchange rate changes on cash and cash equivalents	$ 1,832
Net decrease in cash and cash equivalents	$ (8,666)
Cash and cash equivalents	
Beginning of period	$102,042
End of period	$ 93,376

FIGURE 12.6

Under Armour Statement of Cash Flows

The second section of the statement of cash flows is cash flow from investing activities. Here, adjustments are made to cash that are related to the purchase and sale of property, plant, equipment, and other non-current assets. Through the third-quarter of 2009, Under Armour® had purchased over $16.0 million in property and equipment and $35,000 of trust-owned life insurance policies (see Figure 12.6).

The final section is cash flow from financing activities. The effects of financing transactions like issuance and repayment of debt, issuance and repayment of stock, and payments of dividends are recorded in this section. Under Armour® paid $25.0 million on a revolving credit facility during the third-quarter of 2009 while paying off $5.6 million of long-term debt and borrowing nearly $3.6 million (see Figure 12.6).

Changes to cash in each section are then summed. So,

Changes in Cash in 2009 = Net cash provided by operating activities
    + net cash used in investing activities + net cash provided by (used in)
    financing activities

Changes in Cash in 2009 = $25,657 + ($16,084) + ($20,071)

Changes in Cash in 2009 = ($10,498)

As Under Armour® operates in several nations, cash is affected by changes in the exchange rates between countries. During the third-quarter of 2009, the effect of the exchange rate differences increased cash by $1.8 million. The net increase (decrease) in cash for the period is:

Net increase (decrease) in cash = Changes in Cash in 2009
    + Effect of Exchange Rate Differences

Net increase (decrease) in cash = ($10,498) + $1,832

Net increase (decrease) in cash = ($8,666)

The net increase (decrease) in cash is then added to cash at the beginning of the period to calculate cash at the end of the period.

End of Period = Net increase (decrease) in cash + Beginning of period cash

End of Period = ($8,666) + $102,042

End of Period = $93,376

T-accounts

To track revenues and expenses and create accounts to be entered on balance sheets and income statements, accountants historically have used the **T-system**. Today, organizations often rely on computer software like QuickBooks to create accounts that are used to automatically generate financials. Though computerized software is available and has simplified the accounting process for many firms, an understanding of the T-system will help with the understanding of balance sheets, income statements, and statements of cash flows.

A **T-account** is created using a ledger. **Credits** are entries made on the right hand side of the ledger, or "T." **Debits** are entries made on the left hand side of the "T." For accounting purposes, credits and debits just refer to each side of the "T." Following is a basic T-account:

T-account	
Debits	*Credits*

The balance sheet provides the best example of the application of the T-system. Assets are listed on the left side, or debits side, of the T while liabilities and owners equity are listed on the right side, or credits side, of the T.

Balance Sheet	
Assets	*Liabilities*
	Owners' Equity

Example of the T-System

To fully understand how the T-system and T-accounts work, the transactions of two members of a fitness center can be monitored. Each customer, Customer A and Customer B, is sent a monthly membership charge from the club. The monthly fee is $100. This transaction affects the T-accounts of the two members and the **accounts receivable** account of the fitness center. The accounts receivable account includes money owed to the club by its customers for services or products provided on credit. Here, membership is provided to each customer on credit.

Customer A	
Debits	*Credits*
(A) $100	

Customer B	
Debits	*Credits*
(B) $100	

Accounts Receivable	
Debits	*Credits*
(A) $100	
(B) $100	

Three T-accounts are used for this transaction. The customers each have their own T-accounts and the accounts receivable T-account is used as well. The amount each customer owes is entered on the debits side of the account. The information also is entered on the left side of the fitness center's accounts receivables T-account.

The club also has a cash account (or bank account). Here is the cash T-account:

Cash	
Debits	Credits
$10,000	

Based upon the cash account, the fitness center currently has $10,000 cash in the bank. If Customer B pays her $100 membership, changes will be made to several T-accounts.

Customer B	
Debits	Credits
(B) $100	(C) $100

Accounts Receivable	
Debits	Credits
(A) $100	(C) $100
(B) $100	

Cash	
Debits	Credits
$10,000	
(C) $100	

First, Customer B's T-account is credited with the $100 payment. Next, the fitness center's accounts-receivable account is credited with $100 as Customer B has now paid her bill and she no longer owes that amount to the fitness center. Finally, the fitness center's cash account is debited $100 as the amount Customer B paid is deposited in the center's bank. At the end of the month, the T-account entries are finalized and financial reports are prepared using each account's end of month total.

Customer A	
Debits	Credits
$100	

Customer B

Debits	Credits
$0	

Accounts Receivable

Debits	Credits
$100	

Cash

Debits	Credits
$10,100	

The T-accounts show that Customer A still owes $100. This amount remains in both the customer's account and the accounts receivable account. Customer B no longer owes the club money and her account balance is zero. Finally, the cash account for the fitness center grows to $10,100.

As depicted in this example, it can be seen that asset accounts record increases on the left-hand, or debit side, of the T-account. For liability and owner's equity accounts, increases are recorded on the right-hand, or credit side. Also, this example demonstrates how **double-entry bookkeeping** is used. Generally Accepted Accounting Principles require the use of double-entry bookkeeping. Using this method of bookkeeping, multiple accounts are charged and each transaction has two effects. One requires a right-handed, credit entry (either an increase or decrease), and one requires a left-handed, debit entry (reflecting the opposite).

The method of accounting utilized also impacts T-accounts and the creation of financials. Under GAAP, an organization can operate on an **accrual basis** or a **cash basis**. The preferred method is the accrual basis of accounting. Using this method of accounting, revenues are recognized when they are earned and expenses are recorded when they are incurred. For example, a group sales representative has just sold 500 tickets at $10 per ticket to the Boy Scouts for an upcoming game. The group sales representative creates an invoice for payment and mails it to the Boy Scouts leader. The invoice is for $5,000 and no cash has been exchanged between the two parties. Using accrual-based accounting, the $5,000 is recorded as ticket revenue even though the Boy Scouts have not yet paid for their tickets. Here, the $5,000 is earned and recorded at the time of the transaction. Under a cash basis, transactions are recorded when cash is actually paid or received. Going back to the previous example, if the organization was using cash-based accounting, the $5,000 sale would not be recorded as revenue until the team receives the payment from the Boy Scouts. Here, the transaction would be recorded when the payment was received. Organizations, when formed, can select to use either method of accounting; however, an organization cannot switch between the two methods during the year.

Financing the Operation of a Sport Organization

Understanding how to read and interpret changes in financial statements is just one part of the financial management equation. For all in sport, whether you work for a team where the owner's objective is wealth maximization or winning or whether the sport organization is for profit, not-for-profit, or government owned, a manager in the sport industry will encounter five methods used to finance the organization. These include equity, debt, reinvesting retained earnings, government and gift financing.

Debt Financing

When an organization borrows money that must be repaid over a period of time, usually with interest, **debt financing** is being utilized. Typically in sport, teams issue bonds or borrow from lending institutions, or even in some instances their league, to finance operations through debt. The New York Yankees financed the new Yankee Stadium by borrowing $105 million from a group of banks including Goldman Sachs to pay for cost overruns. Also, the team borrowed more than $1.2 billion through the tax-exempt and taxable bond market (Kaplan, 2009). Debt financing can be either short-term or long-term with short-term debt obligations being repaid in less than one year and long-term obligations being repaid in more than one year. A key to financing operations via debt is that the lender does not gain an ownership interest in the organization. The sport organization's obligation is limited to the repayment of the debt.

Bonds

A **bond** is a promise by a borrower to pay back to the lender a specified amount of money, with interest, within a specified period of time. Private-placement bonds and asset-backed securitizations are two ways sport organizations finance operations through debt. Private-placement bonds have been used to finance the construction of the Wachovia Center, Rose Garden and TD Banknorth Garden (among many others). Here, all revenues from the arena are pledged to repay the amount of money borrowed from the bond holders plus interest. Asset-backed securitizations have been used to finance the construction of venues such as the Pepsi Center in Denver and Staples Center in Los Angeles. Using asset-backed securitizations, specific revenue streams are pledged to repay the bond holders. For both private-placement bonds and asset-backed securitizations, revenue used to repay the debt obligations typically comes from luxury seating sales, naming rights agreements, and the sale of personal seat licenses.

Equity

In contrast to debt financing, in **equity financing** a share or portion of ownership is exchanged for money. Funds for operations, therefore, can be obtained without incurring debt and without having to repay a specific amount of money at a given time. A drawback, however, is that ownership interest will be diluted and there could be a loss of control as additional investors are added. Stephen M. Ross used equity financing to raise capital after purchasing the Miami Dolphins in 2009. He sold minority interests in the team to several partners, including singers Marc Anthony and Gloria Estefan (Talalay, 2009). Few sport organizations issue stock, a common form of equity financing used outside the industry. One of the few, the Green Bay Packers, used $20.6 million of stock proceeds to help finance the renovation of Lambeau Field ("Lambeau Field," 2003).

Professional sport organizations typically do not sell stock to the public to raise equity capital. One reason for this is that little remains hidden when a company is publicly traded. To comply with Security and Exchange Commission (SEC) regulations, annual reports must be made detailing the accounting activities of the organization. Teams often claiming financial hardship while seeking a new publicly funded stadium may have difficulty convincing the municipality of the need if there is significant positive cash flow. Teams also have to answer to shareholders when issuing stock. Stockholder demands for profitability might be counter to winning on the field (i.e. not acquiring a player at the trading deadline because of a near-term financial loss resulting from the acquisition). Concern over public ownership in leagues is so great that since 1960 the NFL has banned public ownership of its teams (Kaplan, 1999).

The Green Bay Packers, however, are an exception to the private norm and the NFL rule. To keep the franchise from leaving Green Bay, Wisconsin, the team went public in 1923. Today, the Packers continue to be exempt from the NFL's prohibition on issuing shares, but the shares they have issued do not appreciate in value and are not traded on a stock exchange.

Despite the reluctance to use equity financing, teams in other leagues have raised significant amounts of capital when doing so. The Cleveland Indians raised $60 million through the team's Initial Public Offering (IPO). The Florida Panthers, Boston Celtics, Vancouver Canucks, and Colorado Avalanche all used equity financing at one time. Today, however, each team is privately held (Kaplan, 1999).

Retained Earnings

In addition to financing through debt and equity, organizations can finance operations or the acquisition of assets through the reinvestment of prior earnings. This reinvestment is a part of the firm's **retained earnings**. The reinvestment of retained earnings is considered a part of equity financing as money not reinvested will typically be sent to the shareholders of publicly traded firms as dividends. However, in sport, financing through the reinvestment of retained earnings should be examined separately from equity financing as the industry, with the exception of sporting goods manufacturers and retail stores, is mostly privately held. Although earnings can be distributed to team owners, in sport they are often used to finance the acquisition of players, improve operations, or make other investments.

The Green Bay Packers reinvest retained earnings to provide a competitive and successful football operation and to preserve the franchise and its traditions ("President's Annual Report," 2005). As the franchise is owned by its shareholders and not a single, wealthy individual, the organization is at a financial disadvantage when reacting to foreseen or unforeseen business challenges. A wealthy individual is able to use personal funds to infuse cash into a sport franchise. The Packers, to increase liquidity, stockpile their retained earnings.

Lambeau Field has been renovated multiple times with the increase of revenues from home games as the primary reason. These new and additional revenues have been used to increase the retained earnings to $232.4 million in 2009. Prior to the 32-month, $295 million redevelopment of the stadium, the Packers had a retained earnings balance of $97.8 million ("Balance sheets," 2010; "Hallowed ground," 2010). With the account balance up to $232.4 million in 2009, retained earnings has grown at an 11.4 percent annualized rate over the past eight years. Over that same period, the Dow Jones Industrial Average decreased 22.0 percent, and the S&P 500 decreased 34.0 percent.

Government

In the sport industry, it is common for private organizations, like professional sports teams, to receive funding from governmental sources. Further, public high schools and universities typically receive a portion of financing through direct or indirect government funding. For all sport organizations, **government financing** may include land use, tax abatements, direct stadium financing, state/municipal appropriations, and infrastructure improvements. Figure 12.7 provides examples of direct stadium financing.

Most stadium and arena projects funded by a governmental agency use either short-term or long-term debt because this debt places less of an immediate financial burden on taxpayers. Bonds are the traditional source of capital improvement revenue for governmental entities. In order to issue bonds, the municipality or district has to receive approval to borrow money from either the voters or the appropriate legislative entity. The process will vary depending on state and local laws in each jurisdiction. Once legal authority to issue bonds is given, the bonds are usually issued on the municipality's behalf by an underwriter—typically a national or regional investment bank.

One of two types of municipal bonds will typically be issued (Bynum, 2003). These will either be revenue bonds or general obligation bonds. Revenue bonds are secured by future revenues generated by the project being funded whereas general obligation bonds are secured by tax revenues and the issuing entity's ability to impose new taxes. General obligation bonds must get voter approval prior to their issue.

Stadia/Arena	Issuer	Funding Source(s)
Giants Stadium	New Jersey Sports & Exposition Authority	State appropriation
Camden Yards	Maryland Stadium Authority	State appropriation
Soldier Field	Illinois Sports Facility Authority	State appropriation
Comerica Park	Detroit/Wayne County Stadium Authority	Limited property tax, county tourism tax
Great American Ballpark	Hamilton County, Ohio	Subordinate sales tax revenue
FedEx Forum	Memphis & Shelby County Sports Authority	Car rental, hotel/motel taxes
Edward Jones Dome	Regional Convention & Sports Complex Authority	State appropriation
Raymond James Stadium	Tampa Sports Authority	Sales tax revenue
American Airlines Arena	Dallas Sports Arena Project	Hotel occupancy, car rental taxes
RBC Center	Centennial Authority	Hotel occupancy tax
Target Center	Minneapolis, MN	General obligation pledge

Source: Fitch Ratings (2002).

FIGURE 12.7

Select Tax-Backed Stadium/Arena Bond Issues

Gift

Gift financing includes charitable donations, either cash or in-kind, made to an organization and is a primary source of operating and investing income for major collegiate sports programs. It is also a supplemental source for minor college programs and non-profit sport organizations. According to Wolverton's 2009 report on fundraising in college athletics, National Collegiate Athletic Association (NCAA) Division I–Football Bowl Subdivision (FBS) schools received over $1.1 billion in cash gifts in 2008.

College athletic programs use revenue from gifts to offset the rising costs of collegiate sport, build or renovate facilities, and grow endowments (see Figure 12.8). Duke University, for example, has raised $13 million per year for athletic scholarships. Other institutions use gift financing to offset losses in institutional (government) financing resulting from state governments cutting funds to state colleges and universities. Most institutions are also seeking to grow their athletic department endowments. Duke University hopes to grow its endowment to $350 million. At one time, Stanford University's athletic endowment was over $500 million and generated $25 million annually for scholarships and additional program needs.

School	Total	NCAA Rank by Total	Gifts for Priority Seating	Gifts for Luxury Suites	Gifts for Facilities	Gifts for Endowments
Louisiana State	$30,435,296	10	$ 4,502,325	$11,854,265	$ 7,324,430	$2,170,736
Mississippi State	$14,029,862	40	$ 7,504,946	$ 3,463,810	$ 2,556,388	$ 496,700
Alabama	$27,900,000	15	$ 6,800,000	$ 8,200,000	$ 8,800,000	$1,200,000
Arkansas	$11,610,987	46	$0	$ 150,000	$ 200,000	$ 50,000
Florida	$45,600,000	2	$23,400,000	$11,600,000	$10,300,000	$ 100,000
Georgia	$36,068,068	5	$29,925,000	$ 3,260,000	$ 1,182,500	$4,494,206
Kentucky	$16,600,000	37	$10,900,000	$ 1,800,000	$ 4,800,000	$ 41,200
Mississippi	$13,462,889	42	NA	NA	NA	NA
South Carolina	$18,189,350	34	$ 1,827,425	$ 1,697,301	$ 1,974,011	$ 100,925
Tennessee	$38,385,450	3	$13,381,302	$ 6,030,168	$14,580,616	$2,478,959
Vanderbilt	$ 8,200,000	48	$ 2,870,000	NA	$ 1,700,000	$2,700,000

Source: Wolverton (2009)

FIGURE 12.8

2007–2008 Southeastern Conference Athletic Donations

Sources of Revenue

For most industries, financial management focuses solely on analysis of financial performance and the financing of company growth. In sport, there tends to be an added emphasis on revenue acquisition. As discussed throughout this text, there are many forms of revenue generated by sport organizations. Most spectator sport organizations derive the majority of their revenues either from ticket sales or broadcasting rights. Minor leagues and the National Hockey League (NHL) are highly dependent on ticket sales. NASCAR, the National Basketball Association (NBA), Major League Baseball (MLB) and the NFL are primarily dependent on broadcasting rights.

The NFL receives the highest percentage of revenues from its variety of national rights fees. On an annual basis, the league receives $4.0 billion per season from network, cable, and satellite operators (see Figure 12.9). The NBA receives a combined $930 million per year from ABC, ESPN, and TNT. Of the major professional leagues, the NHL receives a "paltry" $77.5 million as an upfront rights fee from Versus per season. As a comparison, the Southeastern Conference (SEC) receives $68.4 million annually from its television rights deals with ABC, ESPN, and CBS. For further discussion of other revenue streams, please see Chapters 8, 9, and 11.

	Network TV	Cable	Satellite/ Digital	Total
NBA				$ 930,000,000
MLB	$ 257,000,000	$ 396,000,000		$ 653,000,000
NASCAR	$ 490,000,000	$ 85,000,000		$ 575,000,000
NFL	$1,943,100,000	$1,100,000,000	$1,000,000,000	$4,043,100,000

Source: *Sports Business Resource Guide & Fact Book 2010*

FIGURE 12.9

Seasonal Media Rights Fees of Select Professional Leagues

Conclusion

The sport industry is large and diverse with many factors affecting financial management within the industry. Financial managers strive to maximize wealth while forecasting revenues and planning for expenses. They primarily rely on four financial documents to aid decision-making: budgets, income statements, balance sheets, and statements of cash flows. A budget provides an outline of where money will be spent and where revenue will be generated. The income statement measures flow, or the organization's expenditures and receipts between two periods of time, while the balance sheet measures the financial condition of the organization at a specific point in time.

A statement of cash flows measures cash moving into and out of an organization. For sport organizations, statements of cash flows provide the best picture of the organization's total financial health. Using GAAP, most team owners can use depreciation and amortization expenses to make the income statement look like the team is losing money while the team actually is increasing its cash position.

In addition to reading and interpreting financial statements, financial managers are concerned with the financing of the operation of sport organizations. Debt and equity financing are commonly used across all industries. Sport organizations also rely on retained earnings, government financing and gift financing. These forms of financing will be used to varying degrees based upon the subsector of the industry. Also, the ownership structure of a team and the structure of a league will impact financing decisions.

Finally, financial managers in sport often are tasked to focus on revenue generation. Common forms of revenue generated in sport include ticket sales revenues, revenues from the sale of television broadcasting rights, advertising revenues and sponsorship revenues.

Interview

INTERVIEW 12.1

Gina Rosser
Director, Business Operations
Duke University Athletic Department

Gina Rosser became the Director of Business operations at Duke University in March of 2008. In her role, she supervises daily operation of the business office while also working closely with the Associate Athletic Director of Business on budgetary issues within the department.

Rosser received her master's in business administration (2004) and master's in sport administration (2005) from Ohio University in Athens, Ohio. She worked in Ohio University's Athletic Ticket Office as a graduate assistant while pursuing her sport administration degree. As an undergraduate, Rosser attended High Point University and was a four-year member of the women's basketball team. She received degrees in business administration and sport management from High Point. While a student, Gina worked in various offices within High Point's Athletic Department.

Q: Can you briefly describe your career path?

A: Only after participating as a student-athlete at High Point did I realize that I could have a career in college athletics. During my time there I was able to work in various offices within the department such as Sports Informa-

tion, Marketing and Development. Those experiences led me to pursue a graduate degree in Sports Administration. While at Ohio University I was a graduate assistant in the Ticket Office which was a great learning experience. My objective up to that point was to get a taste of as many areas within college athletics to find my true interest and passion. After graduate school I was hired as the Assistant Business Manager at Duke University Athletics which seemed to be a perfect fit. In addition to my business office responsibilities, I also worked with Game Operations.

After two years at Duke I knew I wanted to concentrate on the business side of college athletics, but my opportunity to advance was limited. I accepted a position at Temple University to serve as their Athletic Business Manager. After six months at Temple my former boss at Duke unexpectedly left. I then returned to Duke as the Director of Business Operations. This move was good for me in that I got a promotion with a raise, but also it brought me back to my home state of North Carolina and to an athletic department with more prominence. I am currently still in the position and am content for the time being.

Q: What was one of the most valuable learning experiences you encountered during your career and how has that experience contributed to your success?

A: I am not sure if there was one specific instance, but overall it has been learning how to relate to people. I really think that intrapersonal skills and recognizing how best to get through to different personalities is important in any sport management job, even one focused upon finance.

Q: What do you see as the most important determinants of a successful financial/business manager? Why?

A: A strong understanding of the department's financial needs, as well as the flexibility of the university, are big factors in succeeding in this position. Maintaining good relationships with campus offices such as Accounts Payable, Procurement, HR, Payroll, and Employee Travel is also important. On the departmental level, it is imperative to be able to communicate effectively with coaches and staff so they can have a good understanding of what is expected of them in the budgeting process and the purchasing limitations they will encounter.

On a personal level, attention to detail, timeliness, and being able to prioritize effectively are essential factors in success. Being approachable and open to answering even the most mundane and repetitive questions definitely helps build trust among coaches and staff.

Q: How has the recent economic recession impacted business operations in college athletics?

A: Overall, the recession has significantly affected college athletics in revenue areas such as fundraising, sponsorship, and ticket sales. Endowment income has also been affected to some degree. Thing have been improving since late 2009, however.

Being a private school with a large endowment has enabled Duke to stay in a better financial position than a lot of other institutions, but as a department we are being held flat in terms of budget preparation for next year. At Duke we have implemented cost containment measures that have reduced unnecessary spending within the department. Coaches and staff are being asked to think about what they really need instead of what they want.

We are asking everyone to come in under budget this year as well as next. A lot of factors are out of our hands, which is why controlling expenses and cutting where possible are vital. For example, we are reevaluating and closely scrutinizing travel in terms of what away trips we take and the method of transportation. We have also moved our sponsorship sales to ISP, which guarantees the department a set amount of revenue each year while shifting the potential financial downside to their sales staff.

Q: What are the biggest financial challenges facing college athletics in the near future?

A: Lack of sponsorship revenue, decreasing annual gifts and major gifts, and the squeeze universities are placing on some departments (because of reduced endowment income) are big issues that we are facing now and will likely face in the near future. These factors will impact team schedules (travel costs), facility improvements, and the overall flexibility of department spending.

Q: In college athletics, what are the primary things looked for in new hires?

A: The primary things would be strong, reliable references, a master's degree, and work experience at a reputable institution. During the interview process good communication skills along with confidence is important. I also want to know that applicants have done homework about the position and institution. If the person will be working directly for me I want to know for sure that their personality will mesh well with mine and that they will be a good fit in our office.

Q: What is your advice to students considering a career in sport business operations and/or sport finance?

A: Prepare with a solid business education and once you get in the field, do everything you can to understand all aspects of finance within your department and university. You want to be able to understand your job completely, as well as what your boss does on a daily basis. Even if you cannot work on the "big picture" items immediately, having a good understanding of the planning and decision-making processes will be key as you advance in your career.

Study Questions

1. What must a sport manager due to be successful in his or her job? Why?
2. What is finance?
3. Of the three sectors of finance, why is financial management the most important sector for the sport industry?
4. What is wealth maximization and why is it an important concept to understand?
5. Of the four commonly used financial statements, which is most important to understand firms in the sport industry? Why?
6. T-accounts are commonly used to track revenues and expenses. What are debits and credits?
7. Either cash or accrual based accounting can be used according to GAAP. What is the difference between the two methods of accounting? Which is the preferred method of accounting? Why?
8. Debt and equity financing are often used in sport. Define debt financing and equity financing and discuss the differences between the two methods of financing an organization.
9. Why are retained earnings, gift, and governmental financing common methods of financing activities in the sport industry? Please provide examples of each method of financing when answering this question.
10. There are many sources of revenue in the sport industry. In professional sport, two are most prevalent. What are the two sources of revenue and how do they impact the financial operations of professional teams and leagues?

Learning Activities

You just purchased an Arena Football 2 team (af2), the Columbia Destroyers. The team is located in South Carolina and requires an infusion of capital. Your previous Chief Financial Officer (CFO) has just left your organization and unfortunately was not good at his job. The financials are a mess. You need to create last year's financial statements for the team's board of directors meeting. The information is not altogether good, but you know how to create financial statements for the club. The facts you do know regarding the financial operation of the club are as follows:

a. No balance sheet, income statement or ledger/T-accounts exist;

b. The club was purchased for $1 million and uses the accrual basis of accounting;

c. The club was capitalized as follows:
   - Borrowed $1,000,000 at 7% interest for seven years (PMT = $185,553; i = $70,000)
   - Investor provided $1,500,000 to fund the new venture

d. The team paid certain costs and expenditures in 2008:
   - Purchased
     —Equipment: $250,000
   - Cash Expenses
     —Player compensation: $195,000
     —Football operations: $459,700
     —Business operations: $497,000
     —Rent: $64,155

e. The team generated cash receipts in 2008 as follows:
   - Ticket sales: 40,000 fans at $16.25 per ticket
   - Concessions: 40,000 fans at $3.50 per fan
   - Parking: $50,000 per year

- Advertising/Sponsorship: $456,000
- Merchandise: 40,000 fans at $2.00 per fan

f. Depreciation:
- All short-term fixed assets depreciated over a 5 year life using the straight line method

g. Other information:
- The football team paid the City 10% for each ticket sold. This is an expense.
- The accounts receivable for ticket sales is $8,000
- The accounts payable for business operations is $100,000
- Don't forget the depreciation, amortization, and interest expenses
- Franchise value amortized over 15 year period
- Tax Rate: 40%

1. Based upon this information, create an income statement for the organization.
2. Based upon the information provided and the income statement completed for Learning Activity 1, create the organization's balance sheet.
3. After examining the income statement and balance sheet completed for the previous learning activities, analyze the financial performance of the club.
   a. How is the team performing currently?
   b. What must it do to improve its financial performance next year?

References

Balance sheets. (2010). *Lambeau locker room.* Retrieved January 25, 2010, from http://www.joe.bowman.net/Balance.htm

Bynum, M. (2003, August). Bonds. Municipal bonds. *Athletic Business,* 90–98.

Foster, G., Greyser, S.A., & Walsh, B. (2005). *The business of sports.* New York: South-Western College Publishers.

Hallowed ground. (2010). *Lambeaufield.com.* Retrieved January 25, 2010, from http://www.lambeaufield.com/stadium_info/history/

Kaplan, D. (1999, June 7). Going public makes company an open book. *SportsBusiness Journal.* Retrieved on September 14, 2005, from http://www.sportsbusinessjournal.com/article/16928

Kaplan, D. (2009, March 16). Yanks get new loan for ballpark. *SportsBusiness Journal.* Retrieved March 17, 2009, from http://www.sportsbusinessjournal.com/article/61849

Kreidler, M. (2009, July 24). State of uncertainty for women's sports. *ESPN.com.* Retrieved on July 24, 2009, from http://sports.espn.go.com/espn/pring?id=4352885&type=story

Lambeau Field. (2003, September 15). *SportsBusiness Journal.* Retrieved February 19, 2009, from http://www.sportsbusinessjournal.com/article/33243

Newport, J.P. (2009, February 28). No entertaining, please—It's golf. *The Wall Street Journal,* p. W4.

President's annual report: 2004–2005. (2005). Green Bay, WI: Green Bay Packers, Inc

Secretary of golf. (2009, February 25). *The Wall Street Journal,* p. A14.

Street & Smith's Sports Group. (2009). *Sports business resource guide & fact book 2010.* Charlotte, NC: American City Business Journals Inc.

Talalay, S. (2009, July 21). Marc Anthony buys stake in Miami Dolphins. *South Florida Sun-Sentinel.* Retrieved on July 21, 2009, from http://www.sun-sentinel.com/sports/miami-dolphins/sfl-marc-anthony-dolphins-s072009,0,3720783.story

Wolverton, B. (2009, January 23). For athletics, a billion dollar goal line. *The Chronicle of Higher Education,* pp. A1, A12–A13, A16.

Suggested Sources

Brown, M., Rascher, D., Nagel, M, & McEvoy, D. (2010). *Financial management in the sport industry.* Scottsdale, AZ: Holcomb Hathaway

Howard, D.R., & Crompton, J.L. (2003). *Financing sport* (2nd Ed.). Morgantown, WV: Fitness Information Technology.

International Journal of Sport Finance Blog (http://ijsf.wordpress.com/)

Lewis, M. (2004). *Moneyball: The art of winning an unfair game.* New York: WW Norton & Company.

Sports Biz with Darren Rovell (http://www.cnbc.com/id/15837629)

SportsBusiness Daily (http://www.sportsbusinessdaily.com/)

SportsBusiness Journal (http://www.sportsbusinessjournal.com/)

SportsMoney—Forbes.com (http://www.forbes.com/business/sportsmoney/)

Interviews

The best way to develop an understanding of the various segments of the sport industry is to read a variety of sources each week and to interact with as many industry professionals as possible. This chapter provides interviews with numerous sport management professionals from a wide variety of segments of the industry. Certainly, attempting to interview someone from every sport industry segment would be impossible, but this chapter is designed to not only cover executives from the most popular sports such as football and baseball, but to also expose the reader to the breadth that the sport industry offers. As you will see, there is not any one "right" career path. However, there are some commonalities you should note: Each interviewee stresses the importance of working hard and networking to launch and build a successful career. While this is not earth-shattering news, if everyone says the same thing, it might be good advice!

Hopefully, one day you will be interviewed for a sport-management textbook. If so, what advice will you offer to the next generation of sport managers?

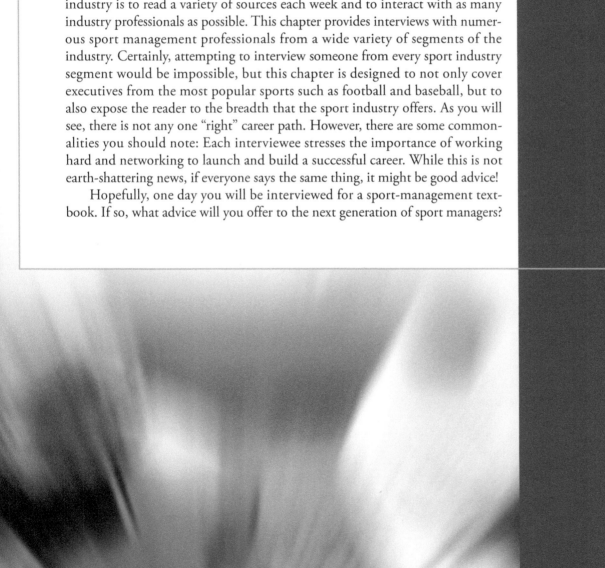

INTERVIEW 13.1

Bruce Popko
Senior Vice President of Business Development
Buffalo Bills—National Football League

Q: Could you briefly describe your career path from undergraduate student to your current position?

A: I was an undergraduate at the University of Pennsylvania but had worked summers for the New York Jets starting at the age of 15. I was hired full time by the Jets after graduation. I then went to NFL Headquarters for three years to work on the launch of NFL Sunday Ticket and then later I worked on the NFL's retail marketing. I was then recruited to the 49ers from the NFL office and spent three years with the team; I then moved to Cleveland and spent seven years with the Browns, handling all revenue generating functions. I spent four years at IMG heading sales for the golf division. I just started with the Bills in May, 2009 and I handle all business development activities.

Q: What have been the biggest challenges you have encountered during your career?

A: The biggest challenges are definitely on the people side of the business—managing a staff, keeping them motivated when the team is not playing their best, and trying to get maximum yield out of (normally) an understaffed situation.

Q: What are some of the biggest issues facing the Bills and the NFL?

A: I think the dynamic of premium seating/hospitality will continue to change. Most teams/stadiums have their seating configured with too many premium seats that are out of the price range of the consumer. The market will go through a natural self-correction, but it will take some time to get demand/supply intersecting in the right spot once again.

Q: Are there specific skills sport-management students should look to develop while still in school?

A: Managing people is a critical skill for success in the sport business. For the sales side, negotiating skills are also a premium.

Q: What specific classes would you recommend students take to best position themselves for a sport-industry job?

A: Sales management, psychology, accounting, and international business.
　　Developing language skills, whether through specific coursework or through other opportunities, will grow in importance in the future (specifically for Spanish and Chinese).

Q: What publications do you regularly read to stay apprised of sport-business events?

A: *SportsBusiness Journal, Brandweek, Ad Age, BusinessWeek* and *The Wall Street Journal*

Q: Would you recommend students pursue graduate school? If so, when should they pursue a graduate degree and what area of study would you recommend?

A: It is "great to have," but not absolutely necessary. A graduate degree certainly helps justify a potential wage scale, but it is not a prerequisite to get hired.

Q: Is there any additional advice or insights you would provide to students pursuing a future career in sport management?

A: I am not a firm believer in the "take any job to get your foot in the door" mentality. I think you can, more times than not, end up in a situation that is not to your liking and/or takes you down a path that is tough to change. Instead, spend considerable time researching opportunities for what you really want to do and then fight with everything you have in you to pursue those potential opportunities in those areas of interest.

INTERVIEW 13.2

Bob Sivik
Director of Inside and Organizational Sales
Cleveland Cavaliers—National Basketball Association

Q: Could you briefly describe your career path from undergraduate student to your current position?

A: I started at Youngstown State University in 1997. After a great career as a student-athlete, I was fortunate to start a career in the sport industry as an Account Executive with the Cleveland Cavaliers. Within eight months, I was promoted to a Sales Consultant. I spent two years selling and servicing accounts until I was promoted to Manager of Inside Sales. I later became Manager of Business Development and then Director of Business Development. I am now the Director of Inside and Organizational Sales for the Cavaliers.

Q: You have spent your sport management career with the Cavaliers. This is unusual for many professionals in sport management. Could you discuss why you have not moved to other organizations since you graduated from Youngstown State?

A: Throughout my career, the Cavaliers have been great to me. From the wonderful teammates to the outstanding ownership, this has been a great home to grow and build long-lasting relationships. There have been opportunities at other organizations in the past few years that might have advanced my career a little faster, but I am not a "title" guy. I like to feel challenged and develop my abilities. The Cleveland Cavaliers have been able to present enough challenges since I arrived here and it is an enjoyable work environment. I have seen some people advance faster by moving and I have also seen some make too many moves. My best advice is to make sure you are surrounded by good people that help challenge you; then you will have a great career and will have a support system in place to help when the tough decisions about potentially moving arise.

Q: What are the biggest challenges you face in your work with the Cavaliers?

A: In general, my biggest challenges are always trying to find a better way to operate. Sometimes it is an obsession, but it will always keep our team motivated to be the best it can be.

We have to make sure we manage success with the Cavs on the floor to ensure our team members are still receiving top-notch training and leadership.

We have been working to create the best fan-development program in professional sports. As most know, the Cavaliers have experienced success over the past few years and we would like to continue to grow our fan base. As part of this development, we are rapidly integrating new technology to make our fans have a more enjoyable experience.

Q: Are there specific job skills sport-management students should look to develop while still in school?

A: Being in sales, I would always recommend learning the art of sales. This is a tool that can be transferable for any position you would take in sports. However, I would not recommend starting in sales unless that is your likely career path.

Q: What specific classes would you recommend students take to best position themselves for a sport-industry job?

A: I would strongly recommend Marketing, Sales, Economics, or other "business" classes. Professional sport may be a fun and entertaining product to consume, but it is still a business.

Q: What publications do you regularly read to stay apprised of sport-business events?

A: *SportsBusiness Journal*

Q: Would you recommend students pursue graduate school? If so, when should they pursue a graduate degree and what area of study would you recommend (e.g., MBA, M.S.–Sport Management, other)?

A: I recommend any chance to learn and to pursue higher education. Education will definitely help throughout your career. Just make sure you are still prepared to take an entry-level position upon graduation.

In addition to formal education, I would recommend studying the career histories of people in your ideal future position. The road you start on will help direct your career path.

Q: What trends are emerging in sport management?

A: Sport teams are looking for more information about industry and team trends, so analytics are becoming more important. Also, servicing current tickets holders has been growing in importance throughout the industry. The ability to sell will remain critically important for individuals and organizations.

INTERVIEW 13.3

Mike Nutter
President
Fort Wayne TinCaps Baseball

Q: Could you briefly describe your career path from undergraduate student to your current position?

A: I graduated from Bowling Green State University in 1995. By graduation I had four summers' worth of experience with the Kane County Cougars where I learned many aspects of the operation from one of the most successful minor-league franchises in the United States. After graduation, I went to work for the Brevard County Manatees for an internship that turned into full-time employment. We had a successful season in 1996 in Brevard County by hosting Florida Marlins Spring Training games as well as the Florida State League's Brevard County Manatees. We also hosted the 1996 Florida State League All Star Game. Following my experience in Brevard County, I went to work for the Nashville Sounds (AAA) in 1997. This was a tremendous experience. In Nashville I was a corporate sales representative and Director of Baseball Operations. Following the 1999 season, I relocated to Fort Wayne, IN where I was the Assistant GM during the 2000 season. Following the 2000 campaign, I was named general manager of the Fort Wayne Wizards. I have been the General Manager, and now Team President, for Fort Wayne Professional Baseball for the past nine seasons. Entering the 2009 season, we moved into one of the best minor-league stadiums in the country (Parkview Field). At the same time, we changed our name from the Wizards to TinCaps (honoring local resident Johnny "Appleseed" Chapman). The 2009 campaign was one of the most successful any team in the minor leagues has ever had at any level. We finished the season with the most wins in the minor leagues, and attracted over 400,000 fans during the season.

Q: What have been the biggest challenges you have encountered in minor league baseball?

A: I have been truly blessed to be surrounded by some of the best people in the country during my tenures with teams. In Kane County, I had the chance to learn while working alongside five future general managers. In Brevard County, I worked with some people who made an impact not only in minor league baseball, but in other aspects of the sport industry. In Fort Wayne, I have been fortunate to work with some of the best young minds in minor league sports. That being said, there are challenges. The economy is always a concern and the economic downturn that began in 2008 has been a major challenge for the industry. Minor League Baseball has an affordable product for families, but the economy can and will impact fans' spending regardless of the price. We certainly try to position ourselves with affordable tickets, great concessions offerings, and a tremendous night of entertainment in one of the best venues in the country, to off-set the issues with the economy. One of the changes I have seen in my 18-plus seasons in baseball is that there is not as much staff turnover from year to year. In the past it seemed as if the business fostered an environment where one had to often move from team to team for promotions. With teams' business operations beginning to dramatically improve, and franchise values continuing to increase, I believe owners and general managers can pay their people better and retain high-performing employees. It is certainly better to be able to develop and pay great people what they are worth, rather than to have to replace and retrain staff members every couple of years. Though staff turnover is still a potential issue, many in the industry have recognized this inefficiency, and worked to change the "move often" mentality.

Q: Can you discuss what you consider the most pressing issues facing minor league baseball and the overall sport industry?

A: The current economic times will dictate success levels for many teams in professional sports. In Minor League Baseball, we are less impacted by the economy, since we have one of the most family-friendly affordable sport products. Fans are able to see future major league talent in over 150 cities across the country for as little as a few dollars. This affordability, combined with promotions, giveaways, and other in-venue entertainment, should keep minor league baseball flourishing in tough economic times.

Another hot topic that many are focusing on is the use of "social media." Facebook, Twitter, et cetera, have become an incredible opportunity to reach segments of our market in a hip, fun, and cost-effective manner. I truly believe over the coming seasons, if they have not already, many teams will hire full-time staff members whose sole job will be to coordinate social media.

Though we are a "baseball" franchise, we focus a lot of time and energy in finding alternative uses for Parkview Field. Having one of the top facilities in the country enables us to be an ideal venue for baseball, but also allows us to host over 150 additional events per season including: concerts (national and regional acts), weddings and wedding receptions, trade shows, charity fundraisers, et cetera. I believe it will continue to be vital for sport franchises to recognize their role in attracting and promoting non-sport or team-specific events. In 2010, Parkview Field will host an Indiana University versus Notre Dame University soccer game, the Midwest League All- Star Game, a Gus Macker Basketball Tournament, several weddings and receptions, class reunions, and numerous other events, many of which have no direct ties to baseball.

Q: Are there specific job skills sport-management students should look to develop while still in school?

A: Sales! The majority of minor league baseball teams have a sales component for front-office employees. I have been with teams where everyone in the front office sold. I think sport-management students should focus on taking sales classes and getting some "real world" sales experience. Additionally, there is a tremendous demand for employment in minor league sports so I encourage students to get internships/summer jobs/experience in your field PRIOR to graduation. In many instances, one can make more money working outside of minor league sports internships, but the experience one receives by working in minor league sports is invaluable and is readily transferable to any other aspect of the sport industry. Regardless of future goals, students should spend considerable time working in the industry prior to graduation so that they have experiences that distinguish themselves from other potential applicants.

Q: What specific classes would you recommend students take to best position themselves for a sport-industry job?

A: Sales courses are a great opportunity to learn the basics of the sales process and to get experience. Sales are vital in most organizations, and the more one understands the process and embraces the opportunity, the greater the chance for career success. I think that along with sales, general marketing classes and communications classes are beneficial as well. Many days are spent with our staff members out in the region speaking with clients and other groups, so the more public speaking experience one has the better they will be able to work in the industry.

Q: What publications do you regularly read to stay apprised of sport-business events?

A: *Baseball America* is a must-read each month. There is a tremendous amount of information involving on-field transactions in minor league baseball as well as coverage of industry trends. *The SportsBusiness Journal* is read regularly by our staff. It provides a good national perspective on the sport industry. *The Migala Report* is one of my favorite periodicals. Dan Migala has a great report and website that can help many keep up with the trends in our industry. *Team Marketing Report* continues to be a good resource for our industry and they are always looking to promote great partnerships, promotions, et cetera, that teams around the country are using.

Q: Would you recommend students pursue graduate school? If so, when should they pursue a graduate degree and what area of study would you recommend?

A: I believe it depends on the students' long-term goals. First off, I believe it would be beneficial for students to have an MBA or M.S.-Sport Management degree. The question is what are they doing and is it needed for their specific role within the organization? We have hired many students with graduate degrees in the past and I would say that they were all extremely successful with us and within our industry. In some cases, the person is being hired for an entry-level position and they can feel like the graduate degree places them above that sort of position, but in our case, it does not. I can only speak on minor league baseball and I would say it would be great to have, but not required. I believe there are many instances in other fields that it would not only be encouraged, but would be required. The majority of our employees that we have hired over the years have had the M.S.-Sport Management and not an MBA. We have also tried to encourage employees over the years to continue their education while a member of our staff. We have one current employee studying for his MBA and another member of management back at school now taking accounting classes. We allow employees to miss some work time and events to allow them to continue to develop and learn, and to hopefully make us a better organization.

Q: Is there a certain sport-business area you see emerging in importance in the near future?

A: I believe social media will continue to be an emerging part of our industry. Much like e-mail 15 years ago, teams on the front line of social media will continue to distinguish themselves from other franchises while being more effective in their marketing and business practices than teams that do not embrace the new trends. The reality is that many folks running teams may not be as capable or knowledgeable regarding social media as some of the students in college today. That could be a great niche for future job opportunities and growth in sport management in the near future.

I believe that marketing in minor league baseball will continue to grow on the national level. There is no greater value, and in minor league baseball we have a franchise in most of the largest 175 metropolitan markets in the country. For example, I believe that companies will soon consider advertising in 150 minor league baseball stadiums for the same price as purchasing a 30-second Super Bowl advertisement. The Super Bowl will always be where the money is in terms of advertising, as nobody can compete with the exposure, but I honestly believe that some companies will continue to look at the realized benefits in the tougher economic climate and realize they can do signage and other elements with every team in the country and get a season-long presence for the same price as 30 seconds during the Super Bowl. The reality is that Super Bowl advertisements are impactful and continue to sell out every year, so Super Bowl broadcasters are not going to be hurting for clients, but some established clients will consider season-long opportunities with minor league baseball and other professional leagues.

Sports have always been extremely popular in our society, and I believe that will continue to be the case. I believe that the value of the product (ticket, experience, exposure, etc.) will continue to hold a lot of weight—perhaps much more during these economic times—than ever before. Many options are extremely difficult for a family to afford, but minor league baseball is usually an exception.

Q: Is there any additional advice or insights you would provide to students pursuing a future career in sport management?

A: Stick with it! There is a great demand to get into this field and it can sometimes be difficult to make the kind of money one could make in other industries right out of college. I have found that students who want to get into sport management who have done their work in terms of sales training, internships, or experience prior to and immediately following graduation, the sky is the limit. It might be a couple of years right out of school making less money than your friends or what you expected, but over time you can make a great income and have a tremendous career in this awesome field. Sports are an incredible part of our society and sport management is a great field to be a part of, but it is hard work—just like any job. If you invest in yourself with attending a great school and get experience along the way, you can be extremely successful in sport management.

INTERVIEW 13.4

Chrissy Baines
Director of Box Office and Retail Operations
Albuquerque Isotopes

Q: Could you briefly describe your career path from undergraduate student to your current position?

A: While pursuing my undergraduate degree in Sport Management at the University of West Georgia, I completed my practicum with West Georgia Sports Marketing. I was able to conduct market research, which provided me much-needed knowledge and experience in the different areas of the business of sport. After graduating, I completed an internship with the Savannah Sand Gnats, a Single-A Minor League Baseball Team, and was then hired full-time as the Director of Merchandise. After working for the Sand Gnats for two years, I was then

hired by the Albuquerque Isotopes, a Triple-A Team in the Pacific Coast League, for a similar position. I have been with the Isotopes for six seasons and currently oversee the Box Office and Retail Operations.

Q: What important skills are needed to work in merchandising?

A: Merchandising involves identifying new trends in products, setting prices, and keeping appraised of licensing guidelines. While other aspects of a sport organization can sometimes be regimented, directing a merchandise operation requires a tremendous amount of creativity. Developing new designs, adjusting logo colors to match garment patterns, or developing store displays requires an ability to visualize and create the future. Since sales can be easily tracked on a daily, weekly, monthly, and seasonal basis, merchandising also involves conducting research to predict what will sell and then analyzing what has been selling, so that adjustments can be made.

Q: Are there specific job skills sport management students should look to develop before they graduate?

A: Communication skills are critical. Students should become well versed in professional etiquette. Understanding how to interact and communicate with customers, co-workers, and the public is crucial to being a successful leader in any industry, but particularly in sports where everything we do is noted by the public.

Q: What specific classes would you recommend students take to best position themselves for a sport-industry job?

A: Any type of sport marketing or business management class is always helpful. Internet-based classes (web design, Internet marketing, etc.) should augment a strong understanding of basic computer programs (Microsoft Office) as well as graphic design programs (Photoshop). An event management class where the students plan and implement an event is particularly helpful as event management requires the use of every class in the sport management curriculum.

Q: What publications do you regularly read to stay apprised of sport-business events?

A: I read the *SportsBusiness Journal* regularly for information about the industry. I am also a news junkie, so I am always reading online at cnn.com and foxnews.com. I also make sure to read my daily local paper to stay appraised of current events in Albuquerque.

Q: Is there a certain sport-business area you see emerging in importance in the near future?

A: Using different social media outlets to market sports will be incredibly important over the next few years. Learning how to market your business or sport through Facebook, Twitter, online blogs, et cetera, is already important but it will likely continue to expand its influence.

Q: Is there any additional advice or insights you would provide to students pursuing a future career in sport management?

A: The industry is competitive, so prepare yourself for what you want to do after graduation. While in school, volunteer or try to obtain a part-time job within the field. Job experience, as well as a strong academic background, are essential to achieve success.

INTERVIEW 13.5

Ricky Lefft

Sports Attorney

Principal, Lefft Law Group
Lecturer, University of South Carolina

Q: Could you describe how you became an agent?

A: I graduated from high school in 1977 from Orangeburg-Wilkinson High School in Orangeburg, South Carolina. I spent my high school years in Orangeburg, which is the home of South Carolina State University, then known as SC State College. My parents were both double alumni of South Carolina State and throughout my life they told me stories about the extraordinary experience they had enjoyed at the College while matriculating there. I was fortunate that when we arrived in Orangeburg the College's music and performing arts programs were amongst the best in the country. Additionally, the SC State Football Program was on the rise under Coach Willie Jeffries' leadership; and a number of professional athletes such as Barney Chavous, Donnie Shell, and Harry Carson played on those teams. I played basketball until my sophomore year and marched for the high school band for three years. I also played in a local band that performed in night clubs during my high school years. As a result of my experiences, I developed a passion for sport and entertainment. When I entered the University of South Carolina as a freshman I knew that I wanted to eventually attend law school and to specialize in the representation of entertainers and professional athletes.

While in law school, I took courses such as labor law, intellectual property, business corporations, and mass communications and media law as a part of my preparation to practice sport and entertainment law. Under the tutelage of two of my law professors, I wrote twelve hours of independent-study papers covering specific research topics germane to these areas of practice.

Prior to entering law school, I was commissioned as a United States Air Force Officer and received a deferment to attend law school. I opted for a career path in systems procurement at Wright Patterson Air Force Base in Dayton, Ohio, as an Officer in Aeronautical Systems Division, which was the largest military procurement organization in the world. During my four-year tenure in the Air Force, I was able to negotiate approximately one billion dollars of contracts for research and development projects and for the purchase of weapon systems such as the F-15E Aircraft system and the Advanced Tactical Fighter, now known as the Stealth fighter. My experience allowed me to interface and interact with executives at the highest levels within companies such as McDonald Douglas Aircraft Company, Raytheon, Northrop, and General Electric. Additionally, I was responsible for overseeing a team of approximately seven other negotiators my last couple of years, and approved and signed approximately another four hundred million dollars in contracts.

After I completed my military commitment, I relocated to Northern Virginia where I accepted a position with a startup company as Vice President and General Counsel. I was responsible for negotiating lease agreements and employment contracts with the executives and other professionals who were hired by the company to lead the new enterprise. I was actively involved in, and led efforts to draft, both the business and strategic plans. I was also responsible for interfacing with potential vendors and venture capital firms.

I then returned to South Carolina to accept a position as Special Counsel with the law firm of Nexsen, Pruet, Jacobs, & Pollard. My initial areas of practice were workman's compensation defense and premise liability defense. I represented companies such as UPS, Food Lion, Shoney's, and B.F. Goodrich. I was subsequently moved to the business division where I represented financial institutions such as NationsBank, First Union Bank, Wachovia Bank, Carolina Capital Investment Corporation, and the Jobs Economic Development Authority (JEDA), where I was responsible for closing commercial transactions and real estate deals. Additionally, I represented a number of privately held companies as outside counsel.

In 1992, I formed the firm's Sport Law practice to represent professional athletes and college coaches. Tubby

Smith was my first college coaching client and Tyrone Legette was my first NFL player client. After building the firm's practice, I founded Synergy Sports International with two other principals in 1997. At our peak we represented approximately 40 professional athletes in football and baseball. In 2003, I sold the firm and joined the University of South Carolina as a faculty member in the Department of Sport and Entertainment Management. I also maintain a separate law practice in which I represent my coaching clients who were not part of the sale.

Q: What have been the biggest challenges you have encountered during your career as an agent?

A: The biggest initial challenges were finding an entry into the business, recruiting quality clients, financing the business to keep it competitive, and retaining the clients once they were signed to contracts. Entry into the marketplace is a major challenge, because agents by nature are not trusting people. The marketplace is very competitive and over-saturated. Agents typically are not willing to train younger agents, because they are fearful that the younger agent will steal their clients. Most financial institutions do not understand the sport agency business and are not willing to finance such companies.

Q: Can you identify what you consider to be the "hot topics or issues" in sport?

A: Despite large revenues in professional football, there is a major fight brewing between the Union and the League. The owners are hoping to turn back some of the gains that the players made during the Gene Upshaw years. The recent transition of leadership in the NFL Players Association may be the worst possible scenario for the players because of the loss of continuity and corporate knowledge.

In college basketball, the emergence of AAU as a major power in men's and women's basketball has corrupted the entire system.

Q: Are there specific classes sport management students should take to develop necessary job skills while still in school?

A: If the sport management program has a business-oriented curriculum, most of the main areas should be covered. However, developing research and writing skills is critically important to future success. Pursuing an MBA is certainly important for long-term success, especially since an MBA should develop marketing and research skills. Law school can hone legal analysis skills. For undergraduates, courses in the following areas can help anyone wishing to become an agent or a member of an executive management team:

a. Legal Training
b. Business and strategic planning skills
c. Contract Negotiation skills
d. Sales and marketing
e. Critical thinking and analysis

Q: What publications do you regularly read to stay apprised of sport-business events?

A: *SportsBusiness Journal,* various news publications, *Sports Lawyers Journal, Marquette Law Review,* various NCAA publications, and biographies of personalities in the industry. Knowledge of current events is critical to achieving ongoing success in this area of the sport industry.

Q: Would you recommend students pursue graduate school? If so, when should they pursue a graduate degree, and what area of study would you recommend?

A: I would strongly recommend that students who are interested in sport representation pursue a joint degree program with a Juris Doctorate and MBA.

Q: What changes are currently occurring in the sport agent industry?

A: Search firms have certainly changed the dynamics in the coaches' representation industry. Hiring a coach at a Division I institution has changed from what it was even 10 years ago. There is a need for coaches to have agents who can represent their interests while navigating a more complex search process.

Q: Is there any additional advice or insights you would provide to students pursuing a future career in sport management?

A: Get more experience in the industry from an institutional standpoint. I suggest that they try to find positions working for a sport franchise and/or a league before seeking to represent players.

INTERVIEW 13.6

Charles Waddell
Associate Athletic Director
University of South Carolina Athletics

Q: Could you briefly describe your career path from undergraduate student to associate athletic director?

A: After a four year NFL career I returned to UNC-Chapel Hill in 1978 and took an entry-level job with the Athletic Department as an Assistant Academic Advisor and Strength Coach. I worked there for three years prior to returning to school to pursue an MBA. I then spent seven years with NCNB (currently Bank of America) as an investment banker before joining the Big Ten Conference as an Assistant Commissioner in 1990. I then joined the Carolina Panthers in 1994 and spent nine years with the franchise before going to Fayetteville State University as a Vice Chancellor for Advancement for two years. In 2006 I came to the University of South Carolina as an Associate Athletic Director, which is the position I currently hold.

Q: What have been the biggest challenges you have encountered during your career?

A: My biggest challenge was maintaining some consistency with the direction of my career path. I have been fortunate to be able to access different sectors of the sport industry, but the lack of consistency has resulted in not being able to achieve some of my career goals as quickly as I had hoped.

Q: What are the biggest issues facing sport managers today?

A: The most pressing issue is how the unstable economy is affecting various aspects of the sport industry. The economy has caused major adjustments to be made by administrators throughout the industry, from local recreation departments to professional leagues.

Q: Are there specific job skills sport-management students should look to develop while still in school?

A: Get used to working long hours and being able to multi-task.

Q: What specific classes would you recommend students take to best position themselves for a sport-industry job?

A: I would recommend a case-study class, a business-of-sport class, and marketing.

Q: What publications do you regularly read to stay apprised of sport-business events?

A: The *SportsBusiness Journal*

Q: Would you recommend students pursue graduate school? If so, when should they pursue a graduate degree and what area of study would you recommend?

A: In an industry that is hyper-competitive, it is always good to have skills that separate one from the pack. Having an advanced degree can help do that. However, I believe if you have a good job that provides good experiences and opportunity for professional growth, it may not be necessary to go back to get a graduate degree.

Q: Is there a certain sport-business area you see emerging in importance in the near future?

A: The fund-raising sector of college athletics is growing rapidly. Facility improvements are critical to an institution's overall success, and the revenue streams from other sources (gate receipts, rights fees from media, etc.) are not growing at the same rate as in the past. Therefore, fund-raising efforts are even more important than they once were.

Q: Is there any additional advice or insights you would provide to students pursuing a future career in sport management?

A: Be patient and persistent.

INTERVIEW 13.7

Leland Barrow
Assistant Sports Communications Director
University of Georgia Athletics

Q: Could you briefly describe your career path from undergraduate student to your current position?

A: I received my undergraduate degree in Journalism, with a focus on newspapers, from the University of Georgia. With full intentions of becoming a legendary sports writer, I took a sports reporter position with a small newspaper in middle Georgia within a month of graduation. I wrote a WIDE variety of stories at the newspaper for two years (and mostly had a great time doing it) until deciding I would be more marketable and have a bigger variety of jobs to choose from if I earned a Master's Degree in Sport Management. I was accepted into Georgia State University's program and completed my degree. I was then offered an internship in the University of Georgia's Sports Communications Department and after a year, I was hired to fill an open position.

Q: What have been the biggest challenges you have encountered during your career?

A: College athletics presents a variety of challenges and most of them I have been able to figure out or overcome by being able to communicate well with other people. The ability to write and speak well is invaluable, especially when much of my job involves multitasking in a high-pressure environment. In sports communications, you have to love, and I mean love, what you do. The time-intensive nature of our jobs sometimes runs head-on with the time you want to spend with your family and free time for yourself. I feel like I get better and better dealing with time management each year, but it helps to have an understanding boss who realizes that there has to be some balance to prevent burnout. In sports, the paycheck can also be a challenge, since most weeks, especially during a team's season, will require 60+ hours of work. Though there is no such thing as "overtime" in this job, it is something that I thoroughly enjoy and I

know that being happy and excited about my job each day outweighs the negatives.

Q: Can you identify what you consider to be the "hot topics or issues" in sport, either directly related to your functional area or the sport industry in general?

A: One hot topic is how to deal with the "here today, gone tomorrow" Internet sites that function mainly as opinionated bloggers rather than as members of the media who conduct thorough analyses for their stories. In sport communications, it is always difficult to make the final determination about the relationship and potential access these groups should have and with the proliferation of Internet sites, the line is becoming more and more blurred each year.

In college sports there will continue to be more issues with how big and powerful conferences and television networks can be—especially with individual institutions trying to maintain some autonomy. Over the next 10 years, the influence of conferences and media outlets will be interesting to observe.

Q: Are there specific job skills sport-management students should look to develop while still in school?

A: While in school I continually tried to develop my communication skills, particularly my ability to write. A good writer cannot be easily replaced, and communication skills make working in ANY office situation much easier. Networking has also been instrumental to my career—establishing, maintaining and expanding your network is paramount. Learning to recognize and understand different jobs and problems within your organization is an important skill, as that enables you to better understand the challenges your co-workers and the overall organization are facing.

Q: What specific classes would you recommend students take to best position themselves for a sport-industry job?

A: Media relations, networking, facility management and sport sociology are all important, no matter which direction someone goes with his or her degree. Although I had to work especially hard in the finance classes since I avoided any and all while pursuing my journalism undergraduate degree, the finance courses are critical and I wish I could retain more of what I learned in graduate school. Those are beneficial in the office and in my personal life.

Q: What publications do you regularly read to stay apprised of sport-business events?

A: I read the local Athens paper, the *Atlanta Journal-Constitution* and the daily publication by the *Sporting News* almost every day. I also try to keep my *Sports Illustrated* magazines from piling up and I read the *Sports Business Daily* as much as I can. I wish I had time to read more, but working in sports communications and having a family does not leave much time for extensive reading.

Q: Would you recommend students pursue graduate school? If so, when should they pursue a graduate degree and what area of study would you recommend?

A: I enjoyed taking a two-year break from my undergraduate degree before starting my master's program. I thought it was key to have a glimpse at every puzzle piece there is in the sport business industry, which is why I would definitely go through graduate school again. Working a variety of internships never hurts, since each provides an opportunity give a thumbs-up or thumbs-down to a career path before beginning full-time. For sports communications, my graduate degree was not a necessity, but it did give me something else on my resume. More importantly, the curriculum broadened my horizons in other sport-related fields in case I decide to go a different direction in my career at some point.

INTERVIEW 13.8

Damon Dukakis
General Manager
ISP Sports
University of California–Berkeley

Q: Could you briefly describe your career path from undergraduate student to your current position?

A: Right out of college, I took a job coaching football at Allan Hancock College. It paid nothing, but they helped me to make a few dollars by proctoring study halls and selling advertisements in the football program. I also helped in the Sports Information Department, which also paid nothing. I worked at a fitness club as well to support myself financially. My second year, I sold signage in addition to advertisements in the program.

After two years, one of the local high school athletic directors left his position and he suggested I apply to replace him. I was only 24 years old, but I applied. I had worked as an assistant to the Athletic Director at one of the other local high schools as an undergraduate student, so I knew a lot about the job and the people in the area. I got the job (which also involved teaching classes) and stayed for two years. I enjoyed the experience, but the over-involvement of parents at this private high school, [a] challenging principal, and low pay led to my decision to move away from high school athletics.

I moved to Sacramento and applied for a position as Marketing Director for Athletics at Sacramento State. There was a huge applicant pool of 75 people, but I was fortunate to possess the skills and experience to get the job. Apparently, selling advertisements and signs at a junior college had more in common with the Sacramento State job than the experience many others had at other institutions. I stayed for three years and then went to fellow Big Sky Conference member Portland State as Associate Athletic Director for External Affairs.

After only a year and a half at Portland State, I was contacted by my old boss from Sacramento State, who had since moved to the University of California–Berkeley. He asked if I was interested in coming back to Northern California and with ISP, the Golden Bears' media rights holder. After much deliberation, and learning that my Athletic Director at Portland State had just accepted a job at his Alma Mater, the University of Wyoming, I decided to head to Berkeley. I have been at Cal for four years and am now the General Manager.

Q: What have been the biggest challenges you have encountered during your career?

A: All of my positions (except high school Athletic Director) have involved generating revenue from the corporate community. The financial challenges at Allan Hancock College, Portland State and Cal are similar—you never have enough revenue. You need to convince people to spend their business' dollars in your athletic department. Although Cal draws over 60,000 attendees per football game and Allan Hancock drew "only" 2,500, it is still just as challenging to prospect, make cold calls, set meetings, present proposals, and try to close sales at the larger school as it is at the smaller one.

Q: Can you identify what you consider to be the main issues facing college athletics and third-party rights holders?

A: With the amount of money changing hands in college sports there are many critics who question the "amateur" status of college athletics. How long will it be before

college athletes claim to be entitled to a share of the revenue (above and beyond their tuition, room and board, and books) that is generated from their performance? This is an important question that underlies everything we do.

Q: Are there specific job skills sport-management students should look to develop while still in school?

A: Ironically, the only sport management-specific class I ever took was Mark Nagel's administration class at Saint Mary's College. Within that class I learned some of the basics of sport marketing. With only one academic class, I did not learn as much as many within my field who have gone through sport-management undergraduate and graduate programs. It certainly would have helped to have a "stronger" academic sport-management background, but this industry is much more about experience and networking than taking specific academic courses before graduation. The most important skill to develop is a strong knowledge of how all the pieces of an organization fit together and affect one another. Knowledge gained through on-the-job training is critical to future success.

Q: What publications do you regularly read to stay apprised of sport-business events?

A: *SportBusiness Journal*

Q: Would you recommend students pursue graduate school? If so, when should they pursue a graduate degree and what area of study would you recommend?

A: I know a lot of people that did not go through a graduate program who are doing fine in the sport management industry. Pursuing an MBA certainly cannot hurt, as the knowledge and information you learn within an MBA program can do nothing but make an individual stronger (as a candidate and in real-world performance). It is certainly important to have a degree on your resume, but it is even more important to be "educated" about the industry you wish to pursue and to have a strong work ethic.

Q: Is there a certain sport-business area you see emerging in importance in the near future?

New technology and media have become critical and they will only grow in importance in the future. More and more content is going to be available online, and a shift away from traditional TV, cable TV, and satellite will continue to occur. The financial model associated with events, both large and small, will greatly evolve over the next 5–10 years due to new technology.

Q: Is there any additional advice or insights you would provide to students pursuing a future career in sport management?

A: Revenue is the backbone of our industry. The proven ability to generate revenue will open a lot of doors. Whether through ticket or suite sales, sponsorship sales, signing rights, and broadcast contracts, bringing in private donations through annual gifts or major gifts, "rain makers" in the industry will always be marketable for advancement.

INTERVIEW 13.9

Heather Ould
Manager, Client Services
NACDA Consulting

Q: Could you briefly describe your career path from undergraduate student to your current position?

A: I graduated with an Exercise and Sport Science degree from the University of Georgia. I worked as a gymnastics coach at the Classic City Gymnastics Academy before becoming a Marketing Research Analyst for Youth and Family Marketing at Strottman International, Inc. The Association County Commissioners of Georgia hired me to conduct research regarding local government operations. These jobs were not exactly what I wanted to do for my career, so I enrolled in a sport management master's program at Georgia State University. While in school, I completed an internship with NACDA Consulting and was then hired full-time.

Q: How does NACDA Consulting work within the college sport industry?

A: NACDA Consulting works with athletic departments to provide solutions to their marketing, sales, and revenue development issues. We provide research that can help an athletic department identify areas of concern or potential opportunity. One of the primary roles we have played for many athletic departments is identifying how they can increase their revenues through sponsorship sales, fund-raising, ticket sales, and merchandising.

Q: What have been the biggest challenges you have encountered during your career?

A: Initially getting my foot in the door was challenging. I was not a college athlete and I did not have an undergraduate degree in marketing, so I had to work harder than many other people who wanted to be in market research and college athletic administration. In both of my career paths, I have had to learn and work from the "ground up."

Q: What are the most pressing issues facing intercollegiate athletics?

A: Maximizing external revenue streams with limited staffing. Most schools could generate additional dollars if they had greater understanding of the marketplace, and more employees to implement new programs or expand existing ones.

Q: Are there specific job skills sport-management students should look to develop while still in school?

A: Students need to study a wide variety of topics, especially if they want to work in college athletics. Within the collegiate sport industry, particularly with smaller institutions, athletics staff members wear many different hats. Therefore, someone with capabilities in multiple areas (marketing, fund-raising, accounting, et cetera) may become invaluable to athletics department. For example, a coach may also serve as a Senior Woman Administrator or a marketing staff member may also have responsibilities in development, ticket sales and corporate partnerships. Even if someone works in a "large" ath-

letic department where there are distinct departments, knowledge and skills across the perspective is invaluable.

Q: What publications do you regularly read to stay apprised of sport-business events?

A: I read the ncaa.org and the *SportsBusiness Journal* for information about the college sport industry. I also regularly check NACDA Daily Review, an online service that provides daily news articles about a variety of topics pertinent to institutions of all sizes.

Q: Would you recommend students pursue graduate school? If so, when should they pursue a graduate degree and what area of study would you recommend?

A: Yes. But, I would recommend working within the business world prior to obtaining a graduate degree. A real-world perspective can then be applied to your studies. If someone is already working within the sport industry I would recommend pursuing an MBA. But if you are working to get into the sport industry, a sport management graduate degree may be more valuable. Certainly, one should investigate the potential career path and networking connections prior to making the decision regarding what program may provide the best opportunity for career success.

INTERVIEW 13.10

Patrick Byrne
Director of Sales & Marketing
AutoZone Liberty Bowl

Q: Could you briefly describe your career path from undergraduate student to your current position?

A: During the summer before I finished my undergraduate degrees at the University of Memphis, I was afforded the opportunity to work in the sport marketing depart-

ment at St. Jude Children's Research Hospital as an intern. The experience was eye-opening to say the least. Not only did it provide the opportunity to meet several prominent sport personalities and learn about the various careers in sports but it also convinced me to pursue a graduate degree in sport business. So the summer following graduation, I began working toward a master's degree in sport & leisure commerce. During the spring semester, I was able to reconnect with the executive director of the AutoZone Liberty Bowl (whom I had met during my time at St. Jude) through a class project. A few weeks later, he called and offered me a position with the AutoZone Liberty Bowl.

Q: What have been the biggest challenges you have encountered during your career?

A: The biggest challenges I've encountered center around my work environment, especially during our peak season. From late November until game day we work for about 12 to 14 hours per day, seven days a week. Early on, I found it difficult to find the energy and focus to work at that pace day-in and day-out. From then until now, I have learned that being organized, good communication, and asking for help are vital to being productive and staying fresh during bowl season.

Q: What are the biggest issues facing the college bowls?

A: The biggest issue over the past couple of years has been whether there should be a playoff in FBS college football. The college bowl system is what makes college football unique from any other collegiate and professional sport. But at the same time, a playoff is the best method for determining a champion. Many people believe the two cannot coexist together. I believe that they can. While a four or eight team playoff would undoubtedly generate unprecedented levels of excitement and the crowning of a true champion, it would only involve a few teams. For the rest of the bowl eligible teams, bowl games would still be an enjoyable and rewarding experience for the fans, coaches, and players.

Q: Are there specific job skills sport management students should look to develop while still in school?

A: I believe that every college student should try to develop a close relationship with a professor and/or peer who can help them identify their strengths and weaknesses relative to their particular field of study. For sport management students, a good work ethic, strong interpersonal skills, and a sound understanding of the sport world are important job skills. Having someone to help you recognize your weaknesses and improve those areas is invaluable . . . and much easier than trying to do it all alone.

Q: What specific classes would you recommend students take to best position themselves for a sport-industry job?

A: Sales training classes and event management classes are critical. A thorough understanding of the sport industry is important but having the knowledge and experience to know what it takes to plan, sell, and execute an event is vital.

Q: What publications do you regularly read to stay apprised of sport-business events?

A: *The Commercial Appeal, Memphis Business Journal, Memphis Daily News, SportsBusiness Journal, ESPN The Magazine, Sports Illustrated,* and *The Wall Street Journal.* Due to the nature of our business, I read local publications more than those that are circulated nationally.

Q: Would you recommend students pursue graduate school? If so, when should they pursue a graduate degree and what area of study would you recommend?

A: I would definitely recommend that students pursue a graduate degree. Attending graduate school was a very enriching educational experience for me. My classmates and professors created a learning environment that made every class and project highly engaging. It was a lot of hard work but fun at the same time.

While a master's degree in sport management is a great area of study, I would recommend that students first consider pursuing a law degree. It amazes me the multitude of careers one can pursue with a Juris Doctor. Many highly successful people in the sport world began their careers as lawyers.

I would recommend that students interested in pursuing a graduate degree enroll upon completion of their undergraduate course work. However, someone who has a few years of real world experience could also benefit greatly from earning a graduate degree.

Q: Is there a certain sport business area you see emerging in importance in the near future?

A: I think that high school athletics, especially football and basketball, will continue to grow as an important area in sport business. The number of televised games, recruiting services, websites, publications, all-star games, showcase games, camps, etc., has grown tremendously over the past decade. As the profile and importance of these entities grow, I believe consumer support and corporate investment will grow as well.

Q: Is there any additional advice or insights you would provide to students pursuing a future career in sport management?

A: Work hard and learn how to sell. The quickest way to get your foot in the door in the sport industry is to have a tireless work ethic coupled with the skills and confidence to sell.

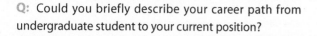

INTERVIEW 13.11

Sally Roach
Executive Director
Township Auditorium
Columbia, South Carolina

Q: Could you briefly describe your career path from undergraduate student to your current position?

A: I have a degree in Broadcasting and Cinema! I worked for two radio stations in their marketing department (and on air!) then spent four years with Ice Capades as their Marketing Director for cities in Canada and the United States. After four years of traveling I was looking for a more "normal" life and thought I might find it with an Arena. I spent 15 months as the Marketing Director of the Five Seasons Center in Cedar Rapids, Iowa. Though marketing was my main responsibility, my boss allowed me to work at different jobs including event management, box office, booking, and contract negotiations. From Cedar Rapids I went to New Haven, Connecticut to work at Veterans Memorial Coliseum as Marketing Director. While there I also assisted with booking, event management, and contract negotiations. I ran my own group sales business in the Washington, D.C., area and I then moved to Los Angeles where I was an event manager at the LA Coliseum and Sports Arena, working with the NBA

Clippers, University of Southern California football team, and international soccer matches. After a brief stay at the Rose Bowl in Pasadena, CA, I moved to Oakland, CA, and was the general manager of the Oakland Arena (now Oracle Arena), home of the NBA Warriors and the Oakland Coliseum, home of the Oakland Athletics of MLB and the NFL Oakland Raiders. After moving to Houston, TX, I was a regional vice president for SMG, a private management company where I had responsibility for nine venues in Texas, Oklahoma, and California. I am the executive director of the TOWNSHIP AUDITORIUM in Columbia, SC, a 3,000-seat, 80-year-old auditorium that underwent a 12-million-dollar renovation in 2010.

Q: What have been the biggest challenges you have encountered during your career?

A: Working in Oakland was a big challenge because there were two venues and three major league teams, each with their own needs and beliefs regarding how the facilities should be operated. In addition, there were numerous lawsuits involving the teams and the city and county that owned the facilities, which often put the facility staff in awkward situations. Staffing the facilities also presented challenges because there was a strong union presence, which made it difficult to reward top-performing employees, and discipline or remove poorly performing employees.

Q: Has working in a male-dominated field been difficult?

A: The hardest thing a woman has to deal with is usually not other people in the industry accepting who we are or what job we do. I have almost always found that I could count on support from both men and women in this business. The hard part is people outside the industry who often have a perception that a woman could not operate a 65,000-seat stadium or a soccer game with 92,000 people. Some of the non-industry people are the ones who often seemed amazed at the success of females in the industry. I do not want to give the impression that there are not any problems, as it was only a few years ago that I had to sue a former employer for wage discrimination, but for the most part this industry evaluates women and men for their abilities. Women should look upon a career in sport and entertainment as challenging for everyone, not just for women.

Q: What are the biggest issues facing sport franchises and facilities?

A: The biggest issue facing sport franchises is retaining season-ticket holders. For our venue, where we do few sporting events outside of some boxing and wrestling matches, attracting and retaining customers is critical. The economy has certainly hurt many customers, and it is a struggle to market our events to people who have multiple choices for their discretionary dollars. Any venue has to provide high-quality customer service, and training our guest-services staff has always been important, but with the economy it has become paramount.

Q: Are there specific job skills sport-management students should look to develop while still in school?

A: Students should observe as many different types of events as they can—even if they "think" they have no interest in pursuing a career in that sport or venue. Understanding how various sporting events operate, or how different venues work with live entertainment shows that attract diverse audiences, is key in this industry. If I only booked shows I personally enjoyed, this facility would have a lot of dark days. While completing an internships or practicum, students should take the time to visit with all the employees and ask about what they do. Knowing how various departments function to make an organization a success is key to being able to be promoted. As students advance their career, they need to learn how to interact with employees, especially those who work "underneath" them. As a manager I have always felt it was important to get to know as many people as possible. Whether they work for me full-time or part-time, they are integral to the facility.

Q: What specific classes would you recommend students take to best position themselves for a sport-industry job?

A: Sport and entertainment management is a business, so it is vitally important students have an understanding of accounting, reading profit and loss statements, and setting budgets. Taking a business law class will enable students to better understand how the law interacts with various aspects of the industry (I took a great law class when I was in college.). Retaining a good lawyer is still critical, but having a basic understanding of the law enables one to know how to interact with their attorney and how to train others to recognize how the law might influence facility operations.

Q: What publications do you regularly read to stay apprised of important developments?

A: I read the local paper for information about our community. New legislation affects the potential events we can do (for instance, mixed martial arts was not permitted in South Carolina until 2009), so it is important to pay attention to what is happening in our local city and state.

Q: Would you recommend students pursue graduate school? If so, when should they pursue a graduate degree and what area of study would you recommend?

A: If their undergraduate degree is in sport management then an MBA would be beneficial; I would not necessarily recommend pursuing an undergraduate and graduate degree in sport management, particularly from the same institution.

Q: Is there a certain sport-business area you see emerging in importance in the near future?

A: The growth and influence of mixed martial arts has been interesting to track. Much of what they have done in marketing and promotions has benefited the entire sport and entertainment industry. How mixed martial arts and other emerging sports compete in a tough economy will be interesting to watch.

Q: Is there any additional advice or insights you would provide to students pursuing a future career in sport management?

A: Being a fan is not enough of a reason to go into this field. The long hours and low pay early in your career means one must have a passion for being involved in events of all types. If you want to be home nights, weekends, and holidays, sport and entertainment management is not a wise career choice. Be ready to move, as better jobs almost always dictate a move out of your current geographical area. Get your foot in the door and start on the path to what you ultimately want to do. Your dream job will not be your first but each job you take should lead toward your eventual goals. Be careful what you wish for, as being in upper management (in my case being the general manager of a building or team) means dealing with politics, budgets, and staff members who often do not get along or fulfill their responsibilities. Those in management also have the responsibility to hire and fire people, which can be an unpleasant experience. Being in this industry is not just about getting your picture taken with a prominent player, performer, or team owner. Try to work for and with people who have something to teach you and be wary of people who throw around a lot of clichés without having a lot of substance!

INTERVIEW 13.12

Dan Carpenter
Director, Corporate Partnerships
Homestead Miami Speedway

Shutterstock, Inc.

Armed with a communications degree from the State University of New York at Geneseo and aspirations of breaking into sportscasting in 1992, my first full-time job was in advertising sales and as on-air talent at WDNY Radio. My first job in professional sport came two years later with the Binghamton Mets in sales, operations, and radio broadcasting. In 1995, I transitioned to a job as a corporate ticket sales representative and public address announcer for the New Jersey Devils. Realizing the need to polish my broadcasting skills in the minors, I left New Jersey in 1997 to work for the Rochester Sports Group (which controlled franchises in AHL Hockey, A League

Soccer and NLL Lacrosse) as a radio broadcaster and the director of sales for three franchises. Four years later, I came to a professional crossroads when I was offered a full-time minor league broadcasting job in the AHL and simultaneously an opportunity to become senior vice president of sales and marketing for Scheer Sports, Inc., a company that operated franchises in the ECHL, arena2 football, and the NBDL. I chose the latter and stopped broadcasting altogether. ScheerSports was sold in 2003, but I was fortunate to earn the opportunity to work in corporate sales and hospitality for Super Bowl XXXIX in Jacksonville, Florida under the joint supervision of the Jacksonville Jaguars and NFL league office. In 2005, I transitioned into motorsports as the director of business development for Memphis Motorsports Park. Four years later, I accepted my current position as director of corporate partnerships for Homestead-Miami Speedway, host of the NASCAR and IndyCar Championships each year.

Q: What have been the biggest challenges you have encountered during your career?

A: Employee retention. Many young successful people leave organizations for immediate gratification rather than staying put to ascend from within their current organization. Sport industry employers can do a better job of retaining their employees, but many employees also need to exercise a bit more patience, especially early in their careers.

Q: What are the biggest issues currently facing the industry?

A: League television deals and labor issues are always at the forefront. The NFL in 2011, and NASCAR in 2012, will have interesting media contract negotiations.

Another more pressing issue is the lackluster economy's effect on sponsors. Many companies are not willing to spend money to continue their sponsorship activities. Most sponsorships' values have not necessarily decreased; there are just fewer "players" in the market, which can drive down the price even when the asking price is justified given the benefits offered.

Q: Are there specific job skills sport management students should look to develop while still in school?

A: This is a "who you know" as much as "what you know" industry. Students should pursue internships and volunteer opportunities to build their network of contacts while enhancing their various business skills.

Q: What specific classes would you recommend students take to best position themselves for a sport-industry job?

A: Classes that develop public speaking, writing, and sales skills are critical. The future of our business will involve social media marketing, so classes that build skills in that area will be beneficial. Taking a sport law course is also helpful. And a "wildcard" class that I would recommend is an acting course. I took some entry-level acting courses during my undergraduate years, which I still refer to 20 years later. I learned to role-play and think through "scenes" and oftentimes, I apply that process to thinking through how I want to achieve my objectives in business meetings by "acting the part."

Q: What publications do you regularly read to stay apprised of sport-business events?

A: *IEG*, Street and Smith *SportsBusiness Journal*, Jayski.com, partnershipactivation.com, The *National Sports Forum*.

Q: Would you recommend students pursue graduate school? If so, when should they pursue a graduate degree and what area of study would you recommend?

A: My perception is that an MBA is still more valued than a master's degree in sport management, but I feel that will eventually change. Having this opinion will probably not make me popular among educators, but I believe pursuing an advanced degree in sport management right after securing an undergraduate degree is not advisable. I know of no industry peer that has financially benefited from an advanced degree without a large degree of practical experience as well.

That being, said, I do know of some people in the sports field who, after three years or so, or maybe even after a decade of work experience, went back to get an advanced degree, and it did benefit them in the workplace immediately afterwards.

Q: Is there a certain sport-business area you see emerging in importance in the near future?

A: I foresee non-marquee teams in the "Big 4" selling uniform sponsorships. Soccer, Lacrosse, NASCAR, and a few other leagues already do this, and when current television deals expire and are renegotiated, the revenue is likely to be lower. Many organizations will then likely seek new revenue sources. I think it is likely the NHL does this first, followed by the NBA, and then maybe the NFL down the road. I am not sure if Major League Baseball ever will pursue this option in the immediate future.

On a broader scale, the role of fantasy sports and social media content is still exploding and has a limitless ceiling to connecting fans with other fans and the athletes themselves.

As for a particular sport, MMA, indoor lacrosse and extreme sports continue to emerge as long-lasting events for athletes and fans alike.

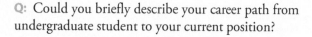

INTERVIEW 13.13

Shawni Sullivan
Director of Events
Rose Quarter

Q: Could you briefly describe your career path from undergraduate student to your current position?

A: I attended St. Martin's College (Lacey, WA) and double majored in Accounting and Business Management. I then went to Ohio University in the Sports Administration and Facility Management Program and earned my MSA in 2001. Following graduate school, I did a 1-year internship in Event Management at Disney Sports in Orlando. Following the internship, I was hired as the Director of Game Operations for Tulane University Athletics. While at Tulane, I oversaw the event management of all sports, with my primary focus being football (at the Superdome), basketball, baseball, soccer, and volleyball. In December 2003, I took a position as an Event Manager at the Rose Quarter (Rose Garden Arena and Memorial Coliseum) in Portland, OR. In December 2006 I was promoted to Director of Events at the Rose Quarter.

Q: What have been the biggest challenges you have encountered during your career?

A: In regards to my career path, I have been extremely fortunate and had the right opportunities at the right time. I was realistic and flexible from the beginning, though. I knew I would have to work from the bottom up and I was realistic with salary expectations. I was willing to go to different areas of the country to pursue the best position for my career path. In regards to my event-management career, it is one that deals with a multitude of personalities: tour managers, coaches, artists/athletes, guests, media, co-workers, promoters, et cetera. One of the biggest challenges is learning to communicate effectively with this diverse group of individuals in a fast-paced, high-stress environment. Being able to remain calm and confident at all times as well as flexible to the changing needs/requests and then to make sure to deliver desired results and provide a fun atmosphere at the same time . . . it's an exciting challenge!

Q: Can you identify what you consider to be the most important issues currently facing the facility management industry?

A: Sustainability is a huge initiative on our campus. We want to be the leader of sustainability in our community and the sport and entertainment industry, so we have already dedicated a lot of time and focus into this initiative, and continue to work on it daily. Also, keeping up with technology is a challenge. Everything from how we market ourselves (i.e. social networking) and our ticketing systems to how we run our buildings and handle the growing size and complexity of shows (the need for tours to continuously "one-up" what the last show/tour did) involves technology that is constantly changing. Also, as new arenas are built, the bar is set a little higher for the rest of us. We continue to get creative to make sure we still stand out as a leader in our industry. The ever-changing world of promoters, ticketing companies, etc. (i.e., paperless ticketing, buy-outs, mergers) and how it potentially impacts how we book and manage shows at our venue is also important. Safety and security continue to be important as keeping guests and staff safe is a primary focus in this industry.

Q: Are there specific job skills sport-management students should look to develop while still in school?

A: Solid communication and multi-tasking skills are important in this business. Also, being flexible is critical in this industry. Students should try to develop their skills as much as possible through hands-on experience in internships, volunteer positions, et cetera. The more actual work experience/exposure one can get, the better. Internships allow students to gain hands-on experience and develop their network of contacts.

Q: What specific classes would you recommend students take to best position themselves for a sport-industry job?

A: Always look to challenge yourself, and look for opportunities to learn. In event management, we work with every area/department, so the more exposure we have to each area, the better. In graduate school, I took a wide variety of classes so I could get a diverse understanding of how each area works (marketing, facilities, sport law, finance, et cetera). I also participated in several volunteer and internship opportunities in order to gain more hands-on knowledge. Once I was out of school and on the job, I asked lots of questions and shadowed other departments to learn their roles and how they fit into the big picture. The more I understand the other departments/areas, the more I have a better understanding of how my decisions affect everyone else. As far as specific classes to recommend, it all depends on a student's interests and long-term career goals. If students have the flexibility to branch out and take a wide variety of classes, then I highly recommend it.

Q: What publications do you regularly read to stay apprised of sport-business events?

A: I read a mix of sports/entertainment/facility management publications—*Pollstar, Sports Business Journal, Facility Manager,* et cetera. Also, I receive several online articles forwarded through various committees on which I serve and associations where I am a member.

Q: Would you recommend students pursue graduate school? If so, when should they pursue a graduate degree and what area of study would you recommend?

A: I believe education is invaluable. However, I have worked with several peers in this industry that do not have a graduate degree but instead have several years of experience and they are definitely leaders in the industry. If somebody has hands-on experience in their profession, that can be just as valuable as a graduate degree. Graduate school was a good fit for me; it exposed me to an industry that I did not know much about and allowed me to become part of a close-knit Ohio University Sport Administration and Facility Management community. What degree somebody should pursue depends on their specific interests. I received an MSA but I also had a double major from my undergrad in Accounting and Business Management so I felt I had a strong business background already. I could have stayed another year and earned my MBA but I felt the best decision for me was to do an internship. I am a hands-on learner, so that is the direction I went after I earned my MSA. I think education is one aspect, but what you do to gain experience and exposure to the area you want to pursue is just as important: internships, job shadowing, volunteer opportunities, working in the athletic department, et cetera. Also, getting out and making contacts/relationships is important, because this industry is a small, close-knit community and those relationships will prove to be rewarding in the future.

INTERVIEW 13.14

Elizabeth Skogman
Marketing Manager
Family Circle Cup

Q: Could you briefly describe your career path from undergraduate student to your current position?

A: During my last semester at the University of West Georgia, I worked full-time as a Ticketing/Marketing Intern at the Family Circle Cup in Charleston, SC. Despite never having been to Charleston before, I accepted the position, loaded all my possessions into my purple Saturn, and drove five hours east from Atlanta. I spent the next five months falling in love with Charleston, being challenged at work, and lamenting to my parents that there was little chance a job would open with the tournament immediately after I finished the internship and graduated. Fortunately, there was a full-time position available and I had put myself in a position to earn the opportunity to stay. I have been promoted twice during my nine years at the Family Circle Cup.

Q: What have been the biggest challenges you have encountered at the Family Circle Cup?

A: I think one of the biggest challenges of working in event management is trying to determine what determines the level of success. Unfortunately, there's no magic formula to know exactly what specific idea or attribute contributed to an event's success. One can make educated guesses about what the local community will embrace, which promotions will be well received, what sponsor interaction the fans will find memorable, and what promotional "stunts" will translate to ticket sales, but sometimes the things you think will work fall short of expectations. During my first years at the Family Circle Cup, our primary challenge was filling our calendar to become a year-round sport and entertainment venue. The tennis tournament was (and still is) our flagship event, but our venue sat idle for a majority of the year. We now host multiple tennis tournaments, about 15 concerts per year, and various community events and festivals. The primary challenge has shifted to choosing the events that provide the best chance for marketing and financial success. Also, objectively evaluating events after they are completed to determine how to improve them for the future can be difficult. Often, one can become personally invested in the event, and it is difficult to take a step back and be constructively critical of your own work.

Q: What are the biggest issues currently facing the sport industry?

A: The state of the economy is always an important issue in the sport industry. Since the economic downturn of 2008, we have had to reevaluate and adjust almost every facet of our business plan—from how we spend marketing dollars to how our consumers, corporate sponsors, vendors, etc. have been affected. In many ways, the economy has thrown "status quo" out the window and necessitated that we become more polished and careful.

Specifically as it relates to marketing, the slow economy has created a lot of opportunity to negotiate advertising rates, trade agreements, and "bells and whistles." Since many companies have cut marketing budgets (which I believe is a mistake in most cases!), there is a lot of available inventory, and media outlets have been quick to reduce rates, throw in color advertisements at no additional charge, and even comp advertisement space in some cases for advertisers who are still spending. At least there's a silver lining!

Q: Are there specific job skills sport-management students should look to develop while still in school?

A: Become comfortable with negotiating! "Negotiating 101" may not be offered at most institutions, but it is such an important skill. Negotiating occurs often in business and in the sport business advertising rates, deadlines, and of course SALARY are critical components of most jobs. The more comfortable and confident you can become at negotiating, the more effective you will be during your career. One of the first real-world questions you will be asked is, "What is your ideal salary?" It is important to be prepared to answer that question!

Q: What specific classes would you recommend students take to best position themselves for a sport-industry job?

A: After you have taken introduction classes (and assuming those do not scare you away), my advice would be to take any class that requires hands-on, real-world application of what you are being taught in the classroom. Find a course where you plan an event, solicit sponsors, build a network, and sell tickets. Experience what it is like to brainstorm (and implement!) creative promotions. Write letters and e-mails with a specific sport business purpose. If you are interested in marketing or ticket sales, learn to use Photoshop. When you graduate, you should be able to list more on your resume than course names and non-sport management part-time jobs.

Q: Would you recommend students pursue graduate school? If so, when should they pursue a graduate degree and what area of study would you recommend?

A: I have not yet pursued an advanced degree, but ideally a person should gain some level of industry experience before enrolling in a graduate program. I learned SO MUCH about what aspects of the industry I enjoyed (and did not enjoy) during my first few years out of school. I think narrowing down your focus via a "real-world" filter helps determine which area of graduate study will ultimately help further your career. Also, once working in the industry, you may discover that a master's degree is not necessary for advancement in many professions.

Q: Is there a certain sport-business area you see emerging in importance in the near future?

A: Technological advances are being made daily that are revolutionizing the ticketing industry. Less than eight years ago, many people were hesitant to order tickets online and now, a vast majority of ticket sales for sporting events occur via the Internet. Companies like Ticketmaster are on the cutting edge of integrating technology into purchasing transactions. Buying a ticket has never been easier, faster, and more streamlined. The ease of purchase translates (hopefully) into a more pleasant consumer experience and higher revenues for events. I think this area of the industry is undergoing rapid and positive change, making it an important focus for many organizations.

Q: Is there any additional advice or insights you would provide to students pursuing a future career in sport management?

A: When you do an internship, STAY IN TOUCH with the people you worked with at the organization. It is amazing that some students spend five months of their life toiling away and building important business relationships only to walk out the door on the last day, never to be heard from again. But, it happens all the time.

Also, it may sound harsh, but remember that coming straight out of school, you are not over-qualified to do anything. During your internships and first several years of full-time employment (and often times even after that!), you should be prepared to make copies, label envelopes, input information into a database, plant flowers, pick up trash, clean restrooms, work late, and work early. I have served birthday cake to kids, stood at the mail centers of random apartment complexes with mascots, done airport shuttle runs in the middle of the night, and (just last year) scanned tickets in the pouring rain. As long as those tasks are being balanced by situations in which you are able to contribute your ideas and talents to the organization, I say "grin and bear it"!

INTERVIEW 13.15

Brent Koonce
Vice President of Basketball Operations
US Sports Camps

Q: Could you briefly describe your career path from undergraduate student to your current position?

A: During my last year of my undergraduate work at the University of San Francisco, I had three different part time jobs and no guarantees about full time employment at any of them. I applied to graduate school, hoping that if no options came through, I could continue to work part time and pursue my graduate degree in sport management.

I knew I wanted to work in the sport and fitness industry, but did not know yet in what specific capacity. I had worked in professional sports with the Oakland Athletics in their Community Affairs Department, at the University of San Francisco's Koret Health & Recreation Center as a Building Supervisor, and had just begun at a small company, US Sports Camps. Looking back it was a unique opportunity to have access and work experience in three distinctly different sport industry jobs.

I did enroll in graduate school and US Sports Camps offered a full-time work opportunity. I have stayed with the company since I was first hired and I am now the Vice President of Basketball operations. I oversee all basketball operations, which include the Nike Basketball Camps, Snow Valley Basketball Schools, and McCracken Camps.

Q: What does US Sports Camps provide its customers?

A: US Sports Camps is the official licensed operator of the Nike Sports Camps. We offer camps in a variety of sports such as basketball, volleyball, golf, et cetera. We strive to provide an opportunity for campers to have fun, to improve their skills, and to meet new friends. The camp industry is different from most in sports and it certainly does not usually attract as much attention as big-time college athletics or professional sports. However, we have thousands of kids who participate in our camps,

and there are certainly thousands more playing sports at other camps across the country.

Q: What have been the biggest challenges you have encountered during your career?

A: Initially, the biggest challenge was to figure out which career path to pursue. Working in professional sport is a rare and unique opportunity. However, professional sport also presents the most competition, a difficult path to advance, and low initial salaries. Though it was initially attractive to dream of working full-time for a professional team, I realized that my personality fit well at an organization like US Sports Camps.

Currently, my biggest challenge is determining which opportunities to pursue and which to let pass. As the leaders in the camp industry, particularly in basketball, many opportunities arise to start new camps or to expand existing ones. It can be difficult to break through the clutter of the marketplace and determine where to assign resources to maximize our chance to succeed. I attempt to look at potential opportunities with a long-term view that will lead to the greatest potential for future success.

Q: Can you identify what you consider to be the "hot topics or issues" in sport, either directly related to your functional area or the sport industry in general?

A: The continued growth and influence of the Internet on the sport industry is fascinating to observe. Our camps are no exception to the expansion of the Internet. For the camp industry, standing out amongst a crowded seasonal business is the biggest obstacle we face. Last year, approximately 70 percent of our signups came via the Web, and that number will continue to grow. Part of the reason for that is convenience and having an information-rich product. We are selling an experience and the Web allows parents to gather information (dates/prices/locations), and ultimately make decisions for their kids that work best for their summer needs and budgets.

For our camps, it is imperative that we continue to upgrade our website and Web presence. Videos and social networking can help drive traffic to our website, but it must also fit our overall goals. Posting videos and embedding them in our website also increases our relevance on the search engines (i.e., Google). I am very interested in studying the continued growth of Twitter and Facebook, and how it will provide marketing opportunities, drive traffic, and ultimately produce revenues.

Q: Are there specific job skills sport-management students should look to develop while still in school?

A: Every job is different, so some specific skills will be needed more in different departments or organizations. However, work experience and relationship building are critical in all areas of sport management. Opportunities to network often come through working for "free" as an unpaid intern or as a volunteer. There are no shortcuts in this highly competitive industry and working for free weeds out many before they even get a full time job (that is usually low paying). The greater one's knowledge of an organization and the overall industry, the better one has to understand how to help the organization achieve success.

When I look at a prospective employee, I will not hire someone with no internship or work experience straight out of college. I believe strongly that we all need to start at the bottom and advance our careers. Highly effective leaders are ones who have experienced what occurs at different levels of an organization. Advancing "from the bottom" shows an individual what various levels of an organization do, and it better prepares that person to interact with various employees

Q: What specific classes would you recommend students take to best position themselves for a sport-industry job?

A: I would always recommend finance classes to anyone who one day would like to be in a managerial role. Regardless of industry or organization, every manager has financial obligations and reporting responsibilities. Being able to manage those expectations can help you immensely. Secondly, many of the sport management classes that examine trends and help students learn to analyze information to make predictions and decisions about the future are especially helpful.

Q: What publications do you regularly read to stay apprised of sport-business events?

A: I have moved to websites for the bulk of my daily information. I used to read the print version of the *SportsBusiness Journal* every week, but I found that much of that information is available from other sources. The Darren Rovell blog on CNBC.com is a good place for quick hits regarding the sport business. I still subscribe to the traditional mediums of *Sports Illustrated* and *ESPN the Magazine,* but that content is increasingly accessible online as well.

Some other blogs that are outside of the traditional mediums like Deadspin.com can also provide content about sports business that the traditional outlets will not cover.

Q: Would you recommend students pursue graduate school? If so, when should they pursue a graduate degree and what area of study would you recommend?

A: I always recommend going to graduate school with some full-time work experience. Ideally, students would come to any graduate program with practical business experience, regardless of the industry. An MBA is invaluable in any industry and provides flexibility if a student later want to leave the sport industry. My Masters in Sport Management was a professional executive program, so it allowed me the flexibility to work and go to school at the same time. That was invaluable.

Q: Is there a certain sport-business area you see emerging in importance in the near future?

Compliance and oversight on all levels will increase in importance. The examples of football coaches Mike Leach (who was fired for abusing his players at Texas Tech University) and Mark Mangino (who accepted a settlement to sever his ties to the University of Kansas after numerous complaints were filed regarding his behavior) are examples where managers not only behaved poorly, but the managers of the managers were unaware of the incidents and could have taken earlier steps to prevent the eventual outcome. Colleges and other sport organizations must be increasingly vigilant in their day-to-day operations. Information is easy to distribute, with nearly everyone owning a cell phone with video capabilities and a Facebook or Twitter account.

Recently, our main camp contact at Nike, Inc. has asked us to get full approval for all images and text mentions from any NCAA institution that we work with via

their Sports Information Director and/or compliance officers. This applies to something as simple as a headshot of a Head Coach in his or her own camp brochure.

The Tiger Woods scandal has also brought to greater light a culture of sports gossip. The success of those businesses reporting on Hollywood gossip can only mean the sport gossip universe will continue to grow. The Woods story had 14 straight days on the cover on *The New York Post*.

Q: Is there any additional advice or insights you would provide to students pursuing a future career in sport management?

A: Go work for free. Meet as many people as possible. Work hard. It can be a tough industry, but also very rewarding if you can find the right career fit.

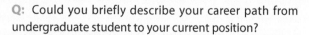

INTERVIEW 13.16

Dan Hazlett
Assistant Director—Intramurals
Georgia Tech Campus Recreation

Q: Could you briefly describe your career path from undergraduate student to your current position?

A: My career path was somewhat uncommon for the sport industry. I graduated with an undergraduate degree in Psychology and decided to pursue a graduate degree in Sport Administration. During my last year of school, I secured a graduate assistant position at the Georgia Tech Athletic Association, but the position was not challenging or fulfilling, so I took a position in the recreation department. I was initially hired on a temporary basis to run the new summer camp program. This led to being hired full-time to oversee the sport club program. Over time I was promoted to my current position. For most people who want to get involved in campus recreation, the typical path is to pursue an undergraduate degree in sport administration or recreation. Then

while in school that person would likely work in the recreation department as a student assistant and then hope to secure a graduate assistant position that pays for a graduate degree. Ideally, the person would be hired as a recreation coordinator after working two years as a graduate assistant.

Q: What have been the biggest challenges you have encountered during your campus recreation career?

A: My biggest challenge has been change. I am not referring to changes in budgets or personnel. Those changes certainly happen and need to be integrated into operations. Change that involves dramatic philosophical shifts due to executive-level hiring at the President—

Vice President—Provost level can be dramatic and sometimes difficult to handle if those new executives do not have an understanding of individual campus units (such as recreation) and their unique operations. In some cases, new management personnel have not taken the time to solicit input before implementing philosophical changes to the entire organization, and that can be frustrating.

Q: What are the most pressing issues in campus recreation?

A: The budget situation on most campuses is critical. More subunits of universities are being asked to financially justify their existence and their operating practices. This can pose some problems in campus recreation. As a result, having the ability to assess and communicate what you are doing has become extremely critical. Establishing goals and objectives that are measurable has become priority for campus recreation programs across the country.

Q: Are there specific job skills sport-management students should look to develop while still in school?

A: I would first have all students continually practice their communication skills, both written and oral. Being able to effectively and succinctly communicate to various levels of the organization is critical. With the direction of many universities, understanding how to develop, implement, and analyze surveys and other research instruments is vital.

Q: What specific classes would you recommend students take to best position themselves for a sport-industry job?

A: Financial management and budgeting (all levels) is critical since eventually employees (who wish to advance in their careers) will be placed in a position where they will manage a budget and need to develop revenue sources. Lastly, I believe research classes that teach basic skills in developing assessment tools are helpful.

Q: What publications do you regularly read to stay apprised of sport-business events?

A: I regularly read all National Intramural and Recreation Sports Association (NIRSA) publications, *Referee magazine* and *Athletic Business* are also helpful. I also read

books by John Maxwell. I have found his books to be extremely helpful and would strongly encourage students to read his books if they are not already assigned as part of a sport business curriculum. Maxwell stands out as the premier conveyor of leadership development tools that provide not only a foundation, but also technical information appropriate for employees at all levels.

Q: Would you recommend students pursue graduate school? If so, when should they pursue a graduate degree and what area of study would you recommend?

A: For management positions in campus recreation, it is required to have a graduate degree. I know of only one person who has an undergraduate degree who is in a position at my level, and that was a unique situation. An MBA would be good to have, but typically the graduate assistants for campus recreation are linked with sport management programs or recreation programs in the College of Education. It might be difficult to work as a graduate assistant and have that funding cover an MBA.

Q: Are there any additional advice or insights you would provide to students pursuing a future career in campus recreation or another area of sport management?

A: I would look at a future career like I would look at life (although work should not be viewed at the same level of importance as life). Things change. People change, technologies change, organizations change, situations change. One of the main constants in work and in life is change. Some changes you can directly control or influence, while many other things will remain out of your direct control. Being in a position where you are prepared to take advantage of an opening or opportunity (that may not be in your current geographic area) may significantly influence overall satisfaction and happiness with your career. One should never assume things will always be the same and equally, one should never assume everything about their job or their life is determined. As soon as you think your life or your job is set, something or someone will take it another direction. When changes occur, you need to be flexible enough to take advantage of the opportunity. Many of the most successful people in campus recreation and sport management achieved success in their careers in jobs or locations they did not anticipate when they began their career.

INTERVIEW 13.17

Terumi Kaibara
Business Development and Project Manager
Green Stamp America, Inc.

Q: Could you explain how sport has helped shape your personality and work ethic?

A: I was born in Singapore and lived in the United States and Japan in the early years of my life. In each country I had to adapt to different cultures and languages. At the age of eight, I returned to Japan to find my gregarious personality posed a challenge in the Japanese culture. However, my love of sports enabled me to break down barriers and assimilate into Japanese culture. Playing basketball helped me learn and share important moments with my friends, as I was always part of a team. I had great success playing basketball as I was a good player on championship teams in junior high, high school, and college.

Participating in basketball and other sports has taught me numerous lessons that are applicable to multiple life situations. For instance, sport taught me an appreciation of team building and creating a common direction for the entire group. Much like business or other aspects of life, playing sports at a high level is important but not just because of winning potential championships. Sport has enabled me to learn about myself and my teammates and to establish common goals. Sport also gave me the opportunity to find common ground when I was experiencing new cultures. My sport experiences extend into everything I do, and my life would be totally different if I had not had my formal and informal sport experiences.

Q: How did your professional sport management career develop after you finished your undergraduate degree?

A: I lived in four different countries in four different stages of my life, and these multinational experiences shaped my dream since I was a little girl—to be a liaison among different countries and people. When I graduated from Waseda University in Japan, I initially worked as a flight attendant at Cathay Pacific Airways based in Hong Kong. The job enabled me to travel, but I knew that I was missing something–a direct involvement in sports.

After my international work experience in Hong Kong, I followed my passion and determination to work in sport management and decided to pursue my master's degree in Sport Administration at Georgia State University in Atlanta. While at Georgia State, I did an internship at the Professional Golf Association (PGA) TOUR in the New Media department which entailed working extensively on the PGATOUR.com website. After earning my Master's degree in 2004, I worked for the Ladies Professional Golf Associations (LPGA), where I started as the New Media Coordinator working for the LPGA.COM website, and eventually became the Manager of Emerging Media and International Television.

While I have always had an interest in a sport management career, I realized that I needed to enhance my global leadership skills to achieve my long-term goals. I recently joined Green Stamp to enhance my business skills. My current position provides an opportunity to develop and implement international strategic plans. I work directly with the Chief Executive Officer and the Vice President, which enables me to see and influence the company's overall operation. These experiences have broadened my perspective regarding how to approach different global problems. Although I left the sport industry temporarily, my passion and heart are still in sport.

My long-term interest in a sport management career is based upon a desire to use sport as a basis to break down cultural barriers and solve problems. Sport gave me the opportunity to adjust to different countries, and I chose to initially pursue a career in international sport management because I wanted to create more opportunities for others to have similar experiences. My long-term career ambition is to open my own international organization to support and help children in underdeveloped countries. An important component of that dream is to help children fall in love with sport and to learn about life through their sport experiences.

Q: What are the biggest differences in the work environment in Japan and the United States? How did you adjust to those differences?

A: Japanese and American cultures are different, and in business that is reflected in the "typical" communication style and decision-making process. A typical Japanese company will have distinctly different supervisory styles, management controls, and inter-department relations. In many ways, the "typical" Japanese employee behaves much like a samurai, having formal duties and loyalties to other members of the organization. In contrast, "typical" American companies have management structures where employees act like a cowboy. An American employee is far more independent in most situations than an employee in Japan. The Japanese emphasis on interdependence and harmony within work groups usually leads to an extensive consultation with pre-meetings, meetings, and after meetings whenever a decision must be contemplated and implemented. American companies are far more likely to have their employees take individual initiative.

Q: As an American-based company, what issues does the LPGA have as it expands it international focus?

A: My experience with the LPGA brought tremendous opportunities to see the existence and advancement of women's sport, and how the LPGA can continue to play a key role creating more opportunities internationally.

During the 2006 Women's World Cup of Golf in South Africa, I observed how golf created opportunities for young girls. The role that the Women's World Cup of Golf had played in the development of the game was evidenced by the 43 percent increase in the number of South African women playing golf from 2000 to 2005. While I was in South Africa helping to operate a junior golf clinic with LPGA professional golfers, girls at first were hesitant to pick up golf clubs for the first time. Even-

tually, the significance of language barriers, citizenship, and religion slowly melted away, and their energy transferred to developing their self-esteem and self-confidence through golf.

In 2010, the LPGA has 129 international players from 28 different countries. The LPGA has worked to support international players and worked to immerse international players in American culture, customs, and language. Each year the LPGA is also expanding the number of tournaments played outside of the United States, which will give tremendous opportunities to grow their fan base internationally. Working in a variety of countries with players from varied backgrounds presents marketing opportunities, but also cultural challenges. Some of the challenges facing the LPGA are similar to other sport leagues as well as businesses in other industry sectors.

Q: What advice would you give to students beginning to study sport management?

A: I highly recommend doing an internship, and while working being aggressive to coordinate lunch with your supervisor and any staff members in other departments. I also think it is crucial to outperform and prove you are different from other interns during the internship program, even in a short period of time. If you perform only as well as the other interns, you will likely not advance in your career at a rapid pace. In order to create an excellent impression, you need to make an effort to do extra and be unique. My internship experience with the PGA TOUR changed my whole life, because it not only opened the door with the LPGA, but it continues to open other doors outside of the sport industry.

Q: What advice would you give to students who know they want to have an international focus to their career?

A: Reading a textbook and talking with others is important, but there is no substitute for living and experiencing a different culture. Obviously, studying or working in a foreign country will enhance your understanding. If you cannot visit or live in different countries while in college, there are still opportunities to dive into international initiatives while on campus. International students who are studying in the United States usually are happy to provide information and contacts from their home country. The global economy has spurred nearly every company to think (and recruit) internationally and on many campuses international activities are regularly occurring. Building an international network while still on campus is important and once a network is developed, it is critical that contacts are maintained. Every sport organization now realizes that the Internet has made the world a smaller place, so the opportunities are limitless if one takes the initiative to develop their international focus.

Q: What publications should students be reading on a regular basis?

A: *SportsBusiness Journal* and *The Wall Street Journal.*

Sport Management Resources

Mark Nagel[1]

> I don't think much of a man who is not wiser today than he was yesterday.
>
> —Abraham Lincoln

> The library is the temple of learning, and learning has liberated more people than all the wars in history.
>
> —Carl T. Rowan

[1] Luke Reasor and Mike Zachrich provided assistance assembling and editing this chapter.

The sport business and its various sub-industries are continually evolving. True sport-industry professionals consistently examine the industry's history, in order to contextualize current changes and trends in standards and best practices, and attempt to identify future areas of opportunity. The best ways to stay abreast of issues in sport management are to continually read related periodicals, maintain membership in appropriate organizations, attend pertinent seminars and conferences, and make use of the nearly limitless body of available information. Since knowledge is power, students should seek to obtain as much information as possible, going beyond that provided in the classroom.

Students interested in a sport-management career should also seek out opportunities to interact with established professionals. Though some professionals have busy schedules that prevent them from conversing with students, many sport managers appreciate the opportunity to return letters or electronic mail from students seeking information or guidance. In some cases, sport-management professionals find time to meet with a "pleasantly persistent" student who seeks to learn more about their past experiences. Nearly everyone who works in the industry began their career "at the bottom" and is willing to give back to the "next generation" if a request is appropriately conveyed. Students should remember that even some of the most powerful sport-business executives, such as National Football League Commissioner, Roger Goodell, began their careers as interns.

This chapter is designed to provide materials and resources to help sport-management students begin their pursuit of a sport business career. It is certainly not an "exhaustive" reference list, since the number and type of potential resources change as rapidly as the overall industry. This chapter hopes to expand students' perspective by highlighting resources relevant to possible careers beyond just the "major" North American sport leagues and Division-I college sport. Though those United States and Canadian leagues and sport organizations will likely continue to be the focus of many students' career aspirations, other sport entities offer exciting and rewarding opportunities. Since the sport industry is constantly evolving, in 10 years new sport organizations (or ones that currently do not even exist) may provide employment opportunities. In 1990 the idea that a national television audience would tune in to freestyle BMX, snow-cross, or snowboarding half-pipe competitions would likely have been considered crazy, but today these and other extreme sports attract large on-site, as well as television and Internet, viewing audiences during the X-Games and DewSport Tour. In addition, several of these sports are now Winter Olympics mainstays.

One of the best resources for students wishing to research organizations and individuals who operate within the sports industry is the *Sports Marketplace Directory*. Most sport management programs will have a copy available for students to examine. Nearly every sport organization has contact information in the 2200-page *Sports Marketplace Directory*, which makes it a valuable resource.

In addition to "sport" resources, this chapter also provides "general" resources that will guide and inspire students beginning a career in sport management (or another field). The listed resources will hopefully spur students to continue to search for greater knowledge of the industry and the potential roles someone may have during their career. In addition, one section of the chapter provides some personal finance materials that students may find helpful as they transition from college to their professional careers.

Academic Organizations and Conferences

There are currently over 250 sport-management academic programs. Most sport-management programs offer specific courses in some or all of the chapter topics covered in this book. Students have an opportunity to enhance their on-campus education by attending academic conferences related specifically to sport management. There are a variety of academic conferences specifically designed to introduce students to the sport industry and provide networking opportunities. Some of the more prominent conferences that focus on providing undergraduate students with sport-industry information include:

Sport and Entertainment Venues Tomorrow Conference
http://www.sevt.org/

Florida State Sport Management Conference
http://www.fsu.edu/~smrmpe/programs/sm/index.htm

Georgia Southern University Sport Management Conference
http://ceps.georgiasouthern.edu/conted/sportconference.html

Southern Sport Management Conference at Troy University
http://troy.troy.edu/healthandhumanservices/khp/ssm2009.html

Sport Industry Networking and Career Conference at George Washington University
http://www.sinc-conference.com/

Sport Management Student Conference hosted by Robert Morris University
http://www.rmu.edu/OnTheMove/findoutmore.open_page?iPage=66650

Sports Events Marketing Experience Conference hosted by Georgetown University
http://www.seme-now.com/

In addition to conferences developed with undergraduate sport-management students in mind, there also are numerous academic organizations that host conferences intended for graduate students to learn about research being conducted in various areas of sport management. Some of the more well-known organizations that host annual conferences include:

North American Society for Sport Management
http://www.nassm.com/

College Sport Research Institute: Scholarly Conference on College Sport
http://www.csriconference.org/

Sport Marketing Association
http://www.sportmarketingassociation.com/

Sport and Recreation Law Association
http://srla.unm.edu/

Sport Management in Australia and New Zealand
http://smaanz.cadability.com.au/

European Association for Sport Management
http://www.easm.net/

Asian Association for Sport Management
http://www.masma.my/pb/wp_63c2d39c/wp_63c2d39c.html

American Alliance for Health, Physical Education, Recreation, and Dance
http://www.aahperd.org/

Professional Organizations

Industry organizations also provide excellent opportunities to network with industry professionals and begin to understand the challenges facing the sport-management industry. Most "practitioner" organizations host a national conference every year and may sponsor local or regional conferences as well. Most industry professionals will attend at least one of their industry conferences and students can often attend at a reduced rate. Students should investigate the many ways professional organizations provide career-development opportunities. Compiling a "complete" list of professional sport management organizations and conferences is certainly difficult, but here are some prominent sport-industry organizations and conferences:

Sport and Entertainment Venues Tomorrow Conference
http://www.sevt.org/

Athletic Business Conference
http://athleticbusinessconference.com/

National Collegiate Athletic Association
http://www.ncaa.org/

National Sports Forum
http://www.sports-forum.com/

Stadium Managers Association
http://www.stadiummanagers.org/

International Association of Assembly Managers
http://www.iaam.org/

Street and Smith's Sports Group World Congress of Sports
http://www.sportsbusinessconferences.com/WCOS/2010/

Travel, Events and Management in Sports
http://www.teamsconference.com/

Sport Lawyers Association Conference
http://www.sportslaw.org/index.cfm

National Association of Collegiate Women Athletic Administrators
https://www.nacwaa.org/

1A Athletic Directors' Association
http://www.d-1a.com

National Association of Collegiate Directors of Athletics
http://www.nacda.com/
(NOTE: NACDA coordinates and administers a variety of sub-organizations related to different athletic departments and athletic-department functional areas)

Collegiate Athletic Business Management Association
http://www.nacda.com/cabma/nacda-cabma.html

Collegiate Event and Facility Management Association
http://www.nacda.com/cefma/nacda-cefma.html

Division I-AAA Athletic Directors Association
http://www.nacda.com/div1aaaada/nacda-div1aaaada.html

Division II Athletic Directors Association
http://www.nacda.com/div2ada/nacda-div2ada.html

Football Championship Subdivision Athletic Directors Association
http://www.nacda.com/div1aaada/nacda-div1aaada.html

International Collegiate Licensing Association
http://www.nacda.com/icla/nacda-icla.html

Minority Opportunities Athletic Association
http://www.nacda.com/moaa/nacda-moaa.html

National Association for Athletics Compliance
http://www.nacda.com/naacc/nacda-naacc.html

National Association of Athletic Development Directors
http://www.nacda.com/naadd/nacda-naadd.html

National Association of Collegiate Marketing Administrators
http://www.nacda.com/nacma/nacda-nacma-main.html

National Alliance of Two-Year College Athletic Administrators
http://www.nacda.com/natycaa/nacda-natycaa.html

Professional Periodicals and Blogs

Though magazines such as *Sports Illustrated* and *The Sporting News* have been prominent sport publications for many years, they have traditionally focused solely on the "action on the field." Recently these publications, as well as daily newspapers such as the *Wall Street Journal* and the *USA Today,* have begun to more extensively cover sport business. Students are strongly encouraged to regularly check these periodicals for information regarding important sport business issues. In addition, it is important to remain abreast of local sport-business activities. Certainly, students should regularly read their local newspaper as well as their local Business Journal (if there is one) for information concerning the business of sport.

Since 1997, Street & Smith's has published the *SportsBusiness Journal.* Since its inception, the *SportsBusiness Journal* has been the "Bible" for weekly sport business information and in-depth coverage of events. The *SportsBusiness Daily* also provides daily online information regarding sport business news. In addition to its afternoon publication, the *Daily* also provides a "Morning Buzz" and "Closing Bell" which enable readers to remain appraised of any breaking news in the industry. The Closing Bell provides links to newspaper and magazine stories concerning sport business from around the United States and Canada. Most sport management professionals read the *Journal* and the *Daily* and students should make reading them a regular part of their professional activities. In addition to publishing the *Journal* and the *Daily,* Street and Smith's SportsBusiness Group also publishes a *Sport Business Resource Guide and Fact Book,* which contains extensive information regarding the sport industry.

There are a variety of publications that cover subareas of the sport management industry. Though the number of periodicals continues to expand each month, some of the established publications include the following:

Athletic Business Magazine
   Online access: http://www.athleticbusiness.com

Athletic Management
   Online access: http://www.athleticmanagement.com/

Facility Manager Magazine.
   Online access:
   https://www.iaam.org/Facility_manager/Pages/Facility_Issues.htm

PanStadia International
   Online Access: http://www.panstadia.com (subscription required)

Sport Travel Magazine
   Online access: http://www.sportstravelmagazine.com/

Stadia Magazine
   Online Access: http://www.stadia-magazine.com

Venue Safety and Security Magazine
   Online access: https://www.iaam.org/vss/pages/issues.htm

Venues Today Magazine
   Online access: http://www.venuestoday.com (subscription required)

The proliferation of Internet blogs and news clips services has created a nearly limitless amount of available content and information. There are now hundreds of sport and sport-business blogs. Though it would be nearly impossible to list every website that may contain pertinent information some of the most well known sport-business sites include:

CollegeAthleticsClips
   http://collegeathleticsclips.com/

Legal Aspects of Sports Blog
   http://www.sportslawprofessor.com/

Money Players
   http://moneyplayers.typepad.com/

SportsBiz
   http://thesportsbizblog.blogspot.com/

Sports Biz with Darren Rovell (CNBC)
   http://www.cnbc.com/id/15837629

Sports Law Blog
   http://sports-law.blogspot.com/

Sports Media Watch
   http://sportsmediawatch.blogspot.com/

The Big Lead
   http://thebiglead.com/

The Sports Economist
   http://www.thesportseconomist.com/

Academic Journals

The following is a list of academic journals that publish research specifically related to certain aspects of the sport industry. These journals typically are designed for "academic" rather than "professional" audiences, though some offer specific articles, book reviews, or commentaries that are written for practitioners. Most of the journals are tailored to a specific sport-management sub area.

Applied Research in Coaching and Athletics Annual
Australian and New Zealand Sports Law Journal
Chronicle of Kinesiology and Physical Education in Higher Education
Coach and Athletic Director
DePaul Journal of Sports Law & Contemporary Problems
Entertainment and Sports Law Journal
Entertainment and Sports Lawyer
European Journal for Sport and Society
European Journal of Sport Management (now *ESPQ*)
European Sport Management Quarterly
Florida Entertainment, Art & Sport Law Journal
Global Sport Management
ICHPER-SD Journal of Research (International Council for Health, Physical Education, Recreation, Sport, & Dance)
International Journal of Applied Sports Science
International Journal of Sport
International Journal of Sport and Exercise Psychology
International Journal of Sport Communication
International Journal of Sport Management
International Journal of Sport Management and Marketing
International Journal of Sport Policy
International Journal of Sports Finance
International Journal of Sports Marketing & Sponsorship
International Journal of the History of Sport
International Review for the Sociology of Sport
International Sports Law Journal
International Sports Studies
Journal for the Study of Sports and Athletics in Education
Journal of Contemporary Athletics
Journal of Hospitality, Leisure, Sport and Tourism Education (JoHLSTE)
Journal of Intercollegiate Sport

Journal of Issues in Intercollegiate Athletics
Journal of Legal Aspects of Sport
Journal of Physical Education, Recreation, & Dance (JOPERD)
Journal of Quantitative Analysis in Sports
Journal of Sponsorship
Journal of Sport & Tourism
Journal of Sport Administration & Supervision
Journal of Sport and Social Issues
Journal of Sport History
Journal of Sport Management
Journal of Sports Economics
Journal of Sports Law & Contemporary Problems
Journal of Sports Media
Journal of Sports Sciences
Journal of the Philosophy of Sport
Journal of Venue & Event Management
Korean Journal of Sport Management
Legal Issues in College Athletics
Marquette Sports Law Review
Michigan State University College of Law Entertainment and Sports Law Journal
National Intramural-Recreational Sports Association Journal (NIRSA Journal)
NISR Journal of Sport Reform
Quest
Recreational Sports Journal
Research Quarterly for Exercise and Sport
Seton Hall Journal of Sport Law
Sport, Business and Management: An International Journal
Sport Management and Related Topics (SMART) Online Journal
Sociology of Sport Journal
Sport History Review
Sport in History
Sport in Society
Sport Journal
Sport Management Education Journal
Sport Management Review
Sport Marketing Quarterly
Sport, Education, & Society
Sporting Traditions, the journal of the Australian Society for Sports History
Sports and Entertainment Litigation Reporter
Sports Lawyers Journal
Sports, Park and Recreation Law Reporter
Texas Review of Entertainment & Sports Law
The Sports Law Forum at Fordham University School of Law
University of Miami Entertainment and Sports Law Review
Villanova Sports & Entertainment Law Journal
Virginia Sports and Entertainment Law Journal
Willamette Sports Law Journal
Women in Sport and Physical Activity Journal

Sport Management Topics

The following sections of this chapter provide resources for various topics directly or indirectly related to pursuing a career in sport management. For each area, the potential list of resources could be nearly limitless as excellent resources are published each day. Each of the subareas contains selected works that may help a person (1) find a sport management job, (2) advance in their career, (3) understand the history or current operations in a specific area of sport management, and (4) better handle the rigors of being a professional in an ever-changing environment. Some of the resources are from the "popular press" while others are written for an "academic" audience. The listing of both types of resources is consistent with the book's overriding goal to link theory and practice in the sport management industry.

Personal Finance

As a student, personal finance may not seem like an important topic and it may seem odd to have a list of books covering finance before the sections discussion finding a full-time position. For many of you reading this book, earning a full-time salary may not occur until a few years into the future. For most students, saving, investing and retirement are not typically discussed on college campuses. However, it is important to begin planning for your financial future IMMEDIATELY—even if you do not currently have a full-time job or any savings. One of the best ways for students to prepare for their financial future (and their eventual retirement) is to start thinking about spending habits–particularly if most purchases are currently made on credit. Digging a financial hole through excessive spending for "unnecessary" items will eventually cause potential problems.

The following books provide some guidance regarding personal finance:

Chatzky, J.S. (2001). *Talking Money: Everything You Need to Know About Your Finances and Your Future.* New York, NY: Warner Books, Inc.

Kiyosaki, R.T., & Lechter, S.L. (2000). *Rich Dad, Poor Dad: What the Rich Teach Their Kids About Money—That the Poor and Middle Class Do Not!* Paradise Valley, AZ: Techpress, Inc.

Levitt, A. (2003). *Take on the Street: How to Fight for Your Financial Future.* New York, NY: Knopf Publishing Group.

Orman, S. (2005). *The Money Book for the Young, Fabulous, & Broke.* New York, NY: The Penguin Group.

Ramsey, D. (2003). *The Total Money Makeover: A Proven Plan for Financial Fitness.* Nashville, TN: Thomas Nelson, Inc.

Stanley, T.J., & Danko, W.D. (1996). *The Millionaire Next Door.* New York, NY: Pocket Books.

Starting Your Career

As you begin to think about securing an internship and a job in the sport industry, it is important to know where you will be applying. One of the most important aspects of seeking a position is to research the industry and the organization you would like to pursue. After researching potential organizations, you should better understand the organization and be able to provide the organization with information about your history, skills, and abilities. In most cases, a potential employer will expect to receive a cover letter and resume before deciding to interview an applicant. In the sport industry, hundreds of people are often applying for each internship or job with a specific organization. In such a competitive marketplace, having a strong, yet concise, cover letter and a well-designed resume are critical.

There are hundreds of how-to resume writing books. Certainly, a resume should be tailored for the desired position. In most cases, a resume's style or format is not as important as making sure it is well organized, is free from spelling and grammar errors, and utilizes action verbs to demonstrate your responsibilities in previous positions. The website *quintcareers.com* offers a variety of resume instructions. Their site that details action verbs is especially informative: *http://www.quintcareers.com/action_verbs.html.*

The following resume and cover letter books may also be helpful:

Bennett, S. (2005). *The Elements of Resume Style: Essential Rules and Eye-Opening Advice for Writing Resumes and Cover Letters that Work.* New York, NY: AMACOM.

Hizer, D., & Rosenberg, A. (2007). *The Resume Handbook: How to Write Outstanding Resumes and Cover Letters for Every Situation.* Avon, MA: Adams Media Corporation.

Ireland, S. (2006). *The Complete Idiot's Guide to the Perfect Resume* (4th Edition). New York, NY: The Penguin Group.

Karsh, B., & Pike, C. (2009). *How to Say It on Your Resume: A Top Recruiting Director's Guide to Writing the Perfect Resume for Every Job.* New York, NY: The Penguin Group.

Whitcomb, S. B. (2006). *Resume Magic: Trade Secrets of a Professional Resume Writer.* Indianapolis, IN: JIST Works

Securing the First Sport Management Opportunity

Of course, writing the "perfect" cover letter and resume is only one part of securing an internship or a job. Other crucial components to launching a successful career include preparing for an interview and researching what to ask for if an offer is made. The following books provide tips on identifying jobs, preparing for interviews, and negotiating salaries:

Dell, D. (2009). *Never Make the First Offer (except When You Should)*. New York: Penguin Books

DeLuca, M.J. (1996). *Best Answers to the 201 Most Frequently Asked Interview Questions*. New York, NY: McGraw-Hill Publishing Company.

Fisher, R., & Ury, W. (1991). *Getting to Yes* (2nd ed.). New York: Penguin Books.

Investor's Business Daily. (2004). *Sports Leaders & Success: 55 Top Sports Leaders & How They Achieved Greatness*. New York, NY: McGraw-Hill Publishing Company.

Krantman, S. (2007). *The Resume Writers Workbook, 3E: Marketing Yourself Throughout the Job Search Process*. Cincinnati, OH: South-Western Educational Publishing.

Levinson, J. C., & Perry, D. (2005). *Guerrilla Marketing for Job Hunters: 400 Unconventional Tips, Tricks, and Tactics for Landing Your Dream Job*. Hoboken, NJ: Wiley Publishing Company.

Mackay, H. (1999). *Dig Your Well Before You're Thirsty: The Only Networking Book You'll Ever Need*. New York, NY: Doubleday.

Oliver, V. (2005). *301 Smart Answers to Tough Interview Questions*. Naperville, IL: Sourcebooks, Inc.

Powers, P. (2004). *Winning Job Interviews: Reduce Interview Anxiety/Outprepare the Other Candidates/Land the Job You Love*. Franklin Lakes, NJ: The Career Press, Inc.

Robinson, M.J., Hums, M.A., Crow, B., & Phillips, D.R. (2000). *Profiles of Sport Industry Professionals: The People Who Make the Games Happen*. Gaithersburg, MD: Aspen Publishers, Inc.

Shropshire, K.L. (2008). *Negotiate Like the Pros: A Master Sports Negotiator's Lessons for Making Deals, Building Relationships, and Getting What You Want*. New York, NY: McGraw-Hill Publishing Company.

Wong, G.M. (2008). *The Comprehensive Guide to Careers in Sports*. Sudbury, MA: Jones and Bartlett Publishers.

Jobs in Sports Links

The following websites provide information regarding internships and jobs in sports. Many of them charge a fee for access to their listings.

http://www.allsportsdirectory.net/
http://www.athleticlink.com/
http://www.internships-usa.com/
http://www.jobsinsports.com/
http://www.ncaa.org/employment
http://www.onlinesports.com/pages/CareerCenter.html
http://www.sportscareers.com/
http://www.sportscareerconsulting.com
http://www.teamworkonline.com
http://www.womensportsjobs.com/
http://www.workinsports.com/

Career Advancement Tips

Once you have been able to secure an initial internship or job, it is important to continue to learn and to stay motivated. There are a nearly limitless number of books designed to help with career advancement. The following books are ones that may be helpful.

Chandler, S. (2001). *100 Ways to Motivate Yourself: Change Your Life Forever.* Franklin Lakes, NJ: The Career Press, Inc.

Johnson, S. (1998). *Who Moved My Cheese?: An Amazing Way to Deal with Change in Your Work and in Your Life.* New York, NY: Penguin Putnam, Inc.

Johnson, S. (2003). *The Present: The Secret to Enjoying Your Work and Life, Now!* New York, NY: Doubleday.

Miller, D. (2004). *48 Days to the Work You Love.* Nashville, TN: Broadman & Holman Publishers.

Miller, D. (2008). *No More Dreaded Mondays: Ignite Your Passion and Other Revolutionary Ways to Discover Your True Calling at Work.* New York, NY: The Doubleday Broadway Publishing Group.

Pink, D.H. (2009). *Drive: The Surprising Truth about What Motivates Us.* New York, NY: The Penguin Group.

Management

Motivating yourself is certainly an important step in career development. However, superior sport managers will be attracted to organizations that are moving in a positive direction and they will work to move their organization forward rather than remaining stagnant. Thousands of books have been written about managing, leading and motivating. Though certainly not an exhaustive list, the following books provide some "general" insights on these topics:

Bolman, L.G., & Deal, T.E. (1997). *Reframing organizations: Artistry, choice, and leadership* (2nd ed.). San Francisco, CA: Jossey-Bass Publishers.

Brown, W.S. (1987). *13 Fatal Errors Managers Make and How You Can Avoid Them.* New York, NY: The Berkley Publishing Group.

Buckingham, M., & Coffman, C. (1999). *First, Break All the Rules: What the World's Greatest Managers Do Differently.* New York, NY: Simon & Schuster, Inc.

Carnegie, D. (1998). *How to Win Friends & Influence People.* New York, NY: Pocket Books.

Collins, J. (2001). *Good to Great: Why Some Companies Make the Leap . . . and Others Don't.* New York, NY: HarperCollins Publishers, Inc.

Collins, J., & Porras, J.I. (2002). *Built to Last: Successful Habits of Visionary Companies.* New York, NY: HarperCollins Publishers, Inc.

Covey, S.R. (2004). *The 7 Habits of Highly Effective People.* New York, NY: Free Press.

Deal, T.E., & Kennedy, A.A. (1982). *Corporate Cultures.* Reading, MA: Addison-Wesley Publishing Company.

Martin, J. (1992). *Cultures in Organizations: Three Perspectives.* New York: Oxford University Press.

Maxwell, J. C. (2007). *The 21 Irrefutable Laws of Leadership: Follow Them and People Will Follow You.* Nashville, TN: Thomas Nelson, Inc.

Russell, B. (2001). *Russell rules: 11 lessons on leadership from the twentieth century's greatest winner.* New York: Putnam.

Schein, E.H. (1992). *Organizational culture and leadership.* (2nd ed.). San Francisco: Jossey-Bass Publishers.

Welch, J. (2003). *Jack: Straight from the Gut.* New York, NY: Warner Books, Inc.

Welch, J. (2005). *Winning.* New York, NY: HarperCollins Publishers, Inc.

Williams, P. (2006). *How to Be Like Coach Wooden: Life Lessons from Basketball's Greatest Leader.* Deerfield Beach, FL: Health Communications, Inc.

Ethics

For many sport-industry professionals a key component of effective management is managing ethically. The following books address ethical dilemmas and provide insights regarding how to be an ethical manager and person:

Badaracco, J.L. (1997). *Defining Moments: When Managers Must Choose Between Right and Right.* Boston: Harvard Business School Press.

Blanchard, K., & O'Connor, M. (1997). *Managing By Values.* San Francisco: Berrett-Koehler Publishers.

Cohen, B., & Greenfield, J. (1997). *Ben & Jerry's Double Dip: Lead with Your Values and Make Money, Too.* New York: Simon & Schuster.

Dali Lama, H.H., & Cutler, H.C. (1998). *The Art of Happiness.* New York: Riverhead Books.

Kabat-Zinn, J. (1994). *Wherever You Go There You Are.* New York: Hyperion.

Rachels, J. (1999). *The Elements of Moral Philosophy* (3rd ed.). Boston: McGraw-Hill College.

Rachels, J. (2003). *The Right Thing to Do: Basic Readings in Moral Philosophy* (3rd ed.). Boston: McGraw-Hill College.

Finance

Sport finance is an important area of sport management, but many students are intimidated by the "numbers." Having an understanding of accounting, budgeting, and economics will position a sport-management professional to not only secure an entry-level job, but also more rapidly advance within the organization.

Brown, M.T., Rascher, D.A., Nagel, M.S., & McEvoy, C.D. (2010). *Financial Management in the Sport Industry.* Scottsdale, AZ: Holcomb Hathaway.

Downward, P., & Dawson, A. (2000). *The Economics of Professional Team Sports.* New York, NY: Routledge.

Fizel, J. (2005). *Handbook of Sports Economics Research.* Armonk, NY: M.E. Sharpe, Inc.

Foster, G., Greyser, S.A., & Walsh, B. (2005). *The Business of Sports: Cases and Text on Strategy and Management.* Cincinnati, OH: South-Western College Publishing.

Humphreys, B.R., & Howard, D.R. (2008). *The Business of Sports [Three Volumes]: Volume 1, Perspectives on the Sport Industry Volume 2, Economic Perspectives on Sport Volume 3, Bridging Research and Practice (Praeger Perspectives).* New York, NY: Praeger Publishing.

Lewis, M. (2004). *Moneyball: The Art of Winning an Unfair Game.* New York: Norton.

Noll, R.G. (1997). *Sports, Jobs, and Taxes: The Economic Impact of Sports Teams and Stadiums.* Washington, DC: Brookings Institution Press.

Quirk, J., & Fort, R.D. (1997). *Pay Dirt: The Business of Professional Team Sports.* Princeton, NJ: Princeton University Press.

Staudohar, P.D. (1996). *Playing for Dollars: Labor Relations and the Sports Business.* Ithaca, NY: Cornell University Press.

Staudohar, P.D., & Mangan, J.A. (1991). *The Business of Professional Sports.* Champaign, IL: University of Illinois Press.

Weiner, J. (2000). *Stadium Games: Fifty Years of Big League Greed and Bush League Boondoggles.* Minneapolis, MN: University of Minnesota Press.

Zimbalist, A. (2004). *May the Best Team Win: Baseball Economics and Public Policy.* Washington, DC: Brookings

Marketing and Sales

Marketing and sales are the lifeblood of any sport organization. Generating interest and creating customers is critical for the sport industry. The following books discuss marketing and sales in general and, in some cases, apply marketing and sales principles to the sport industry.

Cialdini, R.B. (2006). *Influence: The Psychology of Persuasion (Collins Business Essentials).* New York, NY: Harper Paperbacks.

Gitomer, J. (2004). *Little Red Book of Selling: 12.5 Principles of Sales Greatness.* Austin, TX: Bard Press

Gitomer, J. (2008). *The Sales Bible: The Ultimate Sales Resource, New Edition.* New York, NY: HarperCollins Publishers, Inc.

Johnson, S. (2002). *One Minute Sales Person: The Quickest Way to Sell People on Yourself, Your Services, Products, or Ideas—at Work and in Life.* New York, NY: HarperCollins Publishers, Inc.

Levison, J, & Godin, S. (1994). *The Guerilla Marketing Handbook.* Boston: Houghton Mifflin.

Rein, I., Kotler, P., & Shields, B. (2006). *The Elusive Fan: Reinventing Sports in a Crowded Marketplace.* New York, NY: McGraw-Hill Publishing.

Schiffman, S. (1997). *The 25 Most Common Sales Mistakes . . . and How to Avoid Them.* Avon, MA: Adams Media.

Schiffman, S. (2008). *The 25 Sales Habits of Highly Successful Salespeople.* Avon, MA: Adams Media.

Singer, B., & Kiyosaki, R.T. (2001). *Sales Dogs: You Do Not Have to Be an Attack Dog to Be Successful in Sales (Rich Dad's Advisors series)*. New York, NY: Warner Business Books.

Spoelstra, J. (1997). *Ice to the Eskimos: How to Market a Product Nobody Wants*. New York, NY: HarperCollins Publishers, Inc.

Spoelstra, J. (2001). *Marketing Outrageously: How to Increase Your Revenue by Staggering Amounts!* Austin, TX: Bard Press.

Veeck, B. (2001). *Veeck as In Wreck: The Audiobiography of Bill Veeck*. Chicago, IL: University of Chicago Press.

Veeck, B. (2009). *The Hustler's Handbook*. Chicago, IL: Ivan R. Dee, Publisher.

Veeck, M., & Williams, P. (2005). *Fun Is Good: How to Create Joy and Passion in Your Workplace & Career*. Rodale.

Ziglar, Z. (2003). *Selling 101: What Every Successful Sales Professional Needs to Know*. Nashville, TN: Thomas Nelson, Inc.

Law

This book has introduced some important legal aspects of sport. A sport-management academic career will likely include additional coursework in sport and business law. As the law continues to play an increasing role in business and the sport industry, it is important to remain aware of important legal concepts. The following books are excellent legal resources.

Cozzillio, M., & Hayman, J. (2005). *Sports and Inequality*. Durham, NC: Carolina Academic Press.

Day, F.J. (2004). *Clubhouse Lawyer: Law in the World of Sports*. Lincoln, NE: iUniverse, Inc.

Sharp, L.A., Moorman, A.M., & Claussen, C.L. (2007). *Sport Law: A Managerial Approach—Achieving a Competitive Advantage*. Scottsdale, AZ: Holcomb Hathaway Publishers.

Standen, J. (2008). *Taking Sports Seriously: Law and Sports in Contemporary American Culture*. Durham, NC: Carolina Academic Press.

Weiler, P.C. (2000). *Leveling the Playing Field: How the Law Can Make Sports Better for Fans*. Cambridge, MA: Harvard University Press.

Weiler, P.C., & Roberts, G.R. (2004). *Sports and the Law: Text, Cases and Problems*. Eagan, MN: West Publishing.

Title IX

When Title IX of the Education Amendments Act was passed into law in 1972 it was not designed to specifically address interscholastic and intercollegiate athletics. However, since sport is a component of most US educational institutions, Title IX has applied to numerous aspects of educational sport. The following books investigate Title IX and its impact upon sport management.

Blumenthal, K. (2005). *Let Me Play: The Story of Title IX: The Law That Changed the Future of Girls in America*. New York, NY: Atheneum Publishers.

Carpenter, L.J., & Acosta, R.V. (2004). *Title IX.* Champaign, IL: Human Kinetics.

Hogshead-Makar, N., & Zimbalist, A. (2007). *Equal Play: Title IX and Social Change.* Philadelphia, PA: Temple University Press.

Suggs, W. (2006). *A Place on the Team: The Triumph and Tragedy of Title IX.* Princeton, NJ: Princeton University Press.

Agents

Though most sport management programs are not designed to prepare students to become agents, many students desire to enter that field. Attending law school is certainly an important step in understanding contract law and developing the negotiation skills needed to be successful in this highly competitive business. The following resources provide some information about agents, their roles, and the legal environment in which they work.

Crasnick, J. (2005). *Licensed to Deal.* New York: Holtzbrinck Publishers.

Falk, D. (2009). *The Bald Truth.* New York: Pocket Books.

Rosenhaus, D. (1997). *A Shark Never Sleeps.* New York: Pocket Books.

Rosenhaus, D. & Rosenhaus, J. (2008). *Next Question.* New York: Berkley Publishing.

Ruxin, R.H. (2009). *An Athlete's Guide to Agents* (5th ed.). New York: Jones and Bartlett.

Shropshire, K.L., & Davis, T. (2008). *The Business of Sports Agents* (2nd Edition). Philadelphia, PA: University of Pennsylvania Press.

Stein, M. (2008). *How to Be a Sports Agent.* New York: High Stakes.

Sociology of Sport

The sociology of sport involves examining sport in the context of social interactions and sport as a social construction of the people, organizations, and groups involved in sport. Examining sport as a social construction usually occurs from one of three basic paradigms: functionalism, critical theory, and conflict theory.

Adler, P.A. (1991). *Blackboards and Blackboards.* New York, NY: Columbia University Press.

Anderson, E. (2005). *In the Game: Gay Athletes and the Cult of Masculinity.* Albany, NY: State University of New York Press.

Benedict, J., & Yaeger, D. (1998). *Pros and Cons: The criminals who play in the NFL.* New York: Warner Books.

Coakley, J. (2008). *Sports in Society: Issues and Controversies.* (10th ed.). New York: McGraw-Hill Humanities

Eitzen, D.S. & Sage, G.H. (2008). *Sociology of North American Sport: Eighth Edition.* Boulder, CO: Paradigm Publishers

Entine, J. (2001). *Taboo: Why Black Athletes Dominate Sports and Why We're Afraid to Talk About It.* New York, NY: PublicAffairs.

Gems, G.R. (2006). *The Athletic Crusade: Sport and American Cultural Imperialism.* Lincoln, NE: University of Nebraska Press.

Guttmann, A. (2004). *From Ritual to Record: The Nature of Modern Sports.* New York, NY: Columbia University Press.

Hawkins, B. (2010). *The New Plantation: Black Athletes, College Sports, and Predominately White NCAA Institutions.* New York, NY: Palgrave Macmillan.

Higgs, R.J. (1998). *God in the Stadium: Sports and Religion in America.* Lexington, KY: The University Press of Kentucky.

Hubbard, S. (1998). *Faith in Sports: Athletes and Their Religion On and Off the Field.* New York: Doubleday.

Kopay, D. & Young, P.D. (2001). *David Kopay Story: An Extraordinarily Self-Revelation.* New York, NY: Alyson Publications.

Messner, M.A. & Sabo, D.F. (1994). *Sex, Violence & Power in Sports: Rethinking Masculinity.* Freedom, CA: The Crossing Press.

Miracle, A.W. & Rees, R.C. (1994). *Lessons of the Locker Room: The Myth of School Sports.* New York: Prometheus Books

Nixon, H.L. & Frey, J.H. (1996). *Sociology of Sport.* Beverly, MA: Wadsworth Publishing.

Powell, S. (2007). *Souled Out? How Blacks Are Winning and Losing in Sports.* Champaign, IL: Human Kinetics.

Rhoden, W.C. (2006). *Forty Million Dollar Slaves: The Rise, Fall, and Redemption of the Black Athlete.* New York: Crown Publishers.

Ryan, J. (1995). *Little Girls in Pretty Boxes.* New York: Warner Books.

Sage, G.H. (1998). *Power and Ideology in American Sport.* Champaign, IL: Human Kinetics.

Smith, E. (2007). *Race, Sport and the American Dream.* Durham, NC: Carolina Academic Press.

Spindel, C. (2002). *Dancing at Halftime: Sports and the Controversy over Native American Mascots.* New York: New York University Press.

Wetzel, D., & Yaeger, D. (2000). *Sole Influence: Basketball, Corporate Greed, and the Corruption of America's Youth.* New York, NY: Grand Central Publishing.

Wiggins, D.K. (1997). *Glory Bound: Black Athletes in a White America.* Syracuse, NY: Syracuse University Press.

Wolfe, T. (2004). *I Am Charlotte Simmons.* New York: Picador.

Yaeger, D. (2007). *It's Not about the Truth: The Untold Story of the Duke Lacrosse Case and the Lives It Shattered.* New York: Simon & Schuster.

Globalization and Sport

Sport is a global phenomenon that extends beyond national boundaries. Students should be well versed in the structures, institutions and processes that constitute sport in the global marketplace. The way sport is constructed, by whom, and for what purpose, reflects the economic, technological, and cultural forces at work in any given country. Students should not limit their sport-industry aspirations to just their local environment, but should be open to exploring opportunities around the globe. With international sporting organizations and professional leagues in numerous sports from all over world vying to expand into foreign markets, tomorrow's sport managers will have numerous opportunities to excel in the global sport marketplace.

Friedman, T.L. (2000). *The Lexus and the Olive Tree: Understanding Globalization.* New York, NY: Anchor Books.

Friedman, T.L. (2007). *The World Is Flat: A Brief History of the Twenty-first Century.* New York, NY: Picador.

Foer, F. (2005). *How Soccer Explains the World: An Unlikely Theory of Globalization.* New York, NY: HarperCollins Publishers, Inc.

Gems, G.R., Borish, L.J., & Pfister, G. (2008). *Sports in American History: From Colonization to Globalization.* Champaign, IL: Human Kinetics.

Szymanski, S. & Zimbalist, A. (2006). *National Pastime: How Americans Play Baseball And the Rest of the World Plays Soccer.* Washington, DC: Brookings Institution Press.

Whiting, R. (2009). *You Gotta Have Wa.* New York, NY: Vintage Books.

Whiting, R. (2004). *The Meaning of Ichiro: The New Wave from Japan and the Transformation of Our National Pastime.* New York, NY: Time Warner Book Group.

Sport History

Sport-management students should seek to understand sport in relation to the social lives of the people who created, defined, played, and integrated it into their everyday experiences. A historical examination of sport focuses on what sport can tell us about relationships among various groups of people at particular times and places. However, when students engage in historical review, it is important to remember that history is most often written by the "winners," and sport history publications have often been gender-biased. Therefore, it may be appropriate for students to investigate alternative and non-mainstream historical accounts in order to broaden their historical perspectives.

Davies, R.O. (2007). *Sports in American Life: A History.* Hoboken, NJ: Wiley-Blackwell Publishing.

Fitzpatrick, F. (1999). *And the Walls Came Tumbling Down: Kentucky, Texas Western, and the Game That Changed American Sports.* New York, NY: Simon & Schuster.

Gorn, E.J. (2004). *A Brief History of American Sports.* Champaign, IL: University of Illinois Press.

Guttmann, A. (1992). *Women's Sports: A History.* New York: Columbia University Press.

Guttmann, A. (1996). *Games and Empires: Modern Sports and Cultural Imperialism.* New York: Columbia University Press.

Guttmann, A. (2004). *From Ritual to Record: The Nature of Modern Sports.* New York, NY: Columbia University Press.

Jacobs, T., & Roberts, R. (2003). *100 Athletes Who Shaped Sports History.* San Mateo, CA: Bluewood Books.

Rosen, D.M. (2008). *Dope: A History of Performance Enhancement in Sports from the Nineteenth Century to Today.* Westport, CT: Praeger Publishers.

Sports Illustrated. (2004). *Fifty Years of Great Writing: 50th Anniversary 1954–2004.* New York, NY: Sports Illustrated Publishing.

Zirin, D. (2007). *Welcome to the Terrordome: The Pain, Politics and Promise of Sports.* Chicago, IL: Haymarket Books.

Zirin, D., & Zinn, H. (2008). *A People's History of Sports in the United States: From Bull-Baiting to Barry Bonds . . . 250 Years of Politics, Protest, People, and Play.* New York, NY: The New Press.

Resources and Literature Specific to Certain Sports

The following sections provide helpful links and other resources specific to certain sports and/or organizations. Since the "Big Four" professional leagues are extremely popular in the United States there are many resources devoted to the history and business operation in the MLB, NBA, NHL, and NFL. However, as "emerging" sports continue to grow, more authors are devoting time and attention to the development and marketing of those sports. The authors strongly encourage feedback from readers regarding "missing" pertinent sport management resources. Though this chapter's list of resources is extensive, there are likely valuable resources that have been omitted.

Baseball

baseballamerica.com
mlb.com
collegiatebaseball.com
minorleaguebaseball.com
PBEO.com
http://www.baseball-links.com/

Asinof, E. (2000). *Eight Men Out: The Black Sox and the 1919 World Series.* New York, NY: Holt Paperbacks.

Blahnick, J. (1995). *Mud Hens and Mavericks.* New York, NY: Viking Studio Books.

Feinstein, J. (1993). *Play Ball: The Life and Troubled Times of Major League Baseball.* New York, NY: Random House, Inc.

Halberstam, D. (1989). *Summer of '49.* New York, NY: HarperCollins Publishers, Inc.

Halberstam, D. (1995). *October 1964.* New York, NY: Fawcett Books.

Halberstam, D., & Richmond, P. (1992). *Baseball: The Perfect Game.* New York, NY: Rizzoli Publications.

Helyar, J. (1995). *Lords of the Realm.* New York: Random House.

James, B. (1995). *Whatever Happened to the Hall of Fame?* New York, NY: Free Press.

James, B. (1997). *The Bill James Guide to Baseball Managers: From 1870 to Today.* New York, NY: Scribner Publishing.

James, B. (2003). *The New Bill James Historical Baseball Abstract.* New York: The Free Press.

Kahn, R. (2006). *The Boys of Summer.* New York, NY: Harper Perennial Modern Classics.

Keri, J. (2007). *Baseball between the Numbers: Why Everything We Know about the Game Is Wrong.* New York: Basic Books.

Lamster, M. (2007). *Spalding's World Tour: The Epic Adventure that Took Baseball around the Globe—And Made it America's Game.* New York, NY: PublicAffairs.

Marshall, W. (1999). *Baseball's Pivotal Era, 1945–1951.* Lexington, KY: The University Press of Kentucky.

Miller, M. (1991). *A Whole Different Ballgame.* New York: Carol Publishing Group.

Neyer, R. (2003). *Rob Neyer's Big Book of Baseball Lineups: A Complete Guide to the Best, Worst, and Most Memorable Players to Ever Grace the Major Leagues.* New York, NY: Fireside.

Neyer, R., & James, B. (2004). *The Neyer/James Guide to Pitchers: An Historical Compendium of Pitching, Pitchers, and Pitches.* New York, NY: Fireside.

Neyer, R., & Epstein, E. (2000). *Baseball Dynasties: The Greatest Teams of All Time.* New York, NY: W. W. Norton & Company, Inc.

Neyer, R., & Schwarz, A. (2007). *How Bill James Changed Our View of the Game of Baseball.* Skokie, IL: ACTA Sports.

Peterson, R. (1992). *Only the Ball Was White: A History of Legendary Black Players and All-Black Professional Teams.* New York, NY: Oxford University Press.

Schwarz, A., & Gammons, P. (2005). *The Numbers Game: Baseball's Lifelong Fascination with Statistics.* New York, NY: St. Martin's Press.

Seymour, H. (1989). *Baseball: The Early Years.* New York, NY: Oxford University Press.

Seymour, H. (1989). *Baseball: The Golden Age.* New York, NY: Oxford University Press.

Seymour, H. (1991). *Baseball: The People's Game.* New York, NY: Oxford University Press.

Snyder. B. (2006). *A Well-Paid Slave: Curt Flood's Fight for Free Agency in Professional Baseball.* New York: Plume Books.

Sowell, M. (2004). *The Pitch That Killed.* Chicago, IL: Ivan R. Dee, Publisher.

Will, G. F. (1991). *Men at Work: The Craft of Baseball.* New York, NY: HarperCollins Publishing.

Football

Nfl.com
http://www.football-links.com/
Afca.com

Davis, J. (2007). *Rozelle: Czar of the NFL*. New York, NY: McGraw-Hill Publishing Company.

Felser, L. (2008). *The Birth of the New NFL: How the 1966 NFL/AFL Merger Transformed Pro Football*. Guilford, CT: The Lyons Press.

Harris, D. (1986). *The League: The Rise and Decline of the NFL*. New York, NY: Bantam Books.

Maraniss, D. (2000). *When Pride Still Mattered: A Life of Vince Lombardi*. New York, NY: Simon & Schuster.

Meggyesy, D. (1971). *Out of Their League*. New York: Paperback Library.

Mortensen, C. (1991). *Playing for Keeps: How One Man Kept the Mob from Sinking Its Hooks into Pro Football*. New York, NY: Simon & Schuster.

Oriard, M. (2007). *Brand NFL: Making and Selling America's Favorite Sport*. Chapel Hill, NC: The University of North Carolina Press.

Oriard, M. (2007). *King Football: Sport and Spectacle in the Golden Age of Radio and Newsreels, Movies and Magazines, the Weekly and the Daily Press*. Chapel Hill, NC: The University of North Carolina Press.

Oriard, M. (2009). *Bowled Over: Big-Time College Football from the Sixties to the BCS Era*. Chapel Hill, NC: The University of North Carolina Press.

Oriard, M. (2009). *The End of Autumn: Reflections on My Life in Football*. Champaign, IL: University of Illinois Press.

Yost, M. (2006). *Tailgating, Sacks, and Salary Caps: How the NFL Became the Most Successful Sports League in History*. Chicago, IL: Kaplan Publishing.

Basketball

nba.com
fiba.com
http://www.infosportinc.com/h-links.html

Axthelm, P. (1999). *The city game: From the Garden to the Playgrounds*. New York: Buccaneer Books.

Boyd, T. (2003). *Young, Black, Rich & Famous: The Rise of the NBA, the Hip Hop Culture Invasion, and the Transformation of American Culture*. Lincoln, NE: University of Nebraska Press.

Halberstam, D. (2000). *Playing for Keeps: Michael Jordan and the World He Made*. New York, NY: Broadway Books.

Halberstam, D. (2009). *The Breaks of the Game*. New York, NY: Hyperion.

Ham, E.L. (2000). *The Playmasters: From Sellouts to Lockouts—An Unauthorized History of the NBA*. Chicago, IL: Contemporary Books.

Lane, J. (2007). *Under the Boards: The Cultural Revolution in Basketball*. Lincoln, NE: University of Nebraska Press.

Mallozzi, V.M. (2003). *Asphalt Gods: An Oral History of the Rucker Tournament.* New York, NY: Doubleday.

Pluto, T. (1991). *Loose Balls: The Short, Wild Life of the American Basketball Association.* New York, NY: Simon & Schuster.

Pluto, T. (2000). *Tall Tales: The Glory Years of the NBA.* Lincoln, NE: Bison Books.

Pomerantz, G.M. (2006). *Wilt 1962: The Night of 100 Points and the Dawn of a New Era.* New York: Three River Press.

Rosen, C. (2003). *The Wizard of Odds: How Jack Molinas Almost Destroyed the Game of Basketball.* New York, NY: Seven Stories Press.

Rosen, C. (2008). *The First Tip-Off: The Incredible Story of the Birth of the NBA.* New York, NY: McGraw-Hill Publishing Company.

Simmons, B. (2009). *The Big Book of Basketball: The NBA According to the Sports Guy.* New York, NY: ESPN Books.

Smith, S. (1993). *The Jordan Rules.* New York, NY: Pocket Books.

Hockey

nhl.com
TheAHL.com
http://www.kuklaskorner.com/index.php/hockey/hockey_links/

Conway, R. (1997). *Game Misconduct: Alan Eagleson and the Corruption of Hockey.* Toronto, ON: Macfarlane Walter & Ross.

Cruise, D., & Griffiths, A. (1992). *Net Worth—Exploding the Myths of Pro Hockey.* New York, NY: The Penguin Press.

Dowbiggin, B. (2003). *Money Players: How Hockey's Greatest Stars Beat the NHL at its Own Game.* Toronto, ON: Macfarlane Walter & Ross.

Dowbiggin, B. (2007). *Money Players: The Amazing Rise and Fall of Bob Goodenow and the NHL Players Association.* Toronto, ON: Key Porter Books.

Fischler, S. (1995). *Cracked Ice: An Insider's Look at the NHL in Turmoil.* Darby, PA: Diane Publishing Company.

Stein, G. (1997). *Power Plays: An Inside Look at the Big Business of the National Hockey League.* New York, NY: Birch Lane Press.

Willes, E. (2005). *The Rebel League: The Short and Unruly Life of the World Hockey Association.* Toronto, ON: McClelland & Stewart.

NASCAR

NASCAR.com
http://blog.vcu.edu/nascar/

Clarke, L. (2008). *One Helluva Ride: How NASCAR Swept the Nation.* New York, NY: Villard Publishing.

Fielden, G. (2007). *NASCAR: The Complete History.* Lincolnwood, IL: Publications International, Ltd.

Golenbock, P. (1994). *American Zoom: Stock Car Racing—From the Dirt Tracks to Daytona.* New York, NY: Macmillan Publishing Company.

Golenbock, P. (2001). *The Last Lap: The Life and Times of NASCAR's Legendary Heroes, Updated Edition.* New York, NY: Hungry Minds, Inc.

Golenbock, P. (2004). *NASCAR Confidential: Stories of the Men and Women Who Made Stock Car Racing Great.* St. Paul, MN: Motorbooks International.

Hagstrom, R. G. (2001). *The NASCAR Way: The Business That Drives the Sport.* Hoboken, NJ: Wiley Publishing.

Menzer, J. (2002). *The Wildest Ride: A History of NASCAR (or, How a Bunch of Good Ol' Boys Built a Billion-Dollar Industry out of Wrecking Cars).* New York, NY: Touchstone.

Thompson, N. (2007). *Driving with the Devil: Southern Moonshine, Detroit Wheels, and the Birth of NASCAR.* New York, NY: Three Rivers Press.

Yost, M., & Williams, B. (2007). *The 200-MPH Billboard: The Inside Story of How Big Money Changed NASCAR.* St. Paul, MN: Motorbooks International.

Soccer

http://www.fifa.com/
http://www.ussoccer.com/
http://www.ayso.org/home.aspx
http://www.womensoccer.com/
http://www.socceramerica.com/

Chadwick, S., & Hamil, S. (2010). *Managing Football: An International Perspective.* Oxford: Elsevier.

Desbordes, M. (2006). *Marketing and Football: An International Perspective.* Burlington, MA: Butterworth-Heinemann.

Dobson, S., & Goddard, J. (2001). *The Economics of Football.* New York: Cambridge University Press.

Goldblatt, D. (2008). *The Ball is Round: A Global History of Soccer.* New York, NY: Riverhead Books.

Kuper, S., & Szymanski, S. (2009). *Soccernomics: Why England Loses, Why Germany and Brazil Win, and Why the U.S., Japan, Australia, Turkey—and Even Iraq—Are Destined to Become the Kings of the World's Most Popular Sport.* New York, NY: Nation Books.

Markovits, A.S., & Hellerman, S.L. (2001). *Offside: Soccer and American Exceptionalism.* Princeton, NJ: Princeton University Press.

College Sport

NCAA.com
NCAA.org
NAIA.org
NJCAA.org
Rivals.com

Einhorn, E., & Rapoport, R. (2006). *How March Became Madness: How the NCAA Tournament Became the Greatest Sporting Event in America.* Chicago, IL: Triumph Books.

Duderstadt, J.J. (2003). *Intercollegiate Athletics and the American University: A University President's Perspective.* Ann Arbor, MI: The University of Michigan Press.

Gerdy, J.R. (2006). *Air Ball: American Education's Failed Experiment with Elite Athletics.* Jackson, MS: The University Press of Mississippi.

Mandel, S. (2008). *Bowls, Polls, and Tattered Souls: Tackling the Chaos and Controversy That Reign over College Football.* Hoboken, NJ: Wiley Publishing

Sack, A. (2008). *Counterfeit Amateurs: An Athlete's Journey through the Sixties to the Age of Academic Capitalism.* University Park, PA: The Pennsylvania State University Press.

Sack, A.L., & Staurowsky, E.J. (1998). *College Athletes for Hire: The Evolution and Legacy of the NCAA's Amateur Myth.* Westport, CT: Praeger Publishers.

Shulman, J.L., & Bowen, W.G. (2002). *The Game of Life: College Sports and Educational Values.* Princeton, NJ: Princeton University Press.

Sperber, M. A. (1991). *College Sports, Inc.: The Athletic Department Vs. the University.* New York, NY: Henry Holt & Company.

Sperber, M.A. (2000). *Beer and Circus: How Big-Time College Sports Is Crippling Undergraduate Education.* Darby, PA: Diane Publishing Company.

Sperber, M.A. (2002). *Shake Down the Thunder: The Creation of Notre Dame Football.* Bloomington, IN: Indiana University Press.

Tarkanian, J. (2006). *Runnin' Rebel: Shark Tales of "Extra Benefits", Frank Sinatra and Winning It All.* Champaign, IL: Sports Publishing, LLC.

Thelin, J.R. (1996). *Games Colleges Play: Scandal and Reform in Intercollegiate Athletics.* Baltimore, MD. The Johns Hopkins University Press.

Yaeger, D. (1991). *Undue Process: The NCAA's Injustice for All.* Champaign, IL: Sagamore Publishing.

Yaeger, D., & Tarkanian, J. (1993). *Shark Attack: Jerry Tarkanian and His Battle with the NCAA and UNLV.* New York, NY: HarperCollins Publishers, Inc.

Yost, M. (2010). *Varsity Green: A Behind the Scenes Look at Culture and Corruption in College Athletics.* Palo Alto, CA: Stanford Economics and Finance.

Zimbalist, A. (2001). *Unpaid Professionals: Commercialism and Conflict in Big-Time College Sports.* Princeton, NJ: Princeton University Press.

Golf

http://www.golf.com/golf/
http://www.pga.com/home/
http://www.golfdigest.com/
http://www.usga.org/
http://www.lpga.com/
http://www.ajga.org/
http://www.ewga.com/

Callahan, T. (2004). *In Search of Tiger: A Journey through Golf with Tiger Woods.* New York: Crown Publishing.

Clavin, T. (2005). *Sir Walter.* New York: Simon & Schuster, Inc.

Reilly, R. (1997). *Missing Links.* New York: Broadway Books.

Rotella, B. (1995). *Golf Is Not a Game of Perfect.* New York: Simon and Schuster.

Sampson, C. (1999). *The Masters.* New York: Villard Books.

Sounes, H. (2004). *The Wicked Game: Arnold Palmer, Jack Nicklaus, Tiger Woods, and the Business of Modern Golf.* New York: HarperCollins.

Boxing

http://www.eastsideboxing.com/
http://www.wbaonline.com/
http://usaboxing.org/
http://www.womenboxing.com/
http://www.aiba.org/

Boddy, K. (2008). *Boxing: A Cultural History.* London: Reaktion Books.

Newfield, J. (1995). *Only in America: The Life and Crimes of Don King.* New York: HarperCollins.

Remnick, D. (1998). *King of the World.* New York: Vintage Books.

Sugar, B.R. (2006). *Boxing's Greatest Fighters.* Guilford, CT: The Lyons Press.

Ward, G.C. (2004). *Unforgivable Blackness: The Rise and Fall of Jack Johnson.* New York: Random House.

Olympic Games

http://www.olympic.org/
http://www.teamusa.org/

Hoffer, R. (2009). *Something in the Air: American Passion and Defiance in the 1968 Mexico City Olympics.* New York: Free Press.

Lenskyj, H.J. (1999). *Inside the Olympic Industry.* New York: State University of New York Press.

Maraniss, D. (2008). *Rome 1960.* New York: Simon & Schuster.

Pound, D. (2004). *Inside the Olympics.* Toronto: Wiley.

Senn, A. E. (1999). *Power, Politics and the Olympic Games.* Champaign, IL: Human Kinetics

Ungerleider, S. (2001). *Faust's Gold: Inside the East German Doping Machine.* New York: St. Martin's Press.

Young, D.C. (2004). *A Brief History of the Olympic Games.* Carlton, Victoria: Blackwell Publishing

X Games and Winter X Games

http://www.abc-of-snowboarding.com/
http://www.ussnowboarding.com/
http://www.uscsa.com/
http://www.usasa.org/
http://www.ussa.org/
http://www.usskiing.com/
http://www.fis-ski.com/

http://www.isocracing.com/
http://www.usccracing.com/
http://www.sitski.com/pg3.htm

Friedman, G.E. (2000). *Dogtown—the Legend of the Z-Boys.* New York: Burning Flag Press.

Youngblut, S. (1998). *Way Inside ESPN's X Games.* Bristol, CT: ESPN Publishing.

Skateboarding

http://www.thrashermagazine.com/
http://www.nationalskateboardingassociation.com/
http://www.skatenhssa.com/
http://usaskateboarding.org/

Hawk, T. (2002). *Tony Hawk: Professional Skateboarder.* New York: Harper Collins.

Brooke, M. (1999). *Concrete Wave: The History of Skateboarding.* Toronto: Warwick Publishing.

Track and Field

http://www.usatf.org/
http://www.ustfccca.com/
http://www.uscaa.org/index.cfm

Gotaas, R. (2009). *Running: A Global History.* London: Reaktion Books.

Turrini, J.M. (2010). *The End of Amateurism in American Track and Field.*

Figure Skating

http://www.usfsa.org/
http://www.isu.org/
http://www.sk8stuff.com/

Brennan, C. (1996). *Inside Edge.* New York: Doubleday.

Jackson, J. (2005). *On Edge.* New York: Thunder Mouth Press.

Tennis

http://www.tennis.com/
http://www.atpworldtour.com/
http://www.usta.com/
http://www.itftennis.com/
http://www.tennisw.com/
http://uspta.com/

Ashe, A., & Rampersad, A. (1994). *Days of Grace.* New York, NY: Ballantine Books.

Collins, B. (2008). *Bud Collins History of Tennis: An Authoritative Encyclopedia and Record Book.* Washington, DC: New Chapter Press.

Marks, B.L. (2006). *Taking Your Tennis on Tour.* Vista, CA: Usrsa

McEnroe, J. (2002). *You Cannot be Serious.* New York: Berkley Publishing.

Fishing

http://www.asafishing.org/
http://www.igfa.org/
http://www.fishing.net/
http://www.takemefishing.org/
http://www.fishingworks.com/
http://www.iwfa.org/
http://fishingclub.com

Andrews, D.S. (2009). *An Impossible Cast: Glen Andrews and the Birth of Professional Bass Fishing.*

Schultz, K. (2006). *Bass Madness.* Hoboken, NJ: John Wiley & Sons.

Lacrosse

http://www.uslacrosse.org/
http://www.laxpower.com/
http://www.filacrosse.com/?fileid=home&division=women
http://www.lacrosseforums.com/

Fisher, D.M. (2002). *Lacrosse: A History of the Game.* Baltimore, MD: The John Hopkins University Press.

Vennum, T. (2007). *Lacrosse Legends of the First Americans.* Baltimore, MD: The John Hopkins University Press.

Volleyball

http://usavolleyball.org/
http://www.volleyball.org/
http://www.fivb.ch/
http://www.avp.com/

Dearing, J.B. (2007). *The Untold Story of William G. Morgan, Inventor of Volleyball.* Livermore, CA: WingSpan Press.

Strickland, B. (2009). *Inside the Players' Tent: A Year of Professional Beach Volleyball.* BookSurge.

Wurtz, T.J. (2007). *The Score's Wrong.* Bloomington, IN: AuthorHouse.

Other Helpful Links

The following links provide access to important sport management organizations. In many cases, the best opportunity to work in sports is to work for a sport-marketing firm or a sport sponsor rather than for an individual franchise or league.

Sport Marketing Firms

AMG Sports	http://www.amgsports.com/
Axcess Sports and Entertainment	http://www.axcesssports.com/
Axiom Sports & Entertainment	http://www.axiomsport.com/
Edge Sports International	http://www.edgesportsintl.com/
Envision Global Marketing	http://www.envisionglobal.com/
The Gazelle Group	http://www.gazellegroup.com/
General Sports and Entertainment	http://generalsports.com/
GMR Marketing	http://www.gmrmarketing.com/
IMG	http://www.imgworld.com/home/default.sps
IMG College	http://www.imgcollege.com/
Integrated Sports Marketing	http://www.ismsports.net/
International Sports Properties	http://www.ispsports.com/
Keystone Marketing	http://www.keystonemarketing.net/
Knox Sports Marketing	http://www.knoxsports.com/
Millsport	http://www.millsport.com/
National Media Sports	http://www.nmgsports.com/
Nelligan Sports Marketing	http://www.nelligansports.com/
Octagon	http://www.octagon.com/
Premier Sports Management	http://www.premiersportsonline.com/
Sports and Sponsorships	http://www.sportsandsponsorships.com/
Sports Loop	http://www.sportsloop.com/sportsloop/
Team Services LLC	http://www.teamservicesllc.com/
Velocity Sports and Entertainment	http://www.teamvelocity.com/
Wasserman Media Group	http://www.wmgllc.com/

Sport Sponsorship and Research Firms

IEG Sponsorship	http://www.sponsorship.com/
Joyce Julius and Associates	http://www.joycejulius.com/
Performance Research	http://www.performanceresearch.com/
Scarborough Research	http://www.scarborough.com/
Shugoll Research	http://www.shugollresearch.com/
Sponsorship Intelligence	http://www.sponsorshipintelligence.com/content/home.aspx
Sponsorship Research International	http://www.teamsri.com/
SportsEconomics	http://www.sportseconomics.com/index.html
Team Marketing Report	http://www.teammarketing.com/
TURNKEY Sports and Entertainment	http://www.turnkeyse.com/

Sport Branding Firms

Silverman Group	http://www.silvermangroup.com/
Strategic Agency	http://www.strategicagency.com/index.html
Studio Simon Sports Design	http://www.studiosimon.net/

Glossary

80/20 Rule—Revenue-generation "rule" that 80 percent of a sport organization's revenue comes from 20 percent of its customers.

A Duty—An obligation one has to act or refrain from acting. A duty often occurs in response to another person's right.

A Right—The basis upon which someone can make a claim; an entitlement one is due. There are various kinds of rights—legal, human, natural, and moral rights.

Acceptance—An agreement to the terms of an offer as stated.

Access—The extent to which sports organizations, leagues, teams, and athletes make themselves available to the media in terms of coverage and reporting.

Act of God—A defense to negligence in which a person has no liability if an unforeseeable natural disaster causes injury to the plaintiff.

Agenda-Setting—A theory of mass communication which suggests the media exert a significant influence on public perception through their ability to filter and shape media content.

AIO Dimensions—Activities, interests, and opinions of consumers, commonly used for market segmentation.

Alcohol Management—Limits the risks associated with alcohol consumption, as well as reduces facility liability regarding alcohol-related incidents.

Americanization—Implies America's role in processes of globalization. As noted by Kuisel, "Americanization is the import by non-Americans of products, images, technologies, practices, and behavior that are closely associated with America/Americans" (2003, p. 96).

Americans with Disabilities Act—A law signed in 1990 prohibiting discrimination based on disability in employment, state and local government activities, places of public accommodation, and telecommunications; sport facilities are considered places of public accommodation and therefore must be accessible to persons with disabilities.

Arena—Indoor facilities used to host sporting, entertainment, and business events; portable seating designs allow the floor area to be arranged to accommodate multiple tenants.

Base Salary Plus Commission—Combination of a set salary—based on a staff member's experience—and a percent of generated sales (typically between 1–5% on renewed business and 5–20% on new business).

Blog/Blogging—A form of content posted directly to the Internet that is usually subjective and personal in nature. Blogs can be created and maintained by individuals as well as the mainstream media, which opens up the communication process. Blogs also allow for interactivity and direct communication between author and audience.

Bonding—The creation of a unified commitment that holds those in the relationship (marketer and customer or other stakeholder) together.

Brand Equity—The marketplace value that a brand contributes to a product.

Brand—A name, term, design, symbol, or feature that identifies one sport product as being different from another; the mixture of attributes can be tangible or intangible, are usually symbolized in a trademark, and if managed properly, creates value and influence.

Breach of Contract—One party fails to perform essential promises in a contract.

Breach of Duty—The failure to meet the required standard of care in a negligence action.

Capacity—A party must be legally competent to enter into a contract.

Causation—The tie between the breach of duty and the damages in a negligence action.

Chain—A complex network of contractors in disparate global locations involved in manufacturing (often broken down into minute steps) and shipping a tangible product. For example, raw materials may be extracted and shipped from Guatemala, assembled in steps in Sri Lanka, Vietnam, and China, and finally shipped to the U.S. and Great Britain for promotion and point of sale.

Closes for the Next Step—Asking for a client's business or requesting referral information.

Closing—Reaching a sales agreement with a client.

Clutter—Product of too much signage in a facility; decreases the likelihood of advertiser recall, thus diminishing the value of facility advertising.

Commitment and Consistency—A person making a decision will experience pressure from others and themselves to behave consistently with that decision. Depending on a person's past actions, they will be predisposed to making future decisions consistent with those past actions.

Commodification—In a sociological context, commodification occurs when economic value is assigned to something not previously considered in economic terms: i.e., gender, race, sexual orientation. In other words, commodification is treating people, ideas, or things as if they were tradable commodities.

Comparative Negligence—A system that allows a plaintiff in a negligence action to recover some damages even though the plaintiff was also partially responsible for causing the injury.

Compensatory Damages—Damages that are awarded to make up for the actual loss sustained by a party.

Complex Connectivity—Tomlinson's (1999) notion of an ever-densening network of global interconnections and interdependencies that characterize modern life. Rapid increases in technology, modes of communication, travel, and trade have enabled an intensification of global flows. For example, the speed at which intangibles (ideas and information services) and tangibles (products and people) can circle the globe is either instantaneous (Internet, Cable TV, Satellite) or quite swift (plane, train, ship). As a result, cultures and peoples that were once so detached are now incredibly connected and dependant upon each other, especially in realms of politics and economics.

Conflict Theory—Sociological theory emphasizing social and political inequalities and the resulting economic and power differentials; a conflict theory analysis focuses on the inherent and endemic conflicts that arise from economic disparities.

Consideration—Something of value that is exchanged in a contract.

Constitution—A government's foundational document setting forth the operating principles of the government and the limitations on governmental power.

Constitutional Law—the underlying document of the U.S. government, which sets forth limits on governmental power.

Contract Law—A promise or set of promises enforced by courts, which establish a duty to perform between parties.

Contract—A promise or set of promises, the breach of which the law gives a remedy, or the performance of which the law in some way recognizes a duty.

Contributory Negligence—A plaintiff is completely barred from recovery if the plaintiff in any way contributed to his/her own injury.

Crowd Management—Strategy designed to prevent crowd from getting out of control; security, signage, and communication all serve to effectively maintain crowd control.

Cultural (Symbolic) Production—A related process to commodification that involves the inscribing of meaning to a particular product. During the industrial revolution, in order to differentiate one product from another, proprietors of a company would advertise the positive attributes of their product over their competitors. With increasing technologies, sophistication in advertising and marketing, and a decreasing indus-

trial base after World War II, branded corporations turned to cultural meanings to attach symbolic value to their products. For example, while two athletic shoes may be made in the same overseas factory, the symbol inscribed on it denotes a greater value than just the cost to produce it. The cultural meaning and symbolism established by marketing/advertising initiatives bestows the product with greater value for consumers.

Cultural Hegemony—A concept that a culturally diverse society can be ruled or dominated by one of its social classes. Cultural hegemony may also be seen as the dominance of one social, political, or economic group over another group.

Damages—The final element in a negligence action, which involves personal injury or property damage to the plaintiff.

Demographics—Measurable characteristics of the sports audience such as age, gender, income, ethnicity, etc.

Distribution—How sports content reaches the sports audience. The audience itself is taking more of a role in distributing today's content.

Distributive—Retributive justice is concerned with correcting societal imbalances; distributive justice is concerned with the fair allocation of societal benefits and burdens.

Due Process—A constitutional provision that mandates fair treatment for a person who has been deprived of life, liberty, or property by a governmental decision.

Duty—The defendant has an obligation imposed by law to protect the plaintiff from unreasonable risk.

Establishment Clause—A First Amendment provision that protects citizens from the government establishing a state religion or giving preferential treatment to one religion over another.

Ethics—The study of value, very broadly construed. Ethics examines the nature of right and wrong, duty, obligation, freedom, and virtue. It is sometimes referred to as the philosophy of morality, or how people should act. Moral philosophy then is the attempt to achieve a systematic understanding of the nature of morality.

Expenses—Costs incurred by the organization. Common costs in sport include wages, utilities, equipment, and transportation.

External Contingencies—Factors beyond the marketers control that influence marketing strategy.

Fan Cost Index—An index that represents the average cost for a family of four to attend a sport event.

Fan Identification—The personal commitment and emotional involvement customers have with a sport organization.

Festival Seating—Form of general admission ticketing in which spectators are not assigned to a specific seat, but rather a standing/seating area within a facility such as in front of the stage at a concert or outfield berm seating at a baseball game.

Finance—The science of fund management that incorporates concepts from accounting, statistics, and economics.

Financial Bonding—The provision of financial incentives to your customers in order to encourage a continuing customer relationship.

Financial Management—Financial decision-making within a firm with wealth maximization being the goal for most organizations.

Flows—Term used to describe the extent/rate at which people, products, images, information, etc. spread globally. For example, the instantaneous global flow of information via the Internet means that people can learn of current events in distant geographic locations in real time.

Football Bowl Subdivision—A segment of the National Collegiate Athletic Association that is comprised of schools playing the highest level of football (formerly known as Division IA).

Football Championship Subdivision—A segment of the National Collegiate Athletic Association that is comprised of Division I schools that are not playing at the highest level of football competition (formerly known as Division IAA)

Fordism—Concept stemming from Henry Ford's assembly line production of Model-T Ford automobiles. The principles of scientific management pioneered by Frederick Taylor were used to ensure workers performed routinized tasks quickly and effectively without unnecessary steps.

Fragmentation—The splintering of large, mass sports audiences into smaller, niche audiences due primarily to the growth of media channels and options.

Free Exercise Clause—A First Amendment provision that protects individual rights to worship as one wishes.

Freedom of Expression Clause—A First Amendment provision protecting individual rights for verbal and nonverbal expression.

Fulfillment Audit—A post-event report provided to a sponsor that illustrates and highlights what the sponsor received as part of the sponsorship and how the sport property fulfilled the sponsor's corporate needs.

Full Disclosure—A media strategy in which those involved in controversy or crisis try to manage the situation by being as open as possible with the media and proving a free flow of information.

Functionalist Theory, or Functionalism—A sociological theory in which society is viewed as an organized system of interrelated parts held together by shared values and social processes that minimize differences and promote consensus among people (Coakley, 2008).

General Admission—Ticketing system in which seating is available on a first-come, first-served basis; each patron pays a fixed price and can sit in any unoccupied seat in the facility.

Geodemographic Segmentation—Segmenting a market using a combination of geographics, demographics, and psychographics.

Global Heterogenization—Largely in response to the real and/or perceived threat of globally homogenizing forces, this theory asserts that countries, nations, corporations, politics, economies, and cultures are actually becoming more differentiated, not less. In this sense, local difference has intensified by both the reaction to global uniformity by local cultures and through corporations' realization of the value of cultural niches and marketing of local difference. Sport has been argued to play a considerable role in this process, as fans tend to feverishly support place-based teams that reflect a specific locale and its unique cultural nuances.

Global Homogenization—Theory that countries, nations, corporations, politics, economies, and cultures are becoming increasingly the same. More specifically, it generally cites three main forces responsible for the global diffusion of ideas, information, products, and so on, and an accelerated level of cultural convergence/sameness/uniformity: 1. Free market liberal economics, 2. Global corporate structures and technologies, and 3. A consumer capitalist culture. In relation to sport, the processes and structures of global sporting organizations and events can be said to operate much the same, mainly due to the adoption of principles of American business and corporate structure.

Global Hybridity—Essentially a mixture of both homogenization and heterogenization. The hybridity thesis acknowledges that the relationship between local and global forces is much too complex to easily categorize. As such, this theory suggests that a better way to understand globalization is to view it as a global-local nexus, characterized by a complex and ever-changing dynamic between change and continuity, difference and sameness, universality and particularity. As such, global sporting events reflect markers of both local elements (nationalities, cultures, style of play) and global prerogatives (media broadcasting, revenue generation, and marketing).

Glocality—Integral to the global hybridization thesis. Glocalization asserts that global and local forces interpenetrate each other, resulting in unique outcomes in different locations.

Good/Bad—Value terms for things, people, or states of affairs. Saying an action is good/bad is most often associated with a judgment based upon the action's consequences.

Image—How sports athletes, organizations and events, and the information related to them, are portrayed in the media and presented to sports audiences.

Independent Teams—Professional baseball teams that operate without a direct affiliation with any Major League Baseball franchise.

Institutional Logics—A set of material practices and symbolic construction, which constitutes an institution's organizing principles. Such institutional logics (a) determine what are considered acceptable or unacceptable operational means, (b) establish routines, (c) guide the evaluation and implementation of developed strategies, and (d) create precedent for further innovation.

Interactivity—Two-way communication that allows the audience to provide feedback and take part in the communication process. Interactivity has increased with the advent of new media such as the Internet and blogging.

Invitee—A person who is invited by the owner to an establishment with the purpose of conducting business.

Justice—Often seen as synonymous with fairness, is the application of ethics to the structure of society. Justice is commonly divided into two areas: retributive and distributive.

Legality—The subject matter of a contract must not violate the law or it will not be enforceable.

Leveraging (also termed Activation)—The utilization of various marketing strategies to improve sponsor value.

Licensed Merchandise—Granting another entity the right to produce products that bear a trademarked logo.

Lifetime Customer Value—The worth of a particular customer to a company over the course of that customer's lifetime.

Liking—A person's feeling of affection or preference for another person.

Market Segmentation—The process of dividing large, unlike groups of consumers into smaller, more defined groups of people who share similar characteristics.

Marketing—The activity, set of institutions, and processes for creating, communicating, delivering, and exchanging offerings that have value for customers, clients, partners, and society at large.

Marketing Plan—The formal blueprint that marketers follow in the execution of their marketing strategy; the plan includes a SWOT analysis, intended target markets, performance objectives, and resulting strategies for promotion, pricing, and distribution.

McDonaldization—Notion that the four key operating principles of the fast food chain are coming to dominate more and more sectors of American society and the rest of the world.

Metadiscrete Experiential Learning—A learning model, in which staff from partnering sport businesses serve as instructional leaders and facilitators alongside sport-management faculty, that ". . . enhances student understanding of entrepreneurship, sales, sponsorship, event management, and marketing research within the context of the university's sport management program" (Southall, Nagel, LeGrande, & Han, 2003, p. 23). Greater knowledge gain is possible because in a metadiscrete experience, the role of teacher and practitioner are not separate and distinct, but are dual aspects of the same function.

Morality—Concerned with how people act and what they believe to be right or wrong. In practice it is often synonymous with ethics, but morality is also the portion of ethics concerned with interpersonal behavior.

Negligence Law—A part of tort law dealing with unintentional conduct that falls below a standard established by law for the protection of others against unreasonable risk of harm.

Networks—Due to advanced technologies, means of rapid communication, and sophisticated business/management practices, networks have been formed between people, businesses, organizations, and institutions to allow for greater efficiency, accuracy, profitability, and security.

News Cycle—The amount of time it takes for news to reach the general public. The development of new technologies has shrunk the current news-cycle down to just minutes.

Organizational Culture—Pattern of basic assumptions that a given group has invented, discovered, or developed in learning to cope with its problems of external adaptation and internal integration, and that have worked well enough to be considered valid, and therefore, to be taught to new members as the correct way to perceive, think, and feel in relation to those problems (Schein, 1984).

Out-Sourcing—Hiring an outside organization or private contractor to operate facility services such as concessions, security, and maintenance.

Override—Compensation paid to a sales manager for overseeing a sales staff. For example, if a sales manager has five employees that report to him he may receive a 1 percent bonus of the total revenue generated by the five sales-staff employees.

Pay-Per-View—Consumers paying directly for sports content, usually through specialized radio, television, or Internet outlets.

Personal Seat License—Source of facility revenue that requires guests to pay a one-time fee for the right to purchase tickets for a specific seat.

Positioning—Establishing a brand's image in the minds of consumers.

Post-Industrialism—Coming after the industrial age of mass manufacturing, smokestacked factories, and large physical labor workforces (making stuff or things), new technologies, increased global flows, and a changing political and economic climate precipitated de-industrialization and the new post-industrial economy of information services, technology, and the symbolic production of goods and services (selling ideas, meanings).

Prospecting—Searching for and creating new customers.

Psychographics—Variables related to the lifestyle and personality of consumers.

Public Relations—Methods by which sports teams, athletes, and organizations control and manipulate their access and information in regards to the media.

Qualifying the Event—Process of determining if an event is appropriate for a facility.

Reciprocity—A mutual exchange, a return in kind. People react positively and feel obligated to repay others for favorable treatments received.

Referral—When someone gives a salesperson a sales lead (name, address, phone number, and/or e-mail to contact).

Relationship Marketing—Marketing with the conscious aim to develop and manage long-term and/or trusting relationships with customers, distributors, suppliers, or other parties in the marketing environment.

Reserved Seating—Ticketing system used for events that require a designated ticket for each seat; reserved tickets indicate the section, row, and seat a patron is assigned for a specific event.

Revenues—Money coming into an organization. Selling tickets is one common example of generating revenue in sport.

Right/Wrong—Value terms for the permissibility/impermissibility of an action. A judgment regarding an action's being right/wrong is made independent of a decision's anticipated consequences.

Risk Management—Process of identifying, assessing, and treating risks in order to reduce facility liability and ensure a safe environment for employees and spectators.

ROI—Return on investment. Marketing success is measured by the following ratio: revenue generated/costs incurred.

Social Bonding—Providing social or psychological incentives that encourage a continuing customer relationship.

Social Proof—People will do things they see other people are doing. Assuming other people possess more knowledge about the situation, they deem the others' behavior as appropriate or better informed.

Special-Event Facility—Specialized, single-purpose facilities designed to meet the unique needs of a specific tenant or event.

Sport Marketing—All activities designed to meet the needs and wants of sport consumers through exchange processes.

Sport Sponsorship—An opportunity for a sport organization and business partner to utilize two or more marketing mix elements in order to achieve marketing objectives by providing product association, value, and exposure.

Sports Information Director (SID)—Person, usually at the college level, in charge of all media relations between the athletic department and media members. The SID is primarily responsible for dissemination of information to the media and regulating media access to players and coaches.

Stadium—Outdoor or domed public assembly facility that hosts sporting and entertainment events.

Stonewall—A media strategy in which those involved in controversy or crisis try to manage the situation by cutting off the flow of information and/or refusing media access.

SWOT Analysis—A strategic-planning tool used to evaluate an organization's **S**trengths, **W**eaknesses, **O**pportunities, and **T**hreats.

Telemarketing/Teleselling—Marketing/sales approach that features the use of personal selling techniques in a non-face-to-face context and utilizes telecommunications technology as part of a well-planned, organized, and managed marketing program.

Transnational Corporatism—Associated with the ability of corporations to easily bypass national borders and boundaries to promote and sell products and services in various geographic areas; involves a process of marketing toward the sensibilities of local cultural difference.

Virtue—A trait that contributes to something's being good in some way. Virtue may be referred to as "righteous conduct." As a plural, "**virtues**" refers to character traits such as courage, wisdom, self-control, justice, loyalty, and compassion.

Wealth Maximization—The goal or outcome of financial management for most organizations; increasing the overall value of the firm.

Index

DF&P. *See* Disson, Furst and Partners
Dick, R. J., 189
Dick's Sporting Goods, 172
Difference Principle, 108
diffusion theory, 95–96
Digital Sports, 240
directive close, 208
DirectTV, 225–226
discomfort, 95
Disson, Furst and Partners (DF&P), 11
distribution, 218
distribution systems, 235–236
distributive, 109
divine-command theory, 97
division levels, 42
    of college athletic programs, 6–7
    moving around in, 42
    in NCAA, 41–44
Division-I departments, 27–32
Djokovic, Novak, 71
dominant cultures, 25–26
donations, 297
Donoway, Dan, 164
double standards, 20–22
double-entry accounting, 292
Dowd, Maureen, 278
Drucker, P. F., 146, 164
due process, 135
Dukakis, Damon, 317–319
Duke University, 230, 296, 299
duty, 104–105, 122–123

E

earnings before interest, taxes, depreciation and amortization
        (EBITDA), 283
earnings before interest and taxes (EBIT), 283
earnings before taxes (EBT), 283
EBIT. *See* earnings before interest and taxes
EBITDA. *See* earnings before interest, taxes, depreciation and
        amortization
EBT. *See* earnings before taxes
Eckhardt, Shawn, 223
economic environment, 177–178, 240
economic impact, 300
economic networks, 67
egoism, 96–97
80/20 rule, 211
emergency medical care, 129
empathy, 203
employment opportunities
    in college athletics, 300
    competition of, 4
    entry-level, 4, 9, 39–40
    in professional sport franchises, 39–41
    with sport facilities, 49–50, 270
    sport industry links for, 347

    in sport management, 58–59, 346–347
    as sports agents, 51–52, 314, 352
    in sports tourism, 53–54
    talent side of, 39
    volunteers/internships as, 41
employment placement, 54
England, 70
English Premier League (EPL), 72
Entertainment and Sports Programming Network (ESPN), 120, 162,
        222
entry-level employment, 4, 9, 39–40
EPL. *See* English Premier League
Equal Liberty Principle, 108
equipment, safe use of, 129
equity financing, 293–294
Ericson, Jon, 115
ESPN. *See* Entertainment and Sports Programming Network
ESPN: The Magazine, 18, 221, 321, 331
ESPN360, 235–236
Establishment Clause, 134
Estefan, Gloria, 294
ethical decision making
    ethical frameworks in, 101–113
    interrelated components of, 112
    obstacles to, 94–95
    pretenders in, 96–101
ethical egoism, 96
ethical frameworks, 101–113
ethical reasoning, 93–94
ethics, 92
    of care, 110–111, 113
    in decision-making, 92
    failing to act on, 95–96
    of rights, 110–111
    sport industry opportunities in, 349
    in sport management, 112–113
Ettington, D., 25
events, 255
Excedrin, 168
expenses, 280
external contingencies, 177–180
Extra Innings, 236

F

Facebook, 180, 196, 312
facilities. *See also* sport facilities
    college athletic programs requiring, 7
    public assembly, 250
    types of, 250–251
Facility Manager, 327
faculty athletic representative (FAR), 32
Fainaru-Wada, Mark, 232–233
fairness, in athletic competition, 16–17
false promising, 107
Fan Cost Index (FCI), 178
fan identification, 173